Surviving a Japanese
Internment Camp

Surviving a Japanese Internment Camp

Life and Liberation at Santo Tomás, Manila, in World War II

RUPERT WILKINSON

McFarland & Company, Inc., Publishers
Jefferson, North Carolina

LIBRARY OF CONGRESS CATALOGUING-IN-PUBLICATION DATA

Wilkinson, Rupert.
Surviving a Japanese internment camp : life and liberation at Santo Tomas, Manila, in World War II / Rupert Wilkinson.
    p.   cm.
Includes bibliographical references and index.

ISBN 978-0-7864-6570-5
softcover : acid free paper ∞

1. Wilkinson, Rupert. 2. Santo Tomas Internment Camp (Manila, Philippines) 3. World War, 1939–1945—Prisoners and prisons, Japanese. 4. World War, 1939–1945—Personal narratives, British. 5. Prisoners of war—Japan—Biography. 6. Prisoners of war—Great Britain—Biography. I. Title.
D805.5.S28W55 2014   940.54'72520959916092—dc23   [B]   2013041038

BRITISH LIBRARY CATALOGUING DATA ARE AVAILABLE

© 2014 Rupert Wilkinson. All rights reserved

No part of this book may be reproduced or transmitted in any form or by any means, electronic or mechanical, including photocopying or recording, or by any information storage and retrieval system, without permission in writing from the publisher.

Front cover: Liberated internee boys on U.S. Army tank "Ole Miss" at Santo Tomás, *ca.* February 5, 1945 (U.S. Signal Corps, courtesy of MacArthur Memorial Archives, Norfolk, Virginia)

Manufactured in the United States of America

McFarland & Company, Inc., Publishers
Box 611, Jefferson, North Carolina 28640
www.mcfarlandpub.com

To Mary June, and the memory
of our mother, Lorna Wilkinson

Table of Contents

Acknowledgments ix
Introduction: Telling the Santo Tomás Story 1

1. War Clouds Over Eden 9
2. Internment 24
3. A Porous Prison 35
4. Dorms, Shanties, and Sex 49
5. "Cheer Up! Everything's Going to Be Lousy" 68
6. Child's Play 82
7. Power: The Japanese 94
8. Power: The Internees 104
9. Hunger 116
10. Threat vs. Hope 132
11. "They're Here!" 143
12. Aftermath 157
13. Significance 178

Appendix I: Chronology 193
Appendix II: The Camp's "Ten Commandments" 198
Appendix III: The Literature of Santo Tomás 200
Notes 203
Bibliography 221
Index 229

Acknowledgments

Many of the informants who helped me with this book were fellow Santo Tomás internees, though I don't expect them all to agree with all my judgments. In acknowledging interned women and girls whose surnames changed due to marriage, I give their camp family names before their married names.

Among myriad creditors, some warrant special mention. My wife Mary Wilkinson spent hours and hours rigorously editing all chapters, prompting rewrites, advising on pictures, finding gems alongside me in the U.S. National Archives, and listening ad nauseam to "camp" stories. My sister, Mary June Wilkinson Pettyfer, and camp chum, Nicholas Balfour, vividly improved on my own memories, both being older than me. Mary June read draft chapters and made valuable and supportive suggestions; so did my daughter, Camilla Wilkinson. Roderick Hall, whose master bibliography of the wartime Philippines is a memorial to his Filipino family executed in Manila, gave me books, Manila contacts, information, and always encouragement. Curtis Brooks, Liz Lautzenhiser Irvine, and Sascha Jean Weinzheimer Jansen, exceptionally informed ex-internees, provided huge amounts of information, supplemented by Curt's military knowledge and by many documents from Liz as well as from Caroline Bailey Pratt and James Ward. Yukako Ibuki procured and translated the camp guard's logbook and advised me on aspects of prewar and wartime Japan. Yolanda Cruz, Oberlin College biologist, gave me superb, instant tutorials on malnutrition, as well as stories and information from her Philippine past. Margaret Ball, daughter and granddaughter of camp internees, gave all kinds of help, including insights into Manila expat life. In Manila itself, Mary June's son, Robin Pettyfer, a pioneer of videoconferences bridging different Philippine and Indonesian groups, explored the campsite when I could not get to it; he answered various "what where" questions from me, as well as sending me maps and photos. Back here, Adam Thorpe gave generous time and skill, scanning and adjusting the illustrations.

Long before any of this occurred, two people "grandmothered" the book more than they may realize: daughter Clara Klat, by getting me to write an informal memoir, and then Penny Curtis Mellor, another internee's daughter, by suggesting I read more books on the camp to give my account fuller background. Only then did I think of writing a full history of the camp, with some personal basis but more than a memoir.

The chapter on the camp's rescue needs a special mention. It is the first time I have written military history and I wonder if any military historian ever gets everything right, such is the fog of war. In trying to be as accurate as possible while bringing the event alive,

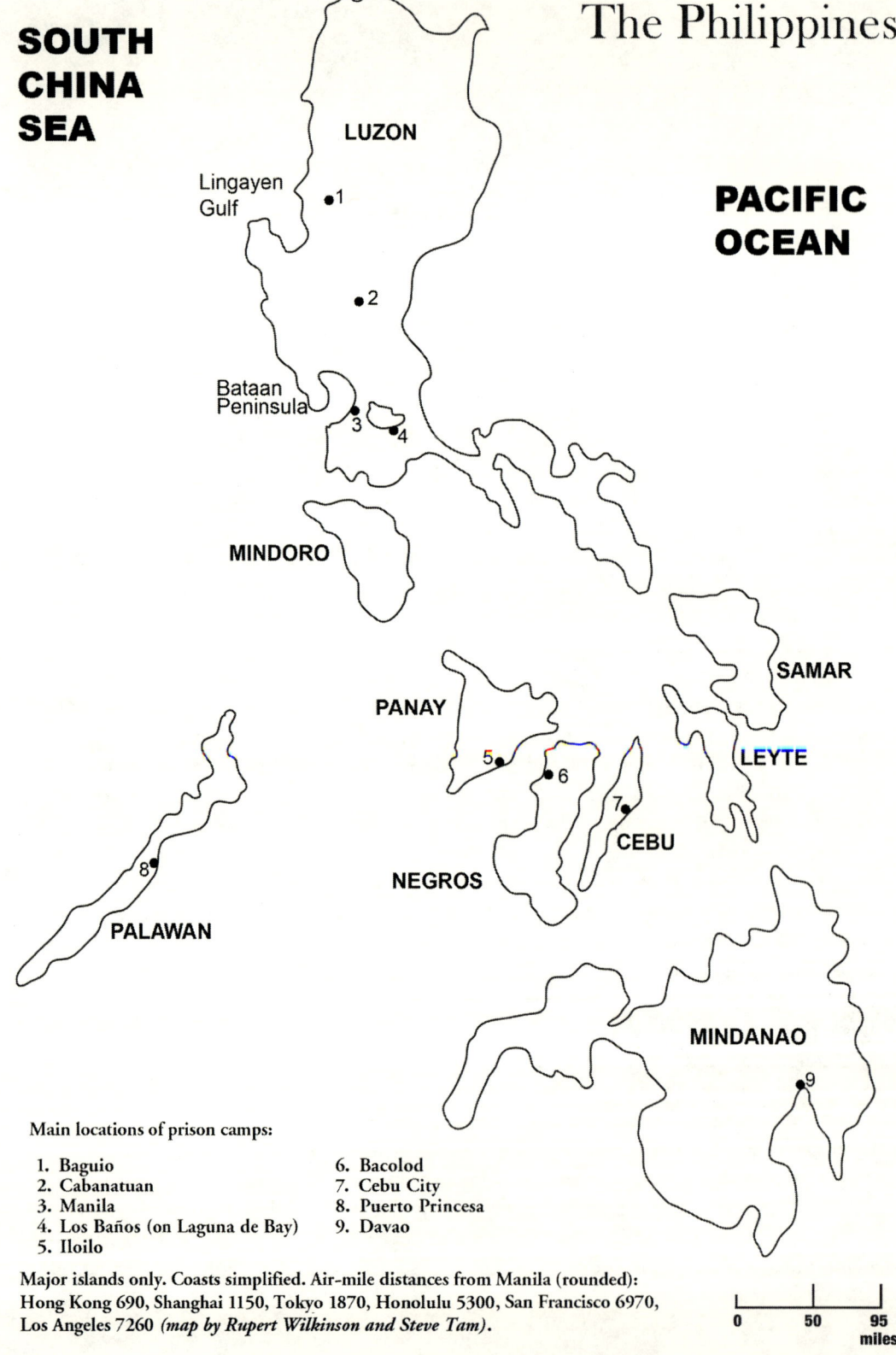

Acknowledgments

I am indebted to Richard Seron, longtime researcher on the subject, and his associate, Lt. Col. Walter Landry (1st Cavalry Division), one of the first American soldiers into Santo Tomás; he was awarded a Silver Star. Both responded generously to shoals of questions from me about the three days in February 1945 when the "flying columns" fought to free the camp. Throughout the book's writing, Richard and I discussed many aspects of the camp's liberation; we used hours of taped testimony by Walter Landry, plus crucial information from Susan Trout, daughter of a flying-column veteran, and interviews with a few surviving liberators (in the list below with their units). Had I relied solely on army-unit reports and published accounts, important aspects of the rescue might have been lost to history.

At library archives, more than routine help came from Eric Vanslander (U.S. National Archives), James Zobel (MacArthur Memorial Library), Suzanne Yupangco and colleagues (Filipinas Heritage Museum, Manila), Naoki Kanno and Satoko Mikado (National Institute for Defense Studies, Tokyo), and Roger Suddaby (Imperial War Museum, London).

I wish I could describe the help given by others; they are too many for that but I do want to name them. I thank Anthony de Alcuaz, Mark Allen, Len Baker, Frederico Baldassarre, Sebastian Balfour, Tika Balfour, May Berenbaum, Lynn Bloom, William Boudreau, Andrew Bridgeford, Dorothy Mullaney Brooks, Mike Browning, Ted Cadwallader, Alexander Calhoun Jr., Craig Comstock, Jay Crawford, Hazel Templer Cripps, Tom Crosby, Keith Cunliffe, Wanda Werff Damberg, Bill Davidson, Patrick Di Matteo (1st Cavalry Division), Roy Doolan Jr., Susan Douglas, Betsy Enriquez, Lettye Staight Falk, George Fisher (44th Tank Battalion), Maurice Francis, Sonia Francisco, Cornelia Lichauco Fung, Susan Go, Lou Gopal, Juergen Goldhagen, Malcolm Green, John Hawkins, Irene Duckworth Hecht, Jeremy Herklotz, Don Hossler, Michael Hurst, Addie Gibb Jensen, Ricardo José, Marie Kish, Iris Krass, Edgar Krohn, Jenny Templer Kyle, Ric Laurence, Benito Legarda, Jr., Karen Kerns Lewis, Barbara Linder, Cortland Linder, Cecily Mattocks Marshall, Edward McCreary, Jr., Connie Hall McHugh, Robert McWilliam (5th Field Hospital), Martin Meadows, Frank Mendez (1st Cavalry Division), Chelly Mendoza (1st Cavalry Division), Alberto Montillo, Leslie Murray, Hitoshi Nagai, James Nelson, Elizabeth Norman, Maita Oebanda, Walter Olson (37th Infantry Division), Peter Parsons, Carol Petillo, Geege Wootten Poston, Ben Richardson, Juan Rocha, Florentino Rodao, Roger Schade, Margo Tonkin Shiels, Jeanne Siegel, Michael Snape, Don Stevenson, Charles Sullivan, Ralph Thompson, Bill Tonkin, Albert Walters, Richard Walters, Terry Wadsworth Warne, and Peter Wrinch.

Not all of these people are still alive. I regret that I started serious work on the camp's history more than a decade after my mother, Lorna Wilkinson, died in 1992. Now and then she mentioned camp experiences, some of which she recounted to Trish Marx for her children's book *Echoes of World War II* (1989) on six wartime children including me (my own comments there are not all correct). But how much more would I have learned had I questioned her systematically? One compensation is that by waiting so long I could use a new generation of memoirs and diaries, some edited by the children and even grandchildren of internees.

Introduction: Telling the Santo Tomás Story

Manila, 3 February 1945. It was after nightfall when six U.S. Army Sherman tanks with an assortment of jeeps and trucks trundled into Calle España, the street running past the main gate of the old Dominican University of Santo Tomás. They waited there while more trucks came up. The force numbered 200 GIs, led by a lieutenant colonel, Haskett ("Hack") Conner. They were the frontrunners of a "flying column" of tanks and motorized infantry — really a series of small detachments — cutting through the Japanese lines to liberate Santo Tomás Internment Camp, the university turned prison for nearly 4,000 Allied nationals.

While the force waited for more tanks to show up (some had got lost), the camp seemed strangely quiet. There was no movement from the guardhouse just inside the gate. No lights from the Main Building, a stone and concrete structure whose massive tower and tall crucifix dominated the camp.

A sizzling sound like a firecracker broke the silence. A Japanese soldier had stepped out of the guardhouse and thrown a grenade. Two GIs shot him dead through the railings, but the grenade had found targets. Shrapnel gashed Colonel Conner's leg and mortally wounded Captain Manuel Colayco, one of two Filipino guerrillas who had helped guide the Americans through the city.

There was no time to wait for reinforcements. The lead tank, "Battlin' Basic," scraped through the gate's arch, showering bits of masonry onto the helmets of riflemen walking beside it. The camp broke into life as jubilant, cheering internees tumbled out of the Main Building to meet the tanks.

Not all the camp was freed that night. The main Japanese garrison, some 68 men, barricaded themselves into their main quarters in another building, along with more than 200 internees. They used the internees as hostages to negotiate "safe conduct" out of the camp early on 5 February. Many were subsequently killed in the fighting that raged through the city, but the "safe conduct" agreement is said to have been unique in the Pacific war.

Just over three years before, on 4 January 1942, the first internees had entered the camp, following the Japanese invasion of the Philippines. In a few weeks Santo Tomás Internment Camp ("STIC" or "the camp" to its inmates) held more than 2,000 American civilians, the largest number imprisoned by the enemy in World War II. (The word "enemy" is important here. America's "relocation centers" for its own Japanese American citizens were much bigger, averaging over 10,000 internees each.) The second-largest group in the camp, the British, numbered almost nine hundred, and about a fifth of the camp through all years.

The STIC internee story is one of dramatic changes, from a life of privilege and access to servants in prewar Manila, the "Pearl of the Orient," to the initial stress and strangeness of internment, and then, remarkably quickly, the creation of a well-organized community, with entertainments, shops, schooling, public health, and access to money and goods from outside. Through 1944, however, as the tide of war turned against them, the Japanese tightened the screws, tried to seal off outside contacts, and repeatedly cut the food supply, even stealing from the camp's own food reserves. By December 1944, deaths from malnutrition were accelerating, with many more walking cases of beriberi; calorie intake was well below 1,000 per day per person. It became a race between mass starvation and rescue by American forces retaking the Philippines. Fear that the Japanese planned outright massacre of the internees, though not confirmed, impelled the U.S. commanding general, Douglas MacArthur, to send the flying column to Santo Tomás in advance of his main assault on Manila.

The story here becomes very personal. Aged eight, I was one of the internees, mostly men and boys, held hostage by the garrison soldiers as they negotiated their passage out of the camp. We were used as a human wall by the Japanese encamped in the corridor behind our dormitories.

After all the internees were liberated, the camp briefly became a forward base in the U.S. army's fight to recapture Manila. The camp's travails were not over. Japanese shelling killed seventeen of the newly rescued internees, plus Filipino workers and a GI (my first sight of bloodied bodies), before the guns were wiped out. But Santo Tomás then became a safe haven in the ensuing Battle for Manila, which devastated the starving city and killed over 100,000 Filipinos.

Throughout their travails, though less at the end, STIC internees retained verve and humor, expressed in coded digs at their captors on the internee-run loudspeakers. They also displayed an impressive range of skills, from plumbing new latrines to medical aid. A strong internee administration, partially elected, worked through a network of committees covering everything from entertainment to running its own jail and the public shaming of thieves and drunks. The internees were not just passive victims. Adjusting old values to new demands, they re-created a society, organizing themselves to survive mentally as well as physically.

How did they do this? How did ordinary people face a world turned upside-down, the loss of home and freedom, and imprisonment by an alien, often frightening enemy? "I wonder how I would have coped," friends have sometimes said to me. There was, of course, no one way of coping. Internment brought out the best in people, the worst in people, and lots of behavior in between. On that score, getting stuck in a prison camp was no different from any other cataclysm that hits a community.

What about the internee leaders — mainly business executives — who ran the camp under Japanese control? How did they adjust to becoming public officials, exchanging profit for collective survival as the measure of success? What compromises did they strike with their Japanese overlords, and why did the Japanese let them govern the camp? Why indeed, for all the turmoil inflicted on internees, did the Japanese treat the "enemy aliens" of Santo Tomás better than Manila's Filipinos, their supposed allies?

The camp's history really started in January 1941, eleven months before Pearl Harbor, when a group of top American business executives rebelled at American and Philippine government inertia, as they saw it, toward the Japanese threat. Working with the Red Cross, they instigated a shelter-building program and urged people to store food and other supplies in case of a Japanese invasion. In December 1941, when invasion was imminent, American and Filipino leaders knew the Japanese would want to intern Allied nationals. They planned to recommend the University of Santo Tomás as a campsite. This enraged the university's clergy faculty, most of whom were Spanish, pro–Franco and pro-fascist.

For the first six months of internment, the Japanese relied solely on the Red Cross and internees' outside connections to feed and supply the camp. Even when the Japanese took belated responsibility for this, they did so via the internee administration, which also brought in extra money and food from outside contacts. Internee leaders walked a tricky line, defending internee interests while placating Japanese power and its need to maintain "face." Internees sometimes accused their leaders of "dictatorship," favoritism, and secret cozying up to the Japanese commandant. The camp's leaders were certainly proactive, and not just inside the camp. A few weeks before the rescue, the top internee administrator, Carroll Grinnell, and several others were taken out of camp by the dreaded Kempeitai (Japanese secret police), tortured, and beheaded, probably for smuggling food and medicine to a military POW camp, Cabanatuan, and communicating secretly with guerrillas.

The camp's most traumatic event happened in its first six weeks: three internee men (two British, one Australian) were badly beaten and then executed for trying to escape. Other internee men were occasionally taken to the military prison, Fort Santiago, for interrogation and torturing, on suspicion of illicit contacts with the outside world. There was also a reverse atrocity during the camp's rescue, when internees savaged a particularly hated Japanese soldier, Lieutenant Nanakazu Abiko, after he was shot by the U.S. Army and mortally wounded. (The names of Japanese in this book are Westernized, putting surname after given name, the reverse of Japanese practice. Initials or rank are used when the full given name is not known.)

In day-to-day life, though, the Japanese guards mostly kept away from internees; sporadic bullying by Abiko and others was mitigated by friendliness to children. The main Japanese atrocity was slow-motion killing through malnutrition. In a final irony, one of the camp doctors, Ted Stevenson, who tended Abiko in his last agony, had been jailed for refusing to delete "malnutrition" and "starvation" from death certificates.

Writing the Santo Tomás story started with my family. In 1934 my parents, Gerald and Lorna Wilkinson, moved from England to the Philippines, where my father began a successful career in the sugar industry and other businesses. At the same time he was working covertly for Britain's Secret Intelligence Service (later also called MI6), reporting on Japanese espionage and military activities. In late November 1941 and again in early December, four days before Pearl Harbor, he warned of an imminent Japanese attack somewhere in the Pacific. His second warning had more impact on his business than the military: the American end of his company turned around in mid–ocean a Philippine-bound ship.

Following the Japanese invasion of the Philippines in December 1942, the U.S. and Philippine commander, General Douglas MacArthur, declared Manila an "open city," not to be defended in order to save it from destruction. On Christmas Eve, MacArthur and his staff moved to Corregidor, the fortress island in Manila Bay that became the last Philippine holdout against the Japanese. My father now a British army major and Britain's liaison officer on MacArthur's staff, went with him to Corregidor and later joined him in Australia, leaving Corregidor by submarine before it fell. The rest of us — my mother, Lorna, aged not quite thirty-four; my sister Mary June, aged eight; and myself, aged five — went into Santo Tomás in early January.

For decades after the war I resisted writing about the camp. I knew that others had, and some of the first-hand accounts by internees seemed self-piteous, especially when compared with much worse camps in Indonesia and the suffering of Manila's Filipinos. In the early 2000s, however, my grown-up children persuaded me to write up my own memories of camp life, if only for the family and maybe a library archive. I inserted in my account some memories (and memory corrections!) from my sister as well as my best friend in the camp, Nick Balfour; my mother had by then died. Then I started to look more closely at other writings on Santo Tomás, as a reality check and to give more context to what I had written.

The literature of Santo Tomás was much larger and richer than I had realized. It comes in two kinds: a wealth of first-hand accounts and various histories. (For more on these, see Appendix III, "The Literature of Santo Tomás.") The first-hand accounts include diaries and some unsung literary gems. They number over twenty-five books (many privately published), plus essays and articles, and three books of cartoons and other drawings. Although the internee government was dominated by men, most of the memoirs are by women. All in all, they portray more hardship than I had realized. At my age, the taunting I got from American kids for being a funny-sounding, "bloody Limey" was usually worse than any fear of the Japanese. I underestimated the stress for adults of being crammed into overnight dormitories in beds cheek by jowl with other families, as well as enduring long lines for toilets; of saying no to hungry children when they asked for more food; of worrying about absent spouses, especially husbands in the hell-holes that passed for Japanese military POW camps. And for all my own, growing hunger, I underestimated the suffering caused by malnutrition and did not share adult worries about how it would all end.

Histories of Santo Tomás range from a few straight narratives about the camp to military histories and books on different camps and internees that *include* Santo Tomás. All historical study of the camp has to start with the three volumes about Santo Tomás and the Philippines under the Japanese by internee Abraham Hartendorp (generally known by his initials, A.V.H.). The writing of these books is a story in itself. An anthropologist, teacher, and journalist, Hartendorp typed away almost daily during internment, muffling his typewriter on a blanket and guarded by fellow internees who kept a lookout for Japanese guards. Hiding his papers in a hollow pillar, he walked out of the camp with 4,000 pages that were later used in the Tokyo war-crimes trials of Japanese commanders and officials. To these he added more research on the wartime Philippines.

None of the books I found does what my book does: give a history that is at once "bottom up" and "top down," combining the experience of internees (what they went through, how they coped, and how they felt — including my own experience and that of my family) with the history and politics that landed them in the camp, shaped the camp, and got most of them out in the end. No one person or group dominates the first-hand accounts, but there are seven eyewitnesses, authors of memoirs and diaries, who appear often enough to bring them onstage here. In order of appearance, they are:

- Tressa Roka, a nurse, interned with her fiancé, Lowell Cates. Working in the camp hospital, her own health deteriorating, she saw the worst of the malnutrition and a lot else. Her secret *Drainpipe Diary* got its name from a drainpipe hiding place; keeping a diary was a serious offense.
- Paul Esmérian, a six-foot-six Gaullist (anti–Nazi) Frenchman not interned until 1943, whose diary — thoughtful, opinionated, vivid — is one of the best accounts we have of wartime Manila and camp life.
- Robin Prising, interned as a boy of eight, whose book, *Manila, Goodbye*, won more literary recognition than any other memoir of the camp.
- Geege (pronounced Geegee) Wootten, interned at 20 without family, not sure if she was in love, and homesick despite a circle of friends. Discovering a talent for drawing, she traded children's portraits for food.
- Emily Van Sickle, wife of a well-to-do business executive, without children, who wrestled with issues of inequality in the camp.
- Margaret Sherk, interned with her small boy, who told of having a baby during internment — this proved controversial, as it was not by her husband, a military POW elsewhere.
- Elizabeth Vaughan, who started in another camp, Bacolod, and wrote a sociology of its life as well as a camp diary. The anxious mother of two small children, whose father was another military POW, she learned of his death while in Santo Tomás.

Many other witnesses also come across these pages. And remarkable characters too, such as Earl Carroll, an internee leader, skilled at knowing when to get angry in the commandant's office (and when not to); Dave Harvey MacTurk, a brilliant dancer and impresario of shows and concerts; and the Chinese American Tun Yem Lee, jailed as the only internee who refused to sign a Japanese loyalty oath (he also refused Red Cross aid as "charity" until his clothes almost fell apart). Japanese characters range from Hitoshi Tomayasu, the camp's first commandant, forced to execute the camp's first escapers but basically benign, to a later commandant, Colonel Yoshie, an eccentric, mercurial fan of baseball, to the proud, immaculate Lieutenant Abiko, commander of the camp guard.

The Santo Tomás saga is one of stories within stories. For example, Luis de Alcuaz, the dynamic young assistant to the university rector (president), appears in the published record here and there as the lynchpin of smuggling chains that brought money, medicine, food, and radio parts into the camp — until he had to go into hiding near the end when Japanese investigators were on his trail. As a professor of chemistry and chemical engineering, Alcuaz also enabled the camp to set up its own soap-making and other operations for public hygiene. What other books don't tell is the way Alcuaz operated within the university to block the largely pro-fascist, Spanish faculty from interfering in the camp — and how he was forced to resign a few weeks after liberation, his presence anathema to the university's top brass and most of its clergy faculty.

On a lower, grubbier level, the history of Santo Tomás needs to make more of children's experiences, though my own memories of the camp's early years are fragmentary. For children especially, life was not just about surviving but also about relating to others and adjusting to big changes while staving off boredom — playing jacks, trading marbles, collecting beetles, and inventing new games. And none of the histories mention the intense community of the Boys' Club, based in several dormitory rooms for boys, especially those without fathers in the camp, run by three men who applied tough love.

Histories of the camp, unlike some of the memoirs, also say little about economic inequality between internees — what some internees called "the haves" versus "have nots." "Have nots" included the improvident, those who did not conserve the big Red Cross food parcels that occasionally came in. But they also included those without contacts in Manila — servants and neutral friends such as the Swiss and Spanish — who could send in food and other things, even fresh laundry, until that was banned a year before the end. Though richer internees were often generous to their own friends, internees did not pool their own resources as much as in a smaller Philippine camp, Bacolod. I knew none of this at the time, not just because of my age but also because economic inequality was — in a very American way — overlaid by an equality of social relations. Former business executives cleaned out latrines as well as serving on committees; William Bryant, the colonial governor of a Philippine province who became a coconut planter, preferred to work in the camp garden rather than join the camp administration. The histories do record, more or less in passing, the creation of a committee to aid "the indigent" (committee minutes initially used that term) but it got little publicity.

What about the Japanese themselves, and the Taiwanese who largely replaced the Japanese guards by the end? From news smuggled into the camp, internees soon realized that the Japanese army treated military POWs much more brutally than civilian internees. The literature on Santo Tomás recognizes this, though it seldom mentions a crucial factor — Japanese military contempt for soldiers who surrendered. Histories and memoirs of Santo Tomás also note that some members of the Japanese garrison were kinder than others, but they rarely try to get into their shoes or feelings, or discuss how they were organized and who had what power.

Understanding the Japanese side of the Santo Tomás story is the hardest nut to crack and we can only take it so far. Most Japanese records of the camp were deliberately destroyed, and we can find no first-hand accounts of Santo Tomás by camp Japanese, nearly all of whom have died.[1] This said, it is now possible to build up a better picture of the Japanese in Santo Tomás, using a mixture of old and new evidence. New sources include a guard logbook, specially translated for this book, reporting the assignments and events of each day.

For all its difficulties, the problem of learning about the camp's Japanese is part of a wider fog of war, which rolled in more thickly at the end. In Chapter 11 I tell the story of the camp's liberation through the eyes of rescuers as well as the rescued. Or rather, I tell it as accurately as I can. Most histories of the liberation get something wrong, passing on the error to other writers. Even eyewitness accounts can record incidents in the wrong order or telescope two events into one. All memory is vulnerable to this, but it is particularly liable to happen when the original events tumbled over each other in the flux and stress of military action. The best the historian can do is to stack up the different accounts, be frank about uncertainty, and judge what most likely happened.

The same is true for claims, repeated in many memoirs, that the Japanese planned to kill all Santo Tomás internees, or all males above a certain age. Between rumor, the incompleteness of Japanese records, and the death of internees who claimed some knowledge of massacre orders, we may never know for sure. Historians have tended to deny it and I think it unlikely (see Chapter 12), although it was never absent as a threat. Many internees believed the Japanese were simply more cruel, more prone to atrocities, than Westerners. They had cause to believe this. But it led me in the final chapter to ponder two things: What do we mean by "atrocity," and why, even today, is there more consensus that massacres by Japanese soldiers, and systematic torture by the Japanese secret police, were atrocities, compared with the Allied firebombing of Japanese and German cities? And when people are conditioned and brutalized to do awful things, how much can we still hold them culpable?

A final note about the book's shape and its sources: This is not an exhaustive history of the camp. Unlike Hartendorp's volumes, I do not tell the camp's story month by month. The chapters in this book are thematic; they follow a chronological sequence but overlap in time. My extensive use of internee memoirs to convey personal experience has its own problems. The most reliable memoirs are diaries, which say what an internee saw, did, and felt that day. Some memoirs amplify the diaries by giving more memories and comments after liberation, and some are purely retrospective, written at differing periods after the war. All kinds are valuable, but again memory can distort. I have tried to limit this by comparing the memoirs with each other, with camp histories, and with what other ex-internees have told me. Few of these people were above twenty years old at the time but several have done considerable research on the camp. As a result of what they told me, I cut out appealing stories from a memoir that contained self-enhancing fantasies.

All written sources, as well as DVDs, tapes, and TV and radio programs, are in the bibliography. I have used the book's endnotes mainly for sources of quotations, issues of fact, and some technicalia.

1

War Clouds Over Eden

In November 1936, Denny Williams, a U.S. Army nurse later interned in Santo Tomás, started work at Corregidor ("the Rock"), the army's island base in Manila Bay. A highlight for Williams was her monthly time-off in Manila, chugging by ferry across the bay to the city. Williams loved the teeming bustle of Manila, even its traffic jams. New American cars competed with horse-drawn *calesas* (carriages) and carts with coconuts pulled by *carabaos* (water buffalos), not to mention darting "auto-calesas," forerunners of the jeepney, stop-anywhere little buses. On the sidewalks, turbaned Moros from the islands' Muslim minority "hurried majestically among crowds of Japanese, Chinese and Filipinos ... all talking rapidly in their own languages and at their own tempo, while over everything was the interminable screeching of odd melodies from Chinese recordings." Williams enjoyed the street theater: Filipino men in undershirts bargaining with peddlers selling *puto*, small sweet rice cakes, dangling off bamboo poles; or the crowd that instantly gathered to shout insults and advice at a cart driver when his hapless *carabao* slipped and fell on a wet street.[1]

Behind the kaleidoscope, as Williams recognized, there were three Manilas: Filipino, Spanish, and American, each permeating the others. Filipino Manila was the city of the great, Tagalog-speaking majority, originally of Malay stock with admixtures of Chinese. Most of Manila's Filipinos were very poor, living in small, crowded dwellings, and working as laborers, servants, and storekeepers or peddlers.

Spanish Manila reflected over three centuries of rule by Spain that ended with the U.S. takeover in 1898 after the Spanish-American War. Especially among the upper classes, many *Manileños* (a Spanish term still used today for Manilans) were *mestizos*—a word that came to mean Spanish-Filipino mixtures and had no overtone of "half-caste" inferiority. The historic heart of Spanish Manila was the "walled city," or *Intramuros*, 400 acres of narrow, cobbled streets, churches and forts. Over the years it had lost some of its gentility to bars, restaurants, and boarding houses, and some of its grand old homes had been subdivided into apartments.

Across the Pasig River from the walled city, the University of Santo Tomás, founded by Dominicans in 1611, was officially more Spanish than Filipino. Its patrons were the pope and General Franco of Spain, officiating through high-level Dominicans in Rome and Madrid. At the outbreak of the war, its top leaders in Manila and all but five of its thirty-eight elite clergy faculty ("the fathers") were Spanish citizens; the five were Americans. The lay faculty were Filipino.

American Manila was the result of U.S. political and economic dominance from the early 1900s, though American and European firms were operating there in the nineteenth century. The city's smartest shopping street, the Escolta, outdid most American Main Streets in its range and quality of American brands. Import-export businesses flourished in Manila, which was also the "head office" for American, European and Filipino enterprises across the country, from sugar to mining. Business opportunities, the widespread use of English, and cheap and plentiful servants, combined with Asian color and Spanish elegance, gave Manila its name as "Pearl of the Orient" for a growing "expat" community. By no means were all expats American but Americans predominated in numbers and culture.

Flying high on American-led affluence was Pan American Airways' glamorous "Clipper" flying-boat service from San Francisco and Honolulu to Manila, inaugurated in 1935 (*Time* magazine put the pilot on its cover) and later extended to Hong Kong. No airliner had the range to fly directly from Honolulu to Manila, let alone from San Francisco, so Pan Am gave its passengers overnight stays on Midway, Wake, and Guam islands as well as sleeping berths on board. The Clippers' final version, the Boeing 314, had a lounge and dining room providing cocktails and fine meals served by white-coated stewards. The Boeings flew up to 72 passengers weekly at a one-way fare, Manila–San Francisco, of $700—over $10,000 today. The flights took almost five days, but steamships took three weeks. The passenger

Expats called prewar Manila the "Pearl of the Orient" for the lifestyle and color they found there. A high point of expat living—for those who could afford it—was the Pan American Airways Clipper flying-boat service from San Francisco with overnight hotel stops at Honolulu and three Pacific islands. The Boeing 314 shown here had sleeping berths despite the stopovers (*courtesy Special Collections, University of Miami Libraries, Coral Gables, Florida*).

lists included business executives and owners for whom time was money but they also featured senior military officers, foreign correspondents, movie actors, and an assortment of the privately rich.

Beneath the metropolitan high fliers the Filipino-Spanish-American mix extended far beyond Manila, across the many islands that made up the country. To the visitor's eye, nothing could be more Filipino than the rice paddies, fishing villages, and *nipa* huts — the standard rural homes, often just one room, roofed with *nipa* thatch made from palms, and standing on stilts above chickens or pigs. Equally Filipino, at the other end of the scale, was the *barong tagalog*, the embroidered over-shirt worn by men on formal occasions.

The most obvious Spanish legacy was the church, ministering to a predominantly Catholic population. The Philippines were and are Asia's only Christian country. Spain also influenced Filipino music. Dance halls and cabarets featured Spanish-Philippine *jota* dances as well as *kundiman* Filipino love songs and American cakewalks and ragtime.

American influence was most obvious in schools and hospitals but also in general attitudes *toward* the Americans. American culture and consumer goods exerted a magnetic pull on many Filipinos. And it was not just materialistic. When war came, the country's new Japanese masters would be infuriated by Filipino affection and support for imprisoned Americans and other Westerners. A cultural pro–Americanism had long flourished, even among some Philippine nationalists. Marcial Lichauco, the first Filipino to graduate from Harvard College before going on to Harvard Law School in 1923, campaigned eloquently for Philippine independence while in the United States of America, encouraged by liberal American friends.

The U.S. political presence in the Philippines had started bloodily. In the Spanish-American War of 1898, U.S. representatives encouraged a Filipino revolt led by Emilio Aguinaldo against a Spanish rule that had become more and more repressive. The United States then rejected the revolutionaries' demand for independence. When Spain finally ceded the Philippines to the United States for $20 million, President William McKinley had decided to "take them all, to educate the Filipinos, and uplift and Christianize them" (some 80 percent had been Catholic for centuries). Despite a strong American Anti-Imperialist League, McKinley rode a tide of U.S. expansionism. Doubting that the revolutionaries could give the islands a unifying government, he and other U.S. leaders saw the Philippines as a source of wealth and a military base, too valuable to leave for other powers to grab.

And so the Spanish-American War was succeeded by the Philippine-American War, or what Americans usually called the "Philippine Insurrection," marked by massacres and other atrocities on both sides. By the time it ended officially in 1902, with the capture and surrender of the revolt's leaders, it had killed about 4,200 American soldiers, 20,000 Filipino fighters, 200,000 Filipino civilians (many through famine), and 90 percent of the country's carabaos — the farmers' main beast of burden and source of milk. Some guerrilla fighting continued for another eleven years.

The regime that followed was colonial without fully believing in it. The basic tone was set by the country's first American civil governor, William Howard Taft (1902–1904), who later became the only man to be both U.S. president and Supreme Court chief justice. He was also the stoutest president ever, weighing in at 354 pounds; he once got stuck in a White House bathtub. In the Philippines his fatness signaled genial relaxation rather than overbearing size. Though he believed that "our little brown brothers" would take a long time to qualify for full self-government, he got on well with the Filipinos and encouraged the country's political development. By 1916, the country had a two-chamber legislature, though the governor and the United States retained extensive economic and military powers. In 1935, after political tussles in both countries, congressional legislation set up a timetable aimed at giving the Philippines full independence in 1946. The following year, the charismatic, mercurial Manuel Quezon was elected president of a new Commonwealth of the Philippines, responsible for most internal affairs. Defense was shared with the United States via an American military adviser, the imperious but politically cunning General Douglas MacArthur.

American power underpinned political change by promoting education and health, including the training of doctors and nurses. When war came, Santo Tomás Internment Camp would benefit from surrounding hospitals that took in seriously ill internees and sent in volunteer Filipino doctors, as well as a public health tradition that stressed hygiene. Economically, though, the American-Philippine system was lopsided, entrenching Philippine dependence on America. Special U.S. trade legislation, permitting tariff-free imports from the Philippines, encouraged exports to the United States of America rather than production for home consumption. In the long run — actually starting under the Spanish — the export-driven expansion of sugarcane plantations reduced rice planting, though admittedly some areas were particularly well suited to sugar. Before the war, the Philippines was barely self-sufficient in rice; it had to be imported in bad years — not a good starting point for when the war came and further reduced rice production.[2]

Americans in the Philippines seldom saw any of this as imperialism. Compared with

Lorna Wilkinson at her parents' English country house, circa 1930.

Rupert and Mary June Wilkinson, a year or two before internment, at our home near Manila. Our father, Gerald Wilkinson, not interned, carried the photograph all through the war.

the Spanish before them and the Japanese after, their power had a light touch. And the export-led policies benefited Filipino sugar kings and other big native producers as well as American and European firms. Socially, though, there was plenty of racism, both conscious and unconscious. For example, Filipino male house servants of whatever age were called "houseboys." The term involved class as well as race, but racism went beyond class distinctions. Up to just before the war, some American companies instructed their young bachelor executives not to marry Filipinas or mestizas. Brent School, the American boarding school in the mountain vacation town of Baguio, excluded Filipinos. So did Manila clubs and golf courses such as the Manila and Army-Navy Clubs, as well as the Elks. However, the Rotary Club and women's charitable organizations were deliberately cross-cultural, though not to the point of approving intermarriage. The exclusive Polo Club dropped its racial bar in the late 1930s when it admitted some elite Filipinos, including President Quezon. Memberships aside, nationality groups tended to socialize with their own sort. This was even true of Americans and British within the expat community.

The Westerners were not all rich, though their standard of living could make them feel that way. The 1930s depression in America had encouraged a range of people, from stenographers to engineers, to seek jobs and find a better life in the Philippines. And find it they did. Soon after internment in Santo Tomás, Tressa Roka recalled her "glorious life" before the war when working as a civilian nurse in a Manila army hospital. After taxiing to work, she would return to her apartment, where her cook/maid, Adoracion, had prepared supper and laid out a freshly laundered uniform for the next day. Her six-hour working day left time in the evenings for swimming or dancing at one of the clubs with her fiancé. On weekends there might be sailing in the bay, and on vacations a trip to Hong Kong or Shanghai.[3]

Following Spanish customs, many business offices closed for two hours in the hottest part of the day (and continued to do so even when air conditioning arrived after the war). Getting to the office by 8 A.M., executives — expat and Filipino alike — would often go home for lunch and a siesta, and then return to the office. At five or six, they would repair to their clubs for drinks with business friends, before going home for supper. They would usually spend Saturday mornings at the office.

The wives and mothers in Western business families seldom had paid jobs; at least one bank banned executive wives from working for money. Spared housework and a lot of childcare by servants, they had a full social life, meeting friends to play bridge or mahjong, and playing tennis, badminton, or golf at the various clubs, as well as business entertaining for their husbands. They also did charitable work. At the Red Cross, my mother, Lorna Wilkinson, helped produce a charity sale of "Mary June" dolls, named after my sister. (Like her, they were blondes, but they annoyed her because their eyes were blue, not her distinctive hazel-brown.)

Our own household was fairly typical of prosperous Western business families living on the outskirts of Manila. Our semi-rural street was aptly named Hibiscus Avenue for the hibiscus and bougainvillea that blossomed along it. Our large garden contained swings, a see-saw, and a big mango tree with low branches well positioned for climbing. A "houseboy" in his twenties, Angel (pronounced Ung-hel) Lodovica, kept the house clean, polishing the floors by moving half a coconut around under his bare foot; the white coconut flesh was the polish. His brother, Anastasia, cooked and did much of the food purchasing along with Eustaquio Pontejo, the driver. Angel's wife, Estolita, was our *lavendera*, doing all the household washing and ironing. All our servants and their families lived in a small bungalow on the property, except for Eustaquio, who walked in from a *barrio* (Filipino neighborhood) nearby.

More unusually among expat business families with young children, our parents decided not to employ a Filipino nanny or *amah*, as they thought that amahs tended to "spoil" the young, giving in to brattish demands. Instead, they brought from England a professionally trained "Norland Nanny" in her sixties, Lucy Evans, who had once been governess to a Siamese (Thai) prince, as she liked to remind us. For us, too, she was officially a "governess" but she was basically a rather censorious nanny. "Evie" was interned with us in the camp and became less important in our lives, whereas our mother became more so.[4]

Our mother had qualities that would make her a bedrock for Mary June and myself in the camp. Slim and very pretty, she came across in a way that some Santo Tomás Americans later saw in other British — "they're reserved but great when you get to know them." Totally accepting her privileges, she accepted adversity, too, when that came along. Modest and practical, with a talent for drawing and painting, she took life as it came. Her background, actually, was not typically British. Born in Hawaii, she had dual British and American passports. Her father, Clive Davies, was board chairman of a Hawaiian company, Theo H. Davies, centered on the sugar business and founded by *his* father, Theophilus, a Welsh minister's son. Clive and family divided their lives between Hawaii and his country estate in England.

Gerald Wilkinson, our father, had married the boss's daughter. A rising young insurance branch manager in England, he took over the Philippine branch of T.H. Davies in early 1935, expanding it from its core business — sugar milling and marketing — into diverse activities including insurance and general merchandising. In time Davies Far East became the most profitable part of the company. Gerald Wilkinson combined dynamism and charisma with thoughtful intelligence and a love of the Philippines. Business enterprise was his passion but, as mentioned in the introduction, he also worked for Britain's Secret Intelligence Service. At first he reported on Japanese business and espionage activities within the Philippines (he was not the only person to mix the two); later, he extended this to Japanese movements throughout the Pacific, swapping intelligence with the Americans.

Ever since its resounding victory over Russia in the Russo-Japanese War of 1904–1905, Japan had been a recognized threat to Western power in the Far East. Within ten years it ruled Korea and had bullied China into giving it economic dominance over part of Manchuria. Between the two world wars, Japan's increasingly militarist governments developed an expansionist foreign policy, driven by army ambitions, hunger for more resources, and a fascist wish to dominate. U.S. exclusion of Japanese immigrants and racist ridicule of the Japanese (well known to Tokyo's elites) made Japan's leaders all the keener to be taken seriously abroad. Economically, they felt that Western colonial empires had left Japan "bottled up" in a race for land and wealth. In 1931 Japan overran Manchuria. In 1937 it invaded the rest of China. At the end of that year, horrific reports and pictures exposed the "Rape of Nanking" (Nanjing), in which the Japanese troops descended to an orgy of rape, mutilation, and massacre, sparing not even tiny children.[5]

U.S. contingency planning for a Pacific war with Japan had started before World War I. The Philippines featured prominently in the planning but assumptions about it varied. In the 1920s and 1930s, many planners believed that the Philippines would initially fall to a Japanese attack: it was too far to reinforce in time. They turned out to be right, but no one at the time was prepared to tell the American people this, let alone the Filipinos. Instead, a series of "Orange" planning reports ("Orange" meant Japan) revolved around the assumption that American and Filipino forces would defend the Philippines, or at least the Manila Bay area, until help came.

At the end of 1940, as Japanese forces advanced across China, opinion divided in Manila about their threat to the Philippines. Many — Filipinos as well as Westerners — discounted it. To them, the Japanese in China were a barbaric but tinpot army. Why else had they taken so long to conquer the "weak" Chinese? They would not dare to take on the Americans in the Philippines and would get a licking if they tried. Some held this attitude right up to the Japanese attack on Pearl Harbor a year later. It was reinforced by Western stereotypes of the Japanese: the copycat manufacturer who sold shoddy goods, the bespectacled pilot who couldn't fly straight.

Others took a different view. Japan was on the move with troops seasoned by years of fighting in China, which was no pushover. They were getting close to Hong Kong and Malaya, and had already seized the Spratly Islands between the Philippines and Indochina. In the Philippines both government and community were being much too easygoing; the country needed military reinforcements from the United States and defense efforts from its own people.

Some leading American businessmen in Manila took this second view. In January 1941, they organized a mass meeting at the Elks Club to air their concerns, first and foremost about the security of Americans but also about the country's defense. Three hundred people attended, including some non–Americans. Out of this meeting came the "American Coordinating Committee," seeking better coordination on security between the different civil and military agencies. Cooling relations between U.S. High Commissioner Francis Sayre, who had wanted more planning for the Japanese threat, and Philippine President Manuel Quezon made this all the more important. Aside from political differences (Sayre was the deeper democrat), the two men were almost exact opposites — Sayre sensitive and thoughtful but outwardly stiff and straight-laced; Quezon flamboyant, slippery, and a talented libertine.

Chaired by Frederic Stevens, a longtime Manila resident and entrepreneur, the Coordinating Committee held weekly lunchtime meetings. It was usually attended by an American military officer and the high commissioner's executive assistant, Claude Buss (who got on better with Quezon than his boss). The committee helped plan the building of air raid shelters as well as evacuation centers for Allied women and children in the event of invasion — a plan never actually used. They also encouraged citizens to stockpile food, clothes, and medicines, for which some laughed at the committee as alarmist. The committee worked so closely with the American Philippine Red Cross that it later became part of the Red Cross, changing its name to the "American Emergency Committee."

Early in 1941, the American committee pressed High Commissioner Sayre to advise all American women and children to return to the United States of America. Sayre nearly did so but then seemed to change his mind. Committee chairman Stevens later called this a "calamity," but Sayre was under pressure from Washington to do so. Already the U.S. government had sent home military families and quietly advised the families of other government employees to go home too. But promoting a general American exodus would signal defeatism and betrayal to Filipinos; it might lose them as allies. To an extraordinary extent not generally realized until after the war, the U.S. State Department tried to prevent American residents of the Philippines from returning to the United States. Having collected up many American passports, from late summer of 1941 the High Commission's passport Officer would not return them to Americans who wanted to leave. U.S. officials also got shipping agents to deny access on ships home. In mid–November, the State Department lifted a rule requiring passports to leave the Philippines and other U.S. "territories," but by then regular civilian sailings to America had stopped.

It seems remarkable now that American expats did not compare notes on all this and make more of a fuss about it. They did not do so until 2004, when 598 ex–Philippine internees and their "descendants" sued the federal government for failure to inform and protect them. The case was rejected on "statute of limitations" grounds: the federal courts held that the plaintiffs could and should have complained earlier.[6] At the time, in fact, many Americans and other Westerners did not have homes elsewhere and did not want to leave. And not all took the war threat seriously. Among those who did were William and Sophie Gibb on Negros island. They had visited Nazi Germany and became very conscious of the short distance between Japan and the Philippines. As early as March 1941, they were worried enough — and rich enough — to fly their eleven-year-old daughter, Allie, by Pan Am clipper to Hawaii, where she stayed with an aunt and uncle and later went to Punahou Academy, Hawaii's top prep school. Allie's father was due to retire and leave at the end of the year. Instead, he and his wife ended up in Santo Tomás.

Meanwhile, the hoped-for military reinforcements from the United States of America did not become reality until July 1941. By then it was too little, too late. July was the crunch month, sealing much of the Philippines' fate, including Japanese invasion and the internment of Westerners. On 2 July, the Japanese invaded French Indochina, taking it in three weeks with a massive deployment of soldiers, aircraft, and ships. In response, the United States froze Japan's American assets and cut it off from American oil, which provided over half of Japanese military fuel needs. Japan, in turn, stepped up its plans for an attack on Dutch Indonesia, which was rich in oil and other resources. Wiping out American bases in the Philippines would protect Japan's attack and its oil tankers from American air strikes and naval action.

Fearing the worst, U.S. President Franklin Roosevelt made new plans to defend and reassure the Philippines. On 26 July, the same day he froze Japanese assets, he absorbed the Philippine army into a new, combined army and air force command, U.S. Army Forces in the Far East (USAFFE), under General MacArthur. Over the next few months, infantry, artillery, and tanks were shipped into the Philippines and paraded before admiring crowds. Building started on new airstrips to accommodate more fighter planes and the vaunted Boeing B17 long-range bomber.

All this looked more impressive than it was. The USAFFE still depended heavily on Filipino troops, many of them green and ill-equipped. Some had to do their training in coconut helmets with obsolete rifles or even sticks. There were flaws at the top, too. At his best, MacArthur was an inspiring and imaginative leader; he was also boastful and prone to self-deception. He accepted that a Japanese attack would come, but as late as November 1941, three weeks before Pearl Harbor went up in flames on 7 December, he pronounced with great certainty that no attack would happen until April.

Other military officers found it hard to shake off a mind-set that had long seen Manila as an ideal posting for the good life — a party town, not a crucible of strenuous effort. Some of this even survived the shock of Pearl Harbor. In late December, John Curtis, a public-spirited British business executive, had arranged with the army to help them find more transport to move out of Manila. When he phoned army headquarters to say, as instructed, that he was "reporting for extra duty," a colonel, who evidently knew nothing about it, told him, "No one in his right mind ever volunteers for extra duty."[7]

By the autumn, however, emergency measures were more palpable. Returning to Manila in September after a six-month American vacation, John Whitesides, a Manila banker, was not allowed by the U.S. government to take his family back with him. A navy warship escorted his ship. The city he found surprised him: store windows taped up, practice air raid alarms and blackout evenings, and troops moving about the city and suburbs. Some gardens, ours among them, acquired big concrete water pipes, perhaps five feet in diameter, as air raid shelters. We children played in ours — the only use they got. When the bombing came, we used a makeshift cellar instead.

Whitesides also noticed that more American men were temporary bachelors. Their families had probably stayed behind after a vacation as well. This was not true of Europeans, whose countries were already war zones and who had further to go, sailing past German U-boats. Due to his intelligence work, my father, Gerald Wilkinson, was worried enough about Japan in early 1941 to book a steamship for the family to Hawaii, but my parents then changed their minds: my mother wanted to stay as long as possible with her husband. They booked again in November, but by then sailings had been cancelled.

Grace Nash, a professional violinist, was in a similar situation. Her husband Ralph headed the Manila branch of a Seattle engineering firm and they had two small boys. By September 1941 she believed war was coming but knew she was in the minority. Ralph wanted her to leave with the boys while he stayed with his company. Grace, niggled that he seemed to put his company ambitions first, did not want to leave him. And maybe it was a false alarm anyway. At a Manila Hotel party on 5 December, a fellow guest remarked, "What a perfect night for a surprise bombing." A navy captain retorted, "Don't be foolish. Why, we could finish off their navy over the weekend." Pearl Harbor was struck two days later.

Due to the time difference, news of the Pearl Harbor attack did not reach Manila until early morning December 8. Even for my father, more primed than most for impending disaster, "the news was staggering ... I sat down on the verandah looking over our peaceful lawn, at its best in the slanting shades of the early morning, to try to grasp the implications of the assault."[8] Events moved quickly after that. Within two days, Japanese bombers had wiped out most of the Philippines' air cover and naval defense as they blasted the Cavite naval base near Manila and key airfields. Many American planes were sitting ducks on the ground. Intermittent bombing through December concentrated on the port but hit other parts of Manila too, including the nearby Intramuros, the Escolta business street, and several schools and a hospital. On 22 December, Japanese troops landed about 120 miles up the coast from Manila and routed the USAFFE defense. MacArthur pulled all his troops into the Bataan peninsula, Manila Bay's western arm that ran out to Corregidor, which became MacArthur's new headquarters.

On 26 December, MacArthur declared that he would not contest Manila, to spare it from fighting. After the Japanese occupation of Manila on 2 January, the Americans and Filipinos on Bataan, fighting tenaciously despite widespread malaria, held out until 9 April. By that time, MacArthur had been ordered by President Roosevelt to leave Corregidor. He escaped by motorboat and then aircraft to Australia, where he set up new headquarters. Corregidor, the Philippines' last holdout, surrendered on 6 May 1942.

Among Manileños themselves, some reacted to Pearl Harbor amazingly fast; others still discounted the threat. When ten-year-old Hans Hoeflein's parents collected him from the American School at lunchtime on 8 December, he saw their car filled with stockpiled groceries. Lawyer Marcial Lichauco immediately bought extra food, medicine, and two bicycles. But when he asked an oil business friend for some drums of gasoline, he was told not to worry: "Our tankers will keep right on coming [from Indonesia]." A movie executive took the same attitude when advised by Lichauco to store up new films while he could.[9]

Among future internees of Santo Tomás, the first group to experience the real horrors of war were nurses. For Tressa Roka and her colleagues, it was no longer a six-hour day. A stream of bloody and mutilated people arrived in hospitals, especially from the bombed docks. Others had near escapes, and sometimes saw people killed, when a bomb came close. For many, though, it was the sheer noise of the explosions and the spectacle — plumes of thick black smoke from the port area and flaming fireworks at night — that had the most impact. There was also what one observer called the "walking effect" of the bombs: a bomber would often release its bombs one at a time, so they became "giant footsteps, walking toward [you]."[10] Streams of Filipinos left Manila, with pots and pans and stoves lashed onto carts and the backs of buses — a signal that the city was sinking.

Eight months before, in early April, President Quezon had established a Civilian Emergency Administration to prepare for an attack, but this did not prevent some disarray. Gasoline was rationed, then not rationed, then rationed again. Air raid sirens went off but no bombers appeared — and vice versa. Blackout rules were better enforced, with a nice variation that pleased one five-year-old. Our Buick (the office car) got the usual black tape over its headlights, but our Pontiac was allowed green headlight bulbs instead, shedding an unusual, soft light.

There was disarray in the military too. John Curtis, the British businessman, was asked to find more transport because the army suddenly found it did not have enough trucks to get all its troops to Bataan. Appointed as army civilian transport officers, Curtis and some young colleagues augmented their polo shirts and shorts with helmets and revolvers. They commandeered all the trucks at a Ford showroom in return for U.S. Army IOUs, and hired Filipino drivers. Curtis also stood in the middle of the road hijacking buses, whose drivers and passengers were surprisingly cooperative. The only resistance he got was from the American army paymaster, who stalled on paying his drivers until Curtis and an associate physically threatened him.

The speedup of war came to our house on the morning of Christmas Eve, when our father appeared in the uniform of an army major — British liaison officer to MacArthur. He had just been told by MacArthur to join him and other staff that evening to go to Corregidor. After packing a suitcase and making various rapid arrangements, he and my mother were driven by Eustaquio to the docks, where they said goodbye to each other, not knowing if and when they would see each other again. On the same day, President Quezon, U.S. High Commissioner Sayre, and their families and staffs also took a boat to Corregidor, between air raids. Like my father, they were later evacuated from the island by submarine. Quezon, already sickening from tuberculosis, felt wretched about leaving the Philippines, and at first resisted it, but he went on to head a government-in-exile in the United States of America.

Mary June and I do not remember Christmas Day, but she is sure our father made a fleeting return visit the day after, probably to recover secret papers. It raised her hopes that somehow we would go on seeing him. Very soon afterward, we moved into the city to stay with friends, the Shannons — probably because that was thought to be safer than on the outskirts when the Japanese came. The Shannons' garden ran down to the Pasig River, across from great oil tanks. This gave us a front-row seat for a spectacle that many Santo Tomás internees remembered poignantly: the river as well as the tanks ablaze. Water burning? How could this be, I asked my mother, so she explained. Before leaving, our army had set

The U.S. Army took this aerial photograph of the university turned camp after it was liberated but when most internees still lived there. The Main Building, with two inner patios on either side of the tower block, contained male and female dormitories, sex-segregated. The Education Building on the right had male dorms, and the Annex, the long building behind the Main Building, was chiefly for mothers with young children. The seminary, on the left of the Main Building, was out of bounds to internees. Beyond the Annex, the street running left to right is Calle Dapitan, the back boundary of the camp. The little huts sprinkled all over are internee "shanties" or "shacks," initially permitted only for daytime use (see Chapter 4). The somewhat H-shaped building in front is an army field hospital, post-liberation, as is the big hedge behind it *(U.S. Signal Corps)*.

the tanks on fire so the Japanese would not get the oil, and the burning oil had poured into the river. I remember thinking that made sense but what a waste. Sad too: it meant the Americans had been beaten. Mary June found it frightening. Would the flames come across to us? They did not but neighbors were concerned enough to put sandbags along the water edge.

For others in the city, a more alarming sight was the hordes of looters breaking into abandoned stores. The army had thrown open its own general stores but looters moved elsewhere too. The French Paul Esmérian described in his diary the tension of waiting for the invader. People "burn their papers, hide what is possible to hide, pour ... bottles of whisky down the sink, so that the Japanese, when they come, will stay sober. They wait, telephoning each other to have the latest news, or to give each other last minute advice, fearing the worst."[11] Among Westerners as well as Filipinos, there were memories of the Nanjing atrocities and fears of rape by the invading Japanese, though people in the Westerners' quarter of Nanjing had seldom been abused. Claude Buss, the high commissioner's

This Army aerial view from behind the Education Building (left) and Main Building (right) shows the isolation hospital (center) near shanties and gardens. It was important in controlling infectious diseases in a closely packed population. The main hospital, however, was formed from the Santa Catalina nuns' dormitory beyond the Education Building, not visible here *(U.S. Signal Corps)*.

assistant, who had volunteered to stay behind in Manila, thought the non–American expatriates generally more stoic than Americans about their uncertain future. For the Americans, national pride was at stake: the Philippines was *their* country in a way that it was not for Europeans.[12] And in contrast with European history, the Japanese attack was the first assault on an American population since Americans attacked each other in the Civil War.

By the last few days before the Japanese arrived, most Americans and Europeans expected to be imprisoned in some way as "enemy aliens." But where? Unknown to almost all of them, a quiet struggle about this had been going on for several weeks.

Working with Claude Buss, the American Emergency Committee had come up with three possible sites for an internment camp: preferably the Santo Tomás campus, but also the American School and the Polo Club, though they had less space. The committee gave the list to Philippine government representatives who met Japanese officers just outside Manila before the Japanese army entered the city. No clear decision came from the Japanese, though they seemed well informed about locations when they did enter, thanks to secret agents in the Japanese business community (well-known civilians suddenly popped up in uniform). In the meantime, several leading Americans, including Christian Rosenstock, a businessman doubling as the army's property administrator, asked Luis de Alcuaz at Santo Tomás to persuade the Japanese, when they came, to make the campus a camp.

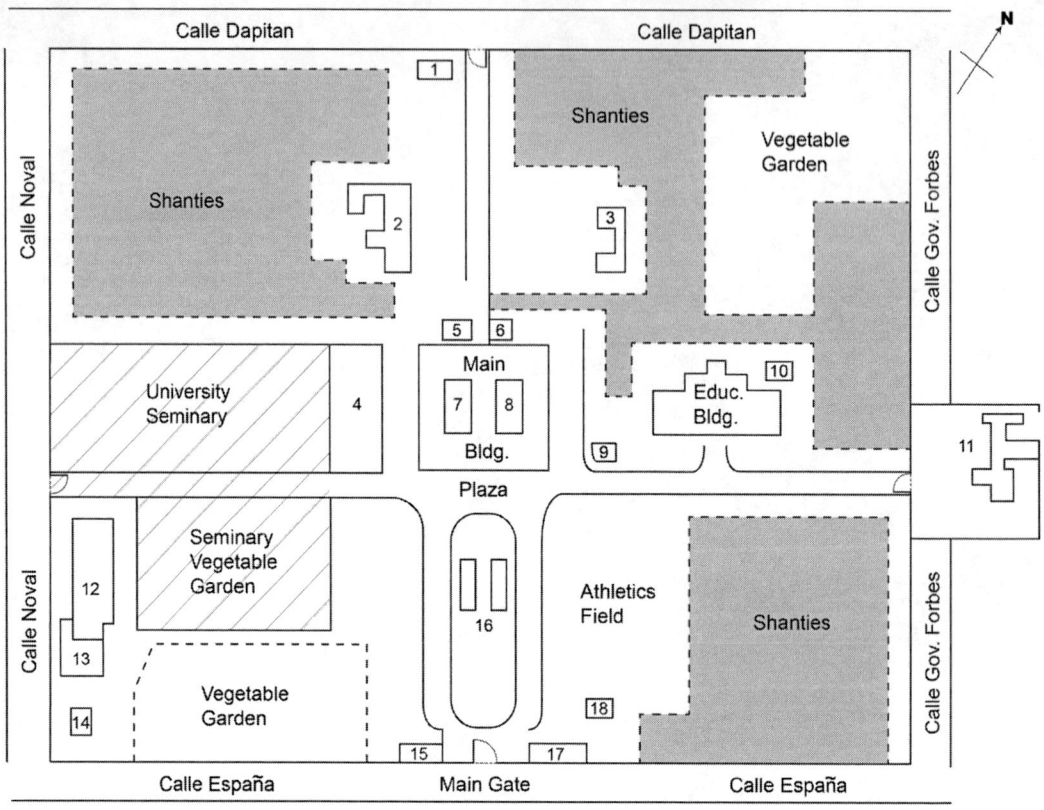

Santo Tomás Internment Camp. The university seminary and seminary vegetable garden on the left were out of bounds to internees. Under Japanese policy against American street names, Gov. Forbes street on the camp's right side was officially changed to Sampaguita, but Filipinos went on calling it Forbes. Key to numbers: (1) Japanese food *bodega* (storehouse); (2) Annex buildings; (3) Isolation hospital; (4) Fathers' Garden (later out of bounds); (5) Main kitchen; (6) Dining shed; (7) West Patio; (8) East Patio; (9) Commandant's office (later moved to the Education Building); (10) Showers and clothes-washing troughs; (11) Santa Catalina Hospital and nuns' dormitory; (12) Gym (mainly dormitory); (13) Water reservoir (former swimming pool) and jail (later moved to the Main Building; (14) Bodega (storehouse); (15) Guardhouse; (16) Pavilions (huts for classes and church services); (17) Garrison quarters (later moved to the Education Building); (18) "Package shed" (for items through main gate.

This diagram-map is not to scale and is based on several versions, especially A.V.H., *The Santo Tomas Story* (1964), 33, and a U.S. Army map (U.S. National Archives) *(map by Rupert Wilkinson and Steve Tam)*.

Aged twenty-six, Alcuaz was the university's youngest-ever full professor of chemistry and the head of two departments, chemistry and chemical engineering. Tough and resourceful, with a presence beyond his years, he was a master of diplomatic language in both Spanish and English. Unlike his Spanish Dominican bosses, he was a Filipino citizen — in fact, a mestizo — and he was pro–American. He was especially close to the family of Louis (Pancho) Francisco, a cultured and well-connected American businessman whose daughter, Pomponette, he married after the war. This intensified his wish to use Santo Tomás to house and protect American and other Western civilians. A devout Catholic, he saw helping the internees as a humanitarian, Christian duty; that, indeed, became his mission.

The university had two chiefs. The senior one, though not officially the president, was thirty-seven-year-old Father Thomas Tascon, chairman of the faculty senate and the country's top Dominican (with the rank of "Provincial"). Junior to him was an older man in his sixties, Father Eugenio Jordan, acting rector (president) while the official rector was away in Spain. Both men had close ties with Franco Spain, which subsidized the university. They disliked the idea of using the campus for American and other internees and were backed by an anti–American Spanish consul general and most of the Spanish faculty. For Tascon and Jordan, Catholic devotion in regard to Santo Tomás meant defending it as a Dominican institution. If they *had* to let in American internees, they would do it reluctantly.

Well before Pearl Harbor, Santo Tomás had been under fire from the Philippine government for propagating fascism. A government pamphlet, "*What Every Filipino Should Know about Propaganda,*" declared that an academic institution (clearly Santo Tomás) had sent students to Madrid to be indoctrinated. These attacks angered the university's leaders but when war broke out, they appointed a three-man Emergency Committee, constituted so as to head off a government investigation of the university's political activities. The committee's chairman was a Spanish father but the other two members were an American father and Alcuaz. Within a few days the university accepted a USAFFE request to the committee to use the campus as a military transit camp and giant motor garage. Classes by then had been suspended, and the campus hummed with trucks pouring in and out of the grounds. Filipino soldiers temporarily occupied two floors of the university's Main Building, with some refugees on the ground floor.

Taking in troops for a short time was one thing, and none too attractive at that, but becoming an internment camp indefinitely was another, though Alcuaz and his Emergency Committee colleagues recommended it. After some resistance, Tascon and Jordan bowed to pressure from American authorities and the Red Cross, agreeing that most of the campus and some of the buildings could be used as a camp. It is not certain how clearly they told the Spanish faculty, many of whom continued to oppose the internment-camp idea. For Alcuaz, it was now a matter of waiting for the Japanese, anticipating the internment of the Franciscos, and doing his bit to make sure when the Japanese arrived that Santo Tomás would be the place.[13]

2

Internment

On Friday, 2 January 1942, Japanese troops entered Manila — men in caps with back flaps, knapsacks and brown helmets on their backs, and officers with sabers. To Fernando Mañalac, a Filipino twelve-year-old, the "elite vanguard," riding in trucks and armored cars, looked "surprisingly tall" and light-skinned as well as husky. But to Erwin Vorster, a German-born Filipino citizen working in his mother's store, the rank-and-file that followed were "scruffy and bandy-legged." "Our conquerors" looked decidedly "comic-opera." Many of them rode into Manila on folding bicycles.[1]

The comic opera moved fast. By the end of Saturday, Japanese soldiers seemed to be everywhere, patrolling key streets, directing traffic, handing out leaflets and notices from motorcycle sidecars — and rounding up Allied nationals. Through the weekend and the next few days, Japanese officers entered the homes, clubs, and hotels of Americans and other Westerners — sometimes courteously, sometimes not. Westerners who could not show that they were neutrals (such as Swiss) or Axis (Germans, Italians) usually had to report for registration at one of several reception centers before moving on to Santo Tomás. Often, but not always, they were advised to take bedding and food for three days. People picked up in the street were often treated more roughly: made to wait in the blazing sun and slapped for talking, before being taken to reception centers.

At the time of the Japanese roundup, Tressa Roka's fiancé, "Catesy" (Lowell Cates, a drug company executive), and another couple had moved into her apartment. Expecting the Japanese to appear any time, Catesy suddenly said to her, "Haven't you something less becoming to wear?" Tressa realized then that fears abut women getting raped were as strong among the men as among the women. Her friend Sophie and she "meekly ... removed all makeup and changed into shapeless and baggy slacks." The rape fears did not materialize: the Japanese invasion of Manila initially established law and order. But when the Japanese did come to collect them, they were offensive in other ways. An officer with a Fu-Manchu mustache, so short that his sword scabbard clanked on the floor, barked questions at them through an interpreter and turned the household upside-down, looking for such hostile items as cameras and binoculars. A shelf full of ornamental Chinese horses, much loved by Tressa, was swept to pieces.[2]

Our own first encounter with the Japanese was different. My sister Mary June remembers the officer who came to the Shannons' Manila house where we were staying as "brisk and quite business-like, but not unfriendly."[3] He gave our mother an hour to pack a suitcase for each of us. We also took light mattresses and (I guess) a bag of food. Mary June's hair was being washed at the time, so she was sent out into the garden to dry it in the sun while our mother and Evie, our governess/nanny, swiftly packed up. Then, piled into a truck with several others, we were taken to Villamor Hall, a big music school, now a reception center. (The Shannons were not interned, as they were Irish Republic neutrals.)

At Villamor, I got my first fright, perhaps my biggest of the whole camp experience. The Japanese separated us by sex into two lines, leading into different rooms. My mother found friends in the male line, a father and son, for me to be with. The son, older than me, had always treated me superciliously, but not now. "We'll take care of you," he said, putting his arm around my shoulders. If he of all people was being nice to me, things must be bad; would I ever see my family again?

After some hours, though, we were reunited. In a big room, teeming with people, my family had found a space for our mattresses. Later, as more people poured in, many would have to sleep on chairs or even on tables. Mary June had found it all "quite fun" at first, like camping out, which she had never done. But then came her turn to be frightened. An official, of indeterminate race, made various announcements. The toilets, he said, were down a long corridor. If we opened any door marked X along the way, we would be "shot."

We do not remember how long we were at Villamor before being taken to Santo Tomás. Some internees spent up to four days in the reception centers; others went into the camp almost immediately; some went straight in. Conditions at the centers were bad: few toilets and washrooms, and no food provided. At one center, a single rusty tap provided the only drinking water. Those who brought food shared it with others who had none. Internees' Filipino servants and neutral friends could bring in food too — a forerunner of what would happen in Santo Tomás.

Meanwhile, the wartime future of Santo Tomás itself was being settled. On Saturday, 3 January, Luis de Alcuaz visited Villamor, ostensibly to turn in a revolver as required by the Japanese. Dismayed to see so many people already crowded into the center, he decided he must waste no time in getting Japanese agreement to using Santo Tomás as a camp. After aggressive cross-questioning by a Japanese officer, he was taken to meet Colonel Seichi Ohta, chief of the military police. To his amazement, he found the police chief stark naked except for a G-string — a measure of his power and status in Manila's humid heat? Displaying university notepaper, Alcuaz persuaded Ohta that he spoke for the university (which was not actually true). Ohta agreed to Alcuaz's proposal for Santo Tomás.

The following day, 4 January, when the first truckload of internees came into Santo Tomás, a group of university fathers with a Spanish flag tried to bar the university's Main Building door. Japanese soldiers pushed clergy and flag aside and opened the building. (The flag was later installed in the building's lobby, where it stayed throughout the war.) The university and the Spanish consul general made a formal complaint to the Japanese authorities, though the university leaders, Fathers Thomas Tascon and Eugenio Jordan, had already conceded to departing U.S. officials that part of the campus, including the Main Building, could be used as a camp. The Japanese told the Spanish fathers to be more cooperative: Spain was a friendly power and the university would only be a camp for a short time(!). In the meantime, Tascon and Jordan recognized Alcuaz's talents as a diplomat as well as an engineer. Apparently unaware of his visit to Police Chief Ohta, they saw him as the best person to deal with the internees and protect university property. On 5 January they made him their "secretary" (executive assistant) and later exclusive university representative to the internees. The university's bosses became more reconciled to the internment camp when they realized that the buildings might otherwise have been made a Japanese barracks or hospital.

To internees entering Santo Tomás, their prison-to-be could have looked a lot worse. Located in a busy neighborhood, the campus occupied sixty acres, with spacious grounds and a few big buildings. An ornate iron fence ran along the front (southeastern) side of the campus. High stone walls bounded the other sides. From the front gate two driveways diverged and then joined at a plaza in front of the massive, four-story Main Building. Behind its façade, embellished with saints on cornices, the imposing, grey Main Building contained two inner patios. Overhead, its tall crucifix, rising from a tower, could be seen for miles. To the right of the Main Building, the three-story Education Building would later house most of the Japanese garrison on its ground floor, with male internees above. Behind the Main Building, a long one-story structure, the Annex, would house mothers with young children. A large gym on the southwestern side of the campus would become a cavernous dormitory for men. But the main sleeping quarters would be in the Main Building, and here lay a serious problem, repeated in the other buildings: the Main Building contained sixty large classrooms and many offices, but no dormitories and few toilets and bathrooms, as the campus's 4,500 students had been commuters. The university retained a seminary building, chapel, and seminary vegetable garden, occupying about a tenth of the campus on the western side, out of bounds to internees.

The first group of internees, about three hundred, came into Santo Tomas in the late afternoon, Sunday, 4 January. They stood around on the plaza with their belongings while a Japanese officer registered them and assigned them to ten rooms on the second floor of the Main Building, men and women in separate rooms. Most had brought some food and shared it. The American Philippine Red Cross was allowed in to serve coffee and rolls and provide first aid if needed. Internee moods ranged from a calm and curious "take it as it comes" attitude to intense anxiety. Some mothers with infants had never changed a diaper or even fed their children; they had left all that to their *amahs*.

Processing and room finding became more hectic over the next few days as thousands more poured in. The Japanese separated Americans from British into different lines to go into different rooms (a policy soon abandoned), and in the rush this made at least one Japanese officer lose his cool. Eight-year-old Robin Prising and his mother entered the camp at a different time from his British father, as he was elsewhere in Manila at the time of roundup. When his mother tried to explain that Robin had a British passport but she an American one, the officer screamed at her, slapped and kicked her — and hurled Robin into the British line. As with my experience at Villamor Hall, kind hands took him in. When the officer moved on, Robin was returned to his shaken and bruised mother, in pain from a damaged ear.

For others, even without such abuse, the plunge from an ordered, comfortable way of life into sudden imprisonment was made worse by a sense of racial indignity. "We now felt very demeaned, frustrated and angry," Geege Wootten told her diary, "at being pushed around by these little, sorry men."[4] Tressa Roka and her fiancé, "Catesy," were especially galled to be sex-segregated in the dorms at night: the day they were interned was their planned wedding day. (They were married after liberation in the ruins of a Manila church.)

For most internees, the first few nights were miserable. My family, assigned to the

Annex, was relatively well off: we had our mattresses. But many had none, and had to sleep on stone floors, padded as best they could by clothing. Some found it felt less hard to sleep on desks. Very few had mosquito nets; internee Eva Nixon counted twenty-seven bites on just one hand her first morning. To keep mosquitoes away from their children, some women smoked cigarettes all night, sleeping when they could the following day (the smoking worked by masking human smell).

On top of that was the crowding, as new arrivals tried to fit in beside the spaces each person or family had carved out. (By the end of the month, living space in the classrooms turned dormitories averaged about 30 square feet per person, a third more than a single bed.) Behavior amid the crowding varied, of course; it could also change. Phyllis Hearnden, a young married British woman, found a very posh mother and teenage daughter reluctant at first to give her space, but when they got to know each other, Mrs. Posh became friendly and helpful.

Noise and interruption at night were incessant, from crying babies to guards tramping in with flashlights to fit in latecomers. A small boy wailed one night, "Mom, when are we going home? I don't like this place." The first few mornings were not much better. On the Main Building's third floor, 350 women and children had to share six toilets, six washbowls and six showers. As early as 6 A.M., there were long lines for the bathrooms. Nobody in them looked too happy but they had to laugh when a small, frail-looking old lady appeared, took one look at the lines, and muttered, "I guess I'll come back next week."[5]

The facilities were often filthy too. The Filipino soldiers who had occupied the Main Building before vacating Manila had left behind blocked drains and toilet bowls full of dried excrement. On the first evening, Clio Mathews, a 29-year-old secretary, had helped a Japanese officer with the spelling of internees' names that he was registering. As a result, she was made room "monitor" for a dorm teeming with women, some of them over twice her age. She set to work with other monitors, cleaning out the toilets. They wrapped rags around their hands, as they had no rubber gloves or, as yet, disinfectant. Internee plumbers who swiftly came in later to fix the waterworks appreciated their work.

The biggest problem, though, was food. On Tuesday, 6 January, the second full day of internment, internees saw a stark notice on the Main Building's front door: "Internees in this camp shall be responsible for feeding themselves." They would also have to find almost everything else, from beds to medicine, but food obviously came first. The Japanese government and army had not thought through the logistics of interning large numbers of civilians. Belated and vague instructions from Tokyo's military high command in February 1942 said that local armies should provide and pay for civilian internees on the same basis as military POWs — which, in fact, meant a harshly low minimum. Until 1944 Japan did not even have a commissary corps for feeding its own soldiers. They were expected to "live off the land," which meant exploiting the local people — not a great way to win them over. Not until July did the army actually start paying for camp feeding and other expenses.

In the meantime, it seemed obvious to the Japanese army in Manila that Santo Tomás's largely business community had the resources and contacts to provide for itself. So the Japanese opened the main gates for several hours each day. Amid a great hubbub, servants and non-interned friends of internees shouted out names or held up placards, so they could pass over food, clothes, bedding, and other items. Not all internees, though, had this backup. They included people who had fled from Hong Kong and China's war zones, hoping to get to Australia or the United States of America, but had put in to Manila when the seas became too dangerous.

Accounts vary on how soon internees got free meals, two a day served initially by the Red Cross to long lines from a small kitchen. One report says that small children got an oatmeal breakfast the first morning. Other accounts vary between 6 January and the end of the month as the start date for general free feeding. By mid–January meal tickets were issued for free meals, initially, it seems, on the basis of need and demand. A restaurant opened but only its coffee was free. Internees who received food through the gate shared with others who did not, but some older people, too proud to ask others for food, nearly starved before the food lines opened.[6] Two Manila grocery companies sent in free food, and over the first few weeks, the Manila electricity, gas and water companies helped the Red Cross and internees build three kitchens: the "central kitchen" with serving bays behind the Main Building, a new kitchen for the children's Annex, and a camp hospital kitchen. New latrines were plumbed, and the Red Cross trucked in a host of supplies, including mosquito nets and thin mattresses. Medicines, though, were in short supply; the Japanese army had confiscated Red Cross stockpiles as military equipment. The generous foresight of two internee doctors provided a nucleus of camp medicines in the early days: just before internment, they stuffed pillow-cases with drugs and brought them into camp, sacrificing some of their own belongings.

A leader in the initial relief operations was Thomas (Tommy) Wolff, an internee and chairman of the Philippine subsidiary of the American Red Cross. Wolff's Philippine background went back to 1899, when he arrived as an American soldier in the Philippine-American War. He went on to become a prominent Manila businessman, while overseeing the growth of the Red Cross in the Philippines. He now worked with other Red Cross internees and Red Cross Filipinos outside the camp to orchestrate Santo Tomás relief as well as attending to numerous other needs, including the destitute families of Filipino soldiers fighting in Bataan. The Red Cross in turn got gifts and loans from Manila business firms, charities and hospitals.[7]

Liaising with Wolff and others was the internees' own organization. This dated from the very first evening of internment. The Japanese officer in charge that day designated Earl Carroll, a thirty-six-year-old insurance executive, as internee leader. Carroll said later he was taken aback by this. He was not yet part of Manila's top business elite, and by his own account he did not look particularly impressive: bespectacled, chubby-cheeked, and short. To some extent he was chosen by mistake. The Japanese officer spoke no English and his interpreter, a Japanese civilian who had worked for a Ford car distributor, mistook Carroll for the American consul general. Other internees, though, had suggested him too: he was known to them as a member of the American Emergency Committee preparing for Japanese invasion. A camp rumor that he was chosen because the Japanese thought he was an earl remains just that — rumor.

However arrived at, the selection of Carroll was apt. Carroll combined dynamism with tact. He also had a track record of reaching out to other cultures. Raised in Alabama by a politically liberal family, he worked in the Philippines as a YMCA organizer in the early 1930s, traveling all over the islands to set up new YMCA chapters. When depression cutbacks eliminated his job, he went to work for a big Philippine insurance company, Insular Life Assurance. Moving to Honolulu, he set up the company's new Hawaiian office, beating off competition by targeting Hawaii's Filipino population. In late November 1941, he left his wife and small son in Hawaii while he returned to the Philippines for what was meant to be just two weeks, exploring an offer of promotion to vice-president for sales back in Manila. Arriving four days before Pearl Harbor, he immediately took on a second, *pro bono* job as American Emergency Committee chairman for southern Manila. He soon had no safe way of getting back to Hawaii.

Carroll's immediate brief from the Japanese was to outline an internee organization, including room monitors, to be approved by the camp commandant when he arrived the next day. In the morning he met with the monitors, chosen the evening before, and other internees whom he knew and thought would be good administrators. The monitors' role was conceived by the Japanese, but the meeting with Carroll fine-tuned it. The job was formidable. In a room of at least 30 men or women (rooms were sex-segregated from teenagers up), the monitor was supposed to keep order, settle disputes, organize cleaning rotas or votes on how to do them, hold evening

Interned at 36, Earl Carroll was the first head of the internee governing committee and also its last. In between he headed the camp's feeding and supply operations. A former YMCA organizer turned insurance executive, he combined tact and firmness in dealing with the camp's Japanese masters as well as with internees. Fellow internee James McCall made this sketch of him three weeks before liberation *(courtesy of McCall family)*.

roll calls to assure the guards that all were present, report special needs for Red Cross or medical help, and represent their roommates at monitors' meetings. Above the monitors, Carroll and colleagues set up the nucleus of four committees, covering health and sanitation, food, recreation, and "discipline" (law and order).

A few hours later, the camp's first commandant, Hitoshi Tomayasu, arrived at Santo Tomás. Though fifty-five years old, he was only a lieutenant, a military police officer. (Subsequent commandants held higher rank as the garrison expanded.) Told of Carroll's plan, Tomayasu said through an interpreter — he spoke no English — that he approved. For him, maximizing internee self-government, including their responsibility for good order, made practical sense, as long as it respected his authority and followed general rules. His initial garrison included just ten guards plus five or six civilian administrators — a total staff of 15–16 in charge of a prison population that soon exceeded 3,000.

Carroll, on his side, wanted to organize strong internee government as fast as possible to minimize Japanese interference in the everyday life of the camp. This applied particularly to law and order. In the first few weeks, internees evolved their own police force under a "discipline" committee. Later they acquired a jail. The commandant encouraged this by threatening collective punishment for misdemeanors not dealt with or prevented by the internees' administration. Preemptive policing started the very first evening when Dan Raleigh, ex–office manager and auditor for Goodyear Tire, "confiscated" crates of alcoholic drinks that an internee had somehow managed to bring in. History does not tell how he did this without major ructions. The next day, Raleigh became head of the new discipline committee.[8] His action was prescient. Throughout the camp's existence, drunk and disorderly behavior, fueled by smuggled booze, became the most frequent law-and-order problem, often landing miscreants in the camp jail.

Two days later, on 7 January, Carroll met with a group of leading American businessmen and ex-government officials who were now in the camp. He offered to hand his authority over to sixty-three-year-old Frederic Stevens, former chairman of the American Emergency Committee. Stevens declined and the group agreed that Carroll should continue as chairman of a Central Committee, a nine-man (no women) internee cabinet. A few of the group joined this cabinet; others formed an "advisory committee" to it. On both committees, British businessmen, representing the camp's second-largest nationality, got a third of the places. The operating committees reporting to the Central Committee soon expanded from the original four.

Writing about all this later, A.V.H.—designated camp historian by the Central Committee—suggested that Carroll was acceptable to the big shots because he was not one of them, a relative newcomer, not a competitor.[9] He had also shown obvious ability in creating an instant government, and he was the Japanese nominee for the job. To try to replace him straight off would be impolitic, even if it had been desirable. That was also a reason to postpone elections for Central Committee places, though dormitory elections for room monitors were held in the third week. (At the end of January the Central Committee was renamed the Executive Committee and elections to it were allowed in July.)

Meanwhile, politics aside, internees were struggling to get used to their topsy-turvy world. In the mornings, married couples, separated at night, would find each other. They might then stand in line for up to an hour to get their meal tickets punched and be served breakfast: cracked-wheat porridge, a roll, and coffee. They would eat fast in a small dining room so as to make room for others, or find a spot on benches outside. The next camp-provided meal would be an early supper: usually stew but sometimes sardines or noodles, with a roll, a cup of tea, and a banana or rice pudding for dessert. Later, there were green vegetables, especially after the camp vegetable gardens got going. By February at the Annex, where its own kitchen was opened up, women and small children were fed three meals a day, including milk and fruit juice for the children. Teenagers, the ill, and men doing heavy work got a lunch too, and others could apply for supper "leftovers" at lunchtime. By 1944, most internees were getting a limited camp lunch.

In the camp's last months, the early "chow-line" meals would be thought a feast, but many internees relied on better fare from servants and friends at the gates—either precooked or ready for cooking on various improvised charcoal stoves. In mid–January, too, one of the commandant's Japanese interpreters was even allowed to set up a sandwich bar, Nagashima's, to be followed in the next few months by other stores and cafes for those with money to spend. The Red Cross, though, advised internees to save their own canned food for the future.

A moving picture of internees, milling about or just lounging in front of the Main Building, would have shown some contrasts. Paul Esmérian, visiting the camp two weeks after its opening, and writing with the eye of a cultured Frenchman, described "women in slacks, wearing lipstick ... walking around as though they were in a fashionable spa. Some [internees are] clean, well dressed, anxious not to 'let things go.' Others slovenly, men unshaved, women with their hair undone." Camp historian A.V.H. described more tolerantly the profusion of beards sprouted by many men, from shaggy Robinson Crusoes to "elaborately trimmed imperials and goatees." Fourteen-year-old Liz Lautzenhiser noticed that stylish women, deprived of dye to keep their hair blonde, took to wearing turbans and bandanas before settling for "two-tone combinations."[10]

Uniting the adults was worry and uncertainty about the future. The best antidote to that was the host of jobs to be done, though some of it was hard physical work in the heat by people not used to it. Tasks ranged from clearing ground and planting to kitchen work or sewing and mending mosquito nets and pillow slips for the new infirmary. A Work Assignment Committee, headed by a tough but fair-minded lawyer, Clyde DeWitt, figured out what jobs needed to be done. It relied initially on social pressure rather than compulsion. Most assignments were just two hours a day. Some did much more, but there were always a few who sought reasons not to pitch in. When an eighteen-year-old declared he was on "vacation," an assembly of his dormitory — the big gym holding 700 men — considered his case. Against "why pick on a kid?" others cried, "Take his meal ticket from him" and "Put him in the Annex with the women and children." The next day he reported for work. By the end of the camp's first month, work assignments became compulsory, handed out by room monitors as advised by the work committee.[11]

Public health and hygiene figured prominently in the jobs. In the camp's close-packed community and tropical climate, disease and infection could spread fast. At the end of the first week, Tressa Roka, plying her trade as a nurse, helped give cholera and typhoid shots in a classroom turned clinic. Strict rules were set up for cleaning — and keeping clean — latrines and dormitories. My first memory of the Annex was a pleasant smell of disinfectant as internees with big brushes sluiced down cement walkways. Digging and filling garbage trenches required a whole gang of men. (Later, the camp found a chemical that would rot garbage into powder, and at the very end there was too little food to produce much garbage of any kind.) Another work gang cleared a wild part of the grounds that had stagnant ponds, a magnet for rats, mosquitoes, and other nasties. In February, children were even organized into a Swat-the-Fly Club, with prizes for the biggest body counts in their jars. A chorus for all this came from the sanitation committee, which put out a bevy of notices and bulletins about hygiene.

The task of converting a nonresidential college into a prison community pulled in a wide range of internee professional backgrounds. Sheer numbers helped produce diverse skills. The camp population totaled nearly 3,400 (three quarters over 18, and 60 percent male) when it leveled off at the end of the first month until further increases in 1943 and 1944. Admittedly, the mix of backgrounds was skewed away from manual workers, as Manila's Westerners had depended on Filipinos for most physical labor. Among men, the biggest group, numbering some 400, comprised various kinds of businessmen and salesmen, but engineers were the next biggest group, numbering almost 200. There were also carpenters, builders, and mechanics of various descriptions, not counting do-it-yourself amateurs who turned their hands to anything from constructing beds to the small toilet seat made by a father for his little daughter so she would not fall into the adult lavatories.

Of the women, nearly half had primarily been "housewives." But women internees provided over thirty schoolteachers and more than sixty nurses, though most of these were army nurses from Corregidor who did not arrive until April, after the island had fallen. There were less than a dozen internee doctors and dentists, but the Japanese allowed Filipino doctors to come in during the day until 1944; there were also druggists and chemists.

On the entertainment front — so important for morale — internees included professional dancers and enough musicians for a band and small orchestra. At the end of the camp's first month came the first of many variety shows. On a stage of planks laid over boxes, the performers did their acts in one of the Main Building's two inner patios before an overflow audience, some leaning out of second- and third-floor windows (the shows moved later to the front plaza). The program featured comic songs and skits, dances, trumpet and accordion solos, and a sword-swallowing act.

The most specialized internee backgrounds were not to be dismissed; one could never tell when they might come in handy. Besides a white-ant expert and a "rope and hemp expert" (the Philippines had been a major hemp producer), the camp had at least one "textile instructor."[12] Outside the Annex one morning, a vociferous dispute broke out between a man and a woman, each claiming the same sheet hanging on a line. Both said it was the other half of a sheet they had cut in two, and showed the other halves to prove it. The Annex's head monitor, a Catholic clergyman, brought in the textile expert. After some peering with a magnifying glass, he found in favor of the woman: her half matched up perfectly. The monitor's diplomatic skills, assisted by churchly power, also came into play: he got the disputants to shake hands. On a bigger scale, the camp benefited from Eddie Tait, a circus owner, who put up a large dining tent — replaced later by sheds. Eddie also became a camp expert on rats.

In October 1942, nine months from the start, versifier (and cartoonist) James McCall looked back, tongue in cheek, at the high-speed, many-skilled creation of Santo Tomás Internment Camp.

> *STIC was built the American way–*
> *Foundation to finish in less than a day.*
> *The skeletal fabric pierced the sky*
> *Ere the ink on the plans had time to dry....*
>
> *'Twas a joy to see the willing hands —*
> *And many of them from foreign lands.*
> *So keen was the wish to cooperate*
> *That guards were needed at every gate....*
>
> *Efficiency experts, advisers, technicians;*
> *Florists and chorists, and noted musicians;*
> *Writers and fighters, and men from the sea —*
> *All willing to serve without thought of a fee....*
>
> *While stern engineers delirious with joy*
> *(Just like kids with a brand new toy)*
> *Got all confused with construction men–*
> *And stood up and shouted — and sat down again....*
>
> *Long before the suites were completed*
> *Committees had formed and asked to be seated.*

All that they needed were adding machines
And office desks and folding screens....
So STIC was built the American way:
Foundation to finish in less than a day....
A perfect Elysium — a haven serene —
The biggest and best that ever was seen.[13]

McCall's way itself was very American — enjoying fast results while spoofing authority. In the following two years, edginess about committee power would get more tense. McCall also captured an eager-beaver heartiness, shown especially by men, making up for losing their regular jobs — but not just the men. When the Recreation Committee organized an ambitious sports program, so many people signed up that the Work Assignment Committee complained that it was taking away volunteers. The program, nevertheless, went ahead, including an eight-team softball league, American football, field hockey, golf on a three-hole course, and — led by the British — soccer and even croquet. Rugby came in later, but not cricket, maybe because the ground was too uneven. (Much later, in the last months of the camp, most people became too weak from hunger to do energetic sports, but that future was hard to visualize in 1942.)

The sports program catered especially to the young, which included 300 children aged six to fifteen. Teenage girls, teenage boys, and younger children each had their own basketball league. Bedlam conditions in the Annex gave special reason to reach as low as possible down the age range. Plunged into a new world with masses of playmates, hordes of Annex children would race down the corridors and outside the building, yelling at top volume. No one remembers how much I was part of this, but one of the antidotes to juvenile anarchy caught up with me. Small boys as young as five and a half (my age) were organized into mini-boxing matches, three one-minute rounds. The events were considered a healthy channeling of aggression as well as being cute. So it was that boxing gloves were strapped on my hands — unnaturally big blobs with an unpleasant leather smell — and I was ushered into the ring to fight a crisp young fellow who seemed to know what he was about. Announced to the audience as Rupert the Battler versus Roy the Champion, I sensed even at that young age what the words predicted. Roy Doolan indeed knew how to box, while I flailed desperately, despite repeated injunctions to protect my face with one glove while hitting with the other. My declared defeat came swiftly but not too soon, and I never returned. I only learned later (a few years ago, in fact) that Roy's father had assiduously trained him, so that he ended up fighting in older age brackets. At camp reunions long after the war, some ex-internees still remembered him as "TNT Doolan." To be fair to the camp elders, the boxing program did include instruction but somehow I had missed it. In TNT's case, the boxing program was not a perfect curb on aggression. When an older boy defeated Roy because his tactics were too defensive, Roy found his adversary later and started beating him up until he ran away.[14]

Sports were not the only provision for the young. Within two weeks, school teaching was under way, starting in an open-air space behind the Education Building that was shaded and relatively cool in the mornings. Not everyone could be enrolled at first, but the program began with over a hundred children at primary and junior secondary level. It concentrated initially on English, arithmetic, and basic science, two and a half hours each morning except Sunday. When the program later expanded, most of it moving to the Main Building's top floor, it took on many more subjects, including college and adult extension courses. A kindergarten started too, in front of the Annex.[15]

Early in the camp's career, internee carpenters built a big playhouse behind the Annex. Nipa-thatched and mostly open-sided, it provided added space for little children to play in when it rained. A small staff there enabled harried parents to get time off. Some parents, inevitably, were more ingenious than others at entertaining very young children. Angela Templer, the wife of a British army officer interned in Hong Kong, had three children, aged from under two to six. Growing up in England, she had learned carpentry from her brother, a keen woodworker. Finding a wooden box and the wheels and handle of an old mowing machine, she made a cart that Jenny, her youngest, could push or ride in. With a friend who had a small son, Templer also collected cans and bottles from a dump so their children could play at being storekeepers.

For teenagers and others, a shed in front of the Annex became a rudimentary social center, hosting weekly square dances; the commandant banned regular "ballroom" dancing as too sexually provocative! Despite prison restrictions, young people sometimes seemed the happiest group of internees. They might miss keenly the odd possession (say, a new bike received for Christmas) but they seldom felt the full anxiety of their parents about the loss of home (had it been looted?) and livelihood. A few had left behind non-interned playmates, but for many, "all my friends are in here," as one put it.[16] Some had missing fathers, in the military or in other camps, but that seemed to worry the young less than their mothers. "Dad" was away as if on business.

For eight-year-old Mary June, the most positive experience of the camp's early days took place in the Fathers' Garden, beside the seminary. Different camp denominations used the garden for open-air services, and it was also used for teaching Sunday school to both Catholics and Protestants. Mary June remembers learning the names of books in the Bible, the Ten Commandments, and the Beatitudes. Maybe they were given a text to color in and decorate. But the important thing, as she remembers it today, was the "very *loving* atmosphere" created by the "wonderful" Sunday school teachers themselves (possibly nuns from the seminary). It was something that would stay with her, a "cushion" of God's love, through the hard times ahead.[17]

3

A Porous Prison

In the early afternoon of Thursday, 12 February 1942, a truck pulled up outside the Main Building. Japanese soldiers took out three men — internees — and hustled them into a barrack room beside the commandant's office. Their cries echoed down the corridors as they were beaten up. In the dormitories that evening, room monitors read out a bulletin, officially from the internee Executive Committee but really from the commandant himself, Hitoshi Tomayasu. It said that three men had tried to escape the evening before. Captured and brought back to camp, they had "apologized" for their "big mistake," and urged no one else to try it. They would not be executed, "the usual punishment for escapees," but would be imprisoned elsewhere. The commandant was angry that his "cooperation" had been so ill rewarded. The next time it would be death for the escapers and punitive "restrictions" for everyone else.

The three men were a forty-three-year-old Australian engineer, Blakey Laycock, and two English merchant seamen in their late twenties, Tom Fletcher and Henry Weeks. Only Weeks was married, with a wife in England; Laycock had a brother and sister-in-law in the camp. At 8 P.M. on Wednesday, after evening roll call, they had slipped out of the building and gone over the wall, but were soon caught in a Manila suburb. Mid-afternoon Thursday, Commandant Tomayasu sent for Earl Carroll, the Executive Committee chairman, and the two monitors of the escapers' dormitories. (Both were British businessmen; the two dorms were mainly British.) Shaking with fury, Tomayasu told them what had happened and shouted that the monitors were liable for extreme punishment for letting the escape happen. He quieted down and relented, though, when Carroll pointed out that the escape had happened *after* the evening roll call, when the monitors reported all were present. Making sure everyone was present through the night was not the monitors' job. Carroll was told to see the three escapers. Laycock, the Australian engineer, was in the worst shape: his face looked like raw meat, the result of fighting back against his tormentors, biting one of them in the arm. The commandant let Charles Leach, the chief internee doctor, examine the men. He found no serious injury beyond very bad bruising. Later that afternoon, the men were taken out of camp.

Two days later, on Saturday, the camp was told a court-martial had sentenced the three men to death. We don't know whether the switch was due to bureaucratic muddle or a change of mind by the Japanese military outside the camp, nor indeed who finally decided the sentence.

The Executive Committee immediately went into a long emergency session, composing an appeal to the Japanese "High Command" that the commandant said he would pass on, having already petitioned for clemency himself. (The committee decided not to base their appeal on the Geneva Convention, as mentioning it might infuriate the military. Japan had never ratified the convention and anyway it did not explicitly refer to civilian prisoners, though early in the war the United States and Japan agreed to apply it to them.[1]) Later in the day, one of the commandant's Japanese interpreters burst into the room and told the committee that the commandant's petition had been turned down. He said the commandant was too upset to see them but would now appeal in person as an "ordinary Japanese citizen." Looking from their second-floor window in the Main Building, the committee witnessed the extraordinary sight of Commandant Tomayasu, clad in a kimono and sandals, walking to his car to be driven off. In the meantime, the commandant's number two, Lieutenant Takahashi, a hard and hostile officer who sometimes seemed to wield almost as much power as the commandant, blocked the committee from making outside contacts. When they finally got through to the American Episcopal bishop, Norman Binsted, who was not then interned and had lived many years in Japan, he appealed to his Japanese contacts, but it was too late. None of the appeals worked.

On Sunday morning, 15 February, as anxious groups of internees gathered, rumors flew about: the men had already been executed; they had been reprieved; the monitors would be shot; Carroll would be shot. Reality came just before noon. Five internees, ordered to be present at the execution, were piled into a police bus along with the commandant and other Japanese. The five were Carroll; the two room monitors; a British Anglican minister, Owen Griffiths; and Ernest Stanley, an internee interpreter for the Japanese. The bus went first to the police station where the three escapers were being held. On seeing their fellow internees, the escapers thought at first it was good news, but the Reverend Griffiths was quickly given the grim job of telling them their fate. The whole party, including soldiers and the condemned men, were then taken to a cemetery where Filipino workers were digging a grave.

Hands tied behind their backs, the three men were lined up while the commandant read the formal sentence (interpreted into English), and Griffiths and one of the monitors, Gerald Pedder, offered such words of comfort as they could. Carroll, too, spoke, declaring that they would not be forgotten at Santo Tomás and were "dying as martyrs to freedom." Laycock exclaimed that they had not been before any court-martial. Weeks said he might by now be a father and asked forlornly if that could be taken into consideration. Fletcher murmured something unintelligible.

After a last smoke — cigarettes put in their mouths by a soldier — the three were seated on the edge of the grave pit and blindfolded, though Laycock tried to refuse the blindfold: "I'll die like a man, not a rat." On the order of Lieutenant Takahashi, in charge of the execution, soldiers fired automatic pistols at the men's hearts. It took repeated volleys to kill them even after they had slumped into the grave. Before they were all dead, Takahashi ordered the Filipino workers to fill in the grave, threatening to shoot them too when they demurred. When the grave was mostly filled, groans still came from it. Several soldiers, one of them laughing, perhaps hysterically, fired into the earth until all was quiet. During the shooting, Tomayasu walked away. Stanley heard him say in Japanese, "It's butchery. They should have had the proper instruments"—meaning rifles, not weak pistols.

The Reverend Griffiths, now clad in cassock and stole, and deeply distressed like the other internees, recited Church of England prayers for the dead. While he did so, the Japanese stood to attention, and when he had finished, several soldiers broke off branches of bougainvillea and planted them on the grave.

The party then returned to the camp, where the news spread quickly. That very afternoon, the commandant permitted a memorial service, and the next morning one of the university's American fathers, Hilary Ahern, held a requiem mass at the seminary chapel (later off limits to internees).[2]

From top to bottom the camp was shaken by the event. Earl Carroll stayed in his room for two days, quietly thinking it over. Thinking back on it later, Ethel Krass wrote a poem of despair:

> *Will the morning ever come*
> *With its healing light?*
> *Will it wash away the stain*
> *Of this evil night? ...*
> *Shall we ever love again*
> *All the sweet birds' song?*
> *Will all beauty always be*
> *Tainted by this wrong?*[3]

The full details, including the behavior of a basically humane but weak commandant and his sadistic second in command, were not released. It was widely believed, even by children like me, that the escapers had had to dig their own grave (untrue) and were buried alive (essentially true), and that the same would happen to anyone else caught trying to escape. The Executive Committee itself put out a circular urging internees to take "every possible precaution to prevent another escape" from the camp.

The awfulness of the event probably did deter escape attempts, as indeed intended.[4] But when they again happened, there were almost no harsh punishments or reprisals, though sometimes this was threatened (more on this in Chapter 7). On the night of 12 February, the very day that the three escapers were brought back to the camp, another internee, Edwin Goldsborough, went missing at evening roll call. To make sure his room monitor did not get blamed for failing to report a missing person, Carroll told the commandant, who made nothing of it beyond searching the camp; Tomayasu may have wanted to keep the escape quiet to protect his reputation for maintaining security. (Goldsborough ended up with Filipino guerrillas but was recaptured two years later and beheaded with a group of guerrillas in the same cemetery as the three initial escapers.)

Despite the trauma, Santo Tomás was not totally oppressive. It was, in fact, a remarkable mixture of authoritarian control, welfare state (austerity style), and commercial enterprise. Like other prisons, it subjected its inmates to numerous rules and regulations, often blared over the camp loudspeakers. They were cut off from news of friends and families; occasionally, the authorities let in piles of held-up mail, but some mail never arrived. For many internees, there was the sense of being ruled over by a people who seemed alien, impersonal, and incomprehensible. Few Japanese could speak English and few internees Japanese. Internee diaries and memoirs portray their rulers as distastefully ludicrous — often sloppily dressed and barking orders in guttural grunts.

The keenest indignity was the rule about bowing. You had to bow to any Japanese person you met, and the Japanese were supposed to bow back less deeply, or simply salute, as befitted a person in a superior position. Although the internee administration included people who had lived in Japan, they did not effectively explain to internees that bowing was embedded in Japanese culture as an etiquette of respect; it was not simply ritual humiliation, though some Japanese used it that way. It had started among samurai warriors as a way of showing no malice to each other while acknowledging hierarchy: top dogs got deeper bows.

In the camp's first two years, the Japanese generally kept away from most internees. Initially there were guards at the Main Building door but that did not last. In the camp's last year there was more contact when Japanese officers and NCOs started officiating at dormitory roll calls and insisted on mass bowing by internees lined up outside their rooms. Internee administrators did a lot of business with the commandant's office, but they were given some autonomy to make their own decisions. This included the essential project of feeding and supplying the camp.

From July 1942, when the Japanese army started providing for the camp, it paid the camp administration an allowance to buy its own supplies — food, medicine, equipment, even gas, electricity and water. This lasted until February 1944, when the army supplied food directly (in decreasing amounts) while allowing some purchases of other items. The allowance started at 70 centavos per internee per day. (On 100 centavos per peso, and two pesos a dollar, the prewar rate, that amounted to about 35 U.S. cents, well under $6 today.) By January 1944, after much complaining by internee leaders, the allowance had gone up to P1.50, but price inflation in Manila far exceeded that increase. Meticulous budget breakdowns by the camp's Finance and Supplies Committee allocated some two-thirds of the allowance to food, with special provision for children, including milk. The camp administration paid some of the cash allowance to outside hospitals, as the formula included hospitalized internees.

As the camp food buyers went out in trucks, with Japanese escorts and Filipino helpers (formerly of the Red Cross), they soon saw that Manileños were as deprived as they. The streets were full of people looking for food they could afford. And the war threats to Manila's economy were only just starting. In time, a host of factors would bring the city to mass starvation — bad rice harvests, heavy-handed Japanese experiments with new grains, disruption of transports by guerrillas, migration to the city from the countryside (where law and order was breaking down), and the economic demands of the Japanese army.[5] Especially parlous was the situation of Filipino families, not interned but with Western husbands and fathers inside the camp. Starting in September 1942, the camp administration made "family aid" payments, and these were permitted even after the Japanese clamped down on outside contacts in 1944, though by then the aid was tiny in relation to Manila's rocketing prices.

The camp's external aid programs also included secret help to military POWs, especially a POW prison camp at Cabanatuan, seventy miles north of Manila. The POWs had a well-organized underground and could make cash purchases but were worse fed and more ill treated than Santo Tomás internees. Some of the money from Santo Tomás went out with the Filipino driver of a food truck, who was a guerrilla; he even brought back receipts!

All of this — indeed, the whole Santo Tomás economy — was subsidized by outside benefactors. Different branches of the Red Cross, national and international, sent in aid ranging from food parcels for each internee to money for the camp. J.O. Bessmer, a Swiss businessman, made four donations in 1943, totaling about $970,000 today—generous in spirit but not really a lot, as some of the money went to three other civilian camps in the Philippines. His import-export firm was supposed to be repaid by the Red Cross.[6]

Individuals weighed in, too. The most remarkable was the university administrator and chemical engineer, Luis de Alcuaz. Besides getting himself made sole university representative to the internees, he became "custodian" of university property in the camp. This enabled him to have an office in the camp, keep out the largely anti–American Spanish faculty, and help the internees in all sorts of ways, some more official than others. Working with internee engineers, he set up the camp's own soap-making and water-purifying equipment, foreseeing that the camp's health might need both. He brought in extra lavatories from a friendly Manila plumbing store and, more dangerously, smuggled in radio bits (a capital offence) so that internees could set up their own secret radios. In 1944, the camp's hunger year, he smuggled in money, medicines, and food. Alcuaz's free passage in and out of the camp also enabled him to visit the family of Pomponette Francisco, who became his fiancée during internment. (Pomponette had been my beloved kindergarten teacher before the war and my family knew the Franciscos and Alcuaz. I remember seeing him, a slim, black-haired man in a sharp white suit, pausing to talk and then bustling off with his briefcase. To a six- or seven-year-old, as I was then, he indeed looked as if he was engaged in important, mysterious business.)

The camp budget and food supply also got help from leading internee businessmen who used IOUs drawn on their own companies or themselves to raise money from a variety of firms and well-wishers. These operations, ironically, were made easier by the very price escalation that caused general distress. A profusion of new bank notes, headed "Japanese Government," inflated the currency and lost so much value that they were soon dubbed

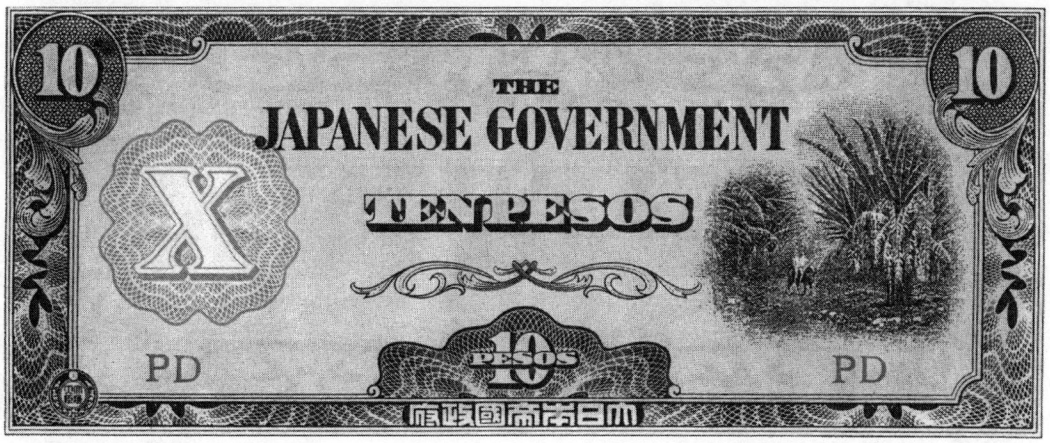

When Japan issued its own currency for the Philippines, it let local army commanders print it. Losing value against the old "Commonwealth" peso, which was banned but secretly used, Japanese pesos were called "Mickey Mouse money." This actually helped Earl Carroll and others get camp supplies from Manila merchants who preferred IOUs in the old currency or in U.S. dollars. The very name, "Japanese Government," printed on the new pesos, was a monument to Japanese imperial stupidity. Imagine taking over a country, declaring it is your liberated ally against Western colonialism, and then printing its money with your own government's name on it. After the war, children used Mickey Mouse money as toy money.

"Mickey Mouse money"; the first issue reportedly carried a faint Mickey Mouse watermark, planted on it by a subversive printing worker (who presumably then vanished to keep his head).[7] By mid–1944, Filipinos were carrying bags of money to market to pay for groceries. Long before this, savvy Manila merchants had figured that Santo Tomás IOUs, redeemable after the war at old "Commonwealth peso" values (two pesos to a U.S. dollar) were preferable to the depreciating currency. Using the IOUs, Earl Carroll and other camp representatives with passes to do business in the city obtained goods as well as pesos. A Filipino bookseller, a Russian Jew by origin, having swapped pesos for IOUs, gave Carroll gratis an extra bundle of pesos, to pass on to Cabanatuan. And a Chinese Filipino rice and corn trader told Carroll to help himself from his corn store, as the Japanese would either confiscate the merchandise or buy it with Mickey Mouse money. Carroll carried off loads of corn in three small horse-drawn carriages.

Some internee executives used the IOU system for private as well as public purposes. George Bridgeford, the camp's chief food buyer, gave some of the pesos, allocated to him from the Japanese payments, to internees who were fellow employees of the British sugar firm, Warner Barnes, to buy extra food and other things from the camp shops that had sprung up. He replaced the pesos with IOUs drawn on Warner Barnes in buying camp food from outside grocers. The camp did not lose, while the Warner Barnes people indirectly got aid from future assets of the company. Carroll Grinnell, president of General Electric in the Philippines, who succeeded Earl Carroll as the top internee leader, lent money to individuals as well as to the camp's finances, mainly interest-free but for individuals to be repaid at two pesos to the U.S. dollar (the prewar rate). Some of the loans by Grinnell and others enabled internees to give money to servants and company employees outside the camp.

Until February 1944, individual internees could get food, bedding, and other items from outside friends and servants at the main gate, though packets of money were officially stopped by late October 1943. For the first few weeks, the scene there was tumultuous. Throngs of people thrust packages through the iron railings to internee couriers, who took them to recipients cordoned off some yards away. Shouts went back and forth ("Hey Pedro, next time bring some cigarettes"), but there was emotion too. Tressa Roka saw "eyes grow moist on either side of the fence" as internees and servants spotted each other. The general hubbub, and the affection and loyalty shown by Filipinos toward the internees, often enraged the Japanese. A Filipino who did not bow deeply enough or committed some other peccadillo might be slapped or kicked; one got his teeth knocked out, while another was tied to a post, flogged, and left for hours in the sun.[8]

In the camp's third week, Commandant Tomayasu's car had difficulty getting through the crowd and he declared he would close down the whole system. When Earl Carroll and two other internee leaders went to see him about this, Tomayasu said he hated seeing the internees fed through the bars like animals, and various Japanese, Germans, and Italians had complained to army headquarters that Santo Tomás looked more like a picnic ground than a prison camp. The commandant relented when Carroll and colleagues proposed changes, which immediately took effect. The front fence was covered with *sawali* (bamboo fiber) matting, though impertinent jackknives soon made peek-holes here and there. Twice a day, visitors filed in through the gate and put their packages, labeled with recipients' names, onto tables manned by Japanese inspectors. After being checked for forbidden items — from liquor to flashlights — the packages were taken by designated internees and put on the grass in alphabetical order. Outgoing parcels, mostly laundry and money, were collected and taken back. Internees, cordoned off about 150 yards further back, were then called by name to collect their items. Shouting, even waving, was forbidden, but internees and visitors evolved coded ways of greeting each other: bobbing up and down, scratching a head, lifting an elbow. A few months later, a shed was built to protect the packages from rain, and this enabled internees, sheltering under its eaves in a downpour, to edge closer to visitors, sometimes even exchanging a few words. In late May 1942, nine-year-old Caroline Bailey was able to speak with her family's house servant, Felipe, when he brought in Winnie, her stuffed bear.

Messages in the packages were officially limited to fifty words and practical needs only on pain of closing down the system again. To prevent this from happening, internee censors headed by Charles Van Sickle, an International Harvester executive, checked many of the packages, rejecting illegitimate messages before Japanese inspectors, doing spot checks, got to them. Internees did not always take this kindly: "Who the hell are you to tell me what to say ... son-of-a-bitch."[9] Message smuggling and miniaturizing became an art form. Messages were inserted into bread loaves, pieces of beef (in waxed paper), even cigarettes, or written on the back of food can labels that were steamed off and then somehow reaffixed. Other message senders simply interspersed brief thank-yous and snippets of personal news in their shopping lists (the censorship was not very thorough).

In early October 1942, another commandant, Akida Kodaki, suspended the whole "package line" system for a week after a crackdown by his guards found twenty-six personal messages buried in outgoing laundry. When the line reopened, a new *sawali* fence, soon dubbed a "spite fence," walled off internees from the shed, to prevent internees and visitors from even seeing each other.

For twenty-year-old Geege Wootten, who had no Manila friends to correspond with (she had been interned in transit from Shanghai to the United States), the message-writers had brought the suspension on themselves and others: "We have been warned often enough." But Paul Esmérian, a bachelor with close friends outside, found "these clandestine messages ... very important," and he managed to outwit the system. Ten months after the crackdown, he was getting and receiving smuggled messages despite being detected by one of Van Sickle's censors and warned that next time his parcels would be removed. Well before then, internees — especially those with Filipino families outside — had found cracks in the new fence to get a sight of family and friends. Over time, the separation broke down further. When a friendly internee rather than a Japanese guard was at the door in the sawali fence, Esmérian managed to exchange a few words with a friend from outside.[10]

Through the package line, my mother received bags of vegetables from our house servant, the aptly named Angel Lodovica, who had extended his prewar vegetable garden and chicken run. He was so generous, indeed, that our Irish-neutral friend, Eileen Shannon, had to stop him, providing fruit and other food herself. Like other internees with servants outside, we also got a laundry service, exchanging dirty items for clean laundry — via Angel. We also received help from assets of Theo Davies, my father's company. Its merchandising manager, Gustav Laurent (a Swiss neutral), had sold the company's big inventory and used the money to buy food and medicines for Davies employees and families. Paul Esmérian and Tressa Roka got outside help too, through friends and servants — and not just staples. Esmérian's diary rejoiced at the arrival of a "beautiful guitar — I've started playing again."[11]

Within two weeks of the camp's opening, some internees were describing themselves as "haves" and "have nots" according to whether they got package-line aid. Two months into internment, Geege Wootten suddenly became a "have," thanks to an outside benefactor, George Milne, Scottish manager of a sugar plantation firm, who was allowed to live outside due to a heart condition. Geege's father, an architect in San Francisco, played bridge with one of the company owners, who got word to Milne asking him to help her. The result was a daily cooked lunch (chicken or pork, vegetables, even dessert) delivered in tiered, enamel pans (a common way of carrying food in the camp). She shared it gratefully with a group of friends.

The spending power of better-off internees showed up in advertisements that peppered the camp's mimeographed newspapers before the commandant closed them in April of the second year. Snack bars were the commonest and the names were often nostalgically Main Street. Art's Dry Goods offered toiletries; Mac's Palm Beach Shop included men's trouser repair. "Gwendolen" touted manicure, pedicure, and head massage services from a dorm room; other businesses used lean-to shacks. Lending libraries also advertised for subscriptions.

Most internees seemed to accept the camp's quasi-capitalist economy—"campitalism," to coin a word. Even Alice Bryant, a liberal who believed most internees had been "over-privileged" and were usefully getting "their corners knocked off," noted that the private resources of those internees who did not line up for the camp "chow" conserved it for those who needed it. (She and her husband borrowed money from outside business contacts.) Emily Van Sickle, the head censor's wife, argued that "money borrowed by individuals helped the entire community," enabling internees to sell all kinds of goods and services from "home-made" cakes and peanut butter to hair cutting. Van Sickle herself, though, felt guilty when she reluctantly hired another woman to do her camp job—cleaning vegetables—so she could spend more time caring for her husband, who increasingly suffered from asthma in 1943. Despite the two-hours-a-day standard job requirement (my mother worked in the vegetable garden), some internees hired substitutes until a new "Labor Code" banned that in September 1944. Tressa Roka exploded in her diary against a minority of "idle women who did little or no work," one of whom kept her hands "manicured and well-kept" by hiring the "destitute wife" of a military POW to do her camp job for her. In Roka's opinion, she should have done the job herself and simply given the money to the poorer internee, who had an ailing mother and two teenage sisters to care for. Later, as camp chow got worse, she "felt sorry for the hundreds who had to rely solely on [it]." Emily Van Sickle came to feel the same but they had no solution, though the Van Sickles gave generously to poorer friends at the end.[12]

The internee administration did try, to some extent, to mitigate inequality. A month from the start it set up an "indigent relief" committee; its name was later changed to the less demeaning "relief and welfare." As well as giving cash to some penniless families, the committee provided them with clothes and personal items—from toothbrushes to sewing kits—supplied by the Red Cross in Manila. The aid was partly financed by a 10 percent surcharge on prices at Aguinaldo's, a Manila department store that had opened a branch in the Main Building very soon after the camp started. It closed down in late August 1942, when the Japanese suspended the whole store in the Philippines for allegedly profiteering and selling illegal goods, but the following year a cash canteen selling extra food was started and this, too, generated aid. Staffed by unpaid volunteers, it sold at cost, plus a small surcharge that went to relief.

As so often happens with financial aid programs, the relief committee's benefits looked bigger to the providers than the receivers — and non-receivers. To get the relief, an internee usually had to apply for it, though some room monitors recommended recipients for Red Cross help. Margaret Sherk, interned with her small son and very little money, said she got no aid from the relief committee and did not even know of it until reading about it after the war. What she *could* see were "hundreds of people with the baskets spread on the grass," eating their lunches from the package line, which she and her little David regularly visited just in case somebody had sent them a package; nobody did. Thinking back on it after internment, Sherk believed that the moneyed "Manila men" who ran the internee government had "no idea ... how the other half were living," while those shortest of food felt too weak to "get up on their hind legs and fight."[13]

Sherk's view was not unique. The British businessman, John Curtis, who had helped the U.S. Army leave Manila (Chapter 1), wrote in 1943 that the camp was "run entirely for the 'haves,' to hell with the 'have-nots,'" though a more senior member of his own firm, Warner, Barnes, was on the relief committee. Curtis exaggerated, but he and Sherk were probably right in thinking that the camp's leaders underestimated the extent of need. Curtis did something about it, too, in keeping with his character. Interned in his early thirties, Curtis was the son-in-law of the British consul in Manila; his wife and baby daughter were not interned and were repatriated along with the consul as part of a diplomatic exchange. An active member of the expat community, Curtis was not obviously unconventional. But he had a strong sense of justice and fair dealing, shaped perhaps by a Quaker family background, though he was not a practicing Friend. A few months into internment, he financially "adopted" a small family, a Russian mother with two small girls, separated from their English father, who was in Shanghai. He wrote in his diary, "The little I was able to give them helped them along and how much they appreciated it." He later found some twenty others, willing to give the same kind of help, once "the idea had been put to them." Concentrating on mothers cut off from husbands and family or business connections, they assisted forty to fifty people. (Curtis left Santo Tomás in the second year to join a new offshoot at Los Baños, where he worked hard helping develop the camp's vegetable growing.)[14]

Curtis was not the first Santo Tomás Good Samaritan. In the camp's first week, Helen Butenko, a young Russian (not interned), started coming into camp, laden with packages for women who, like Curtis' adopted family, had come from Shanghai and had no Manila contacts. Her father, a financier, had once received a decoration from the Japanese emperor. On the strength of this she was allowed to enter Santo Tomás, bringing in food and other items paid for by herself and others. Known to some as the "Angel of the Annex" — the dormitory building for mothers and small children — she continued her missions, usually twice a week, until they were stopped in May 1943.

The uneven flow of private goods and money into Santo Tomás was not the only thing that made it a porous prison. For more than a year, well over a thousand internees had permits ("passes") to live outside, usually in hospitals or their own homes, or those of friends. The system started almost by chance, on the camp's third day. Albert Holland, an energetic thirty-five-year-old, had been trying unsuccessfully to find a mattress for an elderly woman.

Spotting a Japanese officer with an interpreter, he impulsively asked if she could be allowed home. Referred to the commandant's office, he was pleasantly surprised to get releases for the woman and five men on the grounds of age and ill health. The pass system quickly evolved, with formal permits and, later, red armbands issued to internees allowed out. Holland, a member of the internee Executive Committee, got a desk in the commandant's office, with the job of sifting applications for release, talking with doctors inside and outside the camp, and negotiating the cases with Japanese officials. Passes to live outside initially went to hospital cases, ailing people over seventy, mothers with children under the age of one (soon changed to two) along with their other children, and women in advanced pregnancy. Outside the Annex, a friend of Tressa Roka heard a small boy declare sagely to another, "I know how to get out of here.... Just get pregnant."[15] Holland and internee colleagues tried to get extensions for the passes whenever they could, sometimes exaggerating or "prolonging" an illness.

The system favored those with Manila homes or friends to go to, but it reduced overcrowding and the number of people the Japanese had to patrol and supervise. Passes to live at home also reduced the amount the Japanese paid the camp, as this was per internee — no boon to the camp, as the departures did not diminish much what the camp had to pay for electricity, gas, and water. Passes were also extended to a boarding-out scheme for young children, especially those with ailing parents, though others could apply too. At the Holy Ghost College, a girls' convent school near Santo Tomás, a pediatrician, Fe del Mundo, opened (with Red Cross support) a residential kindergarten/boarding school for almost a hundred children under twelve. Several of Geege Wootten's young women friends volunteered to stay there as child-minders for the youngest ones. Every second Sunday the children's parents could visit them, but the experience was often wrenching on both sides. One of the children, eight-year-old Robin Prising, whose ill parents had already left camp, leaving him in the care of a kind room monitor, felt knotted inside as he was packed off in a car to the convent, along with other, younger children who cried as their mothers waved them off with forced cheerfulness. (He later joined his parents at home before being separated again when they went to a hospital and he to two different centers for children; he rejoined his parents back in camp during the last year.) Because the Holy Ghost school offered better feeding than the camp, Margaret Sherk agonized about whether to send her David there but decided in the end that it was better for both of them to stay together: "I will die if I don't have David."[16]

Several private homes, too, offered short-term, foster parenting for camp children who got passes to live there. For almost a year, an Armenian Turkish couple, Alice and Adolphe Ipekdjian, and their Spanish nanny Marie, took in twelve preschool children as a memorial to losing their own baby. Elizabeth Vaughan, cut off from her husband in the Cabanatuan military camp, let her two small children stay with the Ipekdjians for five weeks when her flu became a protracted fever. The Ipekdjians took strict care of their charges, giving them activities while dressing them up in little uniforms. At night, the younger Vaughan child, Clay, aged not quite three, missed his mother dreadfully. His sister Beth (just under four), sleeping in a small bed beside his, placed her hand under his cheek and he put his hand under hers. It was joy of joys when they could visit their mother in the camp and later be reunited with her.[17]

Among those with passes to live at home, bachelor Paul Esmérian became man in the house for two mothers, each with three children, all close friends of his. Being a citizen of

France, not at war with the Axis Powers, he was not interned for nearly eighteen months, and only then because he openly declared himself a Gaullist anti–Nazi. Anne Balfour, the French-born wife of a British colonial administrator interned in Hong Kong, immediately got a pass to live at her home, as her youngest child, Sebastian, was under a year. After she got some bullying visits from Japanese inspectors, Esmérian moved in with her. They were joined five months later by the family of Angela Templer, another wife of a Hong Kong internee. Both families had moved to the Philippines as supposedly safer than Hong Kong. Templer's six-year-old James developed bronchitis with a suspicious spot on a lung, and this made it easy for Bert Holland to get them a pass. Although James never got tuberculosis, the Japanese were acutely afraid of it; TB was a national epidemic, killing a million Japanese every ten years.

The Esmérian-Balfour-Templer ménage became a remarkable cottage industry. A dealer in precious stones before the war, Paul Esmérian was adept at trading in almost anything, from soup and sugar to papayas and even whiskey. Anne Balfour developed a line in *pain d'epicé* (spicy bread), which Paul then sold in the markets. When flour got too expensive, she ran a vegetable stall off her verandah. Then, after the Templers arrived, they moved into high gear, turning out cloth Red Cross nurse dolls and little Santas Clauses for the 1942 Christmas market. At one point they were employing six Filipino *costureras* (seamstresses) and were tickled to get a surprise visit from a Filipino government official, operating under the Japanese, who measured their workroom (former living room, or *sala*) so he could register them as a factory.

When the doll market dried up after Christmas, they embroidered and sold handkerchiefs until cloth became too expensive. Esmérian was the main supplier and salesman for all this, cycling or taking a bus into the markets. He relaxed at home by painting watercolors or reading Pepys, even trying to revive his Greek by reading Aristophanes in the original language, while helping the older children with their own reading. The scene combined prewar social patterns with wartime exigency and enterprise. Always there were money worries but the household still had several servants and Angela Templer bought dancing lessons for her two daughters. She got a loan from Spanish contacts in Manila but paid for the dancing lessons by running a small private kindergarten.

Internees with passes to live at home had to visit Santo Tomás every so often, or send in a representative if too ill, to try for a renewal. In May 1943, the Japanese authorities, worried that too much information was going back and forth between Santo Tomás, the military POW camps, and a growing guerrilla movement, pulled in most internees living outside on a pass. The Templers went back that month, followed by Esmérian in June. The Balfours, unusually, stayed out until June 1944. Anne no longer had a French passport due to her British marriage, but she played up her Frenchness, even telling her bilingual children to speak only French when strangers came by.

Our family, too, spent a year at home, ending in late May 1943. Like the Templers, we were beneficiaries of Japanese TB fears. Our mother got passes for all of us, including our nanny Evie, by contracting bronchitis; a family friend, Susie Yule, who suffered from asthma, brought her two young daughters to live with us. Her husband, Tom, finance director of our family's company, had to stay in camp but was allowed out to visit at least once — prompting a gleeful spy report of their passionate "hugging and kissing" by their seven-year-old Sheila.

Due to family business connections, we had more money to live on than the Balfours and Templers. Our cars, of course, had been taken; our chauffeur, Eustaquio Pontejo, went to work selling pork in a market. My mother's pass, though, enabled us to travel about, by *carromata* (horse-drawn taxis) or by bus. The distressing sight of carromata drivers lashing the welted backs of their horses was not new: my parents had told me that Filipinos and Spanish tended to treat animals badly. What was new and intriguing were the black contraptions on the backs of buses — put there, I was told, to burn charcoal instead of gasoline.[18]

We also got repeat visits from the Japanese, initially to interrogate my mother about her absent husband serving with General MacArthur. While an officer interviewed her, inoffensively, a soldier played with me on our swings. My mother had assured us that "the Japanese like children" and so it seemed. I noticed his shy smile and his complexion, light brown with slightly pink cheeks, not yellow as I had heard the Japanese and Chinese called before the war. (The only yellow soldiers I ever saw were our GI rescuers, who had taken anti-malaria Atabrine.) From this or a later visit, my sister Mary June remembers climbing our mango tree with a Japanese soldier, who then horrified her by gobbling up a bird's egg he found. And when the Japanese had gone, her Shirley Temple doll had gone too, from its little pram left outside the front door. In other Japanese visits, they took our ceiling fans and other furnishings, apparently for officers' quarters.

As in all their behavior, Japanese treatment of internees living out on a pass varied a lot. When Marie Francisco was partly paralyzed by a stroke in early 1942, her husband, Pancho, was allowed to live with her outside to care for her, first at a friend's house and then in a hospital. At the house she received repeated bedside visits from an officer, who seemed to take a shine to her as a mother figure, a surrogate for his own mother or even grandmother. That did not stop, however, a fearsome raid by military police who suspected that Pancho, a leading businessman before the war, was in contact with U.S. forces, especially when they found a prewar calling card from General MacArthur. They made Pancho stand to attention for hours while they interrogated him and took Marie's bedroom virtually to pieces around her, searching in vain for a secret radio. The Japanese also removed furniture and a big painting by Fernando Amorsolo, the Philippines' best-known painter.[19]

Other internees living outside got sudden, rude visits from individual soldiers, barging into their houses, taking what they fancied, and sometimes even giving them dirty laundry to wash. It was generally recognized, though, that the Japanese treated Filipinos much worse. Eight-year-old Jean Weinzheimer was mortified when a laughing soldier pinched her in the breast, but that was nothing to what she saw being done to a Filipino boy, drowned in a bathtub.

At official levels, the Japanese government tried to woo Filipinos toward Japan and Japanese culture, weaning them off Western colonialism, as the Japanese saw it. On top of a shoal of educational and cultural programs, Japan's Military Administration of the Philippines established in October 1943 a puppet Philippine Republic with a senior Filipino politician, José Laurel, as its president. Like other conquered countries, the Philippines were to be a partner to Japan in a Greater East Asia Co-Prosperity Sphere — but very much a junior partner. A mystic racism, tracing Japanese identity to a unique "Yamoto" race, justified Japan's domination of the Co-Prosperity Sphere. Japanese propaganda art linked the essence of the Japanese race to the sun and to light, contrasting the Japanese with darker-skinned and more primitive natives of the southeast Asian countries they had occupied.[20] Sexually, Japanese soldiers in Manila tended to prefer Filipinas to Westerners — which helped protect Western women from rape. But classified ads seeking "hostesses" in the (Japanese-controlled) *Manila Tribune* often specified *mestizas*, who were lighter-skinned. The Chinese, it is true, were often quite light-skinned as well, but after years of plundering and occupying China, Japanese had been taught to despise them as a "coolie" people.

Japanese assumptions of racial superiority had crude effects on ordinary soldiers. They had been raised under a regime that, from long before the war, had censored out popular knowledge of other peoples. They were also subject to the harsh, hierarchical discipline of the Japanese army. Slapped and kicked by superiors for even trivial mistakes, they did the same to Filipinos, their "inferiors"— all the more so when Filipinos did not show proper respect, let alone show enthusiastic gratitude at being liberated from the Americans, as Japanese propaganda said they should.

Among Filipinos and Westerners alike, nothing was more offensive than the Japanese practice of *binto*, or face slapping. Being used to it in their own army, the Japanese military often did not realize how alienating it was. *Binto* and other abuses warmed many Filipinos toward the Americans and their allies, especially now that Westerners were victims too. When internees out on a pass were shopping in the markets, stall holders would often drop their prices, or even insist on charging nothing, when they saw their customer was wearing a red armband.

Despite their generally worse treatment of Filipinos, Japanese soldiers or police would sometimes enter the markets and harass Westerners, whose historic power they still feared: hence the hyper-fear about secret communicating with guerrillas and the military camps. A sudden roundup of internees "on pass" outside the camp happened in early March 1943; Robin Prising and his mother Marie had a near escape from it. They were shopping at the market stall of an aged woman fishmonger, immensely wrinkled with gold hoops in her ears. Suddenly there were shouts in Japanese accents, "American? British? Where?" followed by sounds of a scuffle and a woman's cry: she had obviously been slapped. "Kempeitai [secret police]," whispered the stall holders. The fishmonger seized Marie, pushed her to the ground, and covered her with a shawl. Marie called to Robin to turn around, facing away from the Japanese: his dark hair would hide who he was. The stall holders pointed the Japanese away down a side street and then laughed in victory when they had gone. A young fruit seller, who minutes before had refused to take Marie's money, put them on a carromata, and when they got home, the driver insisted on giving them a choice bunch from a load of bananas rather than being paid. As Robin later saw it, the whole experience was one of love.[21]

Sixty-two Americans, British, and Dutch, including a four-year-old girl, were not so lucky that day. Arrested while shopping or leaving from hospital appointments, they were taken to Fort Santiago, the military police headquarters, where they were kept for two days and, given minimum food, sleeping at night in rows on the floor with rough sacks instead of mosquito nets. One by one, they were questioned: How much money did they have, who had helped them, how sincere was Filipino kindness to them, what was their attitude to the war, and — surprisingly — "are you willing to stay as you are until the Allies win?" At least one internee, Ford Wilkins, was beaten about the head for seeming to lie about the money he had. Exhausted, the group was then trucked into Santo Tomás, where some of the old and ill went into the camp's own hospital.[22]

By the spring of 1943, life outside looked more and more precarious. Arbitrary abuse was far less common in Santo Tomás, where the Japanese regime could keep better control of its soldiers. There were no reported rapes in the camp. Some families, prizing the freedom, wanted to stay out as long as possible, but others were not sorry to return when the general recall came in May. Sometimes the reasons were economic: it was getting harder to make a living outside. But there were security reasons too. Shortly before we ourselves went back, my mother got word from Bert Holland or one of his colleagues negotiating passes: "We think the time is coming when you would be safer inside."

4

Dorms, Shanties, and Sex

On 12 April 1943, Emily Van Sickle returned to Santo Tomás after nearly a year on pass outside, caring for her asthmatic husband in a hospital outside the camp; he came into the camp hospital two weeks later. As she stepped out of the ambulance and looked about her, she saw a familiar "turmoil." "Internees, many of them weary and worn-looking, walked ceaselessly hither and yon, each bent on his own private errand." Now, though, the frontier "village" she had left had become a "full-sized town of many stores, services, and businesses, both private and camp-sponsored."[1]

To newcomers arriving a month earlier, the camp looked comfortable, even bucolic. Alice Bryant and Elizabeth Vaughan were among the 119 men, women and children transferred to Santo Tomás when their camp at Bacolod on Negros island closed down. After eight days crammed into a small cargo boat, with no beds and just three holes in the deck for lavatories, they entered Santo Tomás, exhausted, dirty, and reeking from the boat's load of leaking oil drums. On the grounds in front of the Main Building, they saw internees sitting around on canvas chairs under flowering acacias. To Bryant, the internees who greeted them "looked comparatively well-fed, well-dressed, and carefree." Within a few weeks, though, Vaughan observed even among "seemingly carefree" handball players "a tightness about the mouth ... furrowed brows, [and] quick and cautious whispers after a furtive look around to see that no one [was] in earshot."[2]

What Vaughan probably saw was not just general anxiety but also a struggle for privacy amid the press of people. After curfew, which varied under different regimes from 7 to 10 P.M., internees were confined to crowded dormitories and the corridors and stairs between them until early morning. Many internees also used the dorms during siesta "quiet hours" (1–3 P.M.), enjoined upon the whole camp.

Limited permission to sleep in "shanties" (a.k.a. "shacks") outside the buildings later eased the crowding, but not entirely. In the Main Building, the biggest internee "hotel," a dormitory room usually held thirty to sixty people, depending on its size as a classroom or office before the war. Suitcases and sparse belongings were kept under the beds. People of every age and class shared the same dorm, but not both sexes, except that boys below their teens (like me) usually slept in their mothers' dorms.

The only holdout was an elderly couple who somehow resisted the administration. Mrs. G., a fiery old lady, declared, "I've slept with my husband for forty-five years, and no goddamn Japs are going to separate us now!" They got a special screened cubicle in the corridor where sexes were allowed to mingle, but even that did not wholly mollify Mrs. G.,

The university gym became a big dormitory for men, mainly older ones. This photograph of it, with furled mosquito nets, was taken just after liberation. Two weeks before the end, the Commandant banned sleeping on the balconies following an escape from the gym over the nearby camp wall. The gym was the scene of night-time food smuggling, from an adjoining room of university administrator Luis de Alcuaz, through a hole in the gym's wall hidden behind a bed, to a storeroom off the gym *(U.S. Signal Corps, courtesy of U.S. National Archives, College Park, Maryland).*

who would rage down the passage when people got too noisy for her. She was, though, a devout Buddhist. Tressa Roka found that that her eyes and voice would soften if you asked her about her beliefs. In the end, only death separated them: her husband died of malnutrition in the camp's last month.[3]

Other sleeping eccentricities were allowed too. On the Main Building's ground floor, some men set up a row of beds in a corridor running alongside the two inner patios. Bob Wygle, a mining engineer who became the camp tinker, created a ground-floor cubicle in the triangular space under the main stairs. His twelve-year-old son, Peter, joined him there later, leaving his mother and sister in a regular dorm. Within the dorms, Geege Wootten and her friend, Deede Bowen, made a double bed out of two four-foot-high cabinets, giving more storage space below. In Room 14, and a few others, the whole dorm built upward, sleeping "double-decker," with more space between the beds. Otherwise, they would have been eighteen inches apart.

After our year outside, my own family moved into the Main Building, the three of us

4. Dorms, Shanties, and Sex

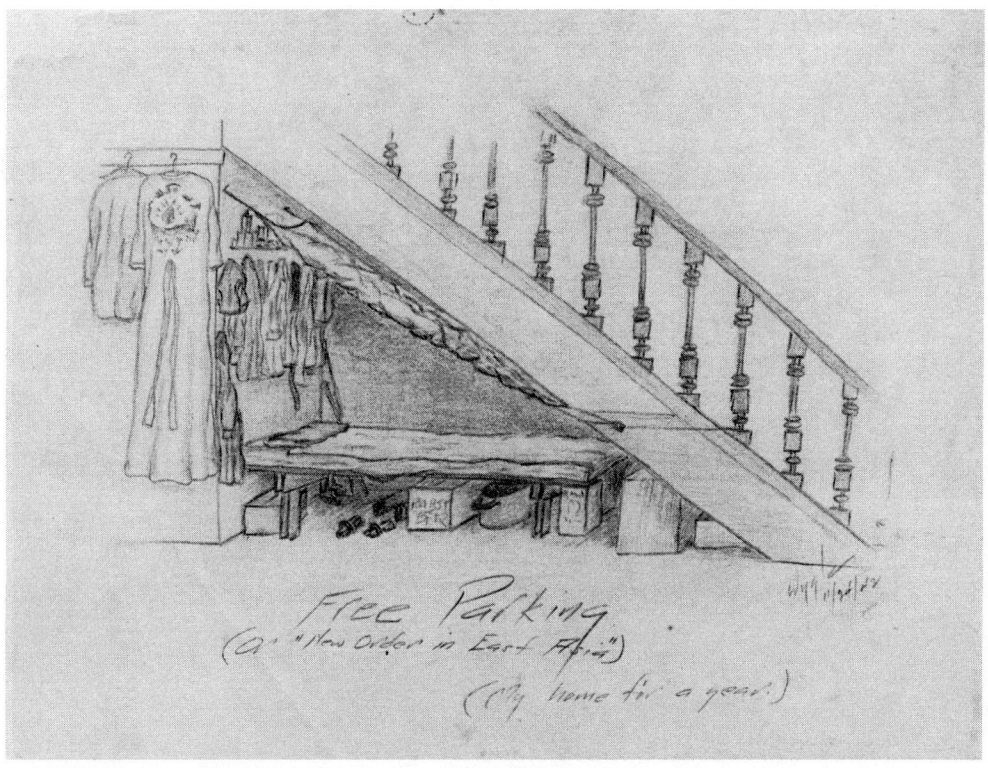

Robert Wygle was a talented eccentric who made bamboo knitting needles and other gadgets for internees. He created his own sleeping space in an alcove under the Main Building stairs, shared part of the time by his son Peter, interned at the age of 11 *(drawing by Robert Wygle, courtesy of Nancy Wygle).*

on the second floor but Evie in a ground-floor room for older people who found stairs a trial (she had broken her leg outside and it was still painful).[4] In our Room 33, as in others, each family group had its own mosquito net, creating a fine-mesh tent around the beds — a semblance of privacy. The nets were effective, but just occasionally, having gone to bed before the others, I would hear the whine of an intruder. "Mum, there's a mosquito in my bed" would bring instant, gratifying attention: my mother entering the tent with Flit spray can — whoosh, whoosh, mosquito silenced.

If the nets warded off mosquitoes, they were good news for bedbugs. The nets hung from lines across the room, and the lines were bedbug highways. Bedbugs, and the itching from their bites, were the bane of Santo Tomás nights; no creatures, after humans, get more mention in camp memoirs. They got everywhere, into the tiniest cracks and holes in furniture, into slippers, into belts. It was not uncommon to see someone suddenly jump up from a chair or slap the back of his or her neck. They caused no real harm, just itchy red welts, but they disrupted sleep: their best opportunities came at night.

Professional blood-suckers, bedbugs are beautifully equipped. They have two tubes to insert into their prey. One sucks out the blood; the other injects an anticoagulant to keep the drink liquid, combined with a temporary anesthetic to give the thief getaway time. Not always enough time, though. A bamboo bed I acquired had many holes in it, just right for

Internee Jerry Sams took this photograph of a men's dorm; it's a rare shot, as cameras were banned. Only a few dorms followed this one in building upward with double-decker bunks to relieve congestion. Sams took the picture in the camp's "good" period, before malnutrition was visible. The moustached man at the bottom left may be Ernest Stanley, former Japan missionary and interpreter for the camp administration. He lived in Japanese quarters part of the time *(courtesy of Gerry Schwede and Lou Gopal)*.

bedbugs. In the morning I would sometimes see a dead bug on my sheet and a smudge of blood beside it. I was intrigued to realize it was *my* blood. The bedbug had been squashed when I rolled over.

Internees did not take this lying down! Many would haul mattresses outside every week, pour boiling water on them, and leave them to dry. Some put the legs of their beds into cans of kerosene. A bedbug squad came by every so often, squirting chlorine into crevices. These measures helped but never won total victory. Teenage twins, Barney and Curtis Brooks, recruited to inject an anti-bedbug powder into wall cracks, caught a live bug and put it into their can of powder. Days later it was alive and well — dampening the brothers' enthusiasm for bug destruction.[5]

In the corridors before lights out (which varied from 8 to 10 P.M.), people gathered in little groups on canvas chairs around small folding tables or college desks. I played checkers in the corridor with Marion Ralston, my first love, who also slept in Room 33. Adults sat around talking, reading, or playing cards. Poker games flourished in the Main Building lobby until a commandant banned them as gambling. Paul Esmérian described the Education Building, accommodating male internees, on a rainy evening in July 1943: "The corridor benches ... are mostly occupied by old men, holding forth on the latest gossip." In the foyer,

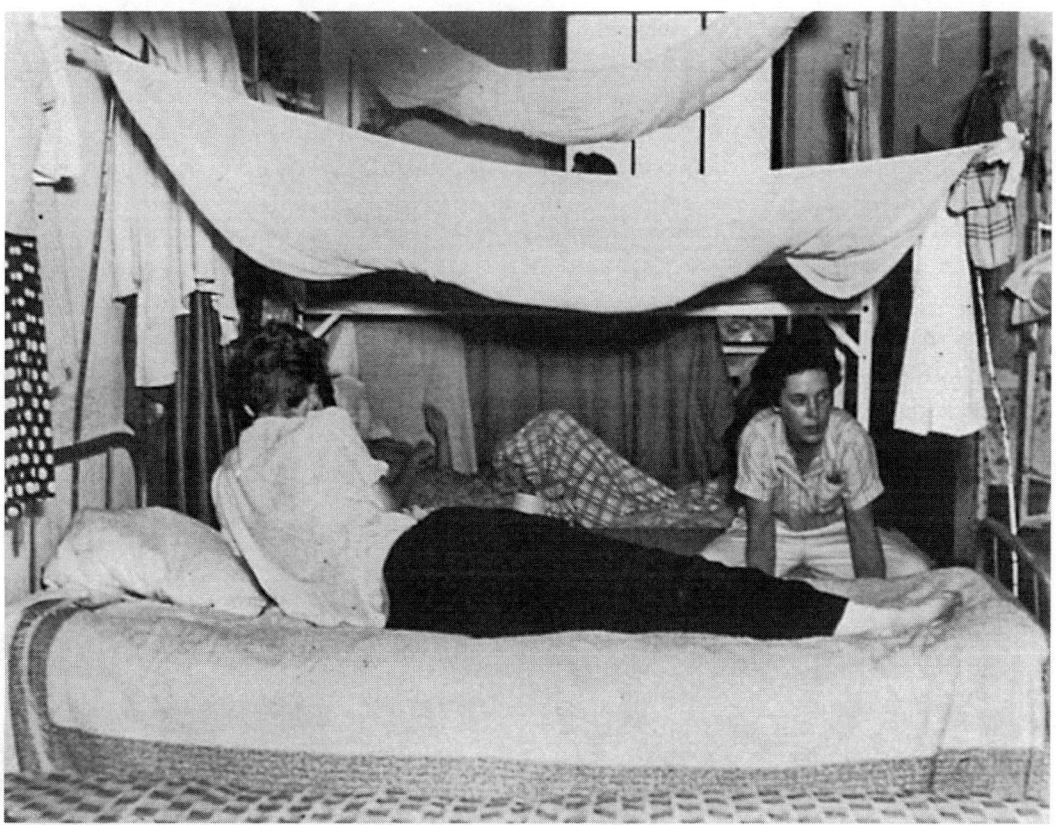

This post-liberation photograph of a women's dorm shows how close the beds were to each other — sometimes less than 20 inches apart *(U.S. Signal Corps, courtesy of Lou Gopal).*

"clouds of smoke, bridge or chess tables, around each of which, seated or standing, are a good half dozen onlookers." He bought a coffee at a small bar serving coffee and cakes, and, hard pressed to find a seat, settled down to read in an old wooden chair whose seat had fallen out.[6]

Because the latrines and shower rooms (sex-divided) remained in short supply, long lines formed in the early morning and late evening. Most lavatory cubicles did not have doors, supposedly to deter lingering. Toilet paper, increasingly scarce, went through several schemes for rationing. At one latrine, when the ration was three sheets per session for men ("one for wiping, one for cleaning, one for polishing") and a fourth for women, the ex-bank manager handing them out called them his "certificates of deposit," a.k.a. "issue tissue" coined by a Japanese instruction. Later, internees were encouraged to use old newspapers and even bottles of water. The *Manila Tribune* was doubly suitable, its inferior newsprint absorbent and easily scrunched up, and its pages full of Japanese propaganda. The water supply itself was unreliable; it would sometimes go off when a woman's hair was all soaped up. Prudent shower-takers made sure a fire bucket of water stood nearby so they could grab it for an emergency rinse.

The showers were open plan: all shapes and sizes could see each other, and often several used the same spray. "If you want privacy, close your eyes," said the sign over one bathroom.

A common culture quickly developed of keeping one's eyes to oneself. But those self-conscious about their bodies, especially teenage girls and young women, found it embarrassing until they more or less got used to it.

In the dorm rooms themselves, packed conditions produced close cooperation; they also sparked conflict. In Room 52A, six women amiably shared the same kimono housecoat, while in Room 45, Geege Wootten tried nervously but bravely to break up a nasty quarrel between two Australians and two Anglo-Indians, all in the dance business. It started with racial and sexual name-calling, ostensibly over a man, and ended in blows: the room became known as "the Fighting 45th."[7] At close quarters, personal habits and carelessness — such as spitting into an ashtray or kicking a bed while walking by — could grate on nerves. Happiness depended in part on whom you slept near. Betty Lehman, whose bed was next to my mother's in Room 33, said just after the war that their friendship was one of the best

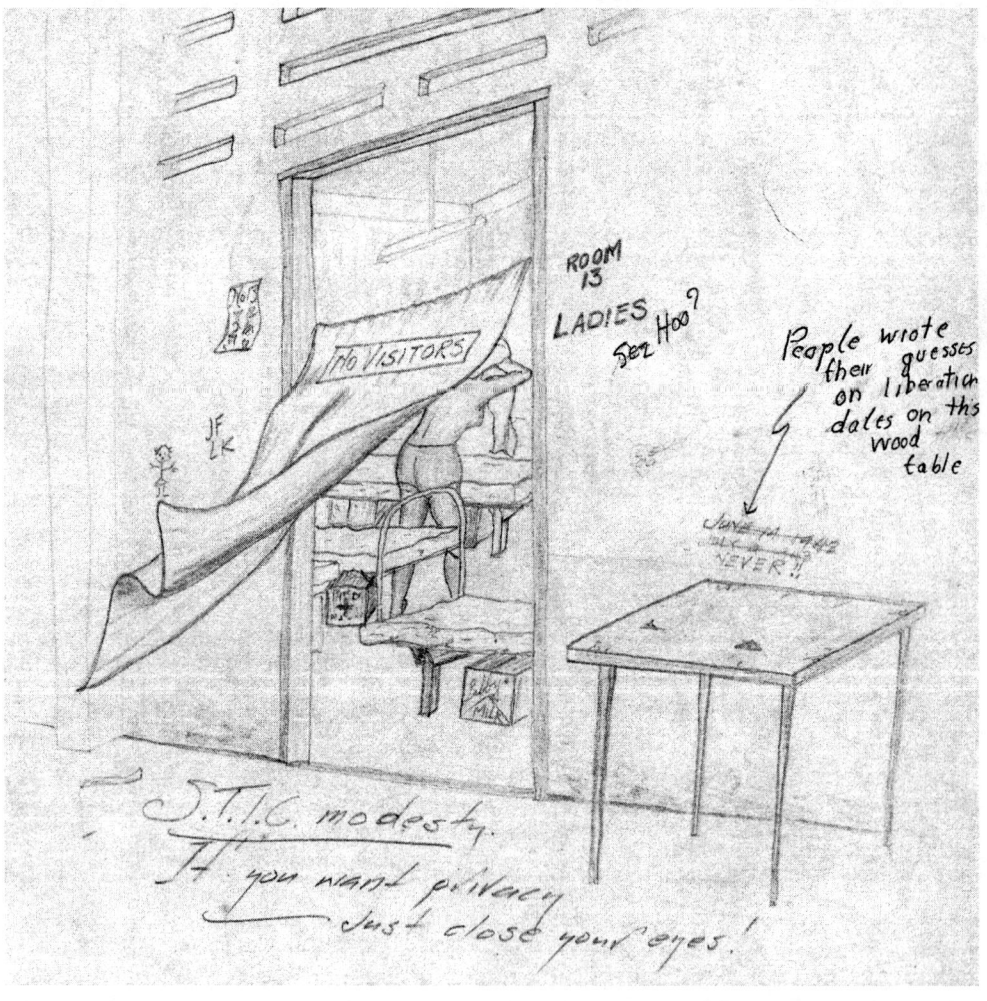

This view into a women's dorm picks up on a camp saying: "If you want privacy, just close your eyes." The drawing also shows a favorite pastime for some — guessing when rescue would turn up *(drawing by Robert Wygle, courtesy of Nancy Wygle).*

aspects of her time in the camp: Lorna was always so "sound and cheerful." And Mary June enjoyed taking care of her toddler, Chris. But in the Annex, among other mothers with small children, Elizabeth Vaughan guiltily confessed to her diary her intense hate at having to sleep next to a "meddlesome, gossipy, middle-aged adolescent" with a "malicious tongue.... I loathe the sight of her, yet she is my roommate for internment, I suppose."[8]

Scant privacy caused other problems too. In the Annex, Margaret Sherk's little David continually wet his bed. She tried to take him to the toilet several times in the night, but often not in time. The smell was trying for others, and he was teased for it by other children. The need for privacy could be sudden and deep. Quite early in the camp's life, a family whose beds were near Tressa Roka's in the Main Building got word from the Red Cross that one of them — their son, brother, uncle — had died in a military POW camp. "They sat on their cots weeping quietly." "If only," Tressa thought, "they had a little corner in which they could be alone in their grief."[9]

Noise was often a hardship, especially in the Annex, where children's cries and yells competed with the clackety-clack of *bakyas* (wooden slippers). Beneath a cupola in the middle of the building, there was a big lecture room like an amphitheater, housing families who put their mattresses and belongings on the bleachers (arena seats). A cluster of Russian women, as volatile as their kids were unruly, made it indeed an amphitheater; the room monitor and others had to break up a series of fights. Jean Weinzheimer (now Sascha Jean Jansen), who slept in the Annex as a young girl with her mother and two smaller siblings, remembers "bakyas flying right through the front door.... The yelling was choice." Relief came in the daytime after her parents had a shanty built. The family trooped forth, singing "Happy Days Are Here Again."[10]

Shanties (a.k.a. "shacks") were an unusual feature of Santo Tomás — little homesteads for families, groups of friends, and even single men. They were banned as sleeping quarters until February 1943, when men were allowed to move to shanties to ease crowding in the dorms, though outside bathrooms did not yet exist. In May, when showers and toilets had been built behind the Education Building, the re-internment of many internees living at home "on pass" induced the commandant to allow some 400 men and accompanied children to sleep in the shanties.[11] The following February, when women were allowed to join their menfolk in the shanties overnight, the wake-up broadcast on the camp's loudspeakers played "Here Comes the Bride."

The first shanty, in February 1942, was little more than a blanket thrown over the back of a disused truck, but Filipinos were soon supplying timber and other materials for more solid dwellings, and even getting permission to come in and build them. A few well-to-do internees had complete, prefabricated shanties rolled through the main gate. Some adept internees built shanties themselves; others used internee contractors. As a market developed, shanties were bought and sold, but several owners, transferred in 1943 and 1944 to another camp (Los Baños), simply gave their shanties to needy friends.

The average shanty was a one-room shack with sawali (bamboo fiber) sides and a nipa (palm thatch) roof. The better ones, ours among them, had wooden floors and were up on stilts, like traditional Filipino nipa huts, to keep out floods and creepy-crawlies and let in more breeze. Most shanties had garden plots, enough to grow a few vegetables in; some had banana trees, and in the Philippines' tropical climate, foliage soon grew up the walls.

Shanties usually contained a small, rough table, folding stools or chairs, a cupboard, and later a cot or two for those who slept in the shanties (we never did). To keep out ants, the legs of our food cupboard stood in small cans of water but the ants quickly crossed on the bodies of their drowned fellows. (I was intrigued by this collective self-sacrifice.) And despite the stilts, a common sound in the shanty was the "geko" from lizards of that name up in the eaves. Outside the shanties, many owners kept a charcoal-burning stove — a simple clay or terracotta pot — for cooking privately obtained food. The shanties in general provided extra storage space. Non-shanty dwellers had to put anything not kept under their beds into a baggage *bodega* (storeroom).

Shanties varied a lot in size and creature comforts. The smallest were often earth-floor lean-tos, enough for just two people. And in the Main Building's inner patios, little cabins — *cabanas* — clustered higgledy-piggledy about each other, some under a shared roof. At the other end of the scale, mini-bungalows boasted several rooms with built-in closets, window seats, and paved gardens. The owner of one of the fanciest dwellings stuck in my memory as the only internee I knew of to have a servant in camp: I could see her doing chores at the shanty window. Eleanor Stone, wife of a Cabanatuan POW, was housekeeper and general factotum to a big, white-haired General Motors vice-president, Edwin Van Vorhees, who had no family in the camp.

Among the smallest "shanties" were the "cabanas" set up in the Main Building's two inner patios. Even these gave more privacy than the dorms, though men could not sleep in shanties until the second year, and women not until the last year *(U.S. Signal Corps, courtesy of U.S. National Archives, College Park, Maryland).*

Van Voorhees obviously had money, but who else could afford shanties? In the camp's first eighteen months, before building materials ran short and prices rocketed, the average shanty cost 100–150 pesos, about $900 today. The most expensive went for over 400 pesos, $3,000 in current dollars.[12] For Isla Corfield and her teenage daughter, Gill, separated from Isla's husband in Hong Kong, these prices were out of sight. Longing for a shanty, they were finally able to rent a patio cabana for two pesos a month (about $15 today) from a woman who was mostly out of camp on a "sick pass."

Another couple, Bill and Sophie Gibb, got a small shanty in return for hair-cutting, Red Cross parcel cigarettes, and vegetables grown on a tiny plot they had drawn lots for. The Gibbs, who were among the transfers from Bocolod camp on Negros, showed that past wealth did not always mean shanty-purchasing power: they had little cash, though Bill had been a loan officer for a Bacolod sugar milling company and they had flown their daughter to Hawaiian safety on a pricey Pan Am clipper. As they had no evident wish to borrow, the best asset they brought was Sophie's hair-cutting skill, learned when she could not find a good enough barber for Bill in Bacolod.

One way or another, over two thousand people — some 60 percent of internees — were using shanties by January 1943, a year from the camp's beginning. Shanties then numbered about 600, including 47 small cabanas. This preponderance did not stop non-shanty people from referring to a "shanty aristocracy," a phrase coined wryly as "shanties" usually meant poor sharecroppers and deprivation. As in modern society, where being a minority can make the poor feel worse, being outnumbered by shanty dwellers could be painful. Of nine moth-

My mother drew this picture of our shanty, up on stilts and made of bamboo, with a *nipa* roof (thatched from *nipa* palm leaves). Banana trees stood on either side. It looked quite like the "nipa hut" homes of rural Filipinos, though we never slept in our shanty at night. A platform on the right-hand side was my den, with a shelf where, for a time, I collected jars of different soils and fluids, even urine (for a *very* short time), plus a jar of leaves with a *salagubang* beetle.

There are almost no pictures of camp shanty interiors, so this is a rare item. It was drawn in November 1942, the camp's first year, when internees could still bring in things from friends or servants outside, as the furnishings here show. Paul and Gladys Schafer, who owned the shanty and had two young boys, shared it with family friends, Mary Browning and her two boys. Mary's husband, Mike, a mining engineer, had volunteered to help the U.S. Army just before Manila fell. Interned in the Cabanatuan POW camp, he died when the unmarked prison ship taking him and other POWs to Japan was sunk by a U.S. submarine *(drawing by Ruth Fisher, courtesy of Michael Browning)*.

ers with children in Elizabeth Vaughan's small Annex room, just three, including Elizabeth, had no shanty and could hear remarks like "How about a game of bingo at the shanty tonight?" The "smell of frying chicken" and the "aroma of coffee" from shanties near the Annex were reminders that many had it a lot better than others.[13]

Vaughan conceded that some shanty dwellers did not have money left over to buy and cook their own food, though they had a private place to take their "chow-line" food to rather than eating it at a long table in a dining shed. There were even internees without children who could afford shanties but did not get them out of a democratic wish to share a common lot, or, in some cases, to do as much as possible for their Filipino families outside. Alaistair Hall, a successful young stockbroker before the war, was quartered in the big gym dorm and had no shanty. Instead, he got passes to visit his Filipino family outside; he also saw them when working as a senior internee orderly at Hospicio de San José, an orphanage turned home and hospital for Philippine-American War veterans and other old men.[14]

Shanties quickly acquired the trappings of American townships. Each shanty area or "town" had a "mayor," initially elected but later appointed as a "district supervisor," though the usual term was "monitor." Shanty rules required owners to pay taxes, a peso a month, to the internee Executive Committee for "camp welfare purposes"; to keep their gardens trim; and to clear adjacent paths.[15] Signs displayed spoofish names for the districts, from Glamourville and Garden Court to Jungletown and Jerkville. Froggy Bottom reflected its swampy site, as well as a pun on Foggy Bottom, the U.S. State Department's nickname, which likewise came from the original marshiness of its site (and, I like to think, the fogginess of its prose). The main paths between shanties got names too. Shantytown, the simplest-named district, recognized the all-important topic of food with allusions to local produce: Camote Avenue, Talinum Lane, Duck Egg Drive. Other districts raised their sights with Hollywood Boulevard, MacArthur Drive, Broadway & 42nd Street, and other high-end inventions.

The advantages of shanty suburbia were obvious to internees coming in from living at home on a pass. Angela Templer, re-interned with her children in May 1943, liked the people in the Main Building room they moved into, some of whom she already knew. Still, she "badly needed a place of our own away from the crowd." She was delighted to get a shanty: "We fetched our meals there from the Annex kitchen and started in to plant the garden."

A month later, Paul Esmérian, finally interned as a French anti–Nazi Gaullist, gladly took up Angela's offer of sharing her shanty. Initially allocated a place in the gym, he was not the only newcomer to be repelled by its "pungent smell" of massed, male bodies, "stripped to the waist." As men and boys were now allowed to sleep in the shanties, Angela's seven-year-old James was happy to have his camp bed moved into the shanty with Paul. Angela and her two daughters would leave the two each evening for their Main Building dorm, where they now had more space. (The following year, April 1944, Angela Templer elected to transfer to a new camp at Los Baños, hoping its rural location would be healthier and feed them better.) For Esmérian, sleeping in the shanty brought the pleasure of moonlit nights, looking out on nipa roofs whitened as if in frost.[16]

A general argument made for shanties was that they reduced overcrowding for everyone. This was dramatized in reverse by a typhoon that struck on the night of 14 November 1943, the worst storm to hit the camp, though not the only one to cause floods. It blew down shanties, especially in Glamourville and Froggy Bottom on the camp's eastern side. That and the floods that came with three days of bucketing rain poured masses of bedraggled shanty people into the corridors and hallways of the buildings, where they camped as best they could. The air there became thick from the crowds of people, damp clothing, and the smoke of kerosene lamps; electricity went off for the three days. Out in the shanties, some overnight sleepers were marooned for a day until reached by rescuers on bamboo rafts. The water came in over some of the buildings' ground floors too.

Our shanty was flooded so much that we could not get to it for several days, but at least we were not among the four hundred-plus — mostly men but some children too — sleeping in the shanties. Though Angela Templer had dug anti-flood ditches around her shanty, it, too, got flooded, and it swayed so alarmingly in the typhoon that Paul Esmérian and James were taken in by shanty neighbors. James then moved temporarily into the Main Building with his family while Paul, after helping his neighbors, adroitly found an Education Building bed vacated by a hospitalized internee. But not everyone found it all stressful. Eight-year-old Angus Lorenzen enjoyed half-wading, half-swimming through floating islands of debris behind his mother when they left the Annex to recover valuables and food from their shanty. Most of it was intact but others lost a lot, especially sugar dissolved by the water. The Templers lost a sack of rice. Our own losses we don't remember, but in all the flooded shanties, the water left a thick slime, which took hours to clean off afterward.

In the meantime, two days after the typhoon hit, the gas supplying the camp kitchens went off for a day. Internees remembered the heroic sight of men wading through the night as they carried heavy stones to make huge charcoal stoves in the dining shed in time for breakfast. The food service never failed, though much in the camp's main vegetable garden was destroyed.

Typhoons aside, the rainy season — roughly late June to November — always caused problems for shanty dwellers, from leaking roofs to quagmires. But it had its advantages: sex. From the start, the Japanese authorities sought sexual restraint — hence the sex segregation of dorm rooms. In part, this reflected a general wish to prevent disorderly and uncontrolled conduct. The camp's first commandant, Hitoshi Tomayasu, actually suggested a "love tent," where husbands and wives could "meet" privately — controlling sex by concentrating it in one spot. We have no details as to how it would have worked: Earl Carroll and other camp leaders stalled on the idea until the commandant seemed to forget it. A more specific motive for controlling sex was preventing pregnancies, along with all the problems that meant for the camp and the Japanese authorities. When an internee, seeking a pass to visit his wife in the hospital, revealed that she was pregnant, an assistant to the commandant declared, "Don't you know the military do not permit interned persons to engage in the business of making babies?"

To stop the business happening in shanties, they had to be open to outside view. As a camp rhyme put it, "in shanties, keep on panties." In heavy rains, though, shanty occupants could close shutters, and that encouraged some couples to get out of their panties. So did the fast-growing foliage that pretty much covered many shanty windows. Most of the activity was very quiet, but not always. When a husband found his wife with another man, a known troublemaker, the interloper might have been strangled if his yells had not brought in neighbors to the rescue.

In December 1942 news of a new pregnancy in camp, involving a nineteen year-old-girl, reached the commandant. On behalf of the couple, who were unmarried, a camp minister and doctor asked the commandant, S. Kuroda, if they could get married. Though a previous marriage had been permitted, Kuroda told them that the military authorities were not allowing any more. Kuroda got the internee Executive Committee to issue stern warnings against breaches of the no-sex rules. If internees did not comply, the committee warned, the shanties would go and, even worse, the camp might be totally segregated. Shanty interiors must be "open to view on at least two sides" and at no times closed when in use.[17]

A week or so later, in early January, the first birth occurred inside the camp; it was premature, giving no time to go to an outside hospital instead of the camp's smaller facility in a former convent dormitory. When Commandant Kuroda demanded to know what other pregnancies there were, the chief camp doctor, Lindsay Fletcher, refused to divulge confidential information. Amid some resentment, women were told by reluctant room monitors to report pregnancies to the commandant within two days. Most of the six who did so said they had conceived while on pass outside the camp, to which Kuroda replied that he had already said internees should not "make babies on pass." He had the pregnant women packed off to an outside hospital, whatever the stage of their pregnancy. The four fathers who could be identified were put in the internee-run jail, three for thirty days and one for ninety (a popular sentence, as he had cheated on a wife outside). The jailed fathers quickly acquired the title "pregnant papas," and Tressa Roka heard some women "chortling" that at last men too were getting a taste of "confinement." For two families, though, it was particularly distressing, as they had small children who had to be sent to the Holy Ghost children's home outside.[18]

Targeting shanties as the main site of sin, the commandant banned all internees from them except mothers and children of twelve years or less, and men over fifty (!) between 10 A.M. and 2 P.M. Internees did not just blame the Japanese. Tressa Roka felt sorry for the "pregnant papas," suddenly split up, but also blamed the fathers for getting her cleared out of her own shanty: "Why do the innocent always take the rap with the guilty?" Geege Wootten's friend Hank Sperry and the two other men who shared his shanty were even angrier. They had built grass-woven sides that could be lowered just when it rained while others had illicitly built shanties almost totally closed in, inviting the general shanty ban — all the more unfair, as pregnancies had occurred in families with mothers and children who were now exempt from the ban.[19]

Areas near the Main Building now sprouted "new ... and original architecture," in the words of Executive Committee minutes, as exiled shanty dwellers camped out in makeshift hovels around their stoves. But the shanty ban lasted only ten days. The shanties were reopened with tighter controls and vigilance against covering up for sex, though the shutters could be closed if, and only if, "necessary to keep out the rain."[20] A year later, on 1 February 1944, as the camp's population approached 4,000, the commandant yielded to repeated internee committee requests that married couples be allowed to sleep in the shanties. This legitimized sex at night in the shanties — another inequality between shanty folk and others. Marriages were permitted too.

In spite of the Japanese efforts, babies were born and conceived throughout the camp's life. In early September 1944, an unofficial survey reported 137 pregnancies, some of them started during the period of maximum shanty restriction, between the "pregnant papas" fuss and the opening up of shanties to couples. No expectant fathers were jailed after the original four, and most babies were born in outside hospitals.[21]

You would expect the stress of internment plus malnutrition in the camp's last year to cause a sharp fall in birth rates. Putting it around the other way, when the camp got a short-lived food bonanza in July 1942 (from a backlog of vegetables and other produce owed to it), camp historian A.V.H. saw an "almost miraculous improvement in vigor and morale," including an upturn in "sex appeal" and more "young couples walking together." The upset of internment did cause some women to stop menstruating for a few months, and a number ceased menstruating altogether. There were also couples who deliberately avoided pregnancy by sexual abstinence, or prudent timing, as contraceptives were hard to get; one father said restraint became easier as malnutrition and worry took their toll on his sex drive. In the camp's last hunger months, Anne Keiffer tried to abort her pregnancy by somehow getting and drinking big amounts of quinine water. She did not succeed; the family later joked that little Patricia, born after liberation, had curly hair because of it. Miraculously, birth rates did not seem to fall much below what would be expected in normal life. Consciously or unconsciously, couples started babies as a life-affirming act of hope. One wife, Grace Nash, said they started a baby thinking they would be out before its birth.[22]

If the Japanese gave up punishing pregnancies and night-time shanty sex, they did not go easy on sexual behavior in public — a position entrenched from the start. Meeting in the morning, three days into internment, Tressa Roka and her fiancé, Lowell Cates ("Catesy"), exchanged their usual kiss, only to be accosted by two Japanese guards, gesticulating and talking fast. "I guess the little runts don't approve of kissing," Catesy said morosely. Racism aside, he was correct. In the middle of the night, a few days later, Tressa and her fifty-five roommates were suddenly awakened by the center light going on to reveal an American internee official with a Japanese guard. The American read out a proclamation from the commandant, forbidding public "display of affection between married or unmarried couples," not even a kiss or holding hands. By then the internee administration had created what was usually called a "morality patrol" or "morality squad" to stop any "indiscreet intimate contact." One evening, the following month, Tressa and Catesy forgot the rules. Sitting out in a patio, they talked emotionally about their hopes for the future, and then hugged each other. A flashlight glared in their faces from one of the patio enforcers. Mechanically and wearily — his heart clearly not in it — he recited, "No demonstration of affection is allowed by order of the Japanese Commandant."[23]

The restrictions enraged internees against their own government as well as the Japanese. In defense, the internee police chief made an argument commonly used by internee leaders: they were administering the commandant's rules to prevent "greater restrictions on the camp" if there were "infractions." In this case there was the specter of dividing the camp into two halves, male and female. It was not clear, though, whether all the rules originated with the Japanese. Anxious not to encourage sexual aggression by the guards, internee administrators tried to discourage some women who they thought were being "entirely too familiar with the Japanese sentries," and they willingly joined the commandant in banning women from wearing shorts in public. The controls also got support from the more prudish internees who disliked having to see romantic goings-on at close quarters. For some of them, only "vulgar" women wore shorts.

The shorts ban ended in late June 1943, when a scarcity of cloth and clothing made the ban impractical: shorts in public were then allowed up to four inches above the knee. And even before then a group of army nurses occasionally and revealingly sunbathed outside their quarters, which were near the shanty of teenager Curtis Brooks, the bedbug hunter. They "exposed glorious female flesh to the gaze of undisguised pubescent lechery as I passed by." Other rules, though, appeared. In the first year, the internee committee banned dancing on the Main Building plaza due to "interference by Japanese soldiers" — whether amorous or hostile was not said. And in January 1943, following the pregnancy fuss, the smooth British tones of the camp's new public announcer, Geoffrey Morrison, brought the command that people sitting out after 6:30 P.M. must do so on chairs — no "lying about on the ground" — due to "critical comments from the commandant's office regarding the conduct of certain internees."[24]

But the morality patrol could not be everywhere. Writing about camp teenagers in the first few months, Chick Parsons observed that "boys and girls ... thrown together in the day" did a lot of "necking ... in the dark corners" of the Main Building, though none of it was very hidden. More inventively, about a dozen teenagers discovered where to find a key to the camp's school rooms on the Main Building top floor. There they would dance and smooch to a single disc on an old record player, wrapped in a blanket to keep down the sound, before leaving and carefully returning the key. They would also dance illegally in corners of the basketball courts to the evening music played on the camp loudspeakers.

Another young group daringly operated a big Main Building elevator, thought to be out of order, raising it to between floors, where they danced and necked. For many more teenagers, the usual pairing ritual was walking between the Main Building and the front gate: "life in the fast lane," as Curt Brooks later quipped. To "go walking" with someone became camp teen idiom for dating. Like their elders, too, teenagers would pair off while listening to the evening music on the plaza. One of the couples, Margo Tonkin and Roger Schade, fell in love. Separated in May 1943 when Roger joined nearly 800 young men recruited to establish the new camp at Los Baños, they exchanged secret notes via the internee driver of a supply truck traveling between the camps.[25]

Sexual restraint was perhaps easier in the 1940s than in today's culture of entitlement: have it all now if you want it. And in the camp's last few months, malnutrition reduced some sex drives. Still, the camp's packed conditions could produce precocious and versatile sex. At least one pair of eight-year-olds, a boy and girl of different families whose beds were next to each other, did some mutual exploring at night, hands reaching out under their respective family mosquito nets. And then there was Emily Van Sickle's curvaceous roommate, Arlene, who would "lie mermaid-fashion on her bed at siesta time, bosoms bare, chin poised appealingly on her palms, buttocks clad in the tightest of tight-fitting shorts." She would sometimes call over a six-year-old boy, engaging him in long conversations while his mother was out of the room taking a shower. Coming back one day and finding the two together, his mother indignantly snatched the boy away and told him never to go near "that woman" again. Arlene enjoyed the label of "that woman." All this was innocent stuff, however, compared with Jack Owens, who used his bed on a Main Building landing to operate a rent-a-bed service. The women in nearby rooms had him moved, but some couples sought midnight liaisons in the women's toilet cubicles until officials threatened to take down the curtains.[26]

In the camp at large, gossipy tongues accused women of using sex appeal to snag a man who could provide them with a shanty and other goodies, not to mention the Romeo who could turn a susceptible young woman into his Girl Friday. The gossips were often right but they underestimated a genuine need for companionship as well as mutual help. The need was poignant when husbands were interned as military POWs at Cabanatuan or in Hong Kong and Shanghai, caught by the war when apart from their families. So it was for Paul Esmérian. He had been in love with Anne Balfour, whose husband Stephen was interned in Hong Kong, long before she finally moved into the camp with her three children in June 1944. In his diary for early August 1943, he said he was overwhelmed by "black thoughts" about Stephen coming to Manila at the war's end.[27] In Santo Tomás, Anne and Paul lived together with the children in the same shanty as husband and wife. By then shanty rules allowed couples and families to sleep in the shanties overnight. Paul resumed his role as surrogate father to the children, as he had outside when living with the Balfour and Templer families. At the end of the war Stephen Balfour was tragically killed by an American bomb after his camp was liberated. Paul proposed marriage to Anne, but for complex reasons she said no.

The most controversial choice by an internee with an absent husband was made by Margaret Sherk, mother of five-year-old David: she had a baby by another internee. Her decision was unusual but the flavors of her story — passion, practical need, dependence but also independence — were not foreign to other internees. Her story is also a rare account of having a baby during Santo Tomás internment.

Paul Esmérian with the Balfour family just after liberation in front of the shanty they shared. Balfours from left to right: Tika, Nicholas, Sebastian, and Anne. Paul, a Frenchman, was interned when he refused to conceal his anti–Nazi Gaullism. Anne's husband, Stephen, a British colonial administrator, was interned in Hong Kong and killed by an American bomb just after being liberated. Unlike us, the Balfour-Esmérian ménage stayed in their shanty overnight, except that Nick (my best friend) moved with me to the Boys' Club dorms *(courtesy of Balfour family)*.

Margaret's husband, Bob Sherk, a mining engineer, had joined the U.S. Army just before the war. He survived the "Bataan Death March," when captive American and Filipino soldiers, many of them weak and wounded from malaria, were marched some sixty miles to their initial prison, subject to torture and summary executions along the way. Bob Sherk ended up at Cabanatuan POW camp.

In Santo Tomás, Margaret met Jerry Sams, who was a risk-taker but also a caretaker. One of the country's top radio experts, formerly working for the U.S. Marines and then the Coast Guard, he reportedly faked illness to get into Philippine General Hospital so he could give radio advice to guerrillas. He also took photos in the camp with an illegal camera.[28]

Jerry slept do-it-yourself on a landing outside the Main Building's university museum. He built his bed with a high frame so he could put two chairs underneath it. (Picking the museum's lock, he once stole a stuffed iguana from it and sneaked it into a friend's bed, with satisfying results.) When Jerry got to know Margaret, David immediately took to him. He let David use his bed for siestas when David was finding it hard to settle in his crowded Annex room. He made him a pail with his name painted on it, for carrying food more easily. And he constructed, out of a metal biscuit tin, a washboard for Margaret, something she had craved.

Jerry, too, was married, with a wife in the United States, but as their love for each other deepened, they envisaged a life together, divorcing their spouses. We have more knowledge of Margaret's side of it. She felt the anguish of a "good girl," raised in a family that abhorred adultery; she also knew the stigma attached to "a woman who forsook her husband when he was away at war." But her love and need for Jerry were stronger. In May 1943, when Jerry was suddenly drafted to Los Baños, she feared she might never see him again. The night before he left they slept together for the first time, knowing she might get pregnant. She did.[29]

After he left, Margaret and David took over Jerry's big bed, and she hid her pregnancy by showering at odd times and hiding a relatively small bulge under loose shirts Jerry had left behind. She also got support from several friends whom she swore to secrecy to forestall the gossips and critics. When she thought she needed a urine test for preeclampsia, her support group nominated one of them, Robert Merriam, to hand her specimen in to the camp doctors as if it was his, since he needed tests for beriberi. The results were reassuring, and the comedy of it lifted her spirits: suppose, they joked, the doctors had found Bob was pregnant. She also confided her news to a woman whose husband had worked with Bob Sherk before the war; she could not accept the pregnancy and severed their relationship. Later on, Margaret borrowed money from camp loan sharks — most of which she eventually repaid at four pesos to every peso borrowed. She bought baby clothes, calcium, and extra food, including duck eggs, whose shells she ground up and ate for the calcium. When a big Red Cross food parcel for each internee arrived in December 1943, she traded cigarettes and coffee for canned or powdered milk, which she stockpiled. Jerry, who had learned of her pregnancy via the valiant inter-camp truck driver, sent in calcium and other items too.

Through underground channels to Cabanatuan, she also explained the situation to Bob Sherk, to whom she had also sent clothes and money. When she finally heard back from him, it was "the most beautiful love letter" she had ever seen. He forgave her and later she learned that he left her all his money. He died before the end of the war on one of the "hellships" transporting POWs to Japan in such appalling conditions that many died before they got there.[30]

As B-day came nearer, Margaret summoned up courage to tell the camp's top internee administrator, Carroll Grinnell. He and a colleague, Alfred Duggleby, were wholly supportive, only regretting she had not told them sooner; the "pregnant papas" fuss was now history. They arranged for her to stay for several weeks at Hospicio de San José, though it mainly catered to old men. Here she met the hardest opposition of the whole saga. Two American army nurses, prickly about giving up space in their big dorm room, refused to let David stay with her, so two of her camp friends agreed to take care of him. Margaret remained at Hospicio but then had her baby at another hospital. According to Margaret, the nurses said they did not want "that brat" born at Hospicio. Ironically, an internee nurse/medical administrator, who stayed with her through the birth, was Mickie Sherk, married to Bob Sherk's brother, who was also in Cabanatuan and later died on the same ship as Bob. While disapproving of what Margaret had done, Mickie did her duty with professional care and tenderness. Still more attentive was Mickie's assistant, Merrill ("Buster") Keeton, an internee with a Spanish wife outside, who did so much the Filipino nurses thought he was the father. Gerry Ann was born on 23 January 1944, three weeks early but in basically sound health, despite an early bout of whooping cough.

Reunited with David and her friends back in the camp, Margaret found that the most unlikely people were most tolerant, and vice versa. A stylish woman, distinguished for her self-preening, gave Margaret a bottle of Johnson's baby oil: the baby, she said, needed it more than "my face." David showed no jealousy; he went around saying, "Have you seen mommy's new baby?" In April 1944, the transfer of some families to Los Baños enabled Margaret and her little family to join Jerry there. Margaret got seriously ill and depressed but Jerry nursed her through it and she breastfed Gerry Ann until the camp was liberated in late February 1945. Jerry got divorced from his wife after the war and married Margaret in 1946.[31]

As a test of Santo Tomás society, the Sherk-Sams story did not show up the camp too badly within its quasi-free-enterprise limits. To get enough for her coming baby and keep it secret, she had felt obliged to use extortionate lenders. And of all people, the meanest to her were army nurses who assumed they were a group apart. Yet she found in the camp a generous and strong support group. In a pinch, friends took care of each other. The camp's leaders pitched in too.

Relationships were complicated for other internees as well, if less dramatically. The camp's prison confines gave no easy escape for couples who wanted to get away from each other. Geege Wootten's friend, Hank Sperry, was unhappily married to Christine, a beautiful young English woman whom he had wedded on a rebound in Shanghai. They had agreed to divorce just before the war, but got interned instead. In the camp, Hank volunteered to be "floor monitor" (over the room monitors on his floor) but withdrew when he realized it would put him in contact with Christine, who had become secretary and lover to the internee administrator, Earl Carroll. So he demoted himself to extra bathroom cleaning — demotion indeed for a former bank manager.

Gossip about Hank and Christine made it difficult for Geege, who was more and more drawn to Hank while wondering if she was in love him and how he felt about her. Serious and quite shy, Hank was fourteen years older than her (interned at 34 when she was 20)

4. *Dorms, Shanties, and Sex* 67

Nearly two-thirds of internees had shanties by the end, but shared facilities like these washtubs remained important (*Corbis*).

and did not want her caught up in speculation about Christine and himself. So he kept an emotional distance beyond mild, if illegal, ankle-stroking when sitting out on the plaza. In May 1943, he joined the first exodus of men to Los Baños, giving his shanty to Geege and leaving some money for her and an ailing older friend of theirs, "Aunt Butsy." On the eve of his departure, Geege cut his hair, and she missed him keenly when he had gone. All came good for her after liberation, when she found a more certain love, marrying an infantry officer, Mac Poston, who had come into the camp; her wedding dress was made of Japanese parachute silk.[32]

Geege Wootten's experience was less arresting than Margaret Sherk's, but it was equally important. It showed that in the camp, as anywhere else, love could grow quietly and uncertainly — in pastel colors, not always torrid hues. Relations between the sexes had to adjust to weird conditions, from crowded, segregated dorms to shanty rules and the morality squad, but romance took many paths and different forms.

5
"Cheer Up! Everything's Going to Be Lousy"

Before he left Santo Tomás for Los Baños, Jerry Sams acquired a refrigerator, which he installed beside his bed on the landing outside the Main Building museum. With Executive Committee permission, he worked on it until it was nearly silent, and concealed it in a handmade wooden cupboard, in case the commandant might not approve. Some forty confederates used it for their small bowls of rice or soup, late-night snacks to bridge the long gap between "chow-line" supper at 4 or 5 P.M. and breakfast at 8. In the wee hours one night, Margaret Sherk, who had inherited Jerry's bed, heard a "rhythmical sort of soft slapping sound." Peeping out — cautiously, in case it was a couple making love — she saw the beanpole figure of Dave Harvey doing a shoeless tap dance in front of the fridge, before getting his bowl of rice.

Dave Harvey — a name known and remembered by almost all internees great and small — was the man who kept everyone going, or so it often seemed. Skinny and tall, with a mop of mousy hair over friendly blue eyes, David Harvey MacTurk was the camp impresario and emcee. He led a team of theatrical and show talent, including his British girlfriend Phyllis Dyer, who sewed costumes, danced, and married him after liberation. One of his Australian "show-girls" said they put more into his shows unpaid than anything they were paid for before the war.

Harvey was an all-around entertainer — comedian, mimic, dancer, singer, script- and song-writer. His dancing was so fluid that his "loose-jointed body" seemed "devoid of any bones," as Tressa Roka put it. In Shanghai he had done a duo with Danny Kaye during Kaye's Far Eastern tour, before coming to Manila for a cabaret trio with two sisters. In Santo Tomás, his signature song was "Cheer Up! Everything's Going to Be — Lousy," making fun of the hardships.[1]

Performances, often organized by Harvey, ranged from full-blown plays and a musical *Cinderella*, with dresses made from mosquito nets, to variety shows with dancing, songs, and burlesques, and quiz contests between different camp groups. Reluctantly, Harvey had to pull back in an early skit, whose double-entendres were thought unsuitable for the young, but his mimicry was not always "politically correct" by today's standards. One of his stock characters was McGillicuddy, an Irish immigrant taking an "Americanization" class. One show invented a mock election with comic speeches and results flashed on a movie screen. McGillicuddy won a place on the internee Executive Committee, beating Mickey Mouse, the Annex candidate, and Clark Gable for the Main Building women. More acceptably today, the Irish and Scots asserted their traditions with Irish folk-singing and Highland flings.

Some skits were done as "radio shows" on loudspeakers, especially when the rainy season drove everyone inside. In January 1943, the main theatrical venue moved from an inner patio of the Main Building to the "Little Theater under the Stars" on the plaza in front. It even had footlights, housed in big powdered-milk cans, which softened the light quite pleasantly. Plaza evenings also featured cinema, usually a required Japanese propaganda film, Walt Disney–type cartoons, and a popular prewar American movie. No cheering or jeering was allowed. Among the Japanese movies, I remembered most vividly the sinking of the U.S. aircraft carrier, the *Hornet*, which actually happened though we told each other at the time that it might have been made up.[2]

By 1943, the entertainment schedule offered something almost every day, including play readings and music in the Fathers' Garden beside the seminary. The range of indoor lectures was extraordinary, from sixteenth century English literature to a talk by a minister on Akhenaton, the Egyptian pharaoh who radically insisted there was only one God. The main fare was the nightly music piped through the public-address "radio" station, KGST, using some three thousand donated records. They were arranged by Cortland Linder, a Norwegian-born shipping executive and musician whose own collection ranged from country and western to grand opera. Linder and a colleague once had stiff words with a rebel who had had enough of "that highbrow stuff" and pulled out the wiring. Others wanted *more* classical music. Based on surveys, different kinds of music were assigned to different evening programs. A minority who wanted more silence lost out.[3]

No one did more for camp morale than impresario Dave Harvey (David Harvey MacTurk), especially up to July 1944, when one of his variety shows got all performances banned: it mocked camp conditions and hinted at the coming Allied capture of Paris. Comedian, songwriter, singer, and dancer, Dave offered self-ridicule as an antidote to self-pity. "Cheer Up! Everything's Going to Be Lousy" was his signature song *(drawing by James McCall, courtesy of McCall family)*.

For camp historian A.V.H., music "did more to keep up the general morale than any other single thing. Virtually the entire camp listened to the evening musical broadcasts." The same was true for choral concerts and organ recitals, even though many listening to music on the front plaza also went there to chat with friends. Angela Templer and Elizabeth Vaughan wrote of the special relaxation and release they found in the Fathers' Garden record concerts on Thursday afternoons and Sunday mornings. Paul Esmérian was transported by a record concert of Mozart followed by Fauré's *Requiem*. Looking around between records, he saw the audience "frozen in unusual poses as if lightning had hit them."[4]

Music comforted the soul and took it beyond the camp walls. So did words and music combined. The camp's first live concert, four months into internment, featured "By Babylon's Wave," Charles Gounod's version of Psalm 137, composed for men's voices. Sung by a male chorus of 40, its cry to God from a people captive in Babylon deeply affected the audience. For churchgoers, Sunday services alternated between different denominations, first in the Fathers' Garden and then later in a big hut in front of the Main Building. Jews met in a classroom on the Main Building's top floor.

Organized "culture" in the camp, from skits to concerts, plus information broadcasts and mimeographed camp newspapers (which were also read on air), did three basic things for internees. It perked up morale and defied anxiety through good humor and coded sassiness toward the enemy regime. It offered relief from the boredom and drudgery of everyday life. And it provided common ground, offsetting inequalities among internees and the tendency of a big camp to splinter into little groups.

Morale boosting operated quite subtly. Dave Harvey laughed at himself as if he were any internee. Two lines from "Cheer Up!" ran, "Don't think that I'm complaining, 'cause it's not really the case/And if I look disgusted, why, it's just my natural face." He offered self-mockery as a substitute for self-pity. Like a vaccine preventing a disease by replicating it, self-ridicule fought self-pity by mimicking it. This theme ran through the spoofish names given to shanty districts and path names, and the jokes we have already observed about privacy (shut your eyes if you want it) and no sex in shanties—even in the camp's popular acronym, STIC. It also appeared in the title of a light-hearted publication, *Internitis*, which suggested internment was a disease, while the first editorial of a mimeographed newspaper, *STIC Gazette*, had fun with paper scarcity by parodying *Time* magazine's streamlined syntax:

> Papershort condition demands abrupt, unceremonious edistyle.... Big stic Grinnell [internee leader] promises noninterference with edithoughts: save libel.... Vox Pop is Sticeditor's aim: wearing no man's collar, our pledge.[5]

The fullest send-up of camp life was "Lost Tribes of the Philippines," a multimedia performance put on in September 1943 as a goodbye (and "don't forget us") to internees about to be evacuated under a prisoner exchange. The narrator, Dave Harvey, was a disconcerted traveler/anthropologist who had stumbled across a strangely retarded community, closed off from the outside world by superior beings, its guards. Actors mimed each scenario against a background of cartoon drawings and subtitles flashed onto a movie screen, with appropriate tunes for different scenes. The visitor consistently misinterpreted the community's primitive habits; it appeared, for example, to burn sacrifices to a god called "Stomach."[6]

Overtly criticizing the Japanese or hailing the Allied war effort was, of course, forbidden, but in August 1943, trumpet player Pendleton ("Bumblebee") Thompson got away with playing "God Bless America" as an encore to something else, and a man's voice in the dark told how Francis Scott Key wrote the "Star Spangled Banner." On another occasion, as Dave Harvey recited the anthem's words in a slow, flat monotone, the audience silently rose to its feet. Symbolic revolts like this helped morale: internees could enjoy a secret one-upmanship over the enemy.

Trouble came, though, after a big variety show on 1 July 1944; at this time, the D-Day landings in June 1944 had filtered into the camp through secret radios. It was a black-face minstrel show — white performers blackened up — still a convention then and not offensive, it seems, to the camp's black Americans, though they included outspoken characters. Unintentionally, the show even had something in common with the coded protests and freedom yearnings in American slave songs. The show started with "Old Man River" and ended with the locomotive song, "Alabamy Bound," the train conductor calling out the redolent names of American towns along the route from north to south. A close-harmony quartet mocked camp food and concluded, "I'll be lucky if I'm out in '53." Nothing too subversive in that, but then a comical but confident "Mr. Sambo" declared, "There'll be a hot time in the old town" — no, not New Orleans — "Paris!" (The city fell to the Allies on 25 August.)

The next morning, the commandant carpeted Dave Harvey and others for several hours, going minutely through the script, objecting to patriotic songs and alleged disrespect of the Japanese, and asking where they got their news. Harvey and the camp's leaders were vague about the news and felt it politic to give apologies, but all stage shows were banned from then on. Two days later, on Independence Day, a procession of children dressed as cowboys, American Indians, soldiers and sailors was led by a small girl carrying a little, hand-painted American flag. That went unnoticed. The Japanese usually attended only adult shows.[7]

With shows closed down, it was left to broadcast music to go on making covert mischief against the camp's masters. From early 1944, reveille broadcasts started at 6:30 A.M. when the commandant added an 8 A.M. roll call to the evening one. The broadcasts opened with a record, often the Andrews Sisters singing "Good morning, good morning, we've danced the whole night through," followed by rasping orders in Japanese to the guards, and then notices and camp news from an internee announcer. The Andrews number grated on some nerves, but the record could vary (my best friend, Nick Balfour, loved "K-K-K-Katie"). It could also be subversive. When the camp was moved from a quasi-civilian authority to more direct army control in January 1944, the reveille broadcast played "You're in the Army Now" and "Who's Afraid of the Big Bad Wolf?" Following the first visible U.S. air raid on Manila harbor eight months later, the broadcast came up with "Pennies from Heaven" and other jubilant songs, and in a lull before the planes came back, the camp heard "Lover Come Back to Me." When the broadcaster played, "Why Don't You Get Out of Town?" the commandant got the message and banned songs with words.

Evening music programs had already got into trouble with authorities outside the camp. Earlier in the year Sousa's "Stars and Stripes Forever" was played so loud that American POWs in the nearby Bilibid prison sang along and stamped their feet. A Japanese officer at the War-Prisoners Headquarters declared that Sousa's march "savored too much of a patriotic air"; evening music was suspended, and then cut to an hour a day at lower volume. In September 1944, evening music was again temporarily suspended when a camp audience applauded "Yankee Doodle."[8]

Cartoon posters, placed in the Main Building's back lobby, were also used to make digs at camp conditions and look forward to liberation. Smart children as well as adults got the point — more, it seems, than the Japanese, who never banned them. Eight-year-old Angus Lorenzen's favorite was the picture of a graduating senior, in cap and gown, penning a letter to his Uncle Sam:

Dear Uncle: This is an urgent invitation to attend my graduation! Only your presence can make this great experience of my life a complete success.
Yours affectionately, Joe Internee.

Joe's bookshelf contained such weighty tomes as *How to Get Fat on H_2O* by Prof. Nip.[9]

Outside the camp, Filipinos also played music and word tricks on the Japanese. In early 1943, during our year out of camp, I came across a Filipino worker at a neighbor's house, squatting on his heels. Looking at me with a mischievous grin, he quietly sang, "God Bless Japa-a-an," to the tune of "God Bless America." Though British and only six, I knew the song and sensed he was really singing for America. Filipinos were also good at word plays. Passing a sentry, boys would smile and bow and say what sounded to the sentry like "*ohayo*," Japanese for "good morning," but was really "*hayop ka*," Tagalog for "you're an animal."

In the camp, the best-remembered political pun was in the reveille notices right after the U.S. Army made its first Philippine landing, on Leyte island, 20 October 1944. In winding up a timetable announcement, Don Bell, a well-known radio commentator before the war, added, "Better leyte than never." Few missed his meaning. For months, the camp had known that U.S. forces were getting nearer. One reason the Japanese-controlled *Manila Tribune* was banned from the camp in mid–June 1944 (though some copies still filtered in) was that the great Japanese military achievements it announced occurred closer and closer to the Philippines, enabling readers to plot American advances—a source of amusement to internees and chagrin to Japanese officials once realized.

The Leyte news came from secret radios. The Japanese never found them despite sudden searches that turned shanties and dorm rooms upside-down. There were at least two radios, each feeding news to different internee leaders. One operation was run by electrician Tom Poole, who brought in a radio at the beginning and moved his sets between various hiding places, including a well, the movie projection apparatus on the plaza, and a series of shanties. Unknown to Poole, George Newman, a mining executive, and Delvin Axe, former "communications supervisor" for Pan Am, built a radio using parts smuggled in by the university administrator, Luis de Alcuaz. Besides a receiver, they also built a transmitter for emergency use, but it was seldom used, if at all, because sending messages increased the risk of detection. Radio expert Jerry Sams and two others also ran a scam on the Japanese, repairing their sets for them but spinning out the repairs while they tuned into the news, and then tinkering with the sets so that they needed more repair later.

To hide their sources, radio operators and one of their "fences," internee official Horace Pond, sometimes delayed and distorted the news so it would sound like a general rumor. In this way, radio news fed rather than contained the camp's hyperactive rumor mill.

Rumors were an important part of Santo Tomás culture. The first wave of them owed more to assumptions of American and Western superiority over the Japanese than to any real news. Following internment, many people could not believe that Allied forces would not be back very soon. Long before Corregidor fell in May 1942, it was reported that masses of U.S. troops had parachuted onto it, and that Australian troops had landed on Luzon. A big acacia tree was just one place where internees met to discuss the latest exciting reports. The good news was bad news to Chick Parsons, who feared that disappointed optimism would backfire into disillusion and loss of morale, for Filipinos as well as internees. In the main this did not happen, but when General MacArthur was taken off Corregidor to Australia, there was resentment at the man scorned by some of his own troops as "Dugout Doug."

5. "Cheer Up! Everything's Going to Be Lousy"

Over time, rumors waxed both positive and negative. As Frederic Stevens noted in his first-hand chronicle of the camp, if rumors were to be believed, both Tokyo and San Francisco were destroyed (long before the fire-bombing of Tokyo), and both U.S. and Japanese fleets were sunk several times over. Near the end, too, there were some rumors, mostly concealed from children, of impending massacre or deliberate starvation, but these mainly surfaced after liberation. Most of the war rumors were optimistic and comforting. Margaret Sherk quoted people who "asked for, and got, good rumors just before they went to bed," to make them "sleep better." When a rumor was proved unfounded, another always came along. Some internees perpetually believed they would be freed within a month; others put it at three months. This optimism could be lethal, inducing internees to ignore their leaders' advice and eat through their Red Cross food parcels, leaving no reserves in the last months of the camp.[10] Other internees, like my mother, were not fooled. When I asked her when would we be freed — "What are the Yanks doing?" — her answer was vague but reassuring: "They're building lots of tanks and ships and planes, and then they'll come back."

"I always HAVE said, and I STILL say: we'll be out of here in ten days"

A prolific rumor factory, the camp produced many stories of imminent liberation. Often preposterous and funny, they were also dangerous, encouraging some internees to eat up too quickly the last big Red Cross cases of food that came to each internee in December 1943 *(cartoon by James McCall, courtesy of McCall family)*.

"Rumortism," as one internee called it, did not go unmocked. A poem, "We'll Be Out Tomorrow," appeared in the camp's first year.

> I heard it stated yesterday by a man who ought to know
> That by tomorrow afternoon we can pack our bags and go
> This information came to him from a most authentic source
> Via his house-boy's cousin's aunt— and verified of course.
> Ten thousand flying fortresses flew over town last night.
> It's too bad we couldn't see them, because of their great height,
> But they dropped a million leaflets, one of which would have been found
> If some Japanese civilians hadn't just then come around....
> This may all sound like a rumor,
> But to me it looks all right,
> So why wait until tomorrow?
> Let's pack our bags tonight.

And in an early variety show, a song, "It's Rumored," written by Dave Harvey and Jim Tulloch, equated rumors with gossip, telling how an ardent fellow invents a romantic rumor to get his girl: "They're saying — can't help listening — a certain pair of newlyweds are soon to be…. It must be you; it must be me."[11]

As camp teenager Curtis Brooks put it many decades later, Santo Tomás was an "almost perfect petri dish for rumors," craved by internees as a "food for the mind and soul." Four things made this so. First, the camp was increasingly isolated from the outside world, yet its fate starkly depended on that world: the more imperfect the information from outside, the more people wanted it. Tressa Roka's fiancé, "Catesy," often said to her, "It's not the internment, it's the uncertainty."[12] Second, the camp had enough community — enough communication between people — for "news" to bounce around fast within the walls. Third, the community was too large for people to verify where a piece of "news" came from and how valid it was, especially as the sources for news from outside were secret. Finally, sheer boredom produced an appetite for rumors, including gossip about goings-on inside the camp as well as the war outside. Several internees even confessed to starting rumors, for the fun of it and perhaps also to feel more important. The boredom and monotony of camp life that made entertainment and rumors all the more important are mentioned by most narratives of Santo Tomás, though they don't stress it much. It is not easy to interest readers by continually saying that each day was just like the last, but that is how it often felt.

"All days were monotonous in their sameness," wrote Margaret Sherk about living in the Annex with her four-year-old David, before they joined up with Jerry Sams. Awakened by David at six, she would go to washing troughs outside to do their "daily laundry"; heat and a limited wardrobe meant more frequent washing. The two would then stand in the Annex kitchen "chow-line" to collect a cracked-wheat breakfast on tin plates. The next hour went on cleaning their spot in the Annex, airing the sheets, and catching bedbugs while David played. David then went to kindergarten at a shanty nearby while Margaret worked in the camp library. An expert book-binder, she mended heavily used camp library and school books while also repairing some private ones to pay for the kindergarten, as David was too young for free school. Meeting David back in the Annex, she would change and wash his clothes if he had fallen in mud, as he often seemed to. After lunch (mainly soup), it was siesta time for David while Margaret (not a siesta person) did chores such as picking worms out of rice in the Annex kitchen. Soon after, it was time to wait in line for an early supper and then read stories or tell nursery rhymes to David back in the Annex before tucking him up in bed. Unless it was her turn for "toilet duty" (issuing paper and cleaning), she listened outside to the broadcast music before coming in at 9 P.M. to be counted at roll call by the room monitor, and then it was lights-out at 10 P.M. Another day done.[13]

For many poor people the world over, such a day would not be particularly arduous, but Santo Tomás internees had known a better life. Camp days varied, of course, for different people. For those without the burden of caring for small children, the main problem was how to fill empty time — especially if you were not an omnivorous reader like Paul Esmérian or the camp financial administrator, Fay Bailey, whose diary recorded the books and plays he read.

Almost all camp memories, though, agree on one thing: the amount of time people spent waiting in line for this or that. In "Lost Tribes of the Philippines," the bemused visitor reported the people's strange custom of "standing, one behind the other," to receive a reward before rushing off to "repeat the performance at some other given point." Waiting in line was not just a camp specialty, but a result of war shortages in general. A saying in Manila was that *Pilipinas* (the Philippines in Tagalog) was now *Pilapinas*—*pila* meaning a line. But it was felt keenly in the camp. "In which queue shall I find you this morning?" an English friend asked Elizabeth Vaughan sardonically in May 1943. About the same time, Tressa Roka reported waiting in "seven long lines" in the same day. It was no joke for Evie, still suffering from her broken leg, who said that standing was more painful than walking.[14]

The most important lines were the "chow-lines." For the main serving point behind the Main Building, four lines sometimes encircled the big building, converging on counters where internees got their meal tickets (issued monthly) punched and dollops ladled onto their plates or pans—each ladle carefully leveled off to make them equal. The only break in chow-line monotony was the cry of "Gangway, hot stuff!" or "Coming through!" as two young men, bare chests shining in the sun, carried a big steaming container through the lines. Families could delegate chow-line collection to one member, a progressively lighter task in 1944 when the dollops got smaller. I did my turn at collecting, in the standard white enameled pans that fitted on top of each other, held together by a metal handle.

Other lining up could not be delegated—at drinking fountains, for instance, and most obviously the toilets and shower rooms. To ease pressure on the women's showers, the camp found a big old bathtub and placed it outside under a faucet so that several women at a time, leaning over it, could wash their hair; that produced another line. Small children were so used to waiting in a line that on an occasion when there was no line for a toilet, Elizabeth Vaughan's three-year-old Clay came running back: "Momee, I can't wee-wee, there is no line." The "package line" at the main gate was a long one too. After it closed, early in 1944, those who had cash could still queue up at small stores selling a few staples such as soya or salt (the items varied). Long before this, Tressa Roka decided to make a game of it, joining a line not knowing what it was for: if the line was long, the item must be good. No wonder, though, "we all complained of exhaustion at the end of the day."[15]

Besides buoying morale and relieving monotony, the entertainment programs offset the camp's tendency to divide into self-regarding families and individuals. Writing as a former anthropologist as well as camp historian, A.V.H. believed that the spread of shanties impaired "community spirit"—"too many people spent practically all the daylight hours in their shanties and took an interest in nothing else." Outside the shanties, too, lack of privacy made people build up a "defensive shell": at the dining tables, people often ignored each other. An ugly breakdown of community spirit occurred in February 1944 when the main-gate "package line" was closed but a new vegetable market opened. It attracted a stampede that appalled Emily Van Sickle: "Men brushed women aside and pounded the stall counters, shouting, 'I'm first. Serve me!'" To prevent this recurring, the camp administration issued ration tickets to groups of internees, compelling them to cooperate on a small-group basis.[16]

Hartendorp also claimed (without making much of it) that inequalities between the relatively rich and the poor divided the camp. Before the package line closed, internee Robert Wygle observed "Manila people with plenty of money or credit" spending big on daily food baskets supplied through the gate. "It used to aggravate a lot of us to smell their pork chops

The Haves and the Havenots

Internees did not make a big political fuss about economic inequality, but it was there from the start. Within two weeks of the camp's opening, internees were calling themselves "haves" and "have nots," according to whether they received food and other things through the main gate from friends and servants outside. Some even got cooked lunches. Inequality diminished when the army stopped private imports in February 1944, but some still had more money than others to buy extra food sold via the Japanese administration or smuggled into camp at rocketing prices (*cartoon by James McCall, courtesy of McCall family*).

frying while our tin 'dishes' held nothing but musty, moldy, bug-peppered 'line chow.'" Elizabeth Vaughan saw an "almost flagrant" spending on extra food and small luxuries that bewildered other internees and, indeed, the Japanese. The same division applied to shanties. Before Tressa Roka and her fiancé got a shanty in December 1942, she recorded being "smitten with envy" over the "Garden Court" homes, with their "orderly flower and vegetable gardens." Even among those with no shanties, it was easy to see that some had much more food under their beds than others: stressful for those with less food and hungry children.

In the camp's first year, Geege Wootten also noticed a difference between Main Building floors — between the tidy-looking Manila residents of one floor, with bridge tables and rattan chairs in the corridor, and the scruffier residents of another floor, mainly transients including seamen caught in Manila when war came, whose corridor furniture was just "ugly benches." Even then, though, elite people dressed down. Men who had been business executives "dressed in simple peasant wear," including *nipa*-straw capes over "bare shoulders and shorts" when it rained.[17]

Equality increased in the camp's final year, 1944 — relatively. People with shanties could still grow vegetables on their own patch while others had to apply for private vegetable lots. The camp administration could import some items for sale, but closure of the package line meant that individuals with money and outside contacts could no longer bring in extra stuff. More people wore patched-up clothes. When I outgrew a pair of shoes, my mother turned them into semi-sandals by cutting off the toe caps. A charitable shipment of pink and blue nighties was quickly transformed into pink shirts and patches for the women and blue shorts and patches for the men. Under the Main Building stairs, women with sewing machines did mending and patching for men without family to do it; the job was still seen largely as women's work even in the camp.

As early as November 1943, the Japanese commandant justified a ban on the private import of basics like rice and sugar, so as to reduce inequity and tensions between internees and not take too much from Filipinos (the needs of the Japanese army were rarely mentioned!). Short commons meant shared wisdom, too. For example, women washing their hair side by side learned that bits of *gugo*-tree bark, well soaked, made a substitute shampoo.

Smaller support groups made a difference, though they could split the camp into different coteries. A group from the San Francisco Bay Area and another from Los Angeles were especially convivial in keeping up spirits. Alexander Calhoun, a camp leader and manager of the National City Bank in Manila, held regular meetings with his fifteen bank staff members, discussing camp business, the war's progress, and what to expect afterward. It reduced the stress of uncertainty. Pan American employees met and shared meals in the same shanty. Through cash resources or credit, some corporation bosses gave financial help to interned employees. Executives of the mining company employing Margaret Sherk's husband before he joined the army cut her in on twenty pesos a month given to each employee for a short time. Elizabeth Vaughan, in a similar position, got no such help.

As we saw in the last chapter, Margaret Sherk could draw on friends as she prepared for childbirth in difficult circumstances. Elizabeth Vaughan, with two small children, seems to have had no support group. Her camp diary mentions almost no friends by name and no relationships in Santo Tomás. Concert broadcasts and the beauties of tropical nature gave her more solace. Her diary describes the coming of the rainy season: "hibiscus bushes ... dropping the scarlet bows that adorn their tresses," while the "dry cracked earth sucks in noisily" the new rain.

None of this helped when on 10 July 1943 she received the news she had dreaded: her husband, Jim, had died of dysentery in Cabanatuan. The news came on a tiny square of notepaper, smuggled to her via an Annex dorm-mate, another Cabanatuan wife. It arrived when everything seemed on top of her, petty by comparison but demanding: getting the children ready for a birthday party where she had promised to help; daughter Beth biting her tongue badly, needing disinfectant from the dispensary; an ink bottle spilled over sheets; an overdue book to be returned to the library. As she went through the day in a whirl of grief ("Oh Jim ... why couldn't I have come to you?"), she felt an "awful loneliness."

No one could have given her much comfort at that hour, but for all her social awareness, Elizabeth Vaughan did not seem able to make the friendships that might have buoyed her up later. Friends were certainly important for Geege Wootten, who in her early twenties missed her separated parents, her father in California and her mother interned in Shanghai. She felt particularly "homesick" for her mother when a set of friends, her "lunch group," was for various reasons breaking up and going their separate ways. It helped later when she got to know better a family with children, the Weinzheimers, who were friendly and hospitable to her.[18]

Social groups in the camp cut two ways. They made individuals feel less alone, but they could also divide the whole society. That made the work of Dave Harvey and others more important than mere entertainment: it united the camp. And when his shows were closed down, their lack was felt in the last months when tempers got more frayed.

Work, too, was important for hearts and minds as well as operating the camp. Like their seeming opposites, the entertainment programs, camp jobs supported morale by making people feel they were not just passive victims; they reduced boredom and induced varied types to work together. In September 1944, a revised "Labor Code," issued by the internee Executive Committee and approved by the commandant, required women to do 1–2 hours of work a day, in addition to "room and floor duties," and men to do 2–3 hours — according to age, physical condition, and type of job, all closely classified. Women with small children could get exemptions; so could people judged by a camp medical board to have "physical or mental incapacity."[19]

The work hours look lenient, but from early 1944 food shortages had started to weaken internees, and the climate was always hot and humid. Midday temperatures in Manila seldom fall below 30C/86F. And many internees did much more than the minimum: some up to a full day. Tressa Roka worked four hours a day as a nurse in the camp hospital until a series of stomach upsets forced her to shift temporarily to three hours a day debugging cracked wheat: "Picking webs, worms and weevils out of cereal for three hours was a tiresome job, but compared to nursing it was a snap."[20]

Internees could combine, or shift between, a variety of camp jobs as well as selling or making things for money or extra food. During Paul Esmérian's relatively short internment (from June 1943), he cleaned Education Building latrines, worked in the camp vegetable garden, went on night patrols guarding the camp from thieves who came over the walls, unloaded Red Cross food kits in the docks, became a nurse's aide in the camp hospital, taught French classes in the camp's education program, and gave private French tutorials for money. Geege Wootten took her turn at dorm and bathroom jobs, from mopping the floor and issuing toilet paper to "room guard duty, [making] sure no strangers came in and stole our meager possessions." For a short spell she worked unpaid selling bananas at cost in a camp bazaar, and later she did rice cleaning and vegetable peeling. In 1944, "feeling the need to move on," she joined two friends who were nursing aides in the camp sanitarium for old and ailing men.

Long before this, Wootten discovered a talent for precise sketching. She drew the children of friends and other internees in return for food, such as a homemade cake or eggs or even a can of spam, but later for money too. Becoming "the village artist" was a "lifesaver," she said, giving her less time to miss her friend Hank and others who had gone to Los Baños, and even helping her forget "how hungry [she] was." Her drawing provided a real service too. As cameras were banned, Wootten's portraits became a valued substitute for photographs. She even drew an internee's picture on a tiny card smuggled to the internee's husband in Cabanatuan.[21]

Camp jobs cut across social class. Soon after Elizabeth Vaughan arrived from Bacolod in 1943 she saw "fourteen or fifteen middle-aged men, without regard to previous wealth

"Do and don't" notices and information bulletins were all over camp buildings. In the financial breakdown (bottom right), the internee administration explained how it spent the 70 centavos a day per internee paid by the Japanese army when it started payments after six months; before then the camp relied on the Red Cross and other benefactors. The internee administration used the cash allocation to buy supplies from outside the camp. The "subsistence" item was probably relief for the very needy. "Family aid" was help to internees' Filipino families living outside. The 70c total was increased several times, but lagged behind inflation. In the last year the army ended cash payments for food and supplied food directly, albeit in diminishing amounts *(drawing by Robert Wygle, courtesy of Nancy Wygle).*

or position, stripped to the waist," sweeping leaves and tending flower beds. The most menial jobs could link people to each other. Peeling vegetables and picking stones, worms, and mouse droppings out of rice — a job almost entirely done by women — was not obviously fun work, but Alice Bryant found it "easy and sociable, [sitting] around a table gossiping." Geege Wootten also liked it, as a chance "to meet some of the other young women in the camp"; it produced "interesting conversations" and made her feel less lonely.[22]

As Wootten's drawing showed, amateur arts and crafts could serve the community — vividly so in the run-up to Christmas, especially the first one, when a mass of wood carving and painting produced free toys for younger children. Free toys appeared during the second Christmas, too, though there was less paint about. But by the last Christmas, in 1944, there was no wood or paint, or indeed energy, for a toy-making campaign.

Among the camp's many DIY mechanics and fixers, the most extraordinary was the mining engineer turned tinker, Robert Wygle. Interned with his wife and two children, Wygle was very much his own man: his eccentric sleeping quarters were described in the previous chapter. He took a dim view of most of humanity, and after liberation became known as a grouser, yet he never charged for the many things he did for his fellow internees, though he might have made some money for his family had he done so. In the camp's first week, he took on the job of digging a pit to bury garbage. Amazed at what people junked in those early days — from nails and wire to cutlery and thermos bottles — he made a "help yourself" pile of salvage, and dipped into it himself for useful bits and pieces. He believed, without objection, that others saw him as "that crazy guy at the dump who will fix anything you have free." Equipped at first with just a heavy broken knife and a chunk of steel as a hammer, he mended pots and pans, bakya shoes and zippers (once having to half-undress a woman to get her unzipped); made wire fly traps for the camp's sanitation department; fashioned containers of all kinds; and, along with others, produced enough bamboo knitting needles to stimulate camp-wide knitting. Shirts and other clothes were knitted, using twine instead of wool. Wygle made bamboo fly-swatters, bamboo whistles for the camp police department — and then whistles for kids who wanted them too. For some months his workshop was a chair under a tree, until he persuaded the camp government to give him a shanty repair shop. When he called for volunteer help, none came except for another mining man, who worked ferociously but blew up so easily at fussy customers that he had to be kept apart from them. A piece in the camp newspaper of November 1942 claimed that Wygle's knitting needles had made him the most popular man among internee women. And in its bureaucratic way, the camp administration recognized Wygle's work by giving him one of its "Community Service Award" certificates for "meritorious service."[23]

There were other social heroes too, though not always so recognized. In the Annex, women could put used sanitary napkins, embroidered with their names and room numbers, into a bathroom bucket of disinfectant. The volunteers, including a high-society lady, who washed the napkins by hand deserved "stars in their crowns," as Margaret Sherk put it."[23] So too the Catholic priest, anonymously celebrated in verse by James McCall in November 1944, three months before the end.

> ... *When you need a cheerful helper*
> *For some task that must be done–*
> *A man to ease your burden*

When grubbing in the sun
— See the Padre.

When you're sick, and weak, and hungry,
And there seems to be no hope,
And the grape-vine has no rumors
And you have to get the dope
— See the Padre.

You will find him with the push cart
And the stinking garbage cans;
Or at the kitchen dish sinks
Scrubbing pots and pans
— He's the Padre.

... Just a common sort of fellow
Is the Roman Catholic priest;
O'er his head there is no halo,
But he understands the East
— He's a Padre.[25]

6

Child's Play

Thursday, January 4, 1945. Up at 6.00—washed—to work. After eating breakfast (we get coconut milk now) cleaned up the shanty. Did the ironing and prepared lunch: greens from our vegetable patch and gravy from the chow-line (thin soup used as sauce). Suntanned with Jeanette out front until 2.00. Then played cribbage in the front lobby with Jeanette, Laurie, and Bill McKinley. To work at 3.45 at the hospital. Rice, gravy, and greens for early supper at the hospital. During roll call back at Main Building heard what sounded like bombing. The rumors now say that the whole of Luzon is under siege. After roll call sat out front with the gang, listening to music.

Mr Cooper died this morning of beri-beri. From 7.00–8.00 pm played bridge in space under Main Building stairs with Terry, Ely, and Ellen. At 8.00 Ely, Jeanette, Punky, Daffy and I took our chairs into the patio, to get chased out 15 minutes later by Applin [internee "Grounds Patrol"].... So we moved into the back hallway. Around 9.30 pm took my shower and went to bed.[1]

Seventeen-year-old Liz Lautzenhiser, who kept this diary, lived with her parents and grandmother in a shanty by day and the Main Building after dark. One of the youngest internees to write a camp diary, she did not start it until just after Christmas 1944. By then widespread hunger had put a stop to classes and athletics. But American aircraft were in the skies, and the U.S. Army landed on Luzon five days later.

Being over sixteen, Lautzenhiser had to work two hours a day. In fact, she started at fourteen, graduating from washing pots and pans in the hospital kitchen to preparing and serving special diet trays. Boys between twelve and sixteen could be assigned jobs too, but the rules for that were vague, and all teenagers got their work assignments reduced or waived for classes during term (usually up to three hours in the morning).[2] At thirteen or so, Peter Wygle, the camp tinker's son, volunteered to be a messenger between different camp offices and work stations, so he could get out of being drafted for something more boring. Some young internees also picked up jobs for money. One of the most enterprising, twelve-year-old Bill Tonkin, did grass-cutting and odd jobs for shanty owners in the camp's first two years, when some internees still had money to spare and the habit of hiring servants had persisted. Tonkin also sold candy to the evening plaza crowd for an internee who imported supplies from Manila relatives through the package line. Tonkin's earnings bought extra food for his eighteen-year-old sister, Margo, and himself when they met for lunch; their parents were in a hospital outside the camp because their mother had had a nervous breakdown.

In their spare time, and there was plenty of it, children and young teenagers played traditional games learned before the war, plus some camp inventions, though the more strenuous pastimes faded out as everyone got weaker. Girls played jacks and hopscotch, and jumped skipping ropes. Some boys played "dog-pile," in which one group formed a "caterpillar" that another group tried to collapse by vaulting onto it. Others dared each other to do something quasi-illegal, such as crawling into manholes. Both sexes climbed trees, until they were cut down for firewood, and played "kick the can," while smaller children played hide-and-seek. Collecting and playing marbles had its aficionados too. I never developed the most expert way of "shooting" or flicking marbles, but I was part of a trading scene that burgeoned in lieu of toy shops. Translucent "puries" and outsize "biggies" swapped for more than one regular-size fellow.

I also collected *salagubangs*, big flying beetles, which my friends and I put into jars with perforated lids, thinking the beetles would happily eat the leaves we put in with them. The enthusiasm was short lived, as the beetles died. Other children did better, as they knew the Filipino trick of tying a long thread to a salagubang's leg so it flew in circles around you until it tired and perched on your shoulder.

Camp conditions made some children inventive. Angus Lorenzen and friends built a miniature volcano from clay in a drainage ditch. Hollowing it out, they lit paper inside it so that it gave out smoke and steam. They also built a catacomb of tunnels and chambers inside a big woodpile, until the wood was taken away for cooking fires.

Although Jean Weinzheimer's shanty was in one of the posher tracts, Garden Court, part of it used to be a city garbage dump containing hidden treasure. Foraging there in the rains, she and friends found surprise items such as porcelain teacups emerging from the mud.

Peter Wygle said he and his group "went nuts" over semaphore and Morse code taken from old Scout handbooks.[3] They signaled to each other in places where the guards could not see them and wrote in Morse code on the margins of their school exercise books. Karen Kerns and her friends formed a club with secret nicknames and codes. Secret writing and signals gave a sense of power, defying the restrictions of prison.

Unusual bits of tropical nature filled in for the absence of playthings. Some boys caught small fish in ponds (before they got hungry enough to think of eating them). Roy Doolan, my age, played with frogs and followed their progression from tadpole to adult — a practical science class. My own science lesson came when I broke open a lizard's egg and, to my horror, a tiny fetus like a tadpole slipped out of it. Its eyes seemed to look at me reproachfully as it slid off into the undergrowth to die. Another scene that always stuck in my mind was walking between the shanties and seeing in my path a beautiful, green grass snake. I knew it was poisonous but a very ordinary-looking tabby cat had jumped on its neck and was shaking it back and forth. The snake was dead, like the cobra killed by the little mongoose Rikki-Tikki-Tavi in Rudyard Kipling's story. I wasn't to know that the tabby would probably end up in someone's pot in the camp's last hunger months.

Most children had little contact with the guards. Some of them were friendly, even patting a head now and again, probably missing their own families. But toward the end, when many of the Japanese were training to go off and fight and were replaced by Taiwanese, some guards looked more hostile and fearful: they surely sensed the retribution that was coming. Most of the time, though, the guards were just seen and heard — sometimes with interest, occasionally with disgust. I noticed their habit of scuffing their feet when marching and imagined it was a way of wading through mud in the jungle. Seeing a bunch of them playing *kendo*— helmeted and laughing as they tried to hit each other with long staves — I was reminded of the quarterstaff play in Robin Hood stories. In the camp's last year, Nick Balfour was amused to see Japanese soldiers doing a practice charge on a fence with broom handles, hitting the fence so hard that they knocked it over. To teenager Liz Lautzenhiser, the guards' grunting at drill sounded like "throwing up."[4]

Children's games could make fun of Japanese customs in a way adults would never dare. When a squad of guards was marching from the front gate to the back, a bunch of kids ran in front of them and bowed, making the squad halt to bow back as etiquette required. The children would then run on ahead and repeat the bowing. Another time, children took turns bowing in front of a single guard, causing him to bob up and down, until he shooed them away. A more unusual target was a commandant's horse, which he kept on a patch of grass near his office. One day in late 1942, Liz Lautzenhiser's friend, Terry Myers, got onto the horse, leaving Liz to watch out for guards. For some amazing reason, no guard appeared.

Much later in the camp's life, spoofing the Japanese could become warlike imitation. In September 1944, Tressa Roka saw eight small children follow twelve marching Japanese, laughing as they imitated the soldiers' swinging arms. She also, though, saw them playing

Child with a toy wagon bowing to a Japanese guard with a bayonet. The guard was supposed to bow back, though not as deeply *(drawing by Paul Esmérian, courtesy of Nicholas Balfour).*

with toy pistols in muddy trenches, pretending to be Japanese, not American, soldiers. "The Japanese soldier was ... the top man": small kids could remember no other.[5]

When children had more personal contact with guards, they triggered — like adults — a range of behavior from fearsome to friendly. In the last year, eleven-year-old Robin Prising and his friends prided themselves on never bowing: when they saw a guard, they avoided him. One day, Robin saw Lieutenant Abiko, the domineering guard commander, coming down a path toward him. Pretending he hadn't seen Abiko, Robin turned and called, "Harry? Harry!" as if looking for someone. The ruse did not work. Yelling with rage, and smelling of saki and sweat, Abiko punched him to the ground and kicked him. He then yelled even louder when his sword scabbard suddenly broke in pieces. Kicking Robin again, Abiko stomped off. Robin nearly vomited with shock and pain but comforted himself with this thought: "How typically Japanese; everything they make always breaks."

Mary Jane Brooks, aged four, got a very different response from a guard. The guards sometimes teased children by throwing peanuts or candy on the ground, laughing as the children scrambled for them. Toward the end of internment, when a guard threw down sticks of chewing gum (Wrigley's, no less), Mary Jane did not get any and burst into tears. Very late that night, another guard, who had seen what happened, visited Mary Jane's shanty with a gift of sugar and meat. Evidently able to speak some English, he told her parents she reminded him of his own little girl. He continued to bring food for the family until just before liberation.[6]

But relating to other children was, of course, more important. Many camp kids had a fuller social life than before the war. In prewar Manila and its suburbs, "there was never a boy next door," as Robin Prising put it. Visiting a playmate had often meant a car and a chauffeur. Still, you could be lonely in the camp too. Unlike Liz Lautzenhiser and the friends she sat out with — "gassing with the gang," she called it — my sister Mary June found that the girls around her had already bonded before the war in the American School; she was an outsider. Nor did she acquire a "best friend" as I did in Nicholas, the Balfour family's son. She often felt bored in the camp, a sense of life going by and wasted; yet she had felt that still more before the war. Suburban isolation was worse than the camp's crowdedness.

For some children, the closest friend they had had before the war was their *amah*, their Filipino or Chinese nanny, and that could be a real loss, for them as well as the amah. In return, they saw more of their parents and often grew closer to them. This was true for my sister, myself, and our mother, though Evie had come with us into the camp and shared our shanty. The real test for the camp here was how it took care of children and teenagers separated from parents who had been hospitalized before internment or soon after. The Holy Ghost boarding school and other establishments outside took in children if they were under twelve, as detailed in Chapter 3, and the Boys' Club dormitories provided a base for boys above eight without fathers or family. But some young people who had no parents in the camp entered a new world without formal provision for them. Their experience was mixed.

At sixteen, Iris Krass was plunged on her own into a dorm of thirty women several weeks after they had been interned; she came in later. Her father was in Hong Kong and her mother and younger sister in an outside hospital, as her mother had a complicated cardiac condition. Iris herself had only just recovered from typhoid. She felt that her dormmates took little interest in her; they were more concerned with their own problems, including who got what space: she remembered a lot of "bed-pushing" and bickering, even some fighting. Her response was an emotional numbness that blotted out her need for others, even her mother, whom she really missed keenly: "I felt anonymous from myself." She threw herself into work, a camp job cleaning vegetables, as well as cleaning internees' dorm spaces for money. Despite her inhibitions, she made friends with a woman in her twenties, Joyce Ford, who was British like Iris. Ford also did cleaning jobs for money but acquired an American boyfriend who provided them both with extra food.

Things later looked up in the dorm. Iris returned there, after a spell in the camp hospital with dengue fever, to find a food parcel on her bed. It came from the Filipino relations of two Hispanic American sisters in the room. The sisters were notorious for grabbing extra space for their big beds but amused everyone by dancing on them. Good-hearted under the flamboyance, they realized Iris needed help. Then Iris' sister, Patricia, came into the dorm, giving her a person to care for, and in the last year her mother was transferred to the camp hospital. Iris went to work in the hospital kitchen so she could see her mother; she also visited other patients, largely because she had long been interested in medicine (she later became a doctor). In spite of all this, she never got over a feeling of isolation from the people about her. She turned to science rather than people. A college-level engineering course showed her how to use calculus in estimating the loads on a bridge. She also copied out a chart she found, tracing the evolution of the heart, digestion, and nervous system from amoeba to humans.[7]

Robin Prising, interned when he was nearly nine, had a more complex time than Iris Krass. He was often separated from his parents. His father, Frederick, had cardiac asthma (a congestive heart ailment) and his mother, Marie, who had painful ear problems, stayed with her husband when he was in the hospital. Lively and intelligent, Robin related well to adults, and two surrogate mothers helped see him through at different times. He felt abandoned and betrayed when his parents left the camp for a hospital in the first month, but the person who stepped in, the wife of a former British consul, was just right.

> A lean, aristocratic lady, Elsie Harrington was in charge of our room in the Annex, a task she performed without fuss, preserving at all times a faint, endearing trace of humor. She kept an eye on me without appearing to do so, saw that I took my meals at the Annex kitchen and that I was safely in bed by eight o'clock curfew after she had called the roll. Unlike my parents, Mrs. Harrington treated me as if I were older than I was and, as a result, I grew up considerably in that brief time.

Later, out of camp, at a care center for women and children beside the hospital where his parents were, he was befriended by Millie ("Ma") Sanders, an African American woman who was as outspoken as she was motherly. The widow of a black Philippine-American War veteran, she had run a boarding house in Manila before the war. Over six feet tall, her imposing build was matched by a long face and eyes that to Robin seemed infinitely wise.

In February 1944, the camp's last year, Robin returned to the camp. He arrived on his own with 200 pesos sewn into the seat of his trousers, money smuggled to him by his parents via a trusted Filipino messenger. Billeted in the gym, he was under the nominal care of "Uncle" John Shaw, an elderly family friend who regaled him with stories of ocean liners and grand hotels before the war. More important, though, was meeting up again with Ma Sanders, who had returned from working at the care center. As she took him in her great arms, all the stresses of his life erupted and he became again a small boy, sobbing as he had not done for months. They ate their meals together with added rice that she bought, and when she saw he had head lice, she seared his scalp with kerosene: a common camp treatment for lice, though it was more of a trial for girls who got their curls chopped off. Since he was not just a small boy but also a precocious operator, she cautiously advised him how to bargain for a chicken with a Japanese guard known to take bribes, which he did for twenty of his pesos. And when Robin came down with a fever, she saw him into the camp hospital, from which he went to the same hospital outside as his parents. All three Prisings eventually returned to Santo Tomás, his mother into a Main Building ground floor, and father and son into part of the Annex that now took fathers. Frederick was still weak from his heart condition, so Robin became housekeeper, cleaning their dorm space, washing their clothes, and even emptying his father's chamber pot at night, to the ridicule of other boys in the room. But he drew closer to his father, enjoying his "affectionate, gruffish sense of humor." Mrs. Sanders disappeared from the story but he never forgot her.[8]

Robin Prising's internment was unusual, moving in and out of the camp, largely separated from his parents. But even when parents and children were solidly in place, there could be problems — at least for the camp as a whole. Parents were generally criticized for not controlling their children enough. By the end of the first year, the camp administration had received many complaints about the "excessive noisiness" of children, especially during siesta quiet hours and the evening broadcasts. They were pictured climbing over the dining tables in muddy shoes and yelling down the hallways. When Mrs. G., the Buddhist anti-noise campaigner in Chapter 4, expostulated to her husband about a "damn kid" racing up and down near their cubicle, the six-year-old heard her, slid to a halt, put his hands on his hips, and declared, "How would you like to have me knock hell out of you?" What happened then we don't know, but Dave Harvey's humor column in the camp paper, *The Internitis*, printed a "warning to Annex mothers: Never strike a child except in self-defense." At the end of the first year, the Executive Committee put out a circular via room monitors and camp school teachers appealing to parents to exert more discipline.[9]

The camp administration did what it could to occupy children with athletic and educational programs, though none of them were compulsory. Among the sports activities, the boxing matches that I had briefly entered in the early days had by early 1943 become a hierarchy combining humor with bureaucratic precision — very "Santo Tomás." Between the Atomweight class for the smallest boys (up to 42 pounds) and Junior Welterweight (140 pounds), there were ten different classes, including Electronweight, Antweight, and Mosquitoweight: no mention of the dreaded bedbug. The formidable six-year-old, Roy Doolan, my conqueror of the previous year and now a Paperweight (54 pounds), was listed in a tournament program as T.N.T. Doolan as if those were his real initials. The sports programs provided communities as well as activities. Len Baker, interned at 14, enjoyed being part of a congenial "gang" that competed with a rival gang at netball. He felt they bonded with their opponents, not just among themselves.[10]

The camp's Education Department ran the whole gamut of courses from grade school through high school to college, adult and business classes. They lasted until the last Christmas recess, December 1944, though air-raid alerts interrupted them during the first big American raids on the Manila docks in September. Roscoe Lautzenhiser, Liz's father and one of the school directors, wanted teaching to resume in January, but by then too few teachers and students felt strong enough to persevere. During the school year (June through

March, to avoid the hottest months of April and May) classes for most students ran for about three hours in the morning, including Saturdays, though some were in the afternoon. Despite the limited hours, the directors were often vexed by students dropping out mid-semester and then wanting to come back.

Bureaucratically, the system looked like an American school or college, with exams, grades, transcripts, course credits, and diplomas. The college section actually constituted itself a "college" with a dean and associate dean, to help students use its credits after the war. Drawing on the camp's variety of professional educators, the camp schools offered much the same range of basic subjects as an ordinary American school, except that the Japanese, ever worried about subversive influences, banned political geography and recent history. Along with adults, high school students could choose from different language classes; Spanish, Tagalog, and French had the most takers, while some adults learned Japanese. Despite paper shortages, optional typing classes ran at least through 1943; they used the backs of official memos. A more obvious sign of imprisonment was the way camp educators teamed up with the Safety Department to promote an optional first aid course. Students passing the course's "final test" got a certificate and a congratulatory letter from the safety director. The letter stressed a "moral obligation" to make the camp safe and conserve scarce medicines by knowing first aid and preventing accidents.

The worst feature of the school system was its location. Most of the high school and college teaching took place on the Main Building's top floor, which was hot and often noisy. Some classes were separated only by blackboards, meaning that teachers had to shout to be heard. The long climb to the top floor also deterred many students when they grew weak with hunger. Not all teaching took place there, however: most grade-school teaching for pupils up to eleven went on in six rooms on the ground floor, but the ages did not divide evenly between them, so that more than one class was taught in the same crowded room. There was also a shortage of textbooks. Students could borrow them from a small library off a Main Building inner patio but often had to read them there or in the patio.[11]

In spite of the problems, the schooling got high marks from some. Karen Kerns, aged nine at internment, later praised "those amazing teachers ... who with so little taught us so much." One of the best experiences was that of Len Baker. His superior record at a British school in Shanghai vaulted him into the high school senior class at age fourteen. A condition was that he take an American history course, for which his teacher assigned him a research paper, defending George III and the British case in the American Revolution. After high school, he took several college courses, which he loved. Among them was a chemistry course taught by Robert Smith, a former pharmacy executive and Stanford graduate, who also ran the camp hospital pharmacy. Smith and Baker did a deal. In return for washing bottles in the pharmacy, Len would get some real-life chemical practice. When the Red Cross sent in a medicinal powder to combat an outbreak of amoebic dysentery, Len learned how to turn the powder into granules and then tablets. His English composition teacher, Harriett Richards, had him write up the process, an exercise in lucid technical writing. She "transformed" his style by getting him to write more informally, he claimed later.[12]

This was the school system and the camp itself at their best, for those willing and able to take advantage of the opportunity. Frontier conditions encouraged people to find new ways of doing things and to move fast and flexibly between different roles, which in Len

Baker's case fed each other; he also earned money cleaning the shanty shared by Pan Am employees. Up on the Main Building top floor, though, Len was relatively lucky. His classes took place at a quieter end of the teaching hall, and his fellow students were more dedicated than others.

Alice Bryant, who tried teaching in the high school, hated it, though she was not a natural complainer. She liked the younger children and some of the older ones, but too many of the teenagers were troublemakers and hard to teach, including a gang of girls who called themselves "the Black Spots" and wrote poison-pen letters to teachers and other students. When two of their leaders were expelled, some of the rest became good students. But the noise abetted unruliness. A senior described to Bryant a typical scene in her class: many not listening to the teacher but talking, reading, or even playing cards. Bryant gave up teaching for dishwashing, and found the company there more congenial.

Between the experiences of Len Baker and Alice Bryant lay a no-man's land of memory. Decades later Curtis Brooks, the camp teenager who remembered so much, could recall hardly anything except a primly Victorian teacher from the American school who had a habit of wringing her hands in displeasure and made her class delete the word "bastard" from an Oscar Wilde play. The only memory that remained with Peter Wygle (interned at eleven) was being repeatedly thumped with a ruler by a grade-school "schoolmarm" and discovering a strange thing called a bidet. (The grade school on the Main Building ground floor used to be the university's "model home" section for domestic science students; Peter and his mates found they could make the bidet go "whoosh" like a fountain.) Robin Prising, returning from the hospital in 1944, and under no firm control by his parents, often played truant. When he did go to school, hunger soon made it easier to dream and look out over the Manila rooftops. What switched him on much more was discovering in the patio library Shakespeare's plays and pictures of famous players — the start of a lifelong involvement with the theater.[13]

The camp had several kinds of libraries, and like Prising, my sister Mary June, my friend Nicholas Balfour, and I got more out of books than the teaching. Nick, at nine, was drawn to "nice secure safe stories" like the Raggedy Ann and Raggedy Andy books. I became a minor expert on Grimm's fairy tales, Hans Christian Andersen, and several other collections in the library. I also enjoyed the elderly rabbit of the *Uncle Wiggily* stories, amused that his car tires were made of German sausages and his steering wheel a carrot, though it worried me slightly that he took a bite every so often from the carrot: what would happen to his steering? By contrast, our memories of camp school are virtually blank. I remember better a camp storyteller, Rosie Rosenbaum. A small, puckish person, she stood at a camp path intersection and told complex stories to a small throng of kids who seemed to follow them more keenly than I did.[14]

Educationally my mother, Lorna Wilkinson, had more impact on me than any teacher or storyteller. In our year out of camp, when I was six, she taught me to read as well as simple arithmetic: she piled up an array of cans and had me add to them and subtract from them. She largely followed the Calvert home-schooling curriculum, which she may have obtained before the war. And when we came back into camp, she brought H. E. Marshall's classic children's history of Britain, *Our Island Story*. Its stories (some openly apocryphal) and arresting color plates intrigued me. My enthusiasm for Robin Hood enabled my mother to pull off a brilliant use of historical myth. When she made me a pair of shorts from some green cloth, I objected. "Green's a sissy color!" "Oh," my mother quietly observed, "Robin Hood and his men wore green." Result: *volte face*. I wore the shorts without further protest. My mother also taught me the counties and county capitals of England by drawing a map with the counties in different colors and their capitals in each. She linked it to Roman history by explaining that "Chester," and towns ending in "chester," came from *castrum*, Latin for a fort. The polymathic Paul Esmérian, living with the Balfour family, was even more of a teacher to Nicholas Balfour and his siblings; among other things, he taught Nick Latin.

My mother was no jingoist but her way of educating me affirmed a pride in being British, an important identity as Brits were the second-largest nationality group in a camp whose culture was predominantly American. We were big enough to be respected but also sniped at, as Nick Balfour and I discovered when the Boys' Club dorms became our part-time base in 1944.

I went to the Boys' Club because my mother thought I needed more male authority. For reasons never really explained, I started having tantrums, especially against Mary June when we were alone in the shanty; I once stabbed her in the thigh with a fork. Mary June did not break a taboo on telling tales but neighbors could hear and see. My mother was no pushover in handling me. The same woman who stroked my head when I was sleepless, and sought out the father of an older boy who was bullying me for money, took my belt to me on two occasions—for calling her a "bloody fool" and for lying that I had taken our garbage pail to the big garbage drums (my shanty job) when I hadn't. Her authority was such that when a church elder caught me after I had flicked sand into a church hut during a service, I implored him so earnestly not to tell my mother that he relented. Still, she felt her discipline needed reinforcement. Nick Balfour was becoming a handful too, in the crowded shanty where Paul Esmérian, Anne Balfour, and her three children slept at night. Anne told Nick he would be happier with other boys, including me. So we moved to the Boys' Club together.[15]

The Boys' Club accommodated about forty boys, from eight years old to mid-teens, in several rooms in the Education Building. It was largely, but not exclusively, for boys without fathers in the camp. We would gather there in the evenings, usually after an early supper, and leave before breakfast. We would sometimes play outside and also return for early-afternoon siestas. The club was run by Bertram Leake, a white-haired former business executive and Scout leader, who combined dignity, warmth, and strictness in equal measures: he was a stickler for precisely made beds and no fidgeting at siesta time. The teenagers included some rough customers and he was not afraid to confront them, using a switch if necessary (the kind used by *carromata* drivers). But it seldom came to that. Before the war, many of the teenagers seem to have attended the free-tuition Bordner High School, not just the private American school. Decades later I surprised Americans as a Brit who knew the American high school drinking song, adapted to Bordner: "Cheer, cheer for ole Bordner High, bring on the whisky, bring on the rye."

The Boys' Club did not work for everyone. Shy loners, who came in without friends, could feel left out. But it worked for Nick Balfour and me. Two other men helped Leake, and the one in charge of our room for younger boys was a reddish-haired Catholic monk in his mid-twenties, John Abrams (Brother Abrams to us). He would read stories to us before lights out, not always with due thought for our dreams; several of us remember vividly Poe's horror story, *The Pit and the Pendulum*. Abrams had an easy-going manner — usually. He had special oversight of the Catholic boys, seeing they went to mass regularly, and when Nick, one of his spiritual charges, laughed at the "Elevation of the Host," Abrams almost elevated *him* by the short hairs behind his ears.

Not as crowded as Main Building dorms, our room had shelves of books for boys and a table in the middle. From the bookcase, Nick escaped the camp by zooming around the Americas with *The Motor Boys*, while I plunged into the jungle as Bomba, a boy Tarzan. More important, though, was the table around which we sat talking and much more. We recited crazy rhymes: "Early in the morning in the middle of the night, two dead boys got up to fight...." We played rock-paper-scissors, checkers, and even chess. We swapped stories of the most fiendish Japanese tortures. And we drew avidly, mostly guns and planes.

The best artist, with a special line in spaceships, was "Mousey." For Nick and me, Mousey was the most memorable boy in the club, though we have never been able to discover his full name. Small but tough, with an enormous jaw, Mousey seemed to have no life outside the Education Building; I have wondered since if he was an orphan who lived in the Boys' Club fulltime. Full of streetwise precocity, it was Mousey who gave me the shocking news of what our parents did to get us born. He was also an adept finger dancer, using two fingers on each hand to imitate tap dancing on the table.

Mousey was one of our best fighters. Club rules, or maybe just our own code, banned hitting in the face or stomach; socking arms or chests was OK, but the preferred mode was wrestling, trying to get your opponent in a neck lock until he said "I give up." Physically timid, I tried to avoid this, and Nick was easily worsted by the smaller Mousey, as he was not strong for his age though tall.

The few of us in the room who were English were barracked for our accents. Our long *a*'s inspired mocking jingles: "the cow wiped its *arse* on a piece of *grarse*." Outside the Education Building, our persecutors drew a British flag in the dust and then trampled it. Nick and others did the same to an American flag; he does not remember how their bravery was punished. Elsewhere, too, much earlier in the camp's existence, six-year-old Angus Lorenzen was ridiculed as a "lousy Limey" for his English accent, which sounded snobbish and precious to some American adults as well as children; they also equated British reserve with stuffiness.[16]

I took heart from small British triumphs: the English bulldog in a story read by Brother Abrams, who beat a champion husky by gripping him and just hanging on, and the quiet Boys' Club Canadian teenager (he counted as British) who out-wrestled an American tough. Like Angus Lorenzen, I happily learned that "Limeys" got their name for smart and doughty reasons: eating limes as seamen to keep off scurvy (or, more apocryphally, throwing lime powder downwind to blind French sailors). Long before this, when sitting out on the plaza, Mary June and I made friends with a handsome, young Pan Am executive, Douglas Willard, who also coached a football team. I hero-worshipped Doug all the more because his lovely companion, Jill (we never discovered her full name), was not only English but also from our home county, Hampshire! My pleasure at finding common roots was not unique ("Oh, you're from Ohio. So am I!") but I had special reason to savor it.

At the age of five or six, perhaps during our year out of camp, I developed a stutter. So, less noticeably, did Mary June. The stress of internment perhaps triggered this, but two of our uncles back in Britain also stuttered. I vaguely remember getting laughed at for that too in the Boys' Club, but my English accent was the main target. I was also called a "bookworm" for reading so much but I counted that no insult. Stutter, Limey accent, bookworm — all produced curious results. Mousey was a leader in taunting us as Limeys, but he would also urge me to "tell us another story about kings and castles and knights." Eager to be wanted, I did not use my bookworm's store of tales as a bargaining chip: no taunting if you want the stories. Instead, I complied.

There were two remarkable things about all this. When I told the stories I stuttered little, if at all, pointing up a unique feature of stuttering. It is perhaps the only disability that can change from situation to situation, depending on the audience and the speaker's confidence toward it. For all the anti–British hazing, my special knowledge was in demand, the situation was comfortably informal, and so I was fluent. But that leads to something else. Why did Mousey and others who so derided Englishness want old-world stories, some of which were manifestly English? It was my first experience of an American desire for roots and lineage that sometimes imitated aristocracy. No Britons would have had the first name of our camp leader, Earl Carroll; we had plenty of real earls. Nor did we go in for the American upper-class John Smith II and III; our kings and queens took care of that. Even John Smith Sr. and Jr., repeating the same name father to son, were not to be found among the non–Americans of our camp. True to American form, the last line of the Bordner High song cheered "our royal sons."

Meanwhile, the Boys' Club was united in feeling superior to our Japanese masters. When their planes flew over, it was commonplace to say they sounded like "pots and pans," and indeed, when we saw and heard American planes again, in September 1944, they seemed to have a smoother hum. Our superiority did not deter us from lucrative work for the Japanese, however, one day a live pig escaped from the garrison and temporarily vanished. Recruited to find it, some of us (not me) supposedly tracked it down to a far wall. In return we were given brightly colored T-shirts and *panucha* cakes, large brown cookies of unrefined sugar — to the fury of Marian Ralston and other girls, who claimed they found the pig. Were we collaborating with the enemy? I doubt it crossed our minds.[17]

In her book, *Stolen Childhoods* (2011), on British children in Japanese camps, Nicola Tyrer hewed to its title by stressing loss and trauma. She included Santo Tomás in her negative picture on the basis of two interviewees, both girls in the camp, including Iris Krass. She cited no memoirs or diaries; the Boys' Club, of course, was not on her map. In the case of Santo Tomás, and some other camps too, she was wrong. The camp's children and teenagers did not lose their childhoods; they reinvented them in many ways, from creating games to reading. As already mentioned, they generally had a fuller social life than before the war and more contact with their parents, if parents were there. Those deprived of parents by illness and/or being boarded out at children's centers often suffered for that, but no more than many upper-class British children sent away to boarding school at age eight. Yes, they got hungry and longed for more food in the last year, and that slowed them down near the end (except for Mousey, it seemed). And some felt a general anxiety in the last year as conditions got worse. But, for reasons to be explored later, the children generally did not suffer as much from hunger and malnutrition as adults, or at least not the older ones. There were virtually no famine pot-bellies, though some teenagers' legs, feet, and faces began to swell with beriberi and a few fainted while waiting in a line.

Day to day, the power that most obviously confronted children was not the Japanese regime but their elders and their peers, like most children everywhere. The adults suffered much more from lost freedoms, worries about the future, and resentment at being forcibly occupied by an alien people. It was among the adults that tensions and power struggles built up between the mass of internees, their leaders, and the Japanese authorities.

7

Power: The Japanese

One of the worst Japanese prison camps was Tjideng Camp for women and children in a poor quarter of Batavia, Dutch East Indies, now Indonesia. Hugely overcrowded, with sanitation so bad that internees had to wade through sewage, it was run by a sadistic commandant, Lieutenant Kenichi Sonei; he was later executed by a Dutch firing squad. Sonei's punishments for supposed transgressions ran from head shaving to public beating to death; for fun, he made boys kill a dog. When the food ration fell to one small bowl of rice a day, and beriberi was rampant, three women plucked up courage to ask if they could have more food and water, and access to Red Cross medicines, to reduce deaths. Sonei's response was to have them beaten and kicked until they were huddled, gashed and bleeding on the ground, and then make them hobble around the camp in the burning sun for three days.[1]

No such event happened at Santo Tomás. Although internees were sometimes tortured and even killed for specific offences, real or imagined, the camp's leaders were always able to complain to the regime. In the camp's last year, no less than nine internee executives and representatives gathered in the commandant's office to argue about work demands. The lack of total oppression made the camp, in a way, more interesting: it had its own politics, marked by friction as well as cooperation between different layers of power. The Japanese army wielded ultimate power; camp commandants did not get the free hand that Sonei enjoyed in Tjideng. But even the army had no one power base or point of view.

At Santo Tomás, there were basically four layers of power. On top there was the Japanese Army outside the camp, which officially included the Kempeitai (secret police). Below it was the camp commandant, his lieutenants, and his office, including civilian officials. Third down was the internee administration: the Executive Committee (later called the Internee Committee) and the managers of departments answering to it. And then there was the great mass of internees, including rule-breakers and critics of the Executive Committee. Room and floor monitors overlapped layers three and four by electing representatives to advise the camp's government.

Because Japanese military doctrine did not approve of surrender by its own soldiers, or even by the enemy's, it did not "think prisoners." So when it invaded countries, it had no clear plan for accommodating prisoners, whether military or civilian. Internment camps, and their governance and provision, had to be hastily invented.

For most of the camp's first two years, its commandant was responsible to a General Affairs Office, later called the State Affairs Office, quasi-civilian but still under the Japanese army.[2] The army took more direct control in January 1944. The earlier arrangement, when the camp largely ran itself and supplemented the army's subsidies with money, food and equipment brought in privately by internees, saved money and manpower for the Japanese army. But the Japanese authorities were sloppy at best and criminal at worst in keeping their side of the bargain. The General Affairs Office or army paymasters above it often delayed the army's monthly payments by a week or more so that the internee administration had to borrow money outside the camp or buy on credit to keep the camp adequately fed. In November 1943, Red Cross aid for internees, including vital medicine, piled up at a Manila dock for over a month; at other times the army seems to have swiped some of the aid. Military needs came first, and as food and almost everything got scarcer in Manila, the temptation to take from the internees grew. At the same time, the Japanese government sometimes rebuffed Red Cross proposals for ensuring greater and more regular aid, perhaps because it did not want to admit the neediness of its prisoners.

And then there was the Kempeitai, which, like other secret police forces, was more or less a power unto itself. Tressa Roka saw a sign of this when she observed a young Kempeitai officer arrogantly bossing around the commandant, though he was a lieutenant colonel in the reserves. Especially in the last year, the camp was prey to sudden inspections and raids by Kempeitai policemen, who took away internees suspected of illicit contact with the outside, such as communicating with the underground, receiving war news, or getting food over the wall. The suspects were taken to Fort Santiago, the gaunt old Spanish fort turned Kempeitai headquarters and prison. They would go into one of the dungeons, a dank room often just ten square feet in size, containing fourteen or so prisoners and a five-gallon gasoline can for toilet — which soon overflowed. From here the suspect would be taken for interrogation and torture. Survivors who returned to Santo Tomás came back as silent specters; their interrogators had told them that if they talked about their experience, their families, if they had any in camp or outside, would be killed.

An early survivor of this treatment was Frederic Stevens, chairman of the prewar American Coordinating Committee that had prepared for Japanese invasion; his son was in a military POW camp, O'Donnell. Stevens was arrested for collecting money for military POWs as well as Santo Tomás internees (all of which he admitted) and for the guerrillas (which he denied). As a Freemason, he was also astounded to learn that he was part of a Masonic-Jewish conspiracy, including Roosevelt and MacArthur, that had fomented war with Japan so it could rule the world. His interrogators at different times sliced and twisted off pieces of skin and made him eat them, knocked out a tooth, suspended him with a rope while they beat him, lied to him that his family was also in Fort Santiago, and told him he would probably be executed. On Good Friday, April 1943, after six months of imprisonment, he was released back to Santo Tomás, half-starved and barefoot.

Two motives emerged in Japan's policy toward civilian internees. The first was the wish to protect them enough to deter Allied retaliation against Japanese prisoners and look civilized. In May 1942, when conditions in Santo Tomás were still quite good, internee leader Earl Carroll, a British woman, and a twelve-year-old American boy were persuaded to give a broadcast indicating that all was basically well, though with worries about the future. A Japanese officer rounded off the broadcast with charges of Allied and Filipino ill treatment of Japanese civilians just before the Japanese army invaded (true in Davao by Filipinos but not in Manila). Throughout internment, an official ban on internee diaries reflected the wish to conceal anything that might look bad.[3]

The second motive, preventing internee subversion, grew stronger as the tide of war turned against Japan and Philippine guerrilla groups became more active. It is often said that the Japanese army's treatment of internees became harsher in revenge for war reverses. Five internees, taken out of camp in the last year and badly beaten up, had brought in transcripts of war news, causing loss of face to the Japanese. But it was not just a matter of pride and revenge. Santo Tomás, with its large population of business leaders and skilled professionals, well connected to the Filipino population, had always posed a "Trojan horse" threat to Japanese power. The amount of self-government allowed to the camp made its internee managers look all the more potent. Western technical prowess did the same. When Francis Cassera, a drug company executive, did experiments in the camp to make a better rat poison, he was hauled off to Fort Santiago for preparing bacteriological warfare. After some days of abuse, he luckily met an interpreter he had known at Columbia, who had the clout to get him released.

The Japanese fears were not all fantasy. Two camp leaders, Carroll Grinnell and Alfred Duggleby, and another internee, Ernest Johnson, had been in contact with the guerrillas, helping them smuggle food and medicine to the Cabanatuan POW camp, and occasionally feeding information to the U.S. military. The Japanese discovery and arrest of Filipino accomplices in late December 1944 led to the three being seized by the Kempeitai, along with another internee, Clifford Larsen, who had done nothing — a case of mistaken identity. Their bodies, beheaded, were found after the camp was liberated.[4]

Long before this, the army had tried to seal off the camp and keep closer tabs on its inmates. The general recall of people living outside "on pass" in May 1943 heralded a bigger change the following January, when the army put civilian camps, along with military POW ones, under its own War-Prisoners Headquarters. Japanese guards now accompanied camp food buyers as they went out into the city. In February, the army ended outside buying altogether, replacing the army's cash payments with direct food supply, plus small payments used for items such as soap. The camp's own funds could still obtain some extra food via Japanese buyers, but the army shut down the package line at the main gate: security now came before the economic advantages of letting internees bring in their own food and other stuff. By then, however, Manila prices were rocketing. Japanese officials outside and inside the camp claimed that the package line was taking too much from hungry Filipinos. Some internees, too, recognized that ending the line removed a burden from friends and servants outside.

The army takeover was followed by a series of controls and crackdowns, all or most of them enjoined by the commandant's military superiors and usually done by soldiers from outside. Squads with fixed bayonets would suddenly descend on a shanty area, seal it off, and search for American magazines, diaries, flashlights, and other "subversive" items. The Fathers' Garden, a place of repose beside the university seminary, was placed out of bounds. Sudden orders required a line of shanties near the wall to be moved back, and then further back. Fay and Althea Bailey had to cut three feet off their shanty and destroy banana trees; several internees helped others drag their shanties away. All privately owned electrical appliances had to be turned in, and the regime shut down the camp's soap-making plant, electrical repair shop, and a small laboratory on the Main Building top floor that was testing rats for bubonic plague.

A morning roll call was added to the evening one, most of them now conducted by

Japanese guards rather than internee room monitors. Filipino doctors and nurses, who had come in to help at the camp hospital and clinic, were turned away, and a series of internee surveys were ordered, starting with men who had particular trades and extended in June to all males between fifteen and fifty. A Japanese cameraman also took photos of all internees in groups of eight. The purpose of these surveys, like some of the other controls, was never clear. Different military interests may have weighed in, ranging from the possible use of internee skills by the Japanese army (seldom done at Santo Tomás) to fear of a camp insurrection aided by guerrillas. A later request from the commandant's office, a week before liberation, for the numbers of males between 18 and 50 became part of claims that the army planned to massacre them, but that was never verified.

In one area, religion, army policy toward Westerners was more lenient but also more manipulative. Army leaders knew how deeply religious belief ran. Japanese nationalists themselves stressed the importance of spirit and "will" against Western materialism and technology. Christian churches continued to operate in wartime Japan, though the government tried to enlist their support. Clergy initially interned in Santo Tomás were told to go home, though some succeeded in staying. Services, including funerals, were always allowed at Santo Tomás.

Realizing that the great majority of Filipinos (79 percent) were Catholic, the army was more tolerant toward the city's Catholic clergy than toward Protestants, though the Catholic archbishop of Manila, Michael O'Doherty, was himself a white Westerner, Irish born. Even so, the army tried to use the churches to promote anti–American loyalty to Japan. Its propaganda corps included a religious section headed by an aggressive lieutenant colonel who had been called out of retirement, T. Nazurawa. When Archbishop O'Doherty drew a firm line between secular obedience and religious independence ("render unto Caesar...") he was confined to his home, but the line more or less prevailed for his clergy.

Not so Manila's Protestants. In a series of browbeating sessions, Col. Nazurawa, aided by a Japanese Protestant minister (his "soft cop"), got most of the clergy to sign a "pledge" of cooperation with Japan's Greater East Asia Co-Prosperity Sphere for its alleged aim of "world peace." They promised not to hold services primarily for people of "hostile nations" and make their buildings available for something vaguely called "military strategy" if duly requested. They reluctantly signed the pledge under ominous threats of personal punishment plus destruction of their churches. The threats turned out to be empty. Four clergy who refused to sign were simply interned in Santo Tomás: they included Dr. Don Holter, who became an active democrat in camp politics and later a Methodist bishop in the United States of America.

The pledge signers were allowed to stay out, giving them a bad odor among Santo Tomás internees, but some clergy volunteered to come in. And in 1944 there were roundups of clergy, nuns, and missionaries, most of whom went to Los Baños via Santo Tomás. In all this, the Japanese army and its propaganda arm, rather than camp commandants, called the shots.[5]

Santo Tomás had seven commandants during its three years, or eight, if you count both Aikida Kodaki and S. Kuroda, who ran the camp as a duo between September 1942 and October 1943. Kodaki was in charge of all Philippine civilian camps but closely managed Santo Tomás, visiting it several times a week. Until the army took direct control in early

1944, most of the commandants were civilians, mainly with consular backgrounds and sometimes togged up in military uniforms. They were succeeded by army officers, though the first of these, Gonshichi Onozoki, was a lawyer in the military reserves (the man Tressa Roka saw getting a hard time from a Kempeitai officer).

Commandant personalities differed, of course, and so did their attitudes toward internees. The first two commandants got on quite well with the camp and its leaders. On leaving in the second month to become chief of Manila's regular police force, Hitoshi Tomayasu wrote an emotional farewell in the camp paper — translated, as he had little English. When he had first met Westerners in Kobe and Shanghai, he said, he had found them "proud and lacking in understanding of the Japanese." In the camp, however, "your cooperation and understanding have brought me a feeling of friendship which I had not thought possible." He appreciated the recognition that "I have always had to work under orders from above." Such cooperation, he believed, would have prevented disputes between nations had it been practiced internationally. His comments about "understanding" applied more to camp leaders than most internees, who resented the sexual restrictions and remembered the first executions, but he seemed to mean what he said. Following the Japanese practice of allocating differently colored armbands for different functions, he gave Executive Committee members new armbands in blue, with his own calligraphy on each as a farewell gesture.[6]

Tomayasu's successor, an English-speaking ex-diplomat, Ryozo Tsurumi, lobbied his superiors energetically to get as much as possible from the Japanese army when it agreed to make regular cash allowances to the camp. He also supported internee leaders in resisting proposals to transfer the camp to inadequate sites outside Manila. In long talks with the British consul general, Stanley Wyatt-Smith, whose family he helped evacuate in a diplomatic exchange, he convinced Wyatt-Smith that he was no warhawk: he disliked the army's brutality. Later, though, he allegedly told an internee, the *Time-Life* photographer Carl Mydans, that he favored a carve-up of the world between Germany, the United States of America, and Japan.[7]

By contrast with the urbane Tsurumi, Lt. Colonel Yasunksa Yoshie, the first regular military officer to become commandant, in 1944, was a clown, sometimes benign and sometimes not. Barely five feet tall, he combined angry obsessiveness with a wish to show off when he had a captive audience. In a public meeting he wildly gesticulated, pranced about, and play-acted to the children. He organized baseball matches between internees and his staff, with himself as pitcher and team captain, pitching badly yet raging at his own team; the internees easily won but tactfully kept the score down and received bananas as a prize. Demanding more athletics while also urging internees to grow more vegetables, he suspended all games when told the internees could not do both. In front of internees, he twice slapped a subordinate, Lieutenant Komatsu, for exceeding orders — once, indeed, for brutally beating up two internees caught smuggling. But Elizabeth Vaughan thought him two-faced, publicly declaring internees could "expect better things" if they kept the rules, yet capriciously turning away an external gift of eggs for the children, having allowed a previous one.[8]

One of the most interesting commandants was Kitaro Kato, the last of the civilians, reigning from November 1943 to February 1944. His looks impressed the fastidious Paul Esmérian: "refined head, an arched nose, long face, clad in a wellcut uniform." He conveyed "understanding"; while commandant, he was learning Spanish. Interned briefly as a diplomat in London, he told internee leaders that he had been treated well there, even getting two eggs for breakfast. After the November typhoon and flood, which worried internees with families living outside, he set up a five-day visiting period when the families could visit their internee husbands and fathers in an area near the front gate. Kato also let members of the internee committee for outside family relief visit affected homes. On another occasion he gave leave for thirteen-year-old Martin Meadows and his father (but not his mother) to have his *bar mitzvah* with non-interned friends at a synagogue outside.

No commandant, though, could be a perfect champion of internees. Internee historian A.V.H. said Kato prowled about the camp more officiously than his predecessors, and he rejected a plea to let the most deprived Filipino families of internees join their husbands and fathers inside. He may have lacked the power; he was certainly unable to stop the closure of the package line and the restriction that followed. When the package line ended, the most Kato could do on the final day was to let friends and relatives bringing packages enter the camp and meet internees. He shared the helpless dismay of internee leaders when the army removed some of the food given by relief organizations and other donors, to be shared out — so the army said — among all Philippine POWs. His relationship with top internee leaders was such that when he left the camp for a post in the Japanese Manila Embassy, Executive Committee Chairman Carroll Grinnell sent him a camp souvenir — a small coconut-oil lamp made out of a Red Cross coffee can. In thanking him for the gift, Kato praised the resourceful American "workmanship" it represented in contrast with the United States' reputation for waste.[9]

Some Japanese, including Kato, disliked the camp's inequality of private wealth and were scoffed at by internees as "socialistic." In the camp's third month, Commandant Tsurumi wanted the internee administration to take over the camp's restaurant and little stores (*tiendas*), eliminating private profit. The administration resisted, preferring instead to tax them: "campitalism" versus "nationalization." Two years later, in March 1944, Kato's successor, Gonshichi Onozoki, temporarily banned private cooking in shanties. Hyper-anxious about fires, he said the army wanted more communal cooking. Shanty dwellers could take their cooking pots to four crowded and very smoky areas. It is hard to know how much the cooking ban really came from the army rather than the commandant, but there was some Japanese concern about shanties (and, indeed, economic inequality) as a threat to communal order.[10]

As a matter of practical power, though, commandants of different stripes tried to head off interference by the army and Kempeitai. To do this successfully, they had to show they ran a tight ship while getting internee cooperation. Escape stories bear this out. After the initial, traumatic execution of three escapers, no one was killed for escaping, though at least sixteen internees went over the wall. Most were men going back and forth in a night to see their Filipino families outside. An unknown number were not detected; others pulled it off by bribing a guard. One temporary escaper, the father of a desperately ill child outside, was detected and the news got through to the army. Commandant Kato jailed him "for the duration" in the internee-run jail; otherwise, Kato said, he would have been treated worse by the military police. He did, though, let the father visit his family for the child's funeral.

Forestalling Kempeitai punishment was not just Kato's policy. Detected escapers were placed in the camp jail or, if drunk or disturbed, classified as mentally ill and put in the hospital, inside or outside the camp. Only two, it seems, ended up in the hands of the military police. Herbert Ward, one of those who tried to visit his family outside, went to Fort Santiago and then Muntinlupa, a prison for special offenders just outside Manila. The other, Mary Ruan Follsom, reportedly joined a guerrilla group but then gave herself up and spent time in Muntinlupa or a mental hospital or both. We don't know how much abuse either suffered. The only escaper to get away permanently was Joseph Eisenberg, who vanished in the night from the gym, the big male dorm by the front wall, two weeks before the camp was liberated. He made it all the way to the 11th Airborne Division, part of the U.S. Army forces on Luzon. The commandant, Lt. Col. Juichiro Hayashi, ordered the gym balconies to be cleared of men and all those under fifty to be transferred out of the gym (most were older). Hayashi sentenced the two gym monitors to seven days in jail; he then pardoned them but warned that anyone caught escaping was liable to be shot. Camp leaders wrote to Hayashi pointing out that neither the monitors nor anyone else were responsible but promising to "exercise care" in preventing escapes. The internee administration had already warned internees not to try to escape, on the usual grounds that a major transgression might bring down collective punishment. Most internees agreed.[11]

Commandants took a harsher line toward Filipino offenders, or let the guards do so. In the first month, a Filipino ice-cream vendor started up in the camp. As Tressa Roka recounted, internees "flocked to him like eager kids" until his third day, when he was taken to the commandant's office and his earnings seized. "When he left the camp, one side of his face was a bloody mess." It is not clear why he fell foul of the commandant, Hitoshi Tomayasu, or his cruel subordinate, Lieutenant Takahashi, who had been so atrocious to the first three escapers. Other Filipino vendors at the time were permitted.

Internee night patrols that caught Filipino burglars who came over the walls often let them go, sometimes "roughing them up" a little first, having found they got a worse flogging if handed over to the guards. In March of the last year, fourteen-year-old Georgia Barnes saw guards beat senseless two Filipino youths. They then gave one of them the Japanese water torture, hosing water into his mouth and jumping on his inflated stomach. The guard logbook reports shooting an "illegally conspiring" Filipino (no detail given) outside the wall after a "fierce fight," though it also says that five Filipino boys were let off with a scolding when they were caught in a grassy paddock for horses.[12]

Lieutenant Takahashi seems to have left the camp soon after the first escapers were executed, but he was not the only bad news for internees. Several other lieutenants under the commandants were extremely unpleasant to those internees they had to deal with. Even basically benign commandants seemed unable to control their offensiveness, though Commandant Yoshie had a go when he slapped Lieutenant Komatsu.

The worst lieutenant was Sadaaki Konishi, supply officer until he left Santo Tomás for the camp's offshoot, Los Baños, in April 1944. Sloppily dressed, in a sweat-stained blouse, he sometimes put his bare feet on the desk when talking with internee officials. His hatred of Westerners was palpable: according to different accounts, he said he would "make the Americans eat dirt" and "before I'm done with you, you'll be eating grass." He enjoyed turning off and on the amount of food he would let the camp buy on its own account: on one day in March he temporarily banned all purchase of eggs, bread, and milk. He was not loved by his own colleagues but seemed to have some clout with hard-liners in the army's prison camps administration. Riled by Konishi's high-handedness, Commandant Kato told the head office that they should give him power to curb Konishi or get a new commandant.

They got a new commandant. Kato went off to a foreign service post in Manila and his successor, the military lawyer Gonshichi Onozoki, had no more success against Konishi.[13]

When Konishi moved to the rural isolation of Los Baños, his hatred found more scope. As the camp's number two, he operated under Major Iwanaha, who seemed virtually senile. On top of ruthless food cuts, he enjoyed playing sadistic tricks. He once told a group of half-starved men they could take all they wanted from several 100-pound sacks of rice if they carried them from the Japanese *bodega* (storeroom) to the camp kitchen. When they had done it, he said he had changed his mind and told them to carry the load back. They got no rice.

On 23 February 1945, a combined force of U.S. reconnaissance troops, local guerrillas, and paratroops dramatically liberated Los Baños, still behind Japanese lines, speeding the internees to safety across a nearby lake in amphibious "amtracs." Many of the garrison were killed, but Konishi was among those who got away. He returned later to massacre in reprisal the inhabitants of the nearest *barrio*, tying them to their nipa huts and then torching the huts. He was hanged in 1946, as was the colonel who had ordered the killings.

Less murderous than Konishi but more hated in Santo Tomás was the camp's guard commander, Lieutenant Nanakazu Abiko — more hated, as he had more contact with internees. Unlike Konishi, Abiko was smartly uniformed and impressive looking. Strongly built, he was said (wrongly) to have been an Olympic swimmer in 1936. By November 1944, and possibly well before, his empire within the camp had expanded to include "farm work" by the guards in the garrison's own vegetable patch, as well as a staff library and documents. Intelligence about internees was his business: part of his job description was preventing internee "manipulations" (illegal activities).[14]

Being responsible for security, he was often the one to issue new orders, which he did rudely and inconsiderately, sometimes changing an order suddenly. When meeting camp leaders he would interrupt and make brusque demands; he had a short fuse. But his main impact on most internees was at the morning and evening roll calls, when internees had to line up outside their rooms, or in designated shanty areas, to be counted by a Japanese officer or NCO and bow to him as he came by. Roll calls came under Abiko, and he was obsessed with bowing and the respect it symbolized. Escorted by soldiers and an interpreter (he had little English), he conducted roll calls personally in different parts of the camp. Robin Prising described what would happen:

> Once the roll was taken, he drilled us in obeisance. These drills represented a course in calisthenics since the proper bow was made from the hips — not the waist — the spine kept rigid and the head dropped close to the ground. After a roomful of prisoners performed the bow in unison, he would snigger and grunt with glee. Then, while we stood waiting in humble silence, his mood would shift; Abiko would start to shout, and the entire room would repeat the bow again and again.[15]

Internees who objected or didn't cooperate got slapped. So did an old man who was sick and excused roll call when Abiko found him sitting in a chair and not in bed.

On Sunday, 28 May 1944, later remembered as Roll Call Day, a combination of miscounting and missing slats in a fence around the adjoining internee hospital led the commandant to think that someone had escaped. At noon, internees had to line up again and stay there for over two hours, and again for an hour before supper, while they were counted and recounted until the mistake was found.

Later in the year, Abiko responded with alacrity when the army called for more punctilious bowing from the waist. Lining up room and building monitors in two ranks, he told them, via his interpreter, that correct bowing expressed due thanks to the Japanese Imperial Army for protecting them. He followed this with half an hour of drill in bowing and a demand that monitors and mayors give the same to their charges.

Abiko's obsession with bowing went beyond roll calls. As Robin Prising had found, he dealt violently with anyone who tried to avoid bowing to him: a common trick was to drop something and pretend not to see him. Prowling around with a small posse of guards, he exuded hostility and threat. Sascha Weinzheimer, the mother of Jean, aged eleven or twelve at the time, pushed her daughter into a hedge to keep out of his way when he was approaching. Another time Abiko came by when Sascha and Jean were waiting in line for some medicine at the small dispensing infirmary just inside the Main Building. An elderly woman, sitting in line just ahead of them, deliberately did not get up and bow. Exploding with rage, Abiko started hitting her with the hilt of his sword. Sascha told Jean not to look and hurried her away.

In Abiko's eyes, his victim had personally insulted him, and she had violated the Japanese code of bowing — which she had. But so had he. Just as Japanese militarism had hardened and distorted the ancient warrior norms of *bushido*, submerging its chivalrous aspects, so Abiko's treatment of bowing made it a matter not of mutual respect, as it was meant to be, but of humiliation. The result was that Abiko got no moral respect but instead fear and loathing; some internees called him "Shitface."

Abiko's reputation, though, made him a camp institution. As a birthday present for Jean, Sascha Weinzheimer made her a big handkerchief from a red blouse she had originally kept for when "the boys" — GIs — arrived. She embroidered into it various place names, words, and phrases of the camp, including "Abiko"! Yet there were signs that Abiko was going to pieces. He was increasingly drunk, or semi-drunk, and meaner in manner when he was. He was not alone; some guards, like internees when they could get it, turned to the bottle. But for Abiko, a vigorous professional soldier, becoming a prisoner officer was a comedown: he reportedly told an internee committee member that he had served in the Guadalcanal campaign in the Solomons southeast of the Philippines. His obsession with bowing showed how a personal, neurotic need for respect could build on and exaggerate a general custom. And prisons, like military boot camps, often give scope for vengeful bullies to take their feelings out on their charges.

Not everyone found him offensive. As one internee put it, if you bowed to him, he would bow back, and that was that. But Abiko, and Konishi too, were just the type and generation of Japanese to feel the full force of prewar anti–Westernism. Internee-to-be Grace Nash, returning with her husband from the United States to Manila via Tokyo in 1937, was struck by Japanese hostility: a former servant who looked past them, store clerks who tried not to serve them, restaurants that turned them away. Abiko and Konishi may well have grown up as young men in this atmosphere before induction into the army, whose brutalizing methods ranged from face slapping to using Chinese prisoners for bayonet practice.

An episode related by Robin Prising's mother, Marie, supports this picture of hostility. Encountering Abiko outside the commandant's office, Marie, who was wearing a sun hat, bowed deeply. Abiko saluted in return, but then, mystifyingly, burst into an angry, scolding torrent and pointed at her head. A Japanese interpreter stepped forward: "In your country, the gentlemen lift their hats to ladies. You will now overcome your colonialist arrogance by lifting your hat to Nipponese men. You will please to remember that you belong to a third-class people."[16]

Whatever the interpreter's own feelings in this case, English-speaking Japanese in Santo Tomás tended to be friendlier to internees, whether because reading and speaking English took them beyond the army's narrow nationalism or because those who *wanted* to learn English were predisposed to understand the West. One such person was Shizua Ohashi, a civilian in the commandant's office (though he sometimes wore a dark olive-green uniform). Slim and dignified, he had come to the Philippines in 1938 as the Manila representative of a Japanese business firm. His English was quite good; he spoke a little Tagalog, too, and according to one internee, he had a Filipino wife. Gerald Rimmer, British vice-chairman of the internee "releases" committee, dealt with him a lot, as Ohashi's jobs included passes to live outside and arrangements with Manila hospitals. Rimmer said later that Ohashi "did his best to protect and help the internees as much as he could, frequently, to my own knowledge, coming between them and the military police." In the row between Commandant Yoshie and internee leaders over vegetable work and athletics, he played a part in stalling the situation until Yoshie calmed down and let athletics continue.[17]

Ohashi was not sweetness and light to everyone, though. At the start of the "pregnant papas" saga, it was he who declared that the army did not allow "the making of babies" by internees. A year later, in December 1943, he refused Paul Esmérian's request to let the French-British Anne Balfour join him in the camp. Having stressed her Frenchness to keep out, she was finding it harder now to make ends meet, and she and her family acutely missed Paul. Six months later, though, he arranged for her to come in but only at the last moment when she was desperate; her house was commandeered for a Japanese couple and their baggage had already arrived.

To Robin Prising, though, Ohashi was a friend in need. Slowly recovering from a terrible fever (maybe dengue) in the camp hospital, he longed to join his parents, also ill, who were out of camp at another hospital, Remedios. Ohashi managed to get him transferred with some delay and difficulty, as it was not truly his decision to make and Remedios might be about to close. Two months later, the army did close Remedios, moving its enemy-alien inmates, mostly elderly, into Santo Tomás. This time Ohashi could not help. Robin was particularly worried for a Mrs. Allen, paralyzed and deaf, who had taught him sign language. When Ohashi visited just after the order to close, Robin asked whether he could cancel the order. Ohashi turned away, his face in sudden misery. He could do nothing more, he said. "I do not give orders. I obey them."[18]

Ohashi was a survivor, serving under almost every commandant from mid-1942 to the end. When liberation came, he kept alive by quickly surrendering. To operate so effectively under different commandants and the army's power, he masked humane sympathy beneath a reserved manner. He kept his wits about him, judging when to push back at power and when not. In this, his situation was quite like that of the camp's internee leaders.

8

Power: The Internees

The heads of the camp's internee administration were all men. The Japanese preferred it that way; Japan's women were excluded from politics. But internee women did not protest. Male leadership reflected expat Manila before the war, where most women who were not nurses or secretaries focused on domestic matters and charity work, leaving "business" to men.

The camp leaders were almost entirely senior executives from Manila's business community, though most were in their early forties or younger. Relative youth became an advantage when malnutrition took its toll. Until 1944 they were chosen by a mixture of elections and appointments by the commandant. The Japanese were often skittish about elections: they wanted to control who they got as top administrators and feared elections; might stir up the animals. In fact, *not* having elections was more likely to cause trouble, until growing hunger made people weaker. Six months into internment, Earl Carroll, the camp's first, Japanese-appointed leader, praised Commandant Tsurumi's knowledge of American" psychology" and persuaded him that electing a new Executive Committee would "make for better cooperation and order."[1] Five Americans and two British (that ratio prearranged) were duly elected, and Tsurumi chose Carroll Grinnell as chairman. Grinnell had only come in fourth in the votes for Americans, but he had worked in Japan and could speak some Japanese.

Early the following year, the commandant duo, Kodaki and Kuroda, cancelled the result of new elections in the wake of the row about shanty sex and "pregnant papas." When several committee members left for the new camp at Los Baños, and were replaced by appointees, protests erupted. The Rev. Don Holter, who had refused to sign the Protestant clergy loyalty oath and now headed an internee relations committee, said it would stop work until the problem was addressed. When the Executive Committee's vice-chairman resigned (to be evacuated under a diplomatic exchange), an election was allowed in early October 1943 to fill the vacancy. Holter won by a landslide. A scheme was started to elect members when the appointed ones had served for nine months, but that came to an abrupt end after the army took over direct control of the camp in January 1944.

In February, the Executive Committee was replaced by a new Internee Administration Committee of just three appointed members (one British), headed again by Carroll Grinnell. It met the army's demand for tighter control, but the commandant, lawyer-soldier Onozoki, did permit an elected three-man body, the Agents, to give direct voice to internees. (The British member, former consul general Thomas Harrington, was the husband of the "aristocratic" room monitor who had been so good to Robin Prising.) Officially the commandant only recognized the Agents as advisors to the Internee Committee, but that did not stop them from making their own complaints about Japanese policies in liaison with the committee.²

The men at the top of this shifting setup included five important characters. Earl Carroll, diplomatic and resourceful, was the young ex–YMCA insurance executive appointed as camp leader on the first day. He did not run for Executive Committee office in the first elections of July 1942, but served under the committee as chairman of the crucial Finance and Supplies Committee handling all supplies from food to medicine. In the next elections he did run for the Executive Committee, collecting the most votes, only to see the results nullified. When an appointed troika replaced the Executive Committee in the last year, he became one of the chosen three.

The most controversial of the five was Carroll Grinnell. He headed the committees from July 1942 to December 1944, when the Kempeitai arrested and executed him for his contacts with the guerrillas and military POW camps. As top man he took the most flak: even Emily Van Sickle, a vehement critic of Grinnell, admitted that he was a scapegoat for all kinds of internee discontent.

Soft-spoken, with spectacles and a moustache, Grinnell was an electrical engineer by training. He had become General Electric's Far Eastern manager, working in the Philippines as well as Japan. He used his own money and business contacts to give and lend money to the camp and to needy individuals; he bought gifts for the non-interned, Filipino children of internees and fruit for oldtimers in the camp. Many internees found him helpful and sensitive, but to others he could be impatient when they asked him about something. He tried to do too much, and the toll showed, especially when he was operating on too little food.

Alfred ("Dug") Duggleby, who was also killed later by the Kempeitai, had been vice-president and consulting engineer for two big gold-mining firms. Vice-chairman of the first Executive Committee, he did not run for office when it became elective. He didn't think much of the average person's ability to elect good people but in the camp's early days he was democrat enough to sleep on a wooden desk until everyone had beds. As head of a "releases committee," dealing with passes to be outside the camp, he smuggled notes between family members when a spouse or parent was in an outside hospital; with the Japanese official, Shizua Ohashi, he helped Robin Prising be reunited with his parents. He also helped the Filipino families of internees.

The internees' finance chief, in charge of the budget, was Alexander ("Cal") Calhoun until he left in May 1943 to become internee leader at Los Baños. He had worked his way up the banking business to become head of the National City Bank in Manila and a leader in the expat community. Strongly anti-racist, he had helped end the Polo Club's ban on Filipino members. In the camp he was attentive to bank employees and was known and respected enough to get the top vote in the first Executive Committee elections. He was no glad-hander: he had a courtly, aloof manner, yet could blow up in meetings. Although he was conscious that he had never been to college, that did not matter when it came to making an argument. In early 1943 the Japanese thought of transferring the whole camp to rural Los Baños, claiming it would provide more space and a healthier climate; it would also distance the camp from subversive Manila contacts. Santo Tomás leaders and doctors protested that the Los Baños site, an agricultural college, was *less* spacious, prone to malaria, and short of water. Their pitch got nowhere until Calhoun wrote an eloquent and personal letter to Akida Kodaki, the Japanese civilian camps chief. The plan was dropped.

The fifth man in the group was Sam Lloyd, the British member of the Internee Committee triumvirate. He was not, at first, the most prominent Briton in the internee power structure, but he made himself generally useful and worked his way up, as he had in the Asian oil industry before the war. A Cambridge graduate (but not from an expensive "public school"), he was interned with his wife, the only one of the five to have a close relative in the camp (their two boys were in Australia). Appointed to the Executive Committee in early 1943, he resigned his place later to make it elective, but was then appointed to the new Internee Committee. Analytical, reserved, and sometimes annoyingly cryptic, he shouldered his share of grumbling at "the Committee," but he was a good sport; he once sang in a Dave Harvey skit. He helped reduce American suspicions of the British, who had got off to a bad start in the camp's early days when a group of them tried to monopolize the Annex kitchen and had to be forced out.[3]

Another Englishman — the camp's mystery man — liaised between the internee administration and the commandant's office. Ernest Stanley, interned at 40, was one of two chief internee interpreters. He stayed closer to the Japanese than his colleague, Frank Cary — so close, indeed, that he was despised by many internees as a quisling. He actually slept in the Japanese quarters during part of his internment. Stanley had learned Japanese as a missionary in Japan. He belonged to an ascetic Christian sect, the Two-and-Twos, so named because they originally proselytized in pairs. Officially attached to the releases department handling outside passes, he struck some internees as unfriendly and unhelpful. At crucial moments, though, he was a friend in need. He prevented a bad scene when, unusually, a group of drunken Japanese came calling on a women's dorm. The women sent an SOS to Stanley, who quickly appeared and jollied the guards away. Behind the scenes, he seems to have given secret information about Japanese plans to camp leaders, and at the end, along with Frank Cary, he helped negotiate an end to the standoff between the U.S. Army and the Japanese garrison, holed up with hostages in the Education Building. A.V.H. and others have claimed he was an Allied secret agent, relaying information to the guerrillas and MacArthur. Whether or not this was true, and we may never know, I believe that Stanley got "in" with the Japanese to be of use to the camp. He accepted, even courted, rejection by his fellows to serve them better.[4]

The business executives who ran the camp from day to day took to bureaucratic government like ducks to water. Capitalists they might be, but big business had passed from the era of titanic individualists to organization men. By the camp's second month, the Executive Committee was presiding over numerous departments, each usually headed by its own committee and chairman. They included departments for clinics and hospitals, sanitation, building and construction, fire prevention, education, religion, "discipline" (later called the Department of Patrols), work assignments, "suggestions and complaints," and a public relations department initially headed by a well-known Associated Press journalist, Russell Brines. A department was added later for regulating shanties. In 1944, the Japanese authorities, seeking clearer oversight, reduced the departments to four—finance and supply, internal affairs, labor, and health—each under the Internee Committee. But that just meant more sub-committees within the four big groupings.

Again, men headed all the departments, except for one woman who co-chaired a recreation committee. Women's committee membership was largely confined to education, recreation, aid to non-interned families, and councils of room monitors. A woman did head the "women's section" of the Work Assignment Department. Another served on the camp court, the Committee on Public Order, but only when women came before it. Internee women seldom ran for high office, though a sixty-five-year-old, Mabel Carlson, got the fourth-highest number of votes, beating many male nominees, in the Executive Committee election of October 1943.

Among the departments, the "medical services" were extraordinary for a prison camp. For much of the time, the department's committee of doctors ran two hospitals, four dispensing clinics in other buildings, a dentist's office created from a machine shop, and a sanitarium for old men on the Education Building's ground floor. One of the clinics, adjoining the Annex, was a children's infirmary too, with about nine beds, constructed out of a cage used by the university for animal experiments. The camp even had an optician, Roy Thorson, who was adept at mending spectacles with bits and pieces, and in the camp's early years he could even send out for new lenses.

From August in the first year, the main camp hospital was the Santa Catalina convent-dormitory, across the road running along the camp's eastern side. It had been housing 8–10 Dominican nuns, their servants, and, before the war, women students. Against Japanese opposition, internee leaders and doctors won the case for moving their main hospital there from a former engineering building, which was too small even after its bits of machinery had been dismantled. But the nuns suddenly rebelled when Executive Committee members visited Santa Catalina and busily announced building changes. Earl Carroll's diplomacy carried the day; the nuns agreed to retain just a wing of Santa Catalina. From this base, as Carroll pointed out, they could minister to the patients. Two nuns actually chose to be interned; internees wondered how they kept their habits so spotless when walking around the camp. Santa Catalina was connected to the camp by making a gap in the eastern wall and barricading off the road that ran along the wall between the camp and hospital.

The camp also had an "isolation hospital," much needed as contagious and infectious diseases were always a threat to a population thrown closely together from diverse places. In the first month nearly a third of internees were diagnosed with respiratory or gastro-intestinal ailments.[5] Throughout internment, internees suffered a lot from dysentery-type illness, but the isolation hospital and strict hygiene rules helped prevent any epidemics worse than measles. (When I caught measles, I ended up in the children's wing. I knew I was in professional hands, and learned some new medical jargon, when a nurse solemnly asked me each morning, "Did your bowels move today?")

Until 1944 internees with major and lengthy illnesses could get passes to stay at hospitals outside. This was subsidized by an allocation from money the Japanese paid the camp, plus the hospitals themselves and benefactors.[6] The Philippine General Hospital donated an ambulance service between all the hospitals in Manila and the camp. Inside the camp, medicines were always short, though that got better after Red Cross shipments arrived in December 1943 and the following August. Doctors generally operated with anesthetics but by 1944 some tooth extractions were being done without them. Used bandages were washed, sterilized, and used again.

The doctors worked heroically. In the big typhoon flood of November 1943, they waded hip-deep at night to make calls on sick internees. Like the nurses, they had to work long hours, especially from early 1944, when the army stopped Filipino volunteer doctors and nurses from entering the camp and closed outside hospitals to most internees. The Internee Committee and Agents complained about the risk and strain caused by the influx of new cases but to no avail; the army was intent on sealing off the camp.

Physical survival was the first of four purposes of the internee administration. Working with camp doctors, the administration tracked internees' calorie intake and weight loss, built up food reserves, and decided how and when to use them when the Japanese army slashed the main food supply. All this took meticulous planning — not to mention imaginative foresight. For example, camp leaders decided they could not indefinitely count on the city's water system, especially if and when Manila again became a war zone. So they emptied, cleaned, and refilled the gym's swimming pool, "to be kept for emergency use."[7] Later they had a well dug on each side of the Main Building. Their foresight was vindicated: in the fighting that followed liberation, the city water supply to the camp temporarily collapsed.

The second purpose of the administration was to maintain law and order. In a close-packed population used to much more freedom, people were frustrated, often fractious about little things, and apt to get on each others' nerves. The result was a host of regulations covering civil behavior as well as obvious misdemeanors like theft. These rules, along with internee police patrols and a prison, also served a third purpose: minimizing Japanese interference in everyday life. Strong self-government by the camp was a trade-off with the Japanese, as it reduced their administrative load. The prison, run by an internee warder, housed rule-breakers caught by Japanese guards as well as by internee patrols. This usually suited the internees and the commandant alike: it helped keep out the Kempeitai military police.

The fourth purpose — really a mission — applied especially to several top leaders. Carroll Grinnell in particular wanted to operate on a larger scale than Santo Tomás. The Committee used Santo Tomás resources to help not just non-interned families but also military POWs, some of whom had wives and children in the camp, and were always worse treated. Many internees took part in this. When Geege Wootten made her small sketch of a Cabanatuan wife, to be smuggled to the husband, she was part of the mission. But for leaders like Grinnell and Alfred Duggleby, contact with the outside world was high policy, albeit secret and dangerous. Ambition to play on a larger stage than the camp may have been part of it, but outside contacts served the camp too. Smugglers brought in food and medicine for the camp after the army tried to seal it off (more on that in the next chapter). And communicating with guerrillas and using secret radios helped camp leaders to judge what was happening in the war outside the camp and when rescue might come.

Within Santo Tomás, the camp government ran what conservatives today might call a "nanny state." A General Code of Regulations, as revised in August 1943, contained seventy "articles," some with many sub-sections, and grouped like U.S. legislation under different "titles." The Executive Committee said it "promulgated" the code but it included rules emanating from the commandant's office — for example, a ban on signaling to people outside the camp. The articles ranged from general prescriptions — "maintaining order and proper sanitation" and respect for "the person, property and rights of others"— to details such as "quiet hours" (11 P.M.–6 A.M., 1–3 P.M.) and no moving of beds without a room monitor's permission. Preventing sickness was prominent. Alongside safety rules, Title IV had plenty to say on "Sanitation and Hygiene." Its ten articles included arrangements for cleaning and inspecting rooms and a lot on personal habits: no spitting, no eating in dorm rooms or bathrooms, and "excreta" had to go where it belonged.[8] Notices and signs supporting the code were everywhere, from myriad "Don'ts" ("Don't Wash Dishes in the Drinking Fountain") to prescriptions for mental health ("Are You in a Rut? Try the Activity Cure").

Competitions and certificates were used too. When teenager Liz Lautzenhiser's room won a weekly competition for cleanest room in the camp, her mother, Mamie, the room monitor, received a "Certificate of Award for Merit" couched in the majesty of legal language: "Be it known by these presents that Room No. 24 under Monitor Mrs. M. Lautzheimer [sic] was duly judged the cleanest and most sanitary room in Santo Tomas Internment Camp." Even Robert Wygle's "Community Service Award" for making bamboo knitting needles and other useful items for the camp praised his contribution to "health and sanitation."

Camp authority won support from the internee press — for all its claims of independence. Editorials in *STIC Gazette* inveighed against lazy and foolhardy "rule-breaking" that incurred collective Japanese punishment, as well as people with "loose tongues" who sought attention by telling unfounded, malicious stories about individuals or the administration. Paper shortages compelled the press to go on air via the camp's PA system, and that included a newsletter of facts and advice, *Campus Health*. Camp broadcasting even featured a Santo Tomás version of the Ten Commandments, the last one starting, "Thou shalt not covet thy neighbor's shanty or his room space...."[9]

Nanny-state officiousness could be irritating, however much needed for order and survival. It was annoying, for example, when officials bustled into a dorm room, measuring spaces between beds to see if one more could be fitted in. Administration media did try to use humor to lighten its injunctions. "'We Crawl by Night' (confessions of a bedbug)" was one of several health and safety posters hamming it up. But official joviality could go awry, at least for Robin Prising, aged eleven, in the camp's last year. In the wake-up broadcasts each morning, he hated the "fake summer camp" cheeriness of the announcer giving out the day's notices "as if they were a commercial for a laxative or deodorant." That and the crooning Andrews Sisters who began the broadcasts were obviously intended to boost morale, but he preferred the barking instructions in Japanese to the guards that came in the middle — at least they sounded real.[10]

A more serious issue was political, sharpened by the speed with which the camp bureaucracy was created. In the first month, a group of men in the gym were so vociferous about an "American dictatorship" and "invisible government" that the new and insecure internee committee deputed the tough lawyer, Clyde DeWitt, to threaten them: if they did not tone down, they would be reported to the Japanese as troublemakers. But after a long meeting with them, DeWitt defused the situation by getting committee members to have more personal contact with the disaffected and be more open about what they did. Tempers cooled but suspicions of undemocracy remained, surfacing again over law enforcement and due process.[11]

While disliking the ban on "undue familiarity of conduct between men and women" (camp rules, Article 12), internees supported a tough line against disruptive behavior. Alcohol in the camp was officially banned, but boozing always went on, thanks to smuggling, bribing

Japanese guards, and home-brewing from almost anything — raisins and pineapples were favorites. In the camp's first few months, "drunk and disorderly" conduct by a few persistent offenders became so serious that the Committee on Order, the nearest equivalent to a camp court, had them paraded through the camp, hands tied behind their backs. At the end of July 1942 the commandant let the Executive Committee set up the internee-run jail. Initially located near the commandant's office, it was moved twice to be less under the eye of the commandant and visiting Japanese. It ended up in a room, about twenty feet by ten, at the front of the Main Building ground floor. Jail sentences usually ran from a day or two to thirty days, but sometimes much more. Until a women's jail was created in another building, women offenders were not jailed but confined to their dorm rooms or given extra work duties, as were some male offenders.

Prisoners stayed in the jail room day and night; it had a toilet, a basin and two pairs of bunk beds. Books were allowed, but other than that prisoners were supposed to be sealed off from outside contact. However, Karen Kerns, aged nine or ten, and her friend, Jean Weinzheimer, talked with Karen's father, Bryan, through a barred window of the Main Building. He had been one of the workers who pushed a garbage cart out of camp until a Japanese guard caught him sneaking in a pot of coconut honey.[12]

For internal camp offenses, in which the commandant had not set a sentence, the Committee on Order was judge and jury; it also arbitrated disputes. In September 1942, another case of drunkenness came up. Aiming to simplify procedures, the committee let the defendant produce just a written statement; neither he nor his counsel could appear before the court or cross-examine witnesses. Unfortunately for the committee, the counsel was Clyde DeWitt. He led a protest that got due process restored — though his client still ended up in the clink. The suspicion remained that camp leaders preferred centralized power to democratic rights.

The following January, the Executive Committee did put a contentious law-and-order issue to a popular vote. By 1,903 to 681, the camp voted to retain the public broadcasting of offenders' names and their sentences, but critics disliked the way that naming-and-shaming lumped together the shameful with the non-shameful (such as Bryan Kerns). Most of the administration's Publicity Department, which ran the public address system, disliked the practice and the announcer resigned when it was upheld.[13]

Higher up the administration, there was an issue about Grinnell's leadership style, especially in relation to the Japanese. In the first year, the Executive Committee told their Japanese-speaking chairman that he was too secretive about what he had learned when talking with the commandant. The commandant might indeed say more if the conversation was confidential but the committee wanted maximum information about Japanese intentions. Grinnell agreed to be more open, but two months later he sailed into another storm when the Executive Committee cancelled New England–style "town meetings." The row dramatized the tension between the committee and the camp population, but it divided the administration too.

The weekly, open-air meetings had started in late September 1942. They were moderated by the Rev. Walter Foley, head of the Religion Department, aided by five "selectmen" — all chosen by election. At the first few meetings an internee administrator answered questions about a particular policy area. By November, though, attendance had grown to 500 and the Executive Committee took fright. It worried that the meetings were stirring up dissension and that questions about food supply might expose secret arrangements for bringing in and stockpiling food reserves, which the committee could not openly admit. But when it suddenly axed the meetings, Grinnell's open letter to Foley was annoyingly vague. The letter implied that handling individual queries through the selectmen would be more peaceful and also more informative.

Ending the meetings divided internee opinion. Some people were not that concerned. Others, including several selectmen, shared committee worries that the meetings might provoke the Japanese. But Foley and his allies were furious. The camp's leaders, he said later, had shown they did not "understand the values of democratic procedure, for which presumably the war was being fought." Far from sowing dissension, Foley believed that the meetings were promoting a "camp unity" based on facts rather than malicious rumor. His letter of protest to the Executive Committee even struck a conservative note, implying that the meetings headed off revolt by provided a "safety-valve" for dissent.

Grinnell felt he was bound to offend, no matter what he did. "We get it coming and going," he told a friend.[14] He felt squeezed between democratic demands and the need to maintain good relations with the camp's Japanese overlords without telling them too much. Internee critics, though, believed that the committee exaggerated the danger of provoking the Japanese so as to give itself a smoother ride. And the fact that the commandant's office often broadcast its orders via committee announcements made it look as if the committee endorsed the orders or was citing Japanese authority for what it wanted to do.

Internees would have got their own back two months later in the elections of January 1943 had the commandant not nullified them. None of the seven-man committee who ran made the top seven. Top vote went to Earl Carroll, camp supply chief, who was not then on the committee. Grinnell's total votes fell by over two-thirds from his votes the previous year, but he was not alone. The votes for treasurer Alexander Calhoun, top vote getter the previous year, fell surprisingly from 1,760 to 131.

Another rebuff was delivered a year later when the new, commandant-appointed troika, the Internee Committee headed by Grinnell, also ran as a slate for the three elected positions of Agent, a direct voice for internees. The voters disagreed they could do both jobs and gave much larger votes to three others. It was not just an attack on Grinnell, but he personified a committee that was seen as a would-be dictatorship. In a show the previous month, Dave Harvey offered to write a book called *Mine Camp* (a play on Hitler's *Mein Kampf*) and dedicate it to Grinnell.

Apart from the court and town-meeting quarrels, hostility to the administration came out in charges of favoritism: that bootleggers could get away with their activities if they sold to "important people," and that some people found it easier than others to get outside passes. Both did happen but not that often.[15] In response to these suspicions, the Executive Committee announced that any Red Cross relief should benefit the whole community, with some preference for women and children; it should not favor the aid's administrators; and it must be accounted for openly.

Criticism of internee leaders seldom extended to inequality. Margaret Sherk, who had been so bitter about Manila's affluent receiving largesse through the package line and said she was never told of special welfare aid, recognized that she was lucky to get help from Jerry Sams. As time went by, though, she played down the inequality of internee fortunes, claiming speciously that everyone had started out equal with just three days' food. In traditional American spirit, she suggested that anyone could make a go of it with enterprise and spunk. Jerry's own enterprise had brought her a new bed space on the museum landing, homemade equipment, and extra food. She herself had had to fight to keep a hot plate from exploitative freeloaders who wanted to borrow it all the time. Given that different people achieved different things, she said, the Japanese set an impossible standard of equality by "criticizing us for not pooling all our resources." Likewise, Emily Van Sickle, who had defended private internee money for the jobs it gave others, claimed that shanty owners had often earned their so-called "privileged status" through hard work. The Van Sickles themselves, with money from "Van's" International Harvester connections, owned one of the grander shanties. At the same time, Emily accused Grinnell of almost everything, from favoritism and insensitivity to incompetence and autocratic behavior. She even endorsed Van's argument that Grinnell should have raised more money than he did and lent it to the camp so that internees without money could eat better. She looked to an individual leader rather than communal sharing to produce more equality and welfare.[16]

Making internees put their surpluses into a common pot, if this were possible, would probably have reduced the food brought through the gate from friends and servants. They were helping specific people, who in turn sought it for their own families, especially when they had children. A test, though, of internees' readiness to share more widely came in 1944. Closing the package line had ended private imports of food and made it harder to smuggle in money, though camp shops still sold some extra food brought in by the Japanese. On 1 August, the evening broadcast announced an army order that adult internees must transfer all their money above fifty pesos each (under $20 today) into accounts at the nearby Bank for Taiwan. No more than fifty pesos could be drawn out each month — half that for children under ten. Derisive laughter greeted the commandant's reasons: protecting the money against robbery and waste, curbing gambling, and enabling the money to accrue interest and last as long as possible. The order was in fact part of a general crackdown on the camp, including covert aid to groups outside, and possibly a wish to equalize internee conditions.

Meeting with Commandant Hayashi and his officials, camp leaders protested vehemently. The initial announcement limited the camp budget as well as individuals to the fifty pesos a month; the camp money had to be banked too. The usually diplomatic Earl Carroll called the order "an outrage" and "persecution"; it meant "starvation, especially of the children." He said every penny was needed now due to Japanese cuts in the food rations and rocketing prices: eggs already cost three pesos each. A strong follow-up protest by the internee Agents said, among many things, that the order amounted to "confiscation," as money left in the bank would lose value from escalating inflation.

Regarding the camp budget, the commandant relented. His civilian official, Shizua Ohashi, negotiated a compromise whereby camp leaders could apply for extra spending above fifty pesos a month. For individuals, though, the fifty peso limit held. The administration invited internees to give from their surpluses to the camp budget rather than simply banking them. Some people just hid their extra money. Of the money turned in, between a quarter and a third was given to the camp — a small proportion but understandable in that internees would want to hold some money back for their families, despite galloping inflation and less and less to buy in the camp. Appeals later in the year produced smaller contributions, some of them for a special coconut milk fund.[17]

If the internees' general giving was only moderate, one group was downright antisocial politically — the fifty-four U.S. Army nurses brought in from Corregidor after it fell in May 1942. On Bataan and Corregidor they had been superb. But in Santo Tomás, plunged into caring for civilians under civilian internee authority, they became a prickly interest group, jealous for their status as military professionals and rivalrous toward a smaller group of navy nurses.

Housed at first in the Santa Catalina convent-dormitory beside the camp, the younger nurses objected when told they all had to move into camp so that Santa Catalina could become a hospital. They gave in resentfully when their commander, Maude Davison, laid down the law — military obedience. But senior nurses worried that their disaffected younger colleagues might turn to prostitution (not unknown in the camp) to make some money. Loans were acquired for the nurses from Grinnell and a former shipping executive, to be repaid out of their postwar back pay. The loans enabled them to buy such extras as duck eggs, papayas, and even hairdos, adding to gifts already received from a German well-wisher. This in turn caused resentment among internee nursing aides who reckoned they worked as hard as the army nurses but ate less well.

The following January, Davison herself led the nurses into a strike when the internee administration said they had to move again, this time into the Main Building out of their quarters in a building beside the Annex, which was needed for an influx of mothers with small children. The strike quickly collapsed when the commandant weighed in: he told them to move or else. The fracas caused bad feeling, and personal style made it worse. They did their job professionally but too often they came across as stiff, unsmiling, and defensive.[18]

The rebelliousness of rank-and-file internees seldom led to direct action against the Japanese. Internees had more opportunity to attack their own administration, a buffer between them and the commandant's office. In the early months there was even some sociability between Japanese guards and internees working at the main-gate package line or on night patrol, especially those internees who spoke a little Japanese. During the long night hours, Japanese sentries sometimes offered the internees a cup of coffee or a cigarette; one gave his Japanese home address for visiting after the war. Six Japanese even signed a tablecloth, on which a British woman, Elizabeth Cunningham, collected over 260 signatures and later embroidered them. Three were women from the same family, presumably working in the commandant's office. We know nothing about them but it showed there was some friendly contact across the usual distance between ordinary internees and the Japanese.[19]

The Japanese, however, were still the enemy. When they parked military trucks in the camp in the last few months, they offered a chance for minor sabotage. Thirteen-year-old Peter Wygle and friends repeatedly got in among the trucks and relieved their tires of air by putting sharp little sticks into the valves.

As for outright, grassroots protests against the Japanese, the most extraordinary episode happened earlier in the last year. Outside the kitchen behind the Main Building, the commandant and some visiting Japanese officers encountered Millie Sanders, the six-foot-plus black American who had befriended Robin Prising. Unable to place her, the commandant asked if she was Canadian. Sanders flared up at this, declared she was a Texas Negro "and proud of it," and told him that "I've got a few things to tell you." She had them taste "the pigfood you've been feedin' us," and even took them into her ground-floor dorm room where "[we live] like a bunch of gypsies." Sanders' natural authority and looks — so different from a white internee — confused and intimidated the officers. Rather than arrest her, they escaped.[20]

Three other episodes dramatized in different ways the relations between internees, their leaders, and the Japanese. In the first, a loose-cannon internee forced the Executive Committee to choose between putting a small minority at risk and endangering the whole camp. In January 1943, Jack Owens, who had operated a rent-a-bed operation (see Chapter 4), got into trouble with his dormmates and room monitor for his unstable aggressiveness. He went to the commandant, complained that he was being bullied, and said he wanted to be moved to another camp. He added self-destructively that he was an ex-serviceman and other internees had been in the military too. The military police took him away, never to be seen again, and the commandant ordered all military internees to report the next day. The Executive Committee defended them, saying many had long ago reported their military service, but it advised military internees to come forward, as the commandant had threatened reprisals against them and the camp if they did not. Some laid low and got away with it, while always fearing they might be found out. In retrospect, it was better not to have reported a military background, but internees and their leaders did not know that at the time.

Thirty men did report and were almost immediately trucked out of camp. As the truck left, Tressa Roka saw a distraught young woman with a baby, sobbing her heart out; she had arrived just too late to say goodbye to her husband. The thirty, plus six from an outside hospital, went to Fort Santiago. Some came back, probably because they had helped the U.S. military without being uniformed servicemen. But others went on to Cabanatuan and then Japan, some of them dying on the way when their unmarked ships were attacked by the U.S. Navy. One survivor, Don Rutter, ended up in a Japanese coal mine where he and other prisoners sabotaged the coal by mixing it with black rocks. When he got dysentery, which would have killed him on twelve hours a day of hard labor, his fellows deliberately broke his foot so he could be laid up in a prison ward.[21]

The second episode, later in the year, was mainly a matter of snarled communications, but that led to suspicions of unfair collusion between the Executive Committee and the Japanese. On 26 September 1943, 127 internees were repatriated under a prisoner exchange. They went by ship to Goa, Portugal's Indian colony, and then by an American ship to the United States, though not all were Americans. They were mainly chosen by the U.S. State Department, with substitutes decided by the Japanese for those who declined the offer to go. Many of them had been living in Shanghai but were caught on shipboard in Manila when war broke out; almost none of them were Philippine residents. This reaffirmed the U.S. prewar policy of doing nothing that might signal to Filipinos and the Japanese that the Americans were abandoning the Philippines. Many internees agreed with this: they did not want to be evacuated if that made it seem less likely that the United States would come back and liberate everyone. In addition, a lot of internees, even the American ones, had no homes in the United States to go to, and conditions were not yet that bad. In a camp poll, over half the adults said they did not want to be repatriated.

This, however, did not make the Executive Committee look good. It was divided as to whether it should try to get old and ailing people put on the list, and it sent mixed messages about who would go. A few days before the ship sailed, the super-commandant, Akida

Kodaki, addressed internees on the plaza. Sniggers came from the audience when he made a candid admission. Some people, he said, had been included because they got on well with the Japanese and would, he hoped, report favorably on the camp. A farewell gathering on the plaza saw the chosen ones leave at 4 A.M., but there was widespread suspicion that many were getting to Goa by "pull" with the Executive Committee as well as the commandant. Some of those added to the State Department selection were ill but many were not.[22]

The third episode, which occurred the following year, pitted internees and the Executive Committee together against the Japanese, though both sides made concessions. The Japanese army demanded that all adult internees sign a loyalty oath. This was part of a general tightening up against "subversion." The oath, issued on 25 April 1944 by the new commandant, Yasunska Yoshie, was a pledge not to "escape or conspire directly or indirectly against the Japanese Military Authorities." This followed some wrangling over language between the commandant's office and the Internee Committee and Agents, with Shizua Ohashi mediating between the two sides. The internee leaders had objected to previous versions, as they seemed too much of a commitment to supporting the Japanese army.

By a vote of 10 to 6, the elected council representing dorm monitors recommended signing the oath, along with a "letter of reservations." The letter's main provisions were that signing the oath did not waive the signer's rights under international law and agreements; it did not require the signer to do anything disloyal to the signer's country; and mere failure to obey orders should not be interpreted as conspiracy. A statement that the oath was not signed by "free will" was cut from the original letter by Ohashi and Commandant Yoshie.

Many still objected, though others thought it did not matter, as it would be signed under duress and promises to enemies carried no weight. In the end, everyone signed the oath or the oath and letter combined — except for one man, Tun Yem Lee. A Chinese American merchant seaman and ship's laundryman, Lee was a total resister. He even refused to take charity of any kind, not Red Cross food kits or clothes from the Red Cross or from friends. His blue shirt and pants fell into such tatters that a bunch of women once grabbed him and sewed patches on him while he stood. When he refused to sign the oath, the commandant's office and Internee Committee hatched their own conspiracy to keep him away from the Kempeitai. They classified him as psychologically incompetent to sign and jailed him for the duration.[23]

Valiant as Lee was, individual disobedience was one thing; general disobedience was quite another. The camp's leaders could not mount total resistance, over the oath or anything else. As well as managing a complex small city, they had to fend off the power of the Japanese army, which ultimately held the whip hand. That required compromise and sometimes surrender under protest. But as the screws tightened in the last year and the camp moved toward mass starvation, internees and their leaders became more united in defending themselves as best they could against their overlords' oppression.

9

Hunger

On 3 October 1944, the U.S. Joint Chiefs of Staff ordered an advance on Japan via Luzon, Iwo Jima, and Okinawa. Two combined forces—sea, air, ground—were already advancing toward the Philippines. The first, coming from the east under Admiral Chester Nimitz, had captured the Mariana Islands. The second, under General Douglas MacArthur, had fought up from Australia along the north coast of New Guinea and set up air bases at Morotai, an island, about 200 miles south of the Philippines.

Bitter fighting on Leyte, where MacArthur made his first Philippine landing on 20 October, took much longer than he expected as he waded ashore. It was not until 9 January 1945 that his troops landed on Luzon. They beached at Lingayen Gulf, the same place where the Japanese had arrived three years earlier. To reach Santo Tomás, 115 miles away, would take almost a month more.

For internees, the approach of their rescuers became a race between liberation and starvation as the Japanese army cut food rations again and again. When they saw American aircraft wheeling and diving over Manila, air raids and food were the two big obsessions. The planes made people impatient: "When will our boys come? Can we hold out?" But they also brought hope. "[On days] when our bombers failed to visit the city," Tressa Roka wrote, "our depression and hunger were more acute."[1]

Back in March 1944, after the Japanese took over the camp's main food supply, "chow-line" meals at the central kitchen were just adequate for some. Breakfast was several ladles of "mush" (boiled rice flour) in coconut milk with a spoonful of sugar, plus tea or coffee and a banana. Lunch was usually a ladle of boiled corn or rice, plus a slice of corn bread and sometimes a bit of coarse greens from the camp gardens. Dinner might be *dilis* (a very salty and skinny small fish) or a little carabao meat boiled with corn, followed by tea and a banana or *calamanci* (Filipino lime). Any milk or eggs that the Internee Committee could get went to the camp hospitals or the Annex kitchen for young children.

In October 1944, fish and meat disappeared from the menu. By early January 1945, a month before liberation, typical chow-line fare was down to one ladle of mush and a cup of hot water for breakfast; a ladle of thin vegetable soup for lunch; and a little stew of mongo beans, rice, and *camote* (Filipino sweet potato) for supper. This delivered less than a thousand calories a day per internee, far below what adults needed to do light work. Many internees had nothing else to live on; they had consumed their last Red Cross food parcels, which arrived in December 1943, and lacked money to buy extra food at exorbitant prices in the camp's dwindling markets. It was worse when lunch was temporarily suspended due to gas failures, shortage of firewood, and air raids.[2]

Though most of the chow-line food came from the Japanese army, it had to be supplemented from the camp's own dwindling stocks; powdered milk, for example, went to young children. The army initially said it would supply 1,750 calories per day for each adult and half that for under-elevens (though the central kitchen served everyone the same). In fact, the army never gave 1,750. By the last month, it was providing less than 800 calories. And this was before kitchen workers had taken out the worst of slimy greens, moldy corn, and rotted camotes, and "cleaned" the rice, removing husks, bits of stalk, dirt, and rat droppings.[3] The fish delivered one day was so bad that it was a fed to a sorry flock of ducks that ended in the pot, producing not much more than gravy. When weevils survived the food cleaning and got into breakfast mush, opinion divided on whether to pick them out or stir them in as protein.

The Japanese also gave short weight on the amounts of rice and corn they said they were providing. When George Bridgeford, internee food supply chief, queried their figures at the commandant's office, he was angrily told he was cooking the books to discredit the Japanese army. In fact, the Japanese were stealing from the camp's own rice and corn reserves, which they insisted on keeping in their *bodega* (storehouse), along with their own cereals. In mid–November 1944, the commandant's office reported that all the camp's rice and corn stocks had been used up. Internee accountants estimated that up to ten tons of corn and rice had gone missing. The Internee Committee challenged the discrepancies. This time the commandant's officials were more polite, but they refused to give exact accounts and said the bodega's contents were secret. In place of the stolen cereal, the army supplied the camp with smaller quantities of camote tops.

From mid–1944, internee leaders, including doctors and a parents' committee, protested repeatedly against food cuts. Using surveys showing serious weight loss among children, they made a special appeal, citing the Japanese reputation for loving their young. Commandants replied that there was no more food; everyone was short, and if adults wanted to give more to their children (which they already did), that was up to them. Again and again, commandants urged internees to grow more vegetables; internee leaders replied that they could not do it on so few calories. The pressure to grow more came from army prison-camp administrators outside Santo Tomás. They wanted internee working hours raised from the standard two hours a day to 3–5 hours for men according to age, and three hours for women. The Internee Committee got the numbers reduced to an official maximum of three hours for men and two hours for women, but the committee also opened up more of the camp for growing and allocated more workers to the task. The Japanese garrison undercut that by seizing an area cleared by internees for its own vegetables. For a time some internees, controversially, got extra food plus tobacco for helping in the Japanese garden. But the ground was not good for growing, and the rainy season delayed what skimpy harvest there was until November. The results mostly went into vegetable stock for soup — often *talinum*, coarse spinach-like greens.

A basic cause of the food problem was Japan's short-sighted and self-defeating exploitation of the Philippine economy. Through 1944, Japanese bodegas in Manila piled up big supplies of rice, destined for Japan but lacking transport to get there, even before the U.S. Navy blocked off the seas. Japanese policies disrupted Philippine agriculture. Farmers, for example, had to kill carabaos to produce meat when they were needed for plowing and milk. And the army added to hyper-inflation by letting local commanders print their own "Mickey Mouse" pesos.

In the countries occupied by Japan, military needs came first. This applied to Allied prisoners as well as native peoples. Feeding Santo Tomás could not be a drain on the army, and when times got tough for the army — especially when guerrilla attacks and U.S. air raids disrupted food transport from countryside to city — grabbing the camp's supplies was a big temptation. Japan itself, unlike the United States, with its booming agriculture, was never able to send food to its troops overseas.

Japanese attitudes to Santo Tomás internees abetted exploitation and hardened hearts toward their plight. In the camp's first year a Japanese visitor noted that the internees were generally better off than Tokyo inhabitants, and as late as January 1944, there was enough money about for shoe-shine boys to operate. The money and the short working hours made it easier to see Santo Tomás's Westerners as rich and lazy. In August 1944, Acting Commandant Onozoki stopped the Internee Committee from using his food buyers to get supplementary vegetables in Manila's markets. Internee "greed," he claimed, should not take food away from "starving Filipinos." We don't know whether Onozoki said this to push more vegetable growing in the camp; the ban was later rescinded.[4] It is true, though, that camp internees as a whole were always better off than many Filipinos living outside. High-risk attempts by burglars to get over the walls did not stop.

In brushing off camp complaints about food cuts, Japanese officials sometimes stressed that their own soldiers were on short commons too. Internees found this hard to believe. Some guards still had fat bellies, and the smell of coffee and frying wafted out of the Education Building, where the commandant's staff had taken up residence on the ground floor. Through most of the year internee Hattie Brantley said she saw guards eating eggs, citrus fruits, and lots of rice. It was especially galling on New Year's Eve 1944, when hungry internees saw truckloads of goodies arrive for their captors' drunken celebration. Still, the official "Japanese soldier's ration" was supposed to give no more than 1,750 calories a day, the amount promised to internees, and not enough to support strenuous work, let alone fighting. Small wonder that individual Japanese soldiers plundered farms, stores and private homes for extra food, and in Santo Tomás they may have hijacked some of the camp stores, either to eat or to sell back to internees at exorbitant prices. In late November 1944, twenty-three of the guards, a good third of the garrison, showed enough symptoms of beriberi to get injections of vitamin B. The guards had done a lot of work trying to produce vegetables that should have helped prevent beriberi, but many of them were Taiwanese suffering from bad feeding elsewhere in the army, where even the low "official" ration was often not met. In late October and early November, more than fifty of them had been drafted in as military "workers," releasing Japanese guards for active service.[5]

But food shortages and army priorities do not explain all the cuts in Santo Tomás rations. In May 1944, the International YMCA was allowed to send in some canned milk, eggs, and flour. In June, the camp received 36,000 pesos from the American Red Cross, almost a third of which went to families of internees living outside. The following month, though, the guards rejected pushcarts of fruit, vegetables and eggs, sent by Manila charities. The carts stood in the heat while the donors' representatives pleaded to be allowed entry. As Tressa Roka bitterly observed, "Our benevolent jailers told them that we had sufficient food and we sadly watched them wheeling away the carts. For this cruelty and falsehood, we hated them." It later transpired that Tokyo had banned all welfare donations to Philippine camps. No reason was given to the donors but it suggested a wish to save face, to not be seen as failing to feed the prisoners.[6]

Back in the camp's "good" years, the internee administration had foreseen that the food situation would get worse. Through 1943, while the Japanese were giving cash allowances to the administration for all camp expenses, the administration held back 2 percent of the food budget to store reserves, especially rice and corn, sugar, coffee, and lard and margarine (for valuable fats). In 1944, when the Japanese took over the main food supply, it still let the Internee Committee use its own money to buy supplementary food via Japanese buyers; this largely went to the camp hospitals and children's Annex. In September, the Japanese let in another monetary gift from the Red Cross, some of which again went to internees' Filipino families living outside. But escalating Manila prices meant the money bought less and less.

To offset the worsening food situation, camp leaders increasingly resorted to money smuggling and then direct food smuggling. One smuggler was Alaistair ("Shorty") Hall, chief internee orderly at the veterans' home outside of the camp. He brought back pesos from camp well-wishers when he reported weekly to the front-gate guardhouse. An internee clerk in the office would hang up an old raincoat Hall carried and remove the pesos from an inside pocket. Luckily for Shorty, security was not exactly post–9/11.

The university seminary was also a source of smuggling. Two of its American fathers had obtained special passes for ministering to the camp and they brought in money and medicines. Just before their passes were stopped, one of them, Fr. Hilary Ahern, set up a scheme with Wanda Werff, a young Dutch internee who worked in Santa Catalina Hospital. At ten each morning, she would look over to the Fathers' Garden of the seminary. If she saw Ahern holding an acacia flower near a statue of Holy Mary, she knew she had an evening assignment. At 10 P.M., after roll call, she would creep out of the Main Building's back entrance and collect a small package of medicine, reaching through the seminary fence to where it was hidden under a bush. Nearly seen once or twice by a guard, she was frightened enough to feel relieved when the good father was not holding a flower. But she kept at it, knowing some hospital patients desperately needed drugs, especially one that strengthened heart muscles weakened by malnutrition.[7]

In March 1944, camp leaders hatched a bigger operation. They enlisted the secret help of seven big-business executives who wrote promissory notes (IOUs) in U.S. dollars, drawn on their companies. The notes were smuggled to Chinese merchants, Swiss firms and others that were prepared to lend pesos at the current rate — five pesos per dollar — to be smuggled back into camp. Two American Philippine Red Cross internees in the camp "guaranteed" eventual repayment by the Red Cross but no one knew for sure that would happen. The leader of the seven, who rounded up the others, was Edwin Van Voorhees of General Motors, the grand shanty owner (see Chapter 4). Without family in the camp, Van Voorhees openly claimed that his main goal in the camp was to look after himself and maybe a few friends. Was this a deliberate smokescreen? He belied his words by putting up $20,000 ($300,000 today). The seven between them produced $120,000, and more contributors came in later.[8]

The chief smuggler was the university administrator, Luis de Alcuaz. As the university's representative to the camp, he had a Main Building office conveniently near that of Earl

Carroll, the camp's supply chief and Internee Committee member. When the commandant came by, Alcuaz got a kick out of pretending to berate Carroll to hide their conniving. Well connected on the outside, Alcuaz would take the IOUs to his money suppliers and bring wads of pesos back into camp; the commandant once gave him a ride in his car when he was carrying 50,000 pesos in his briefcase. Inflation, though, meant a lot of pesos to stuff into a briefcase, so Alcuaz and his accomplices chose another ploy. He hid money in baskets or boxes of fruit, which he took by carromata to the nuns of Santa Catalina Hospital. He operated from a vacant room on the ground floor, separated from the camp optician's office by a partition that did not reach all the way to the ceiling. He would then lob packets of money over the partition to the optician, Roy Thorson. Internees loitering outside signaled if guards were approaching. Once, when a guard was walking toward Thorson's window, Thorson whispered to Alcuaz to stop throwing money over. But Alcuaz did not hear him and kept at it. Thorson desperately kicked packets under chairs and the desk and had just thrown one into the wastepaper basket when the guard peered in. Mercifully, he walked off.

In September 1944, Alcuaz and the others shifted to direct food smuggling. The commandant had stopped the committee buying of rice and corn, and the Japanese now supervised the banking of camp money, making it harder to spend smuggled pesos. Inflation, too, meant the pesos were getting as bulky as the food they bought. When Alcuaz's Main Building office was closed down, he set up a new office in a largely disused seminary building adjoining the gym dormitory. There was no official access between the two, but the wall between dormitory and office had a small iron grille. Announcing he had to make office alterations, Alcuaz opened up the grille and built a second wall of sawali in front of it. Office furniture hid a hole in the sawali. On the other side, the bed of Father David Daly hid the opened grille. Daly, an interned priest, was one of several accomplices; so was the gym monitor.

Through family connections, Alcuaz got Maria Oroso, a professional dietician who ran a government food-packing plant, to send in cans of meat and small bags of beans, ostensibly for the seminary. Night after night, Alcuaz fed cans and food packets to Daly and others while elderly internees snored under their mosquito nets. The smugglers put the food into a furniture storeroom at the end of the gym, before hiding it in hand-carts taking various things around the camp. Some food went out in stretchers, hidden under patients being moved between the gym and Santa Catalina. Seven thousand lbs of mongo beans, a ton of canned meat, and other foods were smuggled in.

For Alcuaz, alone in his office, it was frightening work. Devout Catholic that he was, he prayed a lot. He also left an open bottle of rum on his desk and rubbed some on his face, so he could seem drunk and incoherent if a guard came by. The guards mostly left the seminary alone, but one night Lieutenant Abiko dropped in. He saw a pile of food that Alcuaz had not yet managed to stash away in the cavity between the two walls. "For the monks," Alcuaz explained. "Americans!" shouted Abiko, slapping him. Alcuaz repeated his defense. Abiko left, but in late December Alcuaz got word that the Kempeitai were investigating him. He went into hiding, moving from one trusted friend to another, but still met with the Swiss consul and camp benefactors. Worried that the camp would starve if it became a no-man's land once the Americans arrived in Manila, they planned how to store food inside and outside the camp and even arrange housing for some internees at nearby homes.[9]

But food smuggling could not go far for a population of almost 4,000, though it probably saved some lives at the margin. In late August, a medical survey of the camp revealed alarming weight losses, lack of protein and vitamin B, and attendant ailments, including damage to eyesight. Most of the doctors recommended using up all the camp's meat reserves over two months. They argued that this would prevent deaths and shore up the minimum health the camp needed to move later to an all-rice diet. Three doctors demurred, believing a spend-it-all-now meat policy would have little effect. Much depended, of course, on when the camp would get liberated — which no one could then predict even in Washington, let alone Manila. The Internee Committee went with the medical majority. Besides regular chow-line food, internees got cans of corned beef, or other meat, on the basis of 6 ounces per person per week. The supply, totaling nearly five tons of meat, ran out in late October.

On Christmas Day 1944 the camp kitchens' efforts to give something extra showed the straits they had reached. Help fortunately came from an International YMCA shipment of assorted foods, medicine and other items, allowed in two days before. The usual breakfast mush was sweetened with chocolate, along with a small coffee for each adult. A soybean mash thickened the one course of soup at lunch, and supper was a double serving of fried rice with bits of camote and carabao meat. "Under the circumstances, it was a culinary triumph," commented A.V.H. gratefully.[10] Each internee also got a spoonful of jam and one or two pieces of chocolate: a camp vote had chosen to give it out that way rather than mixing it in with the chow-line meals. In addition, parents clubbed together to pay five pesos for every child under sixteen so that each could get two small pieces of *bocayo*— coconut candy made with brown sugar — at a children's party.

Besides Japanese rations and camp supplements, internees had their own resources. What they had and how they used it varied a lot. In early March 1944 a shipment of mail and parcels came in from American friends and relatives. Elizabeth Vaughan was thrilled to get a parcel from her sister; it included cans of food, chocolate, soap, nice clothes for her children, and even coloring books and crayons. Not all internees, though, got a parcel. More important were the Red Cross "comfort kits" received from several countries.

The last and biggest shipment, from the American Red Cross, arrived in December 1943. Each internee, including infants, received cartons weighing 47 pounds. Contents ranged from corned beef and chopped ham and eggs to margarine, vegetable bouillon powder, dried prunes, and sugar. Among my favorites, at age seven, were little cans of sweet corned pork, which I never met again after the war and still miss today! I was intrigued to discover that the powdered "KLIM" was "milk" spelled backward, and impressed at the claim that each square of the very hard, dense chocolate bars equaled a day's nutrition. The cartons also contained vitamin C tablets, soap, and cold cream. Many internees used the cold cream for frying; Elizabeth Vaughan traded hers for a can of grapefruit juice.

A general shipment came in at the same time, including medicines and clothes. The administration rationed out the clothes by awarding points to each internee: some clothes cost more points than others. Teenager Curtis Brooks got a pair of shoes whose soles were made of cardboard concealed by very thin leather. He figured the manufacturer had cheated the Red Cross, knowing the wearer could not complain.

The comfort kits contained Old Golds and other cigarettes, which nearly scuppered the whole delivery. Tipped off that the Old Gold packets carried propaganda, the Japanese piled up the cartoons before distributing them. They chiseled into the cartons, wrecking cans and packets, as internees looked on, confused and angry. Sure enough, the Old Golds carried a home-front war slogan: "FREEDOM. Our heritage has always been freedom. We cannot afford to relinquish it. The armed forces will safeguard that freedom, if we do our share to preserve it."[11] Guards removed the Old Golds but internees still got the kits. Commandant Kato even apologized later for their rough handling, though his men then did the same to a shipment of medicines. A few days afterward, each adult received thirty cigarette packs but no Old Golds. Right to the end, as the Japanese recognized, many craved a smoke almost as much as food, and it did reduce hunger pangs. The YMCA Christmas shipment in December 1944 included cigarettes and cheap cigars for each adult. My mother, like others, traded cigarettes for cans of meat — though she said later "I felt a bit badly" taking people's food. Grace Nash, with a seven-month-old baby, swapped cigarettes for Pablum formula, which someone else had and didn't need.

A food exchange developed, for selling as well as trading, with offer prices chalked on a blackboard until the commandant banned it. Some men, desperate to help their Filipino families outside, sold much of their kits to send them money. Later, they were allowed to send food, but only if the cans and packets were opened for inspection. Profiteers bought up kit food, to be sold later after prices soared.

The biggest division over the kits was between happy eaters and cautious savers — between those who thought that more kits or rescue itself would come soon, or just couldn't resist gobbling, and those who took no chances and planned ahead, as camp leaders advised. In the first group, one family let their three-year-old stroll about with a chunk of cheese in one hand and a bag of prunes in the other. Among the savers, my mother eked out tiny portions to add to our line chow even when we were hungry all the time — so hungry that my sister and I would meticulously divide the crumbs that fell on our shanty table when a piece of cornbread or hardtack biscuit came our way. The only time she splurged was at our last Christmas dinner when we had more corned beef. "Wow," I said afterward. "I'm actually full." (Other internees also said they felt full — briefly — after Christmas dinner.) We learned after liberation that our mother had worried a lot about our feeding but reckoned that tough rationing was the best way to do it. She made our kits last all the way to liberation. So did others. Four days before the GIs arrived, Tressa Roka and her fiancé, "Catesy," were down to their last four 4-ounce cans of meat, aiming to make each last for three days. Some people had run out a month earlier, even with careful saving.[12]

It was easier to make the kits go further if you had bought up other reserves. In 1943, Alice and Bill Bryant bought brown sugar and cans of sardines and margarine. My mother bought margarine too, which she scraped into our chow-line food. Inventiveness also helped. The Balfour family missed out on the Red Cross kits, as they were not interned until June 1944, but the provisions they brought with them in a big carromata included a crate of live chickens and a duck or two. They kept the birds under the shanty they shared with Paul Esmérian, and had the last thin duckling for Christmas and their last chicken on New Year's Day. The camp's doctors, ever afraid of disease, discouraged poultry keeping, but the commandant approved and even called for more of it in the camp's last month. Anne Balfour collected the eggshells, sterilized them on their stove, ground them into powder using a bottle on a breadboard, and put the powdered shells into her children's food along with raw garlic. (American doctors at a medical checkup after the war said the eggshells' calcium and the garlic's many nutrients had probably made a difference.)

For parents with infants, liquid inventiveness was the name of the game. Before her baby, Roy, was born in September 1943, Grace Nash was determined to breastfeed him right up through liberation — which she did. She drank all she could before and after the birth, including beer repeatedly smuggled to her by a friend who bribed a guard. Sascha Weinzheimer breastfed her little boy, another Roy, until liberation, when he was over three — seriously depleting her own health. Dorothy and Robert Crabb, whose baby Phil was born three months before the end, supplemented the small ration of Lactogen by "fooling him with rice water" as well as pulping bananas. Some pregnant mothers, and mothers with babies, got help from a kindly civilian in the commandant's office, Toshio Hirose, who sneaked in extra food for them.[13]

When it came to growing vegetables, some internees were particularly resourceful. Thieves stole ripe bananas off the Weinzheimers' shanty banana tree, so each month they harvested the tree's big purple blossom, which contained baby bananas and was full of nutrients. Wrapping it in a banana leaf, Sascha Weinzheimer baked it and then mixed it with water and curry powder to make a curry paste. She had learned the custom in Hawaii from a Tahitian grandmother, but she also improvised. Finding weeds that had some bulbs, she replanted them and put the results into the chow-line stew.

Less exotically, enjoyment of "growing stuff" encouraged Roscoe and Mamie Lautzenhiser to apply for and get no less than seven private lots (standard size was four by eleven meters). They ended up providing vegetables for twenty people, on top of Roscoe's job helping to run the school system. Some children made their own gardens. Eleven-year-old Caroline Bailey produced lima beans, Chinese cabbage, and other greens for her family in the last few months. Most internees, though, did not try growing vegetables privately. The ex-missionary Frank Cary, who worked long hours as a Japanese interpreter, thought internees should have done more growing in the past. By the time they really needed the food, digging inferior ground used too many calories to be worth it, or so it seemed.[14]

Private money and credit helped if you had it. There was always food for sale at colossal prices, some of it brought in officially by the Japanese and some sold by profiteers from smuggling and hoarding. In early November 1944, Caroline Bailey's father, Fay, a banker and camp treasurer, bought five cans of Campbell's soup at $10 each (about $150 today). A month later he felt guilty about buying a pound of mongo beans, for which he paid sixty prewar pesos (some $450 today). "It is a crime that if anything can be bought it can't be obtained by the camp for the good of all," he wrote in his diary. Camp treasurer or no, it was too late by then to change an entrenched system of private buying and selling, except that the administration issued ration cards for some basics — salt, sugar, flour, and soap — that it bought and sold.

For people with valuables rather than cash, there were Taiwanese guards who coveted rings, watches, and jewelry to take home to wives and girlfriends. In January, a fine diamond engagement ring could fetch 4–5 kilos of rice plus extras such as tobacco. Internee dealers who got to know "the right" guards negotiated the sale, taking a third or more of the proceeds in food or cash for the risk; some guards took the jewelry without delivering.[15]

None of this stopped malnutrition. By the end Roscoe Lautzenhiser and Fay Bailey felt their legs swelling with beriberi, brought on by lack of protein and vitamin B1, though it would have been worse without the extra vegetables and some vitamins given to Bailey by friends.

Like so much in the Santo Tomás story, the effects of near-famine on different people varied widely, even in the last three months when malnutrition was most dire. Though hungry all the time, like everyone else, I don't remember feeling particularly weak. Mary June, though, was so weak she could only go up stairs one at a time. Approaching puberty put more demands on her body. She in turn worried about how thin our mother looked in the showers. Her bottom was alarmingly wasted — as if it didn't exist. Mary June wondered "how much longer she could go on."

In the Balfour family, eight-year-old Nicholas wept for more mush at breakfast. The three children retained basic health, though Nick slowed down, spending more time lying down and reading in the shanty. Anne Balfour, their mother, confided to her diary that hunger at night was a special torment; it sometimes gave her cramps. Paul Esmérian, surrogate husband and father in the shanty, felt particularly sorry for Tika, just turned seven ("very thin and always ravenous, poor thing"), but his six-foot-six frame took the biggest hit. Though he kept working in the camp garden to the end, by January his ankles were swelling with beriberi and he felt fatigue at the slightest effort.[16]

Captain Walter Landry, one of the camp's liberators, noticed a sharp difference between many men — "walking skeletons" — and women and children who were thin but in "pretty good shape." The photos in this book bear out the difference, though the thinness of children angered GIs. Fourteen-year-old Peter Wygle "thought I was doing pretty well [until the American soldiers] would feel my upper arm and swear they were going to kill every Jap soldier on the face of the earth."

Landry thought the biggest men looked worse. Frank Cary, down to 125 pounds in January from 200 pounds before the war, described himself in a letter he hoped would reach his brother:

> My face is hollowed in with loss of flesh. My neck is sinewy for the same reason. My arms are amusingly tooth-pick like. Each rib is a welt across my body. My abdomen can hit my backbone easily.... Sitting down is much more comfortable with a pillow as my natural upholstering has gone to feed my boiler.

Many other men were like this, except that their skin often hung down in folds whereas Cary's stomach was swollen by water. He had dropsy until vitamin injections in hospital brought relief.[17]

From mid-1944, almost all the deaths were of men, mainly those over 60. In most, if not all, animal species, males are apt to die before females, but malnutrition accentuated this. The "female hormone," estrogen, encourages women to build up more fat than men, whereas men build muscle through the "male hormone," androgen. When food runs short, the body eats into fat reserves before protein-heavy muscle: the fat, though valuable, is more expendable. Men's bodies, with less fat as a buffer, take more out of muscle, which is heavier, volume for volume, and includes heart muscle. In Santo Tomás, the average weight loss of adult men on 20 January 1945, even after two weeks of post-liberation feeding, was 51 pounds — 30 percent of prewar weight. For women, it was 32 pounds, or 24 percent.[18] But they could suffer too. Sascha Weinzheimer — five feet eight inches tall — was down to seventy-four pounds by the end.

Compared with older adults, young children held up remarkably well. It was, of course, distressing for grownups to deny food to a child who did not fully understand why. Working

"Walking skeletons" is how one of the camp's liberators, Captain Walter Landry, described many of the men, in contrast with most women and children. Malnourished men tend to lose more muscle weight than women, who have more fat reserves (which the body uses up first). And the camp gave more food to children than to adults in relation to their size. The five men in this picture were reportedly photographed twenty days after liberation. Their weight averaged 98 pounds, compared with 152 pounds before internment. From left to right: Hugo Winkler, former proofreader; Tom Loft, accountant; Arthur Williamson, merchant; Harold Leney, accountant; and David Norvell, mining executive *(Carl Mydans/Corbis)*.

as a night nurse in a camp children's ward, Tressa Roka found that most of her little patients were awake by five. "Their first question upon wakening would have wrung the heart of a sadist. 'Is chow ready?' they would ask eagerly. 'Pretty soon. Go back to sleep a little longer,' I coaxed."[19]

Old man in the big gym dorm just after liberation. Name unknown *(Carl Mydans/Getty Images).*

Camp feeding, though, did favor small children. Until nearly the end, those under two got eggs several times a week, and small amounts of Lactogen powdered milk. Those over two got milk until late November 1944, and sometimes bananas. Chow-lines usually served the same amount of food to children as adults, though the Japanese gave only half-rations to the camp for children under 13. This reduced adult rations by 7 percent — a sore point to some bachelors. All ages received the 47-pound Red Cross kits.

In June–July 1944 a survey of internees aged up to nineteen found that those between seven and fifteen were most underweight. As malnutrition increased, some teenagers really suffered. Fifteen-year-old Lydia Macleod felt torments of hunger, yet her stomach had shrunk so much she could not always finish all her chow-line food; she gave it away to a friend or to her father. In general, adolescent revving up of metabolism put more demands on teenagers' systems, so malnutrition could make them feel all the weaker. But their basic vitality saw them through, and for a time teenagers got extra portions. They were also, on the whole, less anxious than adults, and anxiety speeds up the body's demand for energy and nutrients. Sonia Francisco, sixteen, developed beriberi by the end, but it did not hurt much: she just felt she had to push each swollen foot forward when she walked. For Curtis Brooks, a year younger, the main problem was peeing at night, probably due to a kidney ailment. He wanted to go six times a night, bumping into other beds and mosquito nets (not popular) and often not quite getting to the toilet in time.

Malnutrition reduced resistance to familiar diseases and introduced new ones. Tressa

Roka soldiered on as a nurse despite barely recovering from dysentery, a well-known complaint at Santo Tomás. At the same time her feet swelled up with beriberi, more painfully than Sonia Francisco's. Other new diseases included scurvy, pellagra, and sprue (fat deficiency), each caused by lack of specific vitamins and nutrients. The results included numbness, irritating skin sores, blurred vision, loss of memory — and death. "Wet beriberi," the commonest new disease, was ultimately dangerous to the heart. Lack of blood protein, and of thiamine (vitamin B1) needed to activate the protein, caused watery blood plasma to leak out of capillaries — hence the swollen feet, hands, and faces. To make up for loss of plasma, the heart valiantly worked faster, straining heart muscles. 42 percent of deaths in the camp's last four months were due, at least in part, to inflamed heart muscle (myocarditis), though beriberi was not the only cause of that.[20]

The camp's death rate accelerated in October 1944, when seven people died. In December the monthly number doubled to fifteen, and doubled again in January to 32. When a man died, his friends sometimes met for a few, brief prayers, and then his body went out to a mass cemetery in a cart pulled by two Filipino boys. Before January, bodies went in a rickety old carromata but then the burial company's one pony died. The reused caskets were sometimes too short for a tall Westerner, so his feet stuck out of the end.

On 31 January, three days before the camp was liberated, the camp's chief doctor, Ted Stevenson, was jailed by an angry commandant for refusing to take the words "malnutrition" and "starvation" off his death certificates. At a meeting about this, Dr. Nogi, the chief Japanese medical officer for prison camps, said the words "stigmatized" the Japanese for food shortages they could not help; internees were actually fed better than Filipinos outside. The Internee Committee and most of Stevenson's colleagues wanted him to comply with the demand: the camp needed every doctor it could get. But Stevenson, a former medical missionary, resisted. He did so not just on grounds of professional principle, but also to make sure that any death reports reaching the International Red Cross pulled no punches. His colleagues stalled but in the end one of them signed the certificates without the proscribed words. Stevenson went into the jail room.

Specious though Nogi's argument was, he got one thing right: internees were spared the scenes of starvation that existed outside the camp. As early as mid–December, the Filipino lawyer, Marcial Lichauco, described "scores of emaciated corpses" on the streets, lying there until pushcarts could take them away, and worse, "the many old men and young children ... lying around not quite dead yet, but soon to die."[21] The cause was Japanese exploitation and mishandling of agriculture (already described) and the disruption of food transport by guerrilla attacks and air raids.

Hunger in Santo Tomás had big effects on behavior. At one extreme there were people who walked around listlessly, staring at the ground. Some called it "the Santo Tomás stare." I remember seeing people at the dining tables gloomily spooning in their thin midday soup, not lifting their elbow to do so. My intolerant young mind thought them depressing and pathetic. At the other extreme, a few internees went mad. Confined to Santa Catalina Hospital, they disturbed other patients by wild singing, cursing, or both.

For many in between, food fantasies trumped sex. "Where's your blonde?" Tressa Roka asked a well-known Don Juan. "Tess," he said with impish gravity, "if Lana Turner stood before me in her birthday suit, I wouldn't give a damn! Unless she had a ham sandwich in her hand."[22] Instead of gossiping about who was going with who or playing card games, internees became obsessed with recipes, copying them out from old magazines, exchanging them, and arguing about the best way to make a fancy cake. Recipe mania had actually started among women in the camp's early months as an antidote to boredom and a way of looking forward to a better future, but hunger intensified the practice and it spread to men. Bill Bryant's roommates gave him a hard time when his wife Alice delayed giving him a lemon pie recipe. Frank Cary found he was looking for food references in every book he read.

On the children's side, Nick Balfour took out library books on cooking and healthy eating; Tika, his younger sister, read recipe books. At the Boys' Club, Mousey invented a lavish four-decker sandwich, fiercely denying that his big jaws could not open wide enough to fit it in. Old games found new motives. Roy Doolan's father saw a group of his friends, sitting in a circle, each in turn making a weird face to see who would laugh first. When Doolan Senior asked what they were doing, one of them said, "We're saving energy." Children hung about the Japanese offices and kitchen, successfully cadging candy and even cigarettes; some parents were in on it. The commandant put an end to that in early December, but he didn't stop ten-year-old Mike Browning and others from picking up the guards' cigarette butts to collect their tobacco. Mike's mother was a heavy smoker and he learned to roll cigarettes for her in dried hibiscus leaves.

The more desperate adults and children scavenged in Japanese garbage cans; their own cans were much emptier by the end. One mother tied her two-year-old to a rope and lowered him into a can, telling him which scrap to pick up. Mary June was among the children who picked up vegetable peelings at the main cooking shed: "You scraped off the skin and ate a tiny bit of [camote] or whatever." Many adults tried boiling weeds; Anne Balfour produced a watery soup from the pigweed growing around her shanty. One or two internees caught pigeons, and by mid-January all cats had disappeared, often into the pots of known "cat eaters," though cat butchers would do the job for you. The commandant encouraged this. Fay Bailey's family lost their black cat, Uling, on 7 December, Pearl Harbor Day, and the camp's prize Persian vanished at Christmas. Dogs had been banned from the camp, but Phyllis and Jag Hearnden lost their beloved dog, Butchie, outside the camp. A message from their servant, Felipe, explained: "No money, my family so hungry, sorry sorry Mum."[23]

And then there was the private smuggling (as distinct from those who smuggled for the whole camp). Through most of 1944, the crew taking out garbage cans brought in sugar, bacon, coffee, and tobacco, using a false bottom in their pushcarts. They gave a bit of it to the camp hospitals and old men in the gym, but most of it they sold at high prices. They were caught and jailed in October, possibly exposed by an internee who had quarreled with a ringleader, but smuggling continued, often by bribing guards. And like the garbage operation, there were mixed motives. Some, Grace Nash's beer smuggler among them, did it for friends and family. Many of the smugglers, though, like the profiteers who hoarded and sold comfort-kit items, marketed food and tobacco for all they could get, jacking up prices for everyone.

In other ways, the camp's hunger months brought out the worst and the best in people. On the "worst" side of the ledger, stealing was not new to Santo Tomás and thieves were punished when caught: jailed or given extra work. In the camp's second month, thefts of Red Cross tools and lumber delayed the camp building program. But thefts increased with

Liberation did not immediately stop internees from doing camp work. Despite their weakened state, these two men still pushed the garbage cart, though more food meant more garbage. During internment, smugglers used a pushcart with a false bottom to take garbage out of camp and bring in food (*Carl Mydans/Getty Images*).

hunger. On the smallest scale, Mary June and I sneaked a spoonful of "KLIM" now and again from our shanty cupboard when each of us was alone there. Mary June felt guiltier about it than I did.

In retrospect, it is not surprising that inequality combined with hunger would encourage stealing, especially if a person was stealing for his or her family. But it was still a shock when it happened. In late December 1944 a man in the Education Building lost nineteen carefully saved cans from under his bed during a cleanup by internees. And the needy suffered too. A friend of Tressa Roka with two small children, who had sold her diamond watch for some rice, lost it all to a thief.

Theft could lead to fights. Tika Balfour watched a fistfight between a shanty neighbor and a man who had stolen bananas from him. She saw the theft and had to identify the thief to a solemn posse of internee patrolmen. It was all quite stressful for a seven-year-old, and she felt badly about it afterwards, as the thief had a wife and children and his victim was a strange fellow who lived alone and seemed to hoard food just for himself.[24]

Internees stole from the camp as well as from individuals — vegetables from the camp garden, even blood serum (protein-rich) from the hospital. The food service was always a problem. In October 1944 a chow-line ticket puncher was caught conniving with other internees, punching four tickets and calling out "six" to the serving women, so the internees could collect two added meals for their families. In the camp's last two months, several teenage servers were fired for what they called "looting"— sneaking camotes into their pockets. (One or two of them also stole food from other internees if they saw it lying around.) Kitchen workers often demanded extra rations for heavy carrying. When not given extra (the policy changed back and forth), they sometimes took it anyway. To some observers, they always looked better fed. In general, the administration tried to equalize rations, favoring only young children and the sick in hospital. When Fr. David Daly in the gym held back some smuggled beans for his frailest old men, he got into a row with the Internee Committee.

The gym was also the scene of a serious fight on the last Christmas Day, again involving food. The gym's chief of security, Mel Cochran, stopped a man from leaving morning roll call early to rush off to breakfast and got knifed before knocking the offender down with a pole. Cochrane survived but two weeks later a fight over food between two elderly residents left one dead of a heart attack. Anger and resentment seemed to thrive on malnutrition. In late December, when two babies were born in Santa Catalina on the same day as a death, some nurses and nursing aides resented the new arrivals: half-starved themselves, they still had so many patients to care for.

Hostility, stealing, and cheating make better copy than quiet unselfishness, but the camp had plenty of that too. Jean Weinzheimer's father was not the only one to "give us kids a spoonful from his plate." Mothers did it as well, but camp nurses believed it was more often the fathers; chivalry was not dead.[25]

Children also gave. After Grace Nash's family moved to Los Baños in 1944, her two older boys, Stan and Gale, aged four and three, would transfer butter beans onto the plate of one-year-old Roy. They all loved the beans, but Stan and Gale could not bear to hear Roy's cries for more; he always finished first. Back in Santo Tomás, Robin Prising shared pieces of comfort-kit chocolate with a solitary older boy who had no family in the camp: "no mother to cook him wild colitis and pigweed stew," as his own did.[26]

Adults also gave to friends as well as family. Several old and frail people became frequent lunch time visitors to the Lautzenhisers' shanty. They got a share of the vegetables grown by Roscoe and Mamie Lautzenhiser on their many plots. More urgently, Anne Balfour pitched in for a young mother, Iris Castleton, with two small boys when they all went into the hospital with stomach ailments. Anne did not know Castleton well but felt upset at her plight: "complete breakdown of her intestines due to lack of food," Anne wrote in her diary. She helped tidy up the Castleton shanty, sent clothes, books, and toys to the family, and deputed Tika to help take care of the boys when they came out of the hospital ahead of their mother.[27]

Despite her own hunger, Anne Balfour saved up enough from the extras she brought into camp in June 1944 to make cakes and good dishes on special occasions. On the camp's last Christmas, Mary June and I received pieces of Balfour Christmas cake; so did Iris Castleton and others in the hospital. They included Bertram Leake, the revered director of the Boys' Club, who had come down with TB. Several of us in the Boys' Club took him small gifts of food from our families. As we came into the ward we saw his familiar white hair and his strong, good face, now hollowed and grey. I can still hear his croaky "thanks a million" as I left his bedside. He died on 7 February, four days after liberation.

Another victim of TB, Walter Stevenson, got help from Charles Van Sickle, the International Harvester executive, and his wife Emily. Having previously bought and saved extra food, they gave Stevenson a few cans of meat, and Charles guaranteed a loan procuring him extra rice and beans from a smuggler; he did the same for two others. The couple refused to buy smuggled food for themselves, as they felt it wrong to make food still scarcer when others needed it more desperately.

Unlike the Van Sickles, who had no child in the camp, the banker and camp treasurer, Fay Bailey, with a wife and young daughter, continued to buy extra food at exorbitant prices, but he did so with qualms, as already mentioned. His camp diary, too, showed how worsening conditions could widen a person's view of what mattered. From the camp's early days he worked hard for it — first as financial "disbursing officer" — but he initially wrote more of private consumption than of public logistics. His camp job got much briefer mention than the stuff he obtained via his servants at the gate or on camp business trips outside, sometimes lunching with Red Cross officials. Steaks, roast chicken, "a perfect lemon pie," vitamins, new shoes for his daughter Caroline — all were recorded so meticulously as to suggest anxiety that it wouldn't last.

Bailey was never without conscience. He lent money to the camp budget and gave the camp all the milk in his allocation from an early Red Cross shipment. He felt sorry for those who had to scrimp on chow-line food alone, and he criticized some friends who, in his view, expected too much from their servants. But the big shift occurred when the package line closed and the camp's food supply started to dive in 1944. His diary then became much more public spirited, more devoted to problems of supplying the camp. Growing threat changed priorities.[28]

10

Threat vs. Hope

Heretofore, internees seemed quiet and orderly, avoiding only the end of the war. With the changed war situation, some now harbor delusions that the turning point of the war is nearing, and mistakenly believe that the Americans will soon land in the Philippines....

When the internees are superficially quiet and orderly, and when duties are long term with few changes, there is a tendency for military discipline and morale to become lax. The utmost effort has been exerted to correct such a tendency. All personnel were made to realize the importance of the situation and of their individual responsibilities. Strict discipline was enforced and supervision was so conducted as to frighten internees into submission and silence.[1]

These comments appeared in June 1944, in a report by the Japanese Army's War-Prisoners Headquarters, Manila, on three camps (including Santo Tomás). The tough talk was clearly aimed at allaying army fears of unruly prisoners. Some of its claims were nonsense. It was obvious that the war had indeed turned and American forces were coming back. The report seems to deny this but it also refers to a "changed war situation." Though U.S. troops would not land in the Philippines for another four months, the Japanese command had already anticipated air raids by trying out its air-raid sirens and imposing practice blackouts. (As blackouts became more common, they hurt camp conviviality by making it harder to sit out in the evening and play card games.)

In May, the army had begun building sentry towers, intended to monitor for (and shoot) escapers as well as "guerrillas and enemy soldiers." Three months later, Santo Tomás guards started a defense training program and dug air-raid shelters for the garrison. They got flooded by rainwater, to the amusement of internees. Less funny was the foxhole dug by a guard smack in the middle of Elizabeth Vaughan's small garden plot. The turned-over soil made it easier to dig there and it wrecked Vaughan's nascent crop of onions, corn, and peanut vines. She protested via the Internee Committee and the foxhole was abandoned, but the damage was done.

Vaughan showed that internees were not "frightened into submission and silence." Still, the impending return of American forces, which brought hope for internees via secret radios and smuggled news, also spelled threat as the Japanese cracked down in response: hence the string of impositions already mentioned, from inspections and police raids to rehearsals in bowing.

132

In December 1944, another report from the War-Prisoner Headquarters declared that the camp garrison's "morale and discipline [had] become lax through unnecessary contact with internees." It said that three guards had been put into "solitary confinement" for smuggling to internees; Carroll Grinnell and three other internees had been arrested for suspected "connections with enemy intelligence and espionage" (see Chapter 7); and First Lieutenant Abiko and a sergeant had attended a course at headquarters for "close-quarters combat." All these items were connected. Maintaining control over the big Santo Tomás population required "discipline" among the guards, most of whom were not now regular soldiers but quasi-military workers; internee interpreter Frank Cary described them as "inferior troops, Formosan [Taiwanese] boys with little or no traditions as fighters."[2] At stake, as the Japanese saw it, was not just the morale and authority of the garrison but also its safety from attack by American forces aided by guerrillas and their contacts with internee leaders like Grinnell.

In September 1944, Tokyo's Army Ministry had issued guidelines for local commanders and commandants on what to do if a camp faced imminent attack. The guidelines were mainly concerned with military POW camps but included civilian ones. They gave local commanders, and maybe commandants beneath them, some options that were not wholly consistent. Commanders, ideally, should prevent prisoners from falling into Allied hands — if necessary, by moving them elsewhere. Alternatively, they might release them. If, however, the prisoners endangered the garrison, they could be neutralized, either by tying up or killing key prisoners or by killing them all and leaving no trace. It should also be done in such a way as not to benefit enemy propaganda or give an excuse for revenge!

The Tokyo guidelines did not rule out the idea of protecting prisoners from air raids. In August and September, before the first raid seen by Santo Tomás internees, Lieutenant Abiko and other Japanese advised internees to dig their own shelters; one or two shanty districts did. Internee leaders thought buildings safer, and so, indeed, did the Japanese running POW camps in Taiwan.[3] But there was always the possibility that a local commander might exaggerate the threat from their half-starved internees and order a massacre, due to panic, malice, or a wish to get prisoners out of the way in a final fight. This happened at Palawan island on 14 December. Mistakenly believing that the nearby American fleet was about to land troops, the island's commanding general had the POWs in Puerto Princesa Camp herded into covered air-raid trenches, which were doused with gasoline and set alight. Most of the prisoners were burned alive or sadistically killed trying to escape. A few miraculously did escape to the guerrillas.

We do not know if internee leaders at Santo Tomás learned of this. But some internees feared a massacre in reprisal at the end. Others wondered if all food would be stopped, starving everyone to death. On New Year's Day 1945, a carousing Japanese officer reportedly said that the internees would never be a threat: "an extremely restricted diet and disease would take care of the situation in due course."[4] The alleged remark got some mileage among internees and it sounded ominous. Did it signal deliberate starvation? Or did it merely mean that physical weakness was making the internees less dangerous? No one knew.

Through much of 1944, Japanese measures to "secure" the camp led to conflicts with internee leaders. Commandants tried to make internees do work that benefited the garrison's defense and welfare, though it was officially agreed that work should be "in the interests of employees." Some battles the Internee Committee won. Orders to build a rifle rack and guardroom floor were rescinded, and a plan to have internees construct the new sentry towers was not pressed. Both sides wanted a new internee-dug drainage ditch for the camp garden, but Carroll Grinnell derailed a Japanese proposal that would have made it into a bigger moat, presumably to obstruct invasion. He got Commandant Yoshie to accept the smaller dimensions without mentioning purposes.

On other construction issues, internees could do no more than modify the demands, if that. When they did, reluctantly, build patrol walkways and pens for the garrison's livestock, they only stopped abusive supervision by officers and guards when some of the workforce went on strike. Under formal protest, internees acceded to demands to build sawali fences, preventing them from seeing their non-interned families at Sunday worship in the seminary.

On several occasions, camp leaders cited the 1929 Geneva Convention, which banned military work by POWs. Maybe this inhibited commandants' demands but the appeal to Geneva was never accepted explicitly. Japan's agreement to abide by Geneva for all war prisoners if the Allies did the same came through the Ministry of Foreign Affairs. It found no favor with the Army Ministry, which could fall back on the fact, if needed, that Japan had not ratified Geneva.[5] Appeals to Geneva also failed when the camp Agents complained and inquired about the police arrest and abuse of the five internees accused of bringing in transcripts of war news (see Chapter 7). What happened to them was only discovered after liberation. The eldest, Everett Harris, died in Manila's Bilibid Prison. The others were transferred to Muntinlupa Prison outside Manila. On 3 February 1945, the day of Santo Tomás's liberation, the guards started shooting groups of prisoners until delayed overnight by Filipino office workers who deliberately mixed up the records. The next morning the guards fled as U.S. forces approached. Guerrillas rescued the survivors, including the Santo Tomás four.

In the meantime, the Japanese authorities removed a thorn in their sides by banishing Clyde DeWitt, one of the three internee Agents, to Los Baños. Seven volunteers for transfer had been allowed to go in October, as they had relatives in Los Baños, but DeWitt (who had no interned family) was told he had to go too. The Internee Committee, backed by the Agents and Council of Monitors, asked Commandant Hayashi to reconsider. Hayashi at first seemed favorable but later said that the War-Prisoners Headquarters was adamant. Was this true? "Maybe, maybe not" (my own favorite phrase of the time amid the camp's uncertainties). What we do know is that DeWitt had been an outspoken critic of the regime, internee as well as Japanese; as a lawyer, he had made much of international law on the treatment of prisoners.

Against these threats on the ground, hope came from the air. 21 September 1944 was the first day the camp saw American planes come back — and how. From morn to eve, intermittent waves of carrier-borne dive bombers and fighters passed over on their way to hit the docks across the river from Santo Tomás and airfields north and south of the city. They came in different formations and patterns, punctuated by bomb explosions, the rattle of machine guns as they strafed as well as bombed their targets, and the answering bangs from anti-aircraft guns.

The camp went wild. People tumbled outside, cheering, waving, and hugging each other, until commanded to get indoors by guards and the public-address system. In the Annex, Elizabeth Vaughan's two children, Beth and Clay, happily asked for and got a lollipop each; they knew she had saved them for "the first air raid when the Americans come." Even a Japanese soldier joined in. When the raids started, Internee Committee members Carroll Grinnell and Sam Lloyd were meeting with Japanese officers. One of them, Lieutenant Komatsu, rushed out several times to see the spectacle and then played the sportsman: "Good bombing. Very daring. Excellent." Lieutenant Abiko simply paced the floor and then told the internees to get out.[6]

The planes came back the next day and then didn't return for three weeks, despite air-raid warnings that made the planes' absence all the more frustrating. When they did come back, at different intervals, they often arrived before the sirens went off. The internees who ran the camp's own sirens usually heard and saw them coming but had to wait until the city's less efficient Japanese-run sirens went off, to "save face" for the Japanese. Internees were told not to look at the planes, either outside or from windows. Violators were taken to the front-gate guardhouse and made to stand all day without moving, looking upward in the blazing heat. Teenager Curtis Brooks got off lightly, though it did not feel like it. Caught looking at an air raid from the Education Building's top-floor corridor, he found himself on the end of a guard's rifle, harangued ferociously before the guard "quit and went off. I spent a subdued afternoon."

The guards, though, could not stop people looking, often creeping under windows to peep out. The spectacle seemed worth the risk. For Nick Balfour, the dive bombers, peeling off one by one over the docks, were "like a ballet." He was also struck by the beauty of some fighters' "gull-wings," with an elegant dip at the fuselage. (They were "bent-wing" Corsairs, the U.S. Navy's fastest planes.) Curt Brooks also described a choreography of sight and sound: the first shimmer of an approaching formation; AA guns booming and puffs of flak; dive bombers "spilling down like birds of prey"; white streamers and a "ripping roar" from their machine guns, and then small black dots falling away from the planes as each released a bomb, making a "spear of spray and debris."[7] Spectators also saw planes shot down, mainly Japanese ones until they entirely disappeared quite early in the raids. Occasionally the flak got an American plane. A gasp would go up around the room or shanty as it burst into flames or lost a wing. Everyone looked for parachutes; they usually appeared but no one knew, of course, what would become of the fliers.

The camp took its own hits. Early in the raids, gas and electricity went off, causing a rush for the faucets as people feared the water would go off too, as it sometimes did. From 25 September to 3 October, the Main Building's central kitchen served no lunch, though it continued for children and the sick at the Annex and camp hospitals. Anti-aircraft shell fragments went though a window and a few shanty roofs; a woman got a scratched face, and a man a gashed arm. In the first big air raid, Geege Wootten and her friends put buckets on their heads, and when the action seemed particularly close, some internees — especially children — dived under beds. (That was when Nick Balfour learned the "facts of life" from Mousey as they lay chattering on the floor during a raid.) A petrified Curt Brooks shot under his bed when AA shells seemed to be coming right at the Education Building.

In late December, land-based planes appeared: fleets of four-engine B24 Liberators (what else could the makers call them?) and, weaving above them, twin-engine P38 Lightning heavy fighters. For a thrilled, fourteen-year-old Peter Wygle, they were the best Christmas present: it meant our side didn't just have carriers but also "real estate" near enough for launching land planes.[8] For me, the P38s brought a special thrill. I was too short-sighted to see American planes until two P38s came over low, their unusual "twin-boom" (catamaran) shapes scudding silver across the blue sky. The arrival of heavy bombers meant bigger explosions, sending waves of air across the camp. Concerned about "concussed" ear drums, adults told children to open their mouths during air raids (I still do it if I hear a sudden big noise). My mother, among others, had us put pencils in our mouths to keep them open. Other, smaller children already wore little "bombsticks" on strings around their necks, to pop them in when planes appeared. The raids produced a new hobby for us children: finding shell fragments and digging out machine-gun bullets, which we then traded like marbles.

On Christmas morning, internees found scattered leaflets that read, "The Commander-in-Chief, the officers, and the men of the American Forces of Liberation in the Pacific wish their gallant allies, the People of the Philippines, all the blessings of Christmas, and the realization of their fervent hopes for the New Year, Christmas 1944."[9] The grand prose was vintage MacArthur. During the night, two weeks before landing on Luzon, he had sent his planes to leaflet Manila. The leaflets gave the camp a fillip but they could not allay disappointment. Many internees had hoped that the previous December's food kits would be repeated, perhaps even on Christmas Day. But no. In the meantime, they tried to keep up the civility of giving their own Christmas presents. Robin Prising's mother, Marie, gave his ailing father, Frederick, six handkerchiefs embroidered from an old bedsheet. Frederick gave his son a toothbrush and some used pencils, and Robin had made him shoelaces from twine blackened with crayon. I gave my mother what I called "a crude cross," two whittled pieces of wood tacked together, but on 15 January, my mother's birthday, I was so hard put to think of anything that I just wrote her a very tidy note: "Dear Mummy, My gift to you is that I will do any errand you ask without grumbling for at least a week. From your loving son, Rupert." Mary June derided it, as an older sister would, but my mother kept it all her life.

While the planes came and went, camp life struggled on and the Japanese tightened their grip. Revised regulations, issued six days after the first air raid, added to the items that internees could not have or use without permission. They included chemicals, electrical appliances, printing equipment, "communication apparatus of any kind," and maps or pictures "detrimental to military operations." Internees could not "assemble in groups" or "execute any new undertaking" unless authorized. In the camp schools, teachers must not criticize the "camp administration" or teach "subjects unfavorable to the Imperial Japanese Army." Two months later, the commandant required camp libraries to turn in lists of all their books, so they could get his *chop* (signed seal of approval). Many of the regulations were simply concerned with camp order and public health, but fear of subversion, even revolt, was palpable.[10]

In early October, the army started using the camp as a military dump, just as the U.S./Philippine army had used it as a motor pool before leaving the city. An army labor unit — some in civilian clothes — took over a big area in the front part of the camp. Trucks were parked, tents set up, and the ground covered with crates of machinery and materials such as rubber. Commandant Hayashi announced that soldiers would sleep at night in the West Pavilion, one of two long sawali huts used for teaching and church services.

The Internee Committee, backed by the internee Agents, protested. The incursion, they said, looked like the use of "non-combatants ... to give protection against bombardment," and it endangered the camp. The soldiers had also taken internee equipment and strayed beyond their designated area, causing "sanitary problems" (translation: urinating and making a mess). Hayashi replied that he would order the soldiers not to take internee property and would stay in a "woodshed portion" of the West Pavilion. He bristled, though, at the idea that internees were being used as a human shield: it was an "insult to the Japanese Imperial Army." All of the Philippines was a war zone, he said, adding the curious claim that Santo Tomás had never been reported to the United States as an internment camp. The trucks and tents soon went, but more stores came in during November — another cause for complaint, as gasoline drums were put dangerously close to Santa Catalina Hospital and soldiers bringing in the stores sometimes stole from the camp garden. (The gas drums were taken away in early January.)[11]

5 December 1944 brought a different kind of incursion, perhaps the most extraordinary event in the camp's history. Reginald Spear, a U.S. Navy frogman, got into the camp, met with internee leaders, and left the same day. His mission was to tell them about the Tokyo guidelines for disposing of POWs if Allied troops approached, including the options of killing or moving them. U.S. intelligence seems to have picked up the guidelines from a code-breaking radio intercept or a captured Japanese submarine. Spear was also to find out what the Internee Committee thought about the camp's future and discuss different rescue scenarios with them, including arrangements for protecting the camp if it were caught up in fighting.

Spear's mission came from the top — President Franklin Roosevelt. FDR knew it would be a political disaster as well as a human tragedy if U.S. troops triumphantly recaptured Manila only to lose thousands of Allied internees to a massacre. There was also a fear that the Japanese might try to ship internees to Japan or Korea to conceal their bad condition — a terrible prospect, as the U.S. Navy had inadvertently sunk unmarked Japanese prison ships, and the ships themselves were a living hell. The Japanese had infiltrated some guerrilla groups in Manila — hence the idea of sending in a new agent who, if caught, could only implicate a few others who had helped him.

Reg Spear was only twenty years old but tough and resourceful. He was known to Roosevelt from other missions and just possibly because an aunt, Mary Ellen Smith, had been a prominent politician and reformer in British Columbia. Though seconded to the U.S. Navy, Spear worked for OSS (Office of Strategic Services, predecessor of the CIA). According to Spear, he secretly met with Roosevelt, whose Maryland mountain hideaway, "Shangri-La" (now Camp David), was near an OSS training base.

Spear's handler was Gerald Wilkinson — my father. Now head of British East Asian intelligence, working with OSS director William ("Wild Bill") Donovan in New York, my father produced Spear's cover story. He would be one of the Canadian engineers exempted from internment to work at the Benguet gold mines near Baguio, about 160 miles from Manila. Benguet had chronic flooding problems and Spear would appear at the camp with written authority to confer about this with internee Alfred Duggleby, former chief engineer at Benguet. The plan counted on minimum phone contact between Benguet and Santo Tomás.

A secret U.S. outfit specializing in forgeries and counterfeit gear kitted out Spear with

Japanese papers and the red armband given to Allied nationals with passes to be outside the camp. During a reconnaissance mission in Indonesia, Spear met navy Lieutenant Commander "Chick" Parsons, who briefed him on the camp's layout and location. Before the war Parsons had been boss of Luzon Stevedoring (cargo handling and tugboats) and a navy reserve officer. Interned in Santo Tomás, he got a diplomatic release to the United States because he had also been Manila's consul general for Panama! Soon he was back, moving by submarine in and out of the Philippines, liaising between guerrillas and MacArthur. He once walked down a Manila street dressed as a Catholic priest, but he was now too well known and too busy to do Spear's job.

Spear entered northern Luzon via one of the submarines operated by the U.S. Navy but lent to MacArthur for special missions. He paddled ashore on an inflatable raft with a seersucker suit in a waterproof bag, to wear for entering Santo Tomás. Filipino and American guerrillas sheltered him overnight and early the next morning they drove him to Tarlac, seventy miles north of Manila, where they put him on a small train with a guerrilla escort. His companion was a woman with a baby—and a revolver under her bag of diapers. In Manila, a guerrilla drove Spear to the camp in a stolen Japanese vehicle. At the gate was a solitary guard, who seemed less interested in Spear's papers than his bag containing twelve packs of cigarettes. The guard took all twelve but gave two back when Spear had the nerve to object.

At the Main Building, an internee sitting just inside the entrance (a "building patrol" official) told him where to find Internee Committee members. As Spear walked off, sixteen-year-old Edward McCreary asked the official who the strange man in the tan suit was. The answer was pure guess and dead right: "He's gotta be a spy."

The Internee Committee had been tipped off about Spear's mission. Even so, when he met the camp leaders, including Benguet's Duggleby, they grilled him in case he was a Japanese plant. Spear blew up: "I've been through hell to get here and probably have worse to get out." Earl Carroll, true to character, calmed everyone down: "Let's hear what the man has to say." Spear gave them his intelligence information and asked for their views. Their main fear, he found, was being starved to death. They discussed an idea for dropping food and medicine if the camp became trapped between opposing armies; an arms drop was out of the question, as the internees were too weak to fight. (In fact, the camp had a secret cache of rifles and ammunition, taken from the university's cadet force armory, and had set up a covert force for handling "emergencies," but that was before malnutrition took its toll.[12])

Before leaving the camp, Spear had a private commission to execute for Gerald Wilkinson: he was to make brief contact with my mother. The committee resisted at first, fearing it would endanger her, but Spear persuaded them to bring her to a convenient spot in the Main Building. As he walked past her, he murmured something like "Hang on. Gerald sent me." He said she was too startled to make much response.

Walking out of the camp, Spear was alarmed to realize he had overstayed the deadline for his driver. He had no problem at the gate and mercifully the driver was still there, bravely waiting amid mounting panic; he had to be restrained from doing a U-turn and racing off at a suspiciously high speed. He drove Spear back to the mountain guerrillas, who hiked him up a trail to their redoubt, "Victory Hill." There Spear used a safe radio to report to MacArthur's staff and others. Later the guerrillas took Spear away in a Japanese-style truck, cutting phone wires as they went, to rendezvous with a submarine.[13]

A month after Spear's mission, the camp garrison belied the fear that inspired it. For several days starting 6 January, a bustle of activity suggested the garrison was about to leave. Phones constantly rang in the commandant's Education Building offices, and his car (a Cadillac!) repeatedly drove in and out of the camp. Commandant Hayashi demanded to see all Internee Committee documents, and mounds of Japanese papers went into two big bonfires. Four trucks took out assorted Japanese supplies, from sacks of rice to bales of wire, and some soldiers left on bicycles with boxes on their backs.

On the second day, Hayashi summoned the two Internee Committee men, Earl Carroll and Sam Lloyd, and interpreters Frank Cary and Ernest Stanley, to meet with him and other officers. He was friendly, offering them rum from bottles laid out on a table. He told them he was now in charge of all Philippine camps, as the camps chief, General Koh, had left. He said he had originally planned to stay in the camp and fight to the last: the Japanese had a different war spirit from that of Americans and believed in total sacrifice for country and emperor. However, to spare the camp's women and children from bloodshed, the garrison would leave the camp sometime that day, to fight in the hills. The Internee Committee would be in charge "until my return or the arrival of the Americans." Despite the scarcity of food in the city, and its huge prices, he would leave behind enough food to feed the camp for fifteen days — or a month "with economy." Internees would be safe if they stayed in the camp and did not provoke the army, though he could understand that they would want to see their Filipino families outside.

After talking about the handover, the internee group was lent Lieutenant Abiko's office. Lunch was brought in to them, and they spoke with several civilian officials, one of them Shizua Ohashi. At their suggestion, Carroll and Lloyd proposed to Hayashi that that his four civilian officers stay in the camp to help with inevitable feeding problems and relations with the army. Hayashi saw the point but said no; he was sure the civilians would want to join him in fighting for the emperor. (They did not.) Shortly afterward, Hayashi appeared to get a message from outside. The garrison's departure was to be postponed, he said. The internees could leave but they must say nothing about the meeting.

The following day, 8 January, more of the garrison left (it had expanded in the previous few months). On the morning of the 9th, though, Hayashi confirmed they would not be leaving. He explained on the camp loudspeakers that he had wanted to leave to save the camp bloodshed but the "condition [for it had] not yet arisen." His main concern now was to find food for the camp, having already had two of the garrison's cattle slaughtered for the camp. He again urged internees to "keep the gardens going at full capacity," but departing soldiers did not cooperate. They stole bananas and papayas, mainly destined for the hospitals and children's Annex, and they took the best gardening implements too.[14]

We don't know exactly what was going on behind the scenes to cause this seesawing between departing and staying, but it echoed disagreement among the top brass. General Tomoyuki Yamashita ("Tiger of Malaya"), the Philippine army's commander, wanted to pull out of Manila and fight in the hills, as Colonel Hayashi envisaged doing. In December and January Yamashita moved his main force out of the city. But the Philippines' top admiral, Denshichi Okochi, and his subordinate, Rear Admiral Sanji Iwabuchi, were determined to fight it out in Manila, using shipboard personnel. Retreat and hill fighting were not their scene. They set up a "Manila Naval Defense Force" and other units. Yamashita felt obliged to leave some army troops behind to help them.[15]

For the next few days, there were more signs of the Santo Tomás garrison packing up to leave, but nothing came of it. Internees' disappointment was offset by news that the Americans had landed on Luzon, at Lingayen Gulf north of the city. In the early morning of 10 January, some shanty people found leaflets dropped during the night, with pictures of MacArthur and a proud announcement to the Philippine people: "MacArthur has returned. General MacArthur keeps his pledges." It clearly referred to a less happy day in March 1942 at a small railway township in Australia, when MacArthur, forced out of the Philippines, made his famous promise, "I shall return."

Internees had other ways, too, of learning about the American landing and advance toward the city, though much of the news was garbled; rumors flew about as to what town they had reached when. Secret camp radios were powerful enough to pick up even the BBC broadcasts. And at local Manila radio news times, Filipinos living near the wall turned their radios up to full volume, different houses taking it in turns to do so. The news of fighting they relayed was Japanese controlled but internees could guess roughly where the U.S. Army had got to.

The day after MacArthur's leaflet appeared, two planes flew so low over the camp that people in the chow-line could see the pilots waving. Everyone broke into cheers. It was exhilarating, but also frustrating: the rescuers were so near, yet so far. As Alex de Tocqeville had said about the French Revolution, a burden becomes more intolerable when the opportunity to remove it is at hand. And hunger and fear about how it all would end — half-suppressed though that fear might be — strained many nerves. As Emily Van Sickle put it, "In the close quarters of shanty areas, one could not avoid hearing words that never should have been spoken: a mother berating her children for wetting the bed; a husband cursing his wife for eating an extra spoonful of rice; a wife swearing at her husband because she was pregnant." Van Sickle also recognized people who quietly got on with it, stayed of good cheer, and worked away at camp jobs even when ailing and weak.[16] Some drew strength from religion. Mary June, remembering her Sunday school teachers' love in the first months, had a "a feeling of God and trusting in God ... not that he's going to make everything all right but he's there, and if we die, not to be afraid of it, because he'll be there." Meanwhile, she would wake each morning and rejoice to be alive. Geege Wootten, whose faith was less certain, still hoped for the "greater joy" of an afterlife, as taught by her church. She also hoped death would be quick if it came. "In the meantime, I concentrated on being alive and observing every moment."[17]

But warfare itself brought comfort. In late January, as the noise of gunfire grew louder and nearer, it was joined by the sound of explosions: the Japanese were clearly blowing up dumps and installations. Could it mean they planned to leave? Now, more than ever, optimists predicted imminent liberation. Others refused to, not wishing to be disappointed. Both moods flourished in the Balfour-Esmérian shanty. Though Anne Balfour had often felt more despondent than she showed, her diary for 30 January named the most likely date of rescue as 3 February — and got it right. Paul Esmérian would have none of such prophesying.

For two days from the evening of 31 January, the garrison again seemed to be leaving the camp — this time without notice. Documents were burned; about twenty soldiers left; trucks took out supplies, including food and cooking equipment. Some of the internees' own rice stocks went, and as they had done a month before, departing soldiers swiped fruits

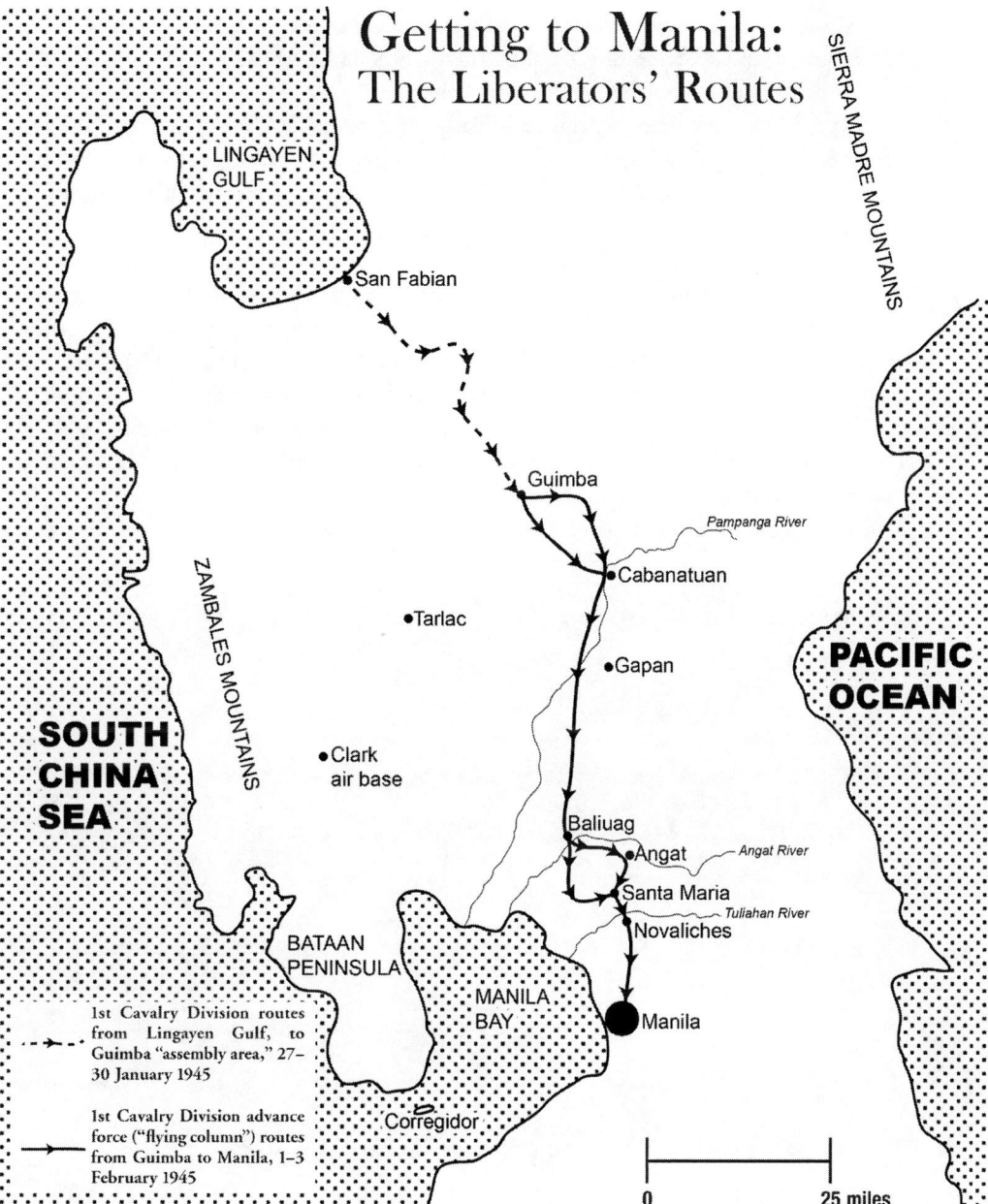

The "flying column" was really two columns, each built around a squadron (small battalion), respectively of the 5th and 8th Cavalry Regiments. They sometimes diverged, the 5th to the east, the 8th to the west. The 8th got to Santo Tomás first. The map does not show a third, reconnaissance column that reached Manila a day later. Coast and rivers simplified. ***Map by Rupert Wilkinson and Steve Tam.***

and vegetables, such they were, from the internee camp garden. The garrison butchered its two biggest hogs and two carabaos. Slaughtering the first carabao was horrible. Refusing to use bullets, the Japanese made internee kitchen staff hit it with a hammer, and when that failed, they used a sledgehammer. Guards took its meat, then let a crowd of waiting internees, including children, rush in with cans to scoop up what was left: offal, ears, hooves. A day later the Japanese killed the second carabao themselves and gave its ninety kilos of meat and bone — mostly bone — to the internee kitchens.[18]

Saturday, 3 February, started bright and early. At 4 A.M. A.V.H. recorded a great "fireworks display" to the south, as green tracer bullets exploded. They were followed by a huge roar. Hartendorp guessed that Fort McKinley military base had blown up its munitions dump. Through the day there were more explosions, the sounds of bombing to the south, gunfire from the north, and smoke from fires all over the city.

At about 5 P.M., a group of dive bombers flew low over the camp. An object fell out of one and landed on a Main Building patio. It was a pair of goggles with a note attached, "Roll out the barrel. Santa Claus is coming Sunday or Monday." (The rear-seat gunner: who dropped it turned out later to be the brother of an interned priest, Fr. Frank McSorley.) The news spread like lightning. At roll call shortly afterward, Cecily Mattocks, aged 13, found everyone in her line quite disorderly, chattering with excitement, and the Japanese guard taking the roll didn't seem to mind.[19]

Deliberately or not, the goggles dropper got the day wrong. Santa Claus came that evening.

11

"They're Here!"

The first internees to hear their liberators coming were shanty folk near the back of the camp. In fact, they *felt* them as much as heard them. A droning sound, like planes in the distance, was followed by the ground shaking. Some thought it was an earthquake before they realized it was tanks. Near the front of the camp, nineteen-year-old Roger Schade thought it was Japanese tanks — until he heard voices speaking English.

Up on the Education Building's top floor, several of us had brought chow-line supper into the Boys' Club, competing to see who could finish last; our mature wisdom decreed that slow eating was more filling. Beyond the camp the gunfire seemed louder than usual. We wondered if this would be the night, but I tried not to hope too much in case of disappointment. Suddenly we heard a burst of cheering. We rushed to the window and saw the other windows lined with men shouting, "THEY'RE HERE!" Looking down toward the main gate, we could see dark hulks with lights creeping up the main drive in the darkness. A flare went up, the best firework I've ever seen, briefly turning night to day and showing up the tanks.

We could not rush to greet them: it was past curfew and the Japanese garrison occupied the floors below us. Not so for Mary June and my mother across in the Main Building. In their dorm room on the east side, second floor, Mary June faintly heard people shouting down below, "They're here, they're here." "Mum, Mum, they're here!" said Mary June. "Oh, they're just shouting," said my mother, loathe to be taken in by one more rumor. But as others made for the door, she gave in. Halfway down the wide stairs they got a prime view. A crowd was milling about in the lobby. Beyond them, through the opened main door, they saw the long gun of a tank. And then everyone burst out singing "God Bless America." At that moment everybody was American.[1]

The camp's rescuers who arrived that night — GIs with tanks, trucks and jeeps — had been driving and fighting for three days. But their mission really started several weeks before in stiff words between two generals. Douglas MacArthur, the Americans' overall Philippine commander, wanted a fast thrust to Manila; he set no formal deadline but wanted to be there for his birthday, 26 January. Lieutenant General Walter Krueger, commanding the 6th Army and charged with taking northern Luzon, wanted a slower advance toward the city. At first he got his way, but at the end of January he had to accept an advance, "flying-column" mission into the city to liberate Santo Tomás and capture key government buildings.

From Lingayen Gulf, where the 6th Army landed on 9 January, Luzon's Central Plain stretched 115 miles south to Manila. On the left — east and northeast — were mountain ranges where General Yamashita was concentrating most of his forces and had now set up his headquarters. Krueger sent well over half his army into these mountain strongholds, where it got into ferocious fighting. He did this largely to protect the left (eastern) flank of a drive to Manila. Unlike MacArthur, Krueger believed that Yamashita might swoop down from the hills and cut off a force advancing on Manila unless it was defended with more troops than MacArthur had given him.[2]

Krueger was not timid. He had landed his army on a treacherous part of the Lingayen beaches, fooling the Japanese as to where he would come ashore. And on 30 January, he authorized a daring heist of the POWs at Pangatian Camp, Cabanatuan, 75 miles north of Manila and still in Japanese territory. The guerrillas and special forces who did this included "Alamo Scouts," created by Krueger two years earlier for behind-the-lines missions. But Krueger also took close interest in his soldiers' welfare. He wanted to keep down casualties by advancing cautiously.

In late January, two of Krueger's divisions captured the big Clark Field airbase 70 miles northwest of Manila. It took them ten days to do it, using flamethrowers to kill the Japanese in a complex of caves and tunnels. On 31 January, one of the divisions, the 37th Infantry, got the green light to advance on Manila. The army's corps commander for the area expected the 37th to be the first into Manila, but it was held up by demolished river bridges and Japanese strong points.

General MacArthur, meanwhile, had been dashing around by jeep and light plane, prodding everyone to move faster. On 30 January, mindful of the Palawan massacre, and warned by guerrillas that the same might happen in Manila, he went all out for a Santo Tomás rescue. He drove into Guimba, 25 miles south of the Lingayen landing spot. Here the 1st Cavalry Division had just arrived from fighting in Leyte. Meeting 1st Cavalry commander Major General Verne Mudge, he gave him an order, much quoted since: "Go to Manila. Go round the Nips, bounce off the Nips, but go to Manila. Free the internees at Santo Tomás. Take Malacañan Palace [government executive headquarters] and the Legislative Building." The cavalry reached the first two objectives in three days but U.S. forces did not get to the Legislative Building, across the Pasig River from Santo Tomás, until a month later; by then shellfire had flattened it.[3]

The 1st Cavalry had a proud tradition of riding horses. Through the 1930s it had partially mechanized into trucks and scout cars, but its horses were still thought useful in difficult terrain. They were not given up until 1943, when the call came to board ship for the Pacific. 1st Cavalrymen called themselves "troopers," not infantrymen, but until they reached Luzon, they struggled through jungles like any other foot soldiers. They retained, though, a liking for fast encircling movement and this was recognized. For their Manila mission, they temporarily reverted to trucks and jeeps, some with mounted machine guns. They were supported by a Sherman tank unit, the 44th Tank Battalion. (Some of the foot-slogging 37th Infantry, disappointed at not getting to Manila first, resented the wheeled advantages of the 1st Cavalry troopers; they called them "feather merchants," an old army term for big mouths who got easy jobs.)

Within 36 hours of MacArthur's "go to Manila" command, General Mudge had put together the "flying column."[4] It was really two columns, plus a third, smaller reconnaissance group that ran into heavy Japanese fire, lost its commander (tank colonel Tom Ross), and reached Manila a day after the others. The two main columns, numbering about 1,900 men, were pretty much cross-sections of the whole division, except they got more vehicles. The nucleus of each was a squadron — a small version of an infantry battalion — from the 5th and 8th Cavalry regiments. Added to each squadron were three tank platoons, totaling sixteen Sherman tanks; medical units in jeeps and ambulance trucks, plus a mobile hospital; wheeled field artillery; and engineers. The field guns were seldom used until they were set up to defend Santo Tomás, but some of them left earlier than the main force to guard a river crossing. The engineers' box of tricks included "dozers" (bulldozers), some of them carried on truck trailers, which could be brought forward to clear roadblocks, fill craters, and grade riverbanks to make fords. The tanks relied on tanker trucks to refuel, but other vehicles carried their own reserve gas cans, and everyone had K-rations ("combat" meal packages) for three days. Some hastily collected Filipino guides were also attached; others were found later.

The two columns had a lot going against them — and for them. On the minus side, they were heading for a city defended by 26,000 Japanese whose commanders were determined to fight to the death; MacArthur grossly underestimated both the numbers and the determination. Along the way the columns met Japanese positions often well concealed from the air. So they did not simply "bounce off the Nips": they got into firefights. The flying columns did not "fly," either. Rivers and blown-up bridges blocked their route. The columns had to zigzag to find an intact bridge or a passable ford. One bridge was so rickety that tanks crossed it one at a time with just their drivers. When they had to ford a river, radios sometimes got wet, putting them out of action.

Going for the columns was the sheer riskiness of their mission. It surprised the Japanese army, which was focused on withdrawing northeast into the mountains, not defending the plain. The columns also had remarkable firepower. Although some thirty Americans lost their lives, with over 130 wounded, the columns' mixture of carbines and machine guns, backed by mortars and rocket-launching bazookas, killed many Japanese for every GI lost.[5] (The tanks' machine guns were faster and more flexible than their main cannon.)

The columns gained, too, from American control of the sky. By the time they set off, nearly all Japanese aircraft had been destroyed. Many had been used up in devastating but expensive *kamikaze* attacks on the fleet that landed the 6th Army: the fleet lost three ships. Marine Corps dive bombers provided the columns' air cover. Taking off from a field near Lingayen, covered by steel mesh, nine planes were constantly overhead. The Marines had only just developed close air-ground support, against army fears that it would cost too many GI losses to "friendly fire." (Aware of this, Marine fliers once "strafed" and scattered Japanese troops without firing a shot because their targets were close to one of the columns.) The planes also helped as reconnaissance, along with the 1st Cavalry's own artillery spotter planes. They reported Japanese movements and the state of river bridges to seven Marine radio coordinators on the ground, riding with the columns' commanders.

The chief Marine coordinator, Captain Francis ("Frisco") Godolphin, was a Princeton classics professor, who spoke to generals as if he was their equal and once got several light planes to land on a highway for an instant conference. He was not the only air coordinator with panache — on either side. When a Japanese radio operator pretended to be American and ordered the planes back to base, Marine radio sergeant Bob Holland heard him, countermanded the order in ripe language, and told his pilots to ask any suspect voice to say, "Honolulu" — the Japanese found it hard to say *L*'s. The intruder did not try again.

The main flying-column force started leaving Guimba at midnight on 1 February. The 5th and 8th Cavalry columns took parallel dirt roads, in detachments 10 minutes apart, to avoid making traffic jams and a concentrated target. The 20–30 vehicles in each column were soon strung out over miles. For much of the journey, they went through barrios with cheering villagers, who showered them with flowers, bananas, and eggs. Catching an egg at 15 miles an hour became a useful skill. When a village was deserted, the troopers learned to watch out for Japanese fire. If that happened, they jumped out and fired back from the roadside, ditches, and hedgerows, then drove on when they could, leaving back-up units, following behind, to take over.

It wasn't always that simple; war seldom is. Approaching Cabanatuan on the first day, a 5th Cavalry unit rolled down a walled avenue. The troopers suddenly discovered that Japanese artillery had turned it into a lethal firing range. At that moment they were well ahead of the tanks. The troopers destroyed a gun with a bazooka, but the situation was too hot to handle. When the tanks arrived, they loaded their casualties onto them and pulled out. One of the wounded, Captain Hughes Seewald, rode on the flat back of a tank with his dead first sergeant. The troopers took another route into Cabanatuan, which by then had been secured by other units. Ambulance trucks then carried the wounded and dead back to Guimba. Later the 5th Cavalry ran into another hot spot but this time their field guns were there to blast away the opposition.

Throughout day one, 1 February, the division's commander, General Mudge, kept personal charge of the columns. He seemed to be everywhere, landing by spotter plane right next to firefights. He personally led troopers onto the Valdefuente Bridge over the Pampanga River, which the Japanese had dynamited, probably planning to blow it up by mortar fire. Mudge and his men saved the bridge by throwing the explosives into the water.

A peppery character, Mudge thought nothing of overruling his subordinates. When an advance troop (company) led by Captain Walter Landry got way out ahead of the 8th Cavalry column, the column's leader, Lieutenant Colonel Haskett Conner, told him to come back. He started to do so when General Mudge reversed the order. Landry and his men went back and forth three times through the village of San Miguel, feted each time by the locals. The main column caught up with them later in the day.

At the end of the first day, Mudge put one of his brigade commanders, Brig. Gen. William Chase, in charge of the columns. With his trim mustache, Chase looked very much a cavalry officer. But he also had a democratic streak. "What would Private Kucinich say about this?" he would ask in pondering a decision. He said it so often his officers affectionately called him "P.K." and he adopted the name as a radio call sign. Like Mudge, he prided himself on being a "front line general," staying close to the action. He often rode in a Marine radio jeep with the 5th Cavalry column.[6]

The columns were so strung out that different bits of them ran into less fire than others. Private George Fisher, gun loader in "Georgia Peach," one of the tanks attached to 8th Cavalry, remembered no firing after Cabanatuan. The main holdup was several hours fording the Angat River. Using their winches, the tanks pulled jeeps and trucks through the river. The rest of the time, Fisher and his crewmates stayed in the tank, driving night and day, except for pauses to refuel from a tanker truck. They took turns to sleep but were too keyed up to do much of that. The tank's big aircraft engine was noisy; it was also hot and smelly inside the tank. Though it had a "blower" and the hatch was open ("unbuttoned") most of

Hull down in the Angat. At several places, including the Angat River crossing here, the flying-column rescue force found the bridges blown and had to make fords, using its tanks to winch the trucks and jeeps across. "Battlin' Basic," the Sherman tank in this photo, was the first one into Santo Tomás. The jeep driver was Marine Technical Sergeant Robert (Bob) Holland, one of seven ground-air coordinators in radio contact with Marine dive bombers overhead; he later wrote a book titled, *The Rescue of Santo Tomas*. The GIs on top of the jeep are taking out his radio equipment to keep it dry. A lot of other vehicles' radio batteries got wet, putting them out of action *(courtesy of the 1st Cavalry Division Association).*

the time, the crew were often stripped to the waist. A store of empty shell cases served as disposable lavatories, which Fisher had the privilege of pitching out through a turret porthole next to him.[7]

On day two, 2 February, the two columns diverged, after fording the Angat at different places. The 5th Cavalry circled left, checking reports of a threat from a Japanese force, hidden on a hill to the east. They repelled heavy opposition but the detour helped put the 8th Cavalry column ahead of them in the race for Manila.

Late afternoon on the third day, 3 February, the 8th Cavalry ground to a halt near Novaliches, thirty miles from Manila. After fighting off Japanese fire at an important crossroads, soon nicknamed "Hot Corner," it reached a bridge across the steep-banked Tuliahan River. It was intact but blocks of explosives on it were visible and the fuse had been lit. Braving Japanese fire, Lieutenant James Sutton, a navy bomb-disposal expert, ran onto the bridge and cut the fuse, though he could not get rid of the explosives. Most of the column crossed the bridge, leaving behind a troop (company) to hold Hot Corner. The 5th Cavalry followed. Later, Japanese guns detonated the explosives and brought down the bridge, which delayed reinforcements following behind.

During the day, both columns shot up Japanese troop convoys, sometimes surprising

Another view of a river crossing by the camp's rescuers. The encouraging crowd of Filipinos meant that no Japanese were about. Most of the population was enthusiastic, but in barrios loyal to the radical Huks further west, other American troops found the villagers unfriendly (*U.S. Signals Corps. Courtesy of U.S. National Archives, College Park, Maryland*).

them as they headed north. The 8th Cavalry, still ahead of the 5th, entered Manila at sunset. Nightfall comes fast near the equator and the darkening city looked ominous. Big city warfare was new to the troopers of both columns: every building and rooftop might have a sniper or gun position — and sometimes did. As jeeps and trucks swept by a large cemetery, snipers fired at them from behind tombstones. Small groups of Japanese vehicles sometimes appeared and were shot up on the hoof, the troopers firing machine guns as they went.

An 8th Cavalry troop with a platoon of five tanks peeled off to take Malacañan Palace, surprising its guards. The troop stayed there, fighting off a counterattack. Another platoon of five tanks got separated from the 8th Cavalry and lost its way: many street signs had been stolen, and almost all American street names had been changed. It withdrew overnight to a field on the outskirts. (The big fireworks I saw that evening were not sent up to light the camp but to show the lost platoon and others where we were.) In the morning the platoon commander recruited a fourteen-year-old boy who scrambled enthusiastically onto the commander's tank and guided the platoon to Malacañan Palace; a siren from a tank there also helped. At Malacañan, they joined the other tank platoon, making a protective semi-circle around the palace.

In the meantime, part of the remaining 8th Cavalry ran into the bloodiest opposition of the three days, which killed ten troopers, a third of all flying-column deaths. One of the troops missed a turning to Santo Tomás and overshot it by several blocks. Driving past Far

Eastern University, the troop leader, Captain Walter Landry, realized the mistake and circled back to Santo Tomás, fighting off Japanese armed trucks along the way. But his three rear platoons, seventy-five men, got separated from the rest. Outside Far Eastern University, all hell broke loose from machine-gun nests plus a "dual-purpose" anti aircraft/surface gun; surprisingly, they had not fired on the front group.

Diving for cover behind their trucks and jeeps, the troopers returned fire. They broke into a university building, shot the Japanese there, and set up their base and aid station in the lobby. Their bazookas silenced some of the Japanese firing from other buildings, but they took heavy casualties when they dashed back to their trucks for more ammunition.

As ammunition ran low, Lieutenant Francis Jerrett decided to get help. Radios were out of action after the river crossings, and Jerrett's jeep had been hit, so he crawled and then ran for it under fire. Somehow he made it to General Chase's "command group," which was coming up behind the 8th Cavalry. Then, eager to rejoin his men, Jerrett returned in another jeep with more ammunition. He did so ahead of any other reinforcements: Santo Tomás was Chase's first objective and he had to get there first.

Back at Far Eastern, Jerrett's driver was killed, shot through the chest, and a shell hit the radiator, knocking over the jeep. Jerrett was thrown clear but when he tried to stand,

Trouble ahead. Approaching Manila, 1st Cavalry Division troopers take cover and prepare for action when firing breaks out further up the column (*U.S. Signals Corps. Courtesy of U.S. National Archives, College Park, Maryland*).

he fell down. He saw his left foot was a bloody mess, dangling and nearly severed. At first there was no outpouring of blood and little pain: his foot was in spasm, and adrenaline kicked in. He managed to scramble behind a big garbage can and then into the captured building. After giving orders to a sergeant, he fainted. By the time a rescue force arrived from Chase, fire from the Japanese had abated; they had lost more men than the Americans. The rescuers got all the troopers out, including dead and wounded. Jerrett's leg was later amputated in a liberated Santo Tomás.[8]

While all this was going on, the front force of the 8th Cavalry — several hundred troopers and six tanks led by Lieutenant Colonel Conner — had reached the camp. As they turned into Calle España, the street beside the main gate, a machine-gun nest at the corner opened fire and got wiped out. So did the guard behind the gate who threw the grenade that gashed Conner's leg and mortally wounded Captain Manuel Colayco. An anti–Japanese patriot working for an American-Australian intelligence unit, Colayco and his fellow guerrilla, Diosdado Guytingco, had joined the Americans as they entered Manila and helped them avoid mined streets. When Colayco was hit, he was placed on an island in the middle of España. Colayco said he felt cold, so Guytingco covered and bound him with his own shirt. By the time the medics arrived, Colayco had gone into a coma.

Moments later, "Battlin' Basic," the lead tank, bashed through the gate, scraping its stone archway. In the darkness, the tank's gunner, Corporal John Hencke, his head outside the turret, misjudged the height of the arch and only just managed to duck. Popping up again, he wondered if he hadn't made it and was seeing St. Peter: a man with a white beard and shepherd's staff stood beside the camp drive. Hencke figured later that his apparition was a seminary father.

As the tanks trundled up the drive, fire came from near the Fathers' Garden on the left. One of the tanks wheeled round and wiped out another machine-gun nest. Before it did so, a second apparition appeared — an elderly white man in khaki fatigues and a baseball cap. He was pointing, at some risk to himself, to the machine gun. The GIs later learned that he was an internee, Charles Schoendube. A Philippine-American War veteran, he had sworn he would help lead the U.S. Army in.

While tanks and troopers on foot were cautiously moving up the main drive, a hundred soldiers climbed over the side walls to get behind the Main Building. By then nearly all the Japanese and Taiwanese garrison, some 68 men, had holed up in the Education Building, but the troopers did not yet know it.

In the Main Building, meanwhile, the sound of tanks from behind the camp had brought a crowd to the back door. A guard shouted at them to stay inside and then hurried off. When the sound of firing came from the front, the crowd moved to the front lobby and heard tanks coming up the drive. Some feared it was the Japanese army come to massacre them, but most were jubilant. Internee patrolmen tried to keep the front door shut and the crowd inside, but not for long. When the first GI appeared, he looked amazingly big, smiling, but with a strange Nazi-looking helmet — the new U.S. issue, deeper than the prewar "tin hats." He was so mobbed he could hardly get out his first words: "All I can say is I'm glad to be with you." A cry went up: "My God, it's Carl Mydans!" Two journalists had appeared — the *Time-Life* photographer, Carl Mydans, and Frank Hewlett of United Press. Mydans was *returning* to the camp: he had been interned there before being evacuated to

Shanghai and repatriated to the United States under an exchange. For Hewlett, the moment was even more emotional. He was about to be reunited with his wife, Virginia, an internee.

Before the first few troopers came into the Main Building, some internees spilled out into the front plaza. Two teenagers went out and came back in, telling their friends inside what they had seen: Abiko — the camp's most hated figure — had been shot and they had been able to kick him on the ground.[9]

Outside in the plaza, a lot happened very fast. In the light of Battlin' Basic's headlights, two Japanese officers appeared and immediately surrendered. They were the civilians, Toshio Hirose and Shizua Ohashi. Shortly afterward, they were taken into the Main Building jail beside the front lobby. "Don't hurt him — he's a fine fellow," a woman internee called out (probably referring to the benign Hirose). She was assured that both would be safe.

Behind the two officers, a third Japanese soldier appeared — Lieutenant Abiko. When he reached for a small shoulder bag, Major James Gearhart shot him from the hip. His experience told him correctly that the bag contained a grenade. Gearhart had succeeded Conner as acting commander when Conner was wounded. A taciturn Westerner who had practiced firing from the hip, he had no time to take measured aim. Another trooper may have shot Abiko too.

Hit in the stomach, Abiko fell, writhing in agony. He had hardly hit the ground when a group of internees, mainly men, set upon him. They kicked him and spat on him, and two women burned him with cigarettes. Men tried to cut off his buttons and insignia as trophies. Some cut at him with knives and possibly his own sword. Others, though, cried, "Knock it off!" — which may have saved one of Abiko's ears from being totally severed.

Two troopers or internees carried or dragged him into the Main Building, leaving him there, where he was attacked again. Robin Prising, entering the lobby from behind, saw a creature, thrashing in his own blood, and remembered not just the violence but the also the cursing: "Don't kill him yet.... Let me get at him ... filthy, yellow-bellied Jap ... I ain't ever gonna bow to you again, Shitface." Again, not everyone went along. Asked by excited friends, "Don't you want to see what they're doing to him?" Geege Wootten said adamantly, "No, I do *not*!" Emily Van Sickle had hated Abiko as much as anyone but was revolted at the "gloating over a dying man's body" and what she later described as a vengeful monster breaking through the "civilized surface of our minds." Robin Prising, eleven at the time, was more confused: he felt guilty about feeling sorry for a hated enemy.

Dr. Ted Stevenson, newly sprung from jail in the Main Building, treated Abiko in the nearby dispensary, which had become a surgery for wounded GIs. Several internee helpers did not want him cared for, especially after a second grenade rolled out of his clothes. Eyewitness accounts differ about the grenade. According to Stevenson, Abiko pulled the pin but it was a dud. Denny Williams, an internee nurse, just said a GI took it and gingerly carried it out.

Stevenson remained the doctor. "War makes animals out of any of us," he said quietly. (A decent error: other animals seldom, if ever, kill or torture in revenge.) After binding up Abiko's wounds as best he could, Stevenson had him carried into a nearby women's dorm, one of several temporarily vacated to take in the wounded. There he got rolled off a bed when its owner declared, "I don't want that pig in my bed." When Abiko died, his body was dumped in a space under the back stairs of the Main Building, with his boots toward Tokyo. This insulted both Abiko and the emperor, as fallen Japanese soldiers were supposed to lie with their heads facing their sovereign. Vengeance did not cease at death.

Vengeance for what? Abiko was infamous not for killing or torturing but for bullying and humiliating — especially among labor gangs and at roll calls. He personified, as Tressa Roka put it, "all that was hateful in our lives," every infliction by every Japanese on up to the war cabinet. The abuse of Abiko was their last chance to "get even" with Japanese power, to *do* something to the Japanese, not just suffer under them.[10]

Abiko's end did not affect the general joy of being rescued, partly because the visible abuse happened quite fast and many internees did not see it. There was, though, distress at the sight of wounded and dying GIs brought into the Main Building as most of the flying columns poured into the camp. Soldiers in stretchers lined the hallway and ground-floor corridors. Internee nurses and other women helped the army medics — boiling water, rolling bandages, or even just murmuring a thank-you to a soldier on a stretcher.

Hero of the scene was Ted Stevenson. Foreseeing that the dispensary might be needed for emergency aid, he had laid in surgical supplies, some of which he himself had brought into camp from his stores as a medical missionary. The only surgeon among the liberated internees, he was joined later that night by an army doctor who was not a surgeon, though qualified to do minor field surgery. Stevenson worked through the night until he collapsed.

The wounded could not go immediately to the camp hospital, Santa Catalina, as it was on the other side of the Education Building, and that was still a war zone. When Gearhart and his men realized the Japanese garrison had taken refuge in the Education Building, they did not seem aware, in the darkness and general hubbub, that internees were there too — 210 men and boys, plus a few women who had been visiting. His tanks moved toward the front of the Education Building, on the east side of the Main Building. Seeing this, Joan Meredith, a British dormmate of my mother, Lorna Wilkinson, ran out to the tanks followed by my mother. "Don't you know our boys are in there?" Joan yelled. She, too, had a son — Guy — in the Boys' Club on the third floor. Another internee yelled a warning from a window on the same floor.

The Education Building situation had actually started before the tanks came. When he heard the tanks approaching north of the camp, Commandant Hayashi called into his office the two Internee Committee men, Earl Carroll and Sam Lloyd, with the two internee interpreters, Frank Cary and Ernest Stanley. Hayashi said he wanted a day's grace in which the U.S. Army would stay outside the gate, letting the garrison leave to fight elsewhere. He sent Carroll and Stanley to contact the U.S. commander. By the time they found Gearhart, however, the tanks were outside the Main Building, the civilians Hirose and Ohashi had surrendered, and Abiko had been shot.

Gearhart gave Hayashi twelve minutes to surrender and then had his machine guns rake the Education Building ground floor. By then, though, the garrison had moved from that floor, all of which they occupied, to the second floor, where they had dorm rooms. Some internees were on the second floor too but most were on the third. Hayashi made no response, so Gearhart then fired on the second floor, having told the internees there by megaphone to take cover at one end of the floor. The garrison was again one jump ahead of him: most had moved onto the top, internee floor. One Japanese or Taiwanese guard was killed, and sporadic rifle-fire from the garrison killed a GI and wounded one or more. Several internees were hurt by stray bullets or floor splinters, and one died of a heart attack after his bedding caught fire. Dr. Lindsay Fletcher, an internee doctor in the Education Building,

According to the photograph archive, the *Time-Life* photographer, Carl Mydans, took this picture after the 1st Cavalry had liberated most of the camp. It supposedly shows three Japanese soldiers standing outside a university building while their boss, the commandant, who was holed up inside the Education Building with the garrison and over 200 internee hostages, negotiated "safe conduct" out of camp in return for releasing the internees. The negotiation succeeded, but there is no record of Japanese soldiers standing outside while it happened. The wall and window behind them do look like the Main Building. The picture might be an earlier Japanese army photograph that found its way into an American collection. I include it as the only close-up picture I have found of Santo Tomás Japanese — probably officers, as they are wearing swords (*Getty Images*).

attended to the wounded, including a Japanese soldier hit in the foot. Hayashi later allowed the dead internee and a wounded one to be taken out.

It was clear that Gearhart had a hostage situation on his hands. Hayashi wanted a safe exit for his garrison and his bargaining chip was the Education Building internees. Some Japanese in a staff car had tried to break out, using a side gate, but had been shot into flames outside the camp.

Between and after the two bouts of firing, a spate of messages went back and forth between Hayashi and Gearhart. Gearhart demanded surrender. Hayashi refused but said he was not hurting the internees. The main message-taker was Frank Cary, the commandant's personal internee interpreter, though Ernest Stanley helped too — at one point shouting up to the commandant from outside the building. Cary went in and out of the building more than five times during the evening and again the next morning. When he asked an American lieutenant to go with him, the young officer refused, saying he was too afraid of Japanese treachery. Cary himself feared that a nervous trigger finger might get him. He walked into the building each time with hands outstretched, shouting in Japanese, "Cary coming in as messenger, unarmed." When he got to the commandant, his main fear was that Hayashi would decide to fight to the death, so he appealed to him not to inflict that on his many Taiwanese guards, who had not signed up to the Japanese army tradition of death before surrender.

In the morning 4 February, Cary took a message from Hayashi to Brig. General Chase, the flying-column commander, who had arrived late the night before. Hayashi proposed releasing the hostages in return for safe conduct out of camp for his garrison. Chase did not like the trade, but he saw no alternative: his first duty was to save the internees. He did not, though, want to release the garrison too early, in case they tipped off the Japanese army outside as to how small and vulnerable the American force was. So he played for time, waiting until more troops came into the camp. He told Hayashi, via Cary, that he was considering the proposal but needed to check with his superiors. A de facto truce followed.[11]

Inside the Education Building a different scenario had unfolded. When they saw the tanks coming in on the night of 3 February, the garrison had barricaded the stairs, one at each end of the building, with tables, chairs, and planks. On the top floor, they blocked the stairs with mattresses and other bedding taken from internees' rooms. Many of them gathered in the corridor that ran along the building behind most of the dorm rooms. They used internees in the dorms as a human wall, including those of us in the Boys' Club. On the other side of the corridor there were only a few rooms and two latrines, in a center section where the building was deeper. (A tank crew had tried to get behind the building, but too many shanties were clustered there to make it a base for firing.)

When the firing started that night, someone told us to get under our beds. The machine-gun fire was deafening: a giant pounding on a colossal typewriter. Tracers flashed outside and occasionally across the ceiling. I was frightened enough — and not frightened enough — to tell myself my life was charmed; I would not die. Before the second bout of firing, the American megaphone told us to move into one of the back rooms. Later we were told we could come back. We spent the rest of the night on the floor under our beds, some of them occupied by sleeping soldiers. Nick Balfour and I had lost our mosquito nets to the guards, so we huddled together under a blanket, occasionally putting our heads out to cool off before being driven back by the mosquitoes. Soldiers sometimes stepped past our beds to peer out of the windows or crouch beside them. In the morning, Nick remembers seeing a hand holding a grenade a foot from his head; its owner was sleeping above us.

Our life as hostages then eased up, aside from no breakfast. We had to stay in our rooms but could go to a latrine if we said "benjo" ("toilet") to a guard. We could also talk to people below our dorm windows. Several boys had emotional conversations with their mothers, including Nick. Anne Balfour called up to him, asked how he was, and said she had a bowl of food waiting for him. That suddenly made him feel tearful and frightened: she was so near and yet so far. But we also bantered with the U.S. Army. (Boy: "What did you eat for breakfast?" GI: "Canned ham and eggs. Not very good." Boy: "Oh yeah?") Food from outside finally arrived in the early afternoon — tall metal containers of hot corned beef and soybean stew — delicious. Some went to the garrison and it was repeated that evening.

During the day of 4 February, several members of the garrison could be seen leaving the building to surrender. Most, if not all, were civilians. Up to nineteen internees escaped, by rope or knotted sheets. The garrison did not try hard, if at all, to stop them. Two or three fell on the way down. One of them, we heard later, broke both legs. A Japanese soldier was also shot in the corridor. It may have been suicide. He knew some English and internees said he had just told them he did not want to fight anymore but not surrender. Several officers, though, inspected his body and claimed he was hit by an American sniper. The commandant complained at a breach of the ceasefire. General Chase gave a qualified apology: he admitted that word not to fire might have failed to reach all his men. On a trip to the latrine, I saw a soldier's body being carried to the stairs. He was the first dead person I had seen, his face curiously waxen, with bloodstains on his uniform.[12]

Outside the Education Building, units of the 37th Infantry Division arrived in the camp during the day of 4 February; that evening they liberated internees and military POWs in Bilibid Prison a few blocks from Santo Tomás. The 1st Cavalry had swept by them, not knowing they were there, and their guards left before the 37th arrived. 1st Cavalry senior officers later claimed that their own troopers' fierce action at Far Eastern University had deterred a Japanese counterattack on the camp, but that was surmise.

Reassured by the reinforcements, General Chase was ready to accept Hayashi's proposal. He sent his second-in-command, Lieut. Colonel Todd Brady, into the Education Building to make final arrangements. Ernest Stanley went with him, and possibly a Japanese American interpreter too, Sergeant Ken Uyesugi. Commandant Hayashi met them General Patton-style, his hands on two pistols, but they got down to business and agreed on procedure. In the morning, a 1st Cavalry troop would escort the garrison several blocks out of the camp. The garrison could take rifles, pistols, and swords, but not grenades or machine guns.

And so it happened. Before 7 A.M. on 5 February, the garrison was escorted across the camp. Few internees were about then, and the troopers silenced them when they started jeering. Flanked by troopers and Stanley, the garrison kept orderly ranks as they passed through the gate. One of them carried a wounded soldier on his back. But when the two sides parted company, the garrison broke and ran, disappearing between houses. An angry, mortified Hayashi could not stop them.

What happened to most of them we do not know. About eight got themselves captured by American soldiers and returned to Santo Tomás as POWs. Other writers usually say that the rest were killed by guerrillas or by U.S. troops around Malacañan Palace who did not know of the safe-conduct agreement. Nobody has produced evidence to support this assertion. According to a newspaper article, Hayashi's body was found in the hills. If true, he got his wish of leaving Manila to fight elsewhere.[13]

All in all, Hayashi and the hostages had served each other. He had not turned on us, as the gloomiest internees had feared. Instead, he used us as a lever to achieve an exit without bloodshed and without surrender.

When we rose on the morning of 5 February, our captors had gone. We could not leave straight away, though, as the army wanted to check the building for explosives. When a lieutenant came into the Boys' Club we crowded around him. Nick Balfour remembers we were less fascinated by his deep helmet and shiny yellow face, tinctured by anti-malaria Atabrine, than by his pistol. Drawing pistols had been one of our favorite pastimes, and here was the real thing. Downstairs, meanwhile, adults who had been released looted the Japanese quarters, removing ornaments, rugs, and food. During the siege, Frank Cary had stopped looters from breaking into a Japanese food store at the end of the Education Building, incensed that they would take it just for themselves. But that was a different era.

Early on 5 February 1945, following the "safe-conduct" agreement, 1st Cavalry troopers escorted the Santo Tomás garrison for several blocks out of the camp. Lieut. Tom Barrow is front left, beside the commandant, Lt. Col. Juichiro Hayashi. Front right in a white shirt is British internee interpreter Ernest Stanley. According to vague reports, most of the garrison died in fighting soon after but Hayashi survived to die in the hills as he wished. Some of the guards returned to the camp as prisoners. A negotiated withdrawal like this is said to have been unique in the Pacific war *(Carl Mydans/Getty Images)*.

Finally liberated, we raced downstairs, laughing and yelling, to join our families. In our shanty my mother produced a can of Christmas plum pudding we had been saving for liberation. Mary June had been eying it but Lorna would not open it "till Rupe's here." When she did, we saw it had gone bad.

A week before we might have eaten bits of it anyway. But our life of famine was over.

12

Aftermath

At 4:15 [A.M.] Dodie, Joan and I went out front and sat in a jeep with soldiers till 6:0. They gave us biscuits, chocolate, gum and coffee. God, what a fantastic dream. One of them (Desmond) was wonderful. Only 19 and boy what looks. —
Diary of Lydia Macleod, 16, liberation night, 3–4 February 1945

Lydia was lucky. Many GIs were setting up machine guns and field guns around the camp in case the Japanese counterattacked or were on watch outside the Education Building. Others just slept and slept, in their vehicles, or on the ground, or in hastily dug foxholes, making up for the last three days.

But Lydia's diary got it right. Liberation meant GIs and food, though the main food trucks, some driving through enemy fire, did not reach the camp until 6 February, day three of liberation. Until then some concealed food — mainly mongo beans, corned beef, and canned milk, plus cans of meat from a Japanese storeroom — supplemented the camp kitchens' meager stocks. Residue of the Alcuaz smuggling operation, the food cache had been hidden somehow in the gym when Lieutenant Abiko's prowling made it too risky to transfer to the camp kitchens. Some internees, who had saved a tiny hoard of comfort-kit cans, broke into them avidly. But the food situation was more precarious than they realized those first few days.

GIs gave generously wherever they could. In the rush to Manila the soldiers had not eaten all their K-rations, so they shared candy as well as canned and packeted food with internees of all ages but especially children — and went on doing so after the army took over the kitchens. Anne Balfour was disgusted at how much cadging children did, including cigarettes for their parents. In Balfour's spirit, my mother told us not to ask for food, so I just hung about the GIs until one gave me a half-eaten can of beef in gravy. I bore it proudly back to the shanty, where Mum said I could have it all. Mary June brought back candy from a GI and *lent* it to our mother, or so she thought, to suck before giving it back to her. She was dismayed when Mum innocently chomped it up. Later, when the army cooks started their own bread-making, a GI gave Mary June a slice with nothing on it. She thought it "the most wonderful thing in the world, eating it very slowly — like a box of chocolates today."[1]

Of course, GI-internee relations went beyond food. "So big, so healthy, so gentle" is how many internees saw their rescuers. The rescued, in turn, reminded the soldiers of their families back home, though distressingly reduced. After months of ferocious warfare, lib-

Lt. Col. Haskett (Hack) Conner, shaving out of a helmet on his jeep, at a liberated Santo Tomás. Conner led the first of the two flying columns to reach the camp. His leg shows the bandaged wound he got from a grenade outside the gate, which mortally wounded his guerrilla guide, Manuel Colayco *(courtesy of 1st Cavalry Division Association).*

American soldiers killed just before liberation were buried in the camp the day after the U.S. troops came in, and some internees attended the burials. The bodies later went to a Manila cemetery *(Sgt. Ira Rosenberg for U.S. Signal Corps., courtesy of U.S. National Archives, College Park, Maryland)*.

erating and feeding the internees was something special and good. Several liberators even claimed that the internees had had a tougher time than they did. As former private first class Pat DiMatteo put it, "we were trained to expect the worst"; the internees were not. "We were a mutual admiration society," recalled Lieut. Colonel (then Captain) Walter Landry. The soldiers admired internee parents for the sacrifices they had made for their children. They also made friends with youngsters, letting them crawl over the tanks and even handle their carbines; one GI was accidentally shot dead.

Romance was in the air, and not just crude sex. Many women, married or not, had saved a little make-up for "when the boys come." As some soldiers pointedly said, they had seen no white women since leaving Australia or the United States. For a shy teenager or young woman, their ardor could be too much; advances had to be batted off. Others felt safer in numbers, socializing in twos and threes. But lots of young women acquired boyfriends. When their beaus went off to fight again, their faces more grim than before, some came back; others didn't. Geege Wootten saw an internee father desperately trying to find a husband for his pregnant daughter; she never knew if he succeeded. A few internees, like Geege herself, became GI brides.[2]

For boys like me, the military equipment that poured into the camp made it a new paradise. Even the smell of oily metal was exciting. I was intrigued by the different vehicles that appeared, not just tanks and jeeps but also super–jeep "command cars," water tankers, amphibious DUKWs, and exotically hybrid "half-tracks"— trucks with wheels in front and tank treads

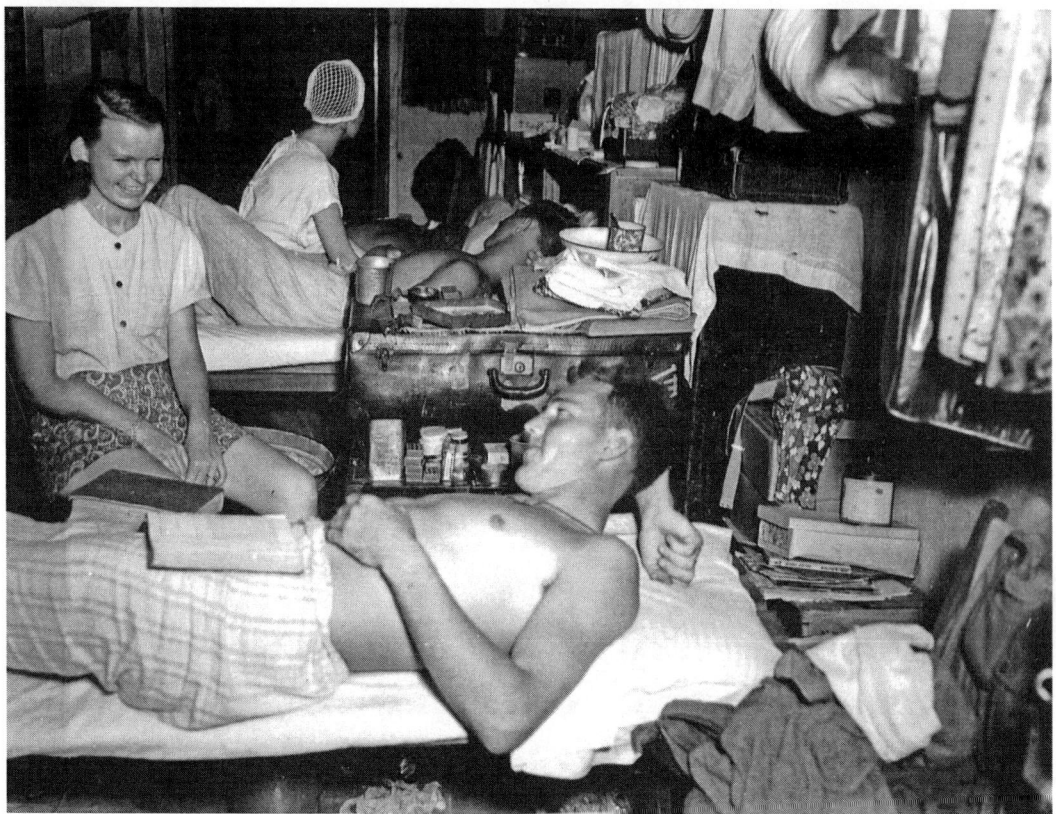

Bedside ministry. Betty Coote, interned when she was fifteen, gives good cheer to wounded Private First Class Lynwood Clemson — and vice versa *(U.S. Signal Corps, courtesy of U.S. National Archives, College Park, Maryland).*

behind. I also saw my first Filipino guerrilla, a wicked-looking fellow fully up to the part: hefty, long hair, pleased-with-himself grin, and two bandoliers criss-crossed on his chest.

But these were just spectacles. Some boys more enterprising than me, Nick Balfour included, got near to the field guns that started firing out from the camp two days after liberation. They scooped up spilled gunpowder, poured small amounts into empty shell cases, lit them with K-ration matches, and whoosh — there went a mini-rocket. No one, amazingly, got hurt. Camp health and safety rules, so assiduously promoted during internment, could not keep up with the new military scene.

A sight that Nick and I missed because of our detention in the Education Building was Abiko's body. Through the first day, 4 February, it lay on view at the back of the Main Building, placed so that people could file past it and out of the building through a side door. They soon needed the fresh air, as the stench rose in the tropical heat. But for many internees it was a "must-see" spectacle. Some of them, including small children, spat on Abiko as they went by. The attraction, though, was not just cheap revenge and ghoulish curiosity. Seeing the body gave "reassurance," as one internee put it: the hated, feared oppressor was laid low. At the end of the day, Abiko's body was buried in the camp along with two other Japanese or Taiwanese soldiers, well away from internee and GI dead. Before finally taking the body away, the army took a hands-off attitude to Abiko's treatment; troopers sympathized with internee feelings and had other things on their minds.³

The reappearance of some former guards, taken prisoner outside the camp, gave internees another sign that the tables had turned. Housed in a shed near the Annex, they were put to work in a camp storeroom. Some internees, including children, jeered at them with mock bows, but others objected, declaring that Americans should not stoop to "the level of the Japanese." After a while they were more or less left alone before being trucked to detention elsewhere.⁴

Internee triumph peaked on the morning of 7 February, when Douglas MacArthur paid a brief visit to the camp. A Stars and Stripes had already been draped, amid patriotic singing, over the Main Building entrance. As an excited throng gathered about MacArthur, an eight-year-old boy burrowed through the crowd and touched the great man's wrist. I can still picture the faded khaki of his sleeve, almost orange in the bright sun. Not long after I heard an adult say that "Rupert shook hands with General MacArthur." Camp "rumortism" lived on.

Sherman tank "Ole Miss" acquires visitors outside the Main Building. For some boys like me, the army hardware was as exciting as the GIs — but the soldiers had a great relationship with children and other internees, who reminded them of their folks back home *(U.S. Signal Corps, courtesy of MacArthur Memorial Archives, Norfolk, Virginia).*

Eight members of the Japanese garrison were captured outside the camp after they were escorted out; some had changed into civilian clothes. This photograph shows them being taken to a shed in the camp, where they were accommodated and given work. Japanese soldiers seldom surrendered but most of the prisoners were probably Taiwanese. The dejected posture of the man in the middle, an older Japanese soldier, suggests the shame the Japanese military accorded surrender *(U.S. Signal Corps, courtesy of U.S. National Archives, College Park, Maryland)*.

MacArthur was luckier than the internees. A few hours before he arrived, several Japanese shells hit the camp. No one was seriously hurt then, but heavier shelling started just after he left. It continued off and on for the next four days. Shells and mortar bombs hit the plaza, the front and west sides of the Main Building, the front of the Education Building, the gym, and some shanties. The shelling killed seventeen internees, a GI, and at least nine newly arrived Filipino workers. Many more were wounded, some hideously maimed. Dorm rooms became a mass of debris and severed limbs before army squads swiftly came in to rescue and clean up; five teenage boys joined in as stretcher bearers. Internee Eva Nixon, in her twenties, saw a friend decapitated before her eyes. A young girl on the plaza survived a shell blast but her nose was sheared off. Most internees, though, were not hurt, and many (our family included) saw no one actually being killed or wounded. Some realized they had had near escapes: "if I'd been at that spot five minutes before...." As is so often the case in war, luck was crucial and capricious.

I did see some ghastly sights. Along a ground-floor corridor of the Main Building, I

Captured Japanese or Taiwanese being interrogated and watched by American soldiers behind the Main Building. The soldier squatting at the left of the seated group seems to be a Japanese American interpreter. Some internees found it hard to accept that people who looked Japanese could be on their side *(U.S. Signal Corps, courtesy of U.S. National Archives, College Park, Maryland).*

saw a line of stretchers with people in them lying quite still, gashed by horrible wounds, one of them a big hole in the back, as black as it was red. Were they alive or dead? Down a corridor to the surgery, I watched medical orderlies bearing an old lady in a chair above their heads. She was crying hysterically and spattering their white tunics with diarrhea. I confess I felt sorrier for the orderlies than for her.

Mary June and I have total amnesia as to where we sheltered, though she does remember hitting the ground when sniper bullets pattered trees above her. Terrified, she crawled to the nearest building. The Balfours and others spent some time in the private, cave-like shelter of Edwin Van Voorhees, the grand shanty owner. Thirteen-year-old Peter Wrinch heard a whistling shell and jumped into a foxhole with a GI before scampering to safety in a building. Most of the shelling came from the south, from the front side of the camp, so many internees huddled at the back of the Main Building or behind the Education Building. The army evacuated the most vulnerable rooms.

But life went on. The shells came at intervals that people learned to calculate. In the lulls they collected food from the central kitchen at the back of the Main Building, chatted with each other and the GIs, or anxiously searched for missing relatives and friends. Alas,

Two days after the camp was liberated, some internees unfurled without fanfare an American flag over the Main Building entrance. A crowd gathered and started singing softly "God Bless America." Many wept, including GIs — and then cheered *(U.S. Signal Corps, courtesy of MacArthur Memorial Archives, Norfolk, Virginia).*

12. Aftermath

Yank, the U.S. Army magazine, put on its cover this photograph of field gunners and internee boys. Aware that it was surrounded by much larger Japanese forces, the U.S. Army fired out from the camp shortly after arriving. The field guns soon left for combat outside the camp, but the Japanese then shelled the camp off and on for five days, killing more than twenty people, mostly internees, before U.S. troops found and destroyed the guns (Yank, *30 March 1945, courtesy of Liz Irvine*).

they did not always get the intervals right. A soldier told Emilie Brooks, mother of the teenage twins Curtis and Barney, that she could collect some things from her evacuated room. She tried to and was killed by a shell. Eleven days earlier her husband, Bernard, had died of heart failure due to malnutrition.

By 12 February, the shelling had ended: the U.S. army had destroyed the Japanese guns. Finding and trading the camp's collection of shell fragments again became a hobby for children, as it had after the September air raids. And the army set to work repairing rooms and restoring the damaged water system. As a stopgap measure, engineers dug outdoor latrines, enclosed by bamboo walls. They could best be called "shitpits." You inched your bottom along a plank over the pit, hoping you would not fall, splat, into the many-hued, brown mass below. The smell was not popular in nearby shanties.

There were two tragic ironies about the shelling. The first lay in the sheer shock of getting attacked after being rescued. The internees were more assaulted than they had been during internment, when they were supposedly in more danger. The shelling, though, had one thing in common with the years of internment: it came from outside the camp. For all the offensiveness of some garrison officers, the Japanese army itself had always been a greater threat. Security raids, Kempeitai arrests, and even the basic food cuts came from outside.

The second irony was that the camp's rescuers may have encouraged the shelling. Even after reinforcements arrived on 4 February, the army felt vulnerable to counterattack from much larger Japanese forces. By 5 February, two days before the first Japanese shell hit the camp, U.S. army field artillery was firing from inside the camp, guided by observers atop the Main Building. Back in September, internee leaders had protested to the Japanese for doing much the same thing: using the Main Building tower for military "signaling." The tower made a highly visible target. Of course, it's possible that the Japanese would have shelled the camp anyway. By the time they started U.S. artillery had left the camp. At the very least, though, the American commanders failed to anticipate retaliation, though they acted fast when the shells struck.[5]

The shelling did not destroy the camp's new vitality. "The camp is an extraordinary sight," Paul Esmérian wrote on 11 February, the last day the shells fell.

> Filipino workers, washer-women, Chinese cooks, wounded soldiers, civilians ... tent canvases, queues, refugee internees, sleeping in the passageways ... almost incessant explosions. The hissing of shells flying across the camp. The soldiers, tall, well-fed, all smiles. The poor internees can still hardly believe their luck, all skin and bones, but beaming with happiness. The Red Cross distributes sweets, letters, chewing gum. Among all this apparent disorder, magnificent organization.... The meals are delicious and served on time. Magazines are distributed — regular news broadcast at 11:30 am.[6]

The new feeding had some instant effects, for good and bad. A boy in the Boys' Club, where we continued to sleep after the siege, showed a dramatically good effect, though not to my credit. Before liberation, I used to pick on him, compensating for being worsted by other, tougher boys. Though he was older and taller than me, he was rather sad and passive and I found I could sock him with impunity. When we returned to the Education Building, he looked different, his face already fuller. "You're not going to sock me anymore," he said quietly. And I didn't. Maybe the whole zeitgeist of liberation strengthened him. But food was surely part of it.

The downside of army feeding was eating too much too soon, despite warnings. Many

Hot work in the tropics. Though the army soon set up field kitchens, internees continued to operate the big camp stoves for some days after liberation. Here, three days after the army came in, are three internee cooks and a Filipino, one of many brought in by the army to work in the camp *(U.S. Signal Corps, courtesy of U.S. National Archives, College Park, Maryland)*.

internees became seriously sick, their starved bodies unable to absorb a sudden flow of rich nutrients. Their experience helped give rise to a new, emergency science of "refeeding" — controlled dieting after starvation — which benefited prisoners liberated later from other camps. But even the best diet, backed by care from army doctors and nurses, could not cancel in a single stroke the damage done by malnutrition. In the week following liberation, the same number died from malnutritional illness as the week before: a death a day on average.

A limited number of refugees were allowed to join the camp, especially the Filipino families of internees; some went into the university seminary rooms. Internees learned of terrible things happening outside. The "Battle for Manila" had begun, a block-by-block struggle that would leave Manila the most destroyed Allied city in World War II after Warsaw. Of the more than 100,000 who died, many were killed by American and Japanese shelling but even more died from massacres as Japanese soldiers turned on the people they had alienated. I was told only some of this: of houses torched and their residents gunned down as they fled. Adults did not tell me how the soldiers had gone into orgies of abuse: raping women before mutilating and then killing them; bayoneting babies before the eyes of parents about to be killed too.

Private cooking continued too. Besides shanty stoves owned by internees, there were camp-provided stoves, as used here by a small family *(Corbis)*.

Had a massacre been planned for the camp as well? Internees and a few troopers relayed reports of a plan to kill all internees, or all male adult internees. Some versions claimed that MacArthur had got wind of this and that 4 February, the day after the tanks arrived, was to be the massacre day. Perpetuated by many memoirs and other writings about the camp, the claims were made with great certitude and flaky evidence.

The fact is that the garrison had shown no sign of organizing for a massacre and every sign of wanting to get out. When tanks were heard behind the camp, interpreter Frank Cary and other internees cooperated with guard commander Abiko in urging shanty people to move into the Main Building, but that was to protect them from gunfire, not herd them in for a massacre. Some shanty people came in; others didn't. (Anne Balfour did so but only after the tanks had entered; she put her two younger children into my mother's bed while both adults spent the night in the corridor.) The garrison itself had already withdrawn most of its guards into the Education Building.[7]

In the Tokyo war-crime trials of 1946, General MacArthur's lawyers deployed every damaging detail they could but no massacre plan for Santo Tomás. Postwar diplomacy did not silence the general either. His *Reminiscences* (published 1964) pulled no punches on Japanese behavior. In January 1945, he said, he was alarmed by "reports from my various underground sources" that the guards at Santo Tomás and other camps were getting "more and more sadistic." But he never mentioned a premeditated plan.[8]

After liberation, some internees decided to stay in the Philippines, picking up the pieces of their often-wrecked homes and businesses. Others wanted to wait a while, to make contact with friends and family elsewhere in the Philippines if they were still alive. But most ended up leaving, usually by ship to the United States (some British and Dutch went to Australia). It was a long wait — more than two months for most people — until the navy could spare the troop transports and anti-submarine escort vessels to take internees across the Pacific. How the army decided who went when was never clear; it seemed to depend on luck, special needs, and occasionally sheer pushiness by an internee. But the internees, so fractious in the past, did not complain much at the process: they accepted their liberators' authority.[9]

More than a hundred internee nurses and seamen left first in mid–February. A slightly larger group left a week later, including the orphaned, teenage twins, Barney and Curtis Brooks. As they flew in an army transport plane to their ship at Leyte, they passed right over a flotilla of boats churning across part of Laguna de Bay, the Philippines' biggest lake, southeast of Manila. What they saw were the amphibious "amtracs" racing to rescue the internees of Los Baños beside the lake.

The biggest exodus from the camp — over 2,100 internees, including our family and the Balfours — was in mid–April. Until then, and indeed until the camp was finally closed in July, it was run by the army. The basic living quarters were unchanged but the army laid on what amenities it could, including movies, variety shows (aided by internees), and the occasional jazz concert. Through February, shell flashes and the sounds of gunfire were a backdrop to the shows, as house-to-house fighting destroyed the old walled city across the river. Camp historian Hartendorp contrasted "people sitting on chairs and benches, in comparative safety" with "men killing and being killed" two miles away.

Passes were still needed to go out, in order to control who came in and make sure internees visited only safe areas, but that did not shield them from dreadful sights — and smells. When a soldier friend of the Weinzheimer family took them on a jeep tour, they saw many bodies, especially Japanese ones, as the Filipino dead got collected more quickly. Although lime was poured on bodies to suppress infection and smell, there was still a strong stench.[10]

When it was safe to do so, we visited our home out near Quezon City, a Manila suburb. Or what was left of it. It had burned to the ground, probably due to an electrical fault in a storm. Mary June and I were sadly struck — as one often is — by how small an area the ground plan covered. Our mother concealed whatever shock she felt; out-of-camp friends had already given her the bad news. We joyously met our servants, who had survived largely by expanding their vegetable garden; we're not sure if they had stayed with country relatives for part of the time. Our parents later paid them arrears for every year of our internment. Other employers did the same.

Visits out of camp were breaks in the waiting. Mary June and I remember the wait differently. She recalls the sheer pleasure of no longer being hungry, of having new energy — no longer "creeping around with one's mind in neutral." I remember increasing boredom and frustration: when were we going to "get out of this dump"? In sociological language, my *absolute deprivation* had gone down but my *relative deprivation* — measured against what I hoped for and expected — was going up. For adults, there was also the anxiety of wondering how they would cope on the outside. This was probably more acute for men, who were more likely to be going back into the job market. Even if they had company jobs to return to, would they be up to it? Had they fallen behind modern know-how?[11]

A change in army personnel did not help psychologically. The camp's first U.S. commandant, Colonel Pete Grimm, was well known to some internees. Before the war he had been a manager of Luzon Stevedoring, port management. He left in two weeks, though, for the big task of clearing Manila harbor, which reportedly had more sunk ships than any other port except Naples. The two lieutenant colonels who in turn succeeded him were basically bureaucrats. Their staffs did not have the rapport with internees enjoyed by the initial liberators, who had gone off to fight in the bloody battles outside. As time went by, the administrators were more apt to see internees as burdensome welfare cases than gallant, rescued innocents.

The biggest failure of the army officials was their treatment of Luis de Alcuaz, the university's executive secretary and chemistry professor, who had helped select the campus as a campsite and then smuggled in aid. Fr. Thomas Tascon, the Franco Spanish chief of the university, had valued Alcuaz for his abilities and useful connections with the American population, but had fallen out with him over policy and style. Alcuaz was tactful when he wanted to be but could also be brusque and, to some, high-handed. When Tascon spoke at a dinner honoring some visiting Japanese officials, Alcuaz told him he was talking pro–Japanese propaganda and stopped the university printers from publishing his speech. The Spanish faculty, too, took offence when the Japanese put up a sign outside the university seminary banning entry to the camp without the permission of Alcuaz, who had been designated "custodian" of the camp's university property. Tascon suspected and appeared to oppose Alcuaz's food smuggling. There were also disputes about allocations of space between camp and university.

When the shells hit Santo Tomás after liberation, Alcuaz opened university offices, including Tascon's, for internees evacuated from dorms and shanties. Alcuaz claimed he had no time to tell Tascon: the internees needed immediate shelter. A month later, Tascon pressured Alcuaz into resigning before being fired outright. Army officers rudely bundled him out of his two offices without any apparent awareness of what he had done for the internees, much less any provision or employment for him on leaving the university. Complaints by Alcuaz's supporters, including the Catholic archbishop in Manila, cut no ice with the army;

Wedding of Luis de Alcuaz and Pomponette Francisco, Manila, 14 April 1945. A professor of chemistry and chemical engineering at the University of Santo Tomás, Alcuaz was a major benefactor of the camp, where Pomponette (my much-loved kindergarten teacher before the war) was interned. Against opposition from the university's Franco Spanish authorities, Alcuaz helped get it chosen by the Japanese as the campsite. During internment, he smuggled food, money, medicine, and radio parts into the camp. Increasingly at odds with the university's leaders, he was forced to resign as professor and university administrator after the camp was freed. He was later awarded the Medal of Freedom, the USA's highest award for civilian service in World War II *(courtesy of de Alcuaz and Francisco families)*.

it was steering clear of university politics. General MacArthur later made amends by awarding Alcuaz a Presidential Medal of Freedom, given for outstanding civilian service against the enemy. By then Alcuaz had married his interned fiancée, Pomponette Francisco, and moved to California, where he became (appropriately) a food-industry chemist.

There is no room here to write about our three-week, troopship voyage to the United States, kitted out with clothes by the Red Cross and cuddly stuffed creatures for the small children.[12] But I do want to highlight one moment: when Alice Bryant first saw the lights of San Francisco. In 1940, the Bryant couple had left their eight-year-old daughter, Imogene, with relatives in the United States — Alice's father presciently predicted a prison-camp future in the Philippines. Now, as the Golden Gate Bridge approached, she looked back, and then forward to meeting Imogene, now 13.

> The wilderness, the dark night, lay behind us. It might have been worse — the worst things had been those that had not happened to us. It had not been hell — just purgatory. The purgatory of anxieties, of absence from loved ones, of lack of privacy and constant milling about in a mob, of the steerage-class way of living, of good rumors proved false, of hunger, of uncertainty, of fear of what the Japanese might next do to make us uncomfortable.
>
> All that was behind us. The future lay spread out bright just ahead. Its details we could not see: the military band; the relatives who met us on the dock; the Red Cross girl who served us orange juice ... while the customs inspector passed our suitcases in thirty seconds ... our lovely daughter herself, almost as tall as I [who] threw her arms around me.... As choirs of angels sang in my mind's ear, we swept through the Golden Gate.[13]

Re-entering mainstream society was happier for some internees than others. It depended not just on their ages and camp experiences — what they were coming *from* but also on who and what they were going *to*. Our own re-entry was as good as it could be, at least until our plunge into the conventions of English boarding schools and their denial of privacy (as bad as the camp's).

Our ship, USS *Ebberle*, went to Los Angeles. After it docked at San Pedro harbor, we had the thrill of meeting of meeting father and husband, Gerald Wilkinson. Resplendent in the uniform of a lieutenant colonel, British Army intelligence, he had wangled special permission to come on board. A week followed with family and business friends in San Mateo, where two neighborhood boys, Hank and Danny, "adopted" me, helping make up for my loss of Nick Balfour. We spent the rest of the summer with other friends on the banks of the Hudson River. They generously lent us a cottage on their property, while my father commuted to New York, winding up his intelligence work and preparing for his return to the Philippines to rebuild his business.

In the fall we returned to England, to the big country house of my mother's parents. Postwar austerity Britain, often rainy, was like a black-and-white movie after our technicolor summer, but Mary June was thrilled to discover so many relatives after years of boredom and loneliness in the Philippines. We stayed on with our grandparents in the school holidays, while our parents spent much of each year in the Philippines. Leaving children in boarding schools was common practice when the British upper classes worked abroad; they did not set up overseas "American Schools."

Re-entry for the teenage twins, Curtis and Barney Brooks, was less happy than ours. The loss of their parents in the camp was part of it but not all. For fifteen months, until

Family reunited, May 1945. Like many internees, Dr. Theodore (Ted) Stevenson was separated from his family. Vacationing in the United States in 1941 with his wife Beatrice and three small sons, he planned to return with them to his work as a medical missionary in Canton. The United States government let only him go because of the threat of war. The attack on Pearl Harbor interrupted his journey; he got as far as Manila. In Santo Tomás, Stevenson was jailed when he refused to take "malnutrition" and "starvation" off death certificates; he himself had lost 50 pounds. Sprung from jail when the U.S. Army arrived, he went straight to work operating on wounded GIs. Stevenson family from left to right: Davy, Billy, Beatrice (Bunny), Donny, and Ted *(courtesy of Donald Stevenson).*

they went away to college, they stayed with their mother's brother, a doctor, and his wife on Staten Island, along with two unmarried adult daughters. Their good intentions could not fill a gap. For years Curtis felt a "brooding sense of loss," which at first he could not define — had he not, after all, been liberated? — until he realized it was loss of community; family friends in the camp had given the orphaned twins a close-knit support group. Later he discovered that other internees, too, missed the ties they had forged in the camp when they faced common hardships and shared a common purpose: survival. Now they were on their own amid a people of plenty who gave them material comforts but could not comprehend what they had been through; American history seemed to have passed them by.[14]

The full story of how the camp's many alumni graduated into postwar society is not for this book. Again, there were big differences, including health. Malnutrition left some permanently impaired. Damage to one's heart, stomach, eyesight, teeth, and bone density (osteoporosis) was particularly common. But many people suffered little in the long term.

Camp-born friendship: Lettye Staight Falk and Lorna Wilkinson, England, 1964. "I got to know people I wouldn't have otherwise," my mother said about the camp afterward. When they met in camp, the two seemed very different: Lettye a tough Texan; Lorna an English lady. But they had the same sense of humor and the same warmth, and they stayed close friends all their lives. Neither may have known in the camp that their husbands had both had double careers before the war in business and intelligence; both had also predicted an imminent Japanese attack before Pearl Harbor was hit. But unlike my father, who joined General MacArthur before Manila fell, Ronny Staight was interned in Santo Tomás — and never found out by the Japanese.

Psychological effects were no less varied. For some, the change was just too much. Memories of death and near-death; the years of being at the mercy of unpredictable, alien captors; anxiety about coping in the new world; even freedom itself— no more prison routines, no more U.S. army welfare state — all this could lead to depression, sleeping problems, lapses in memory and concentration, and other disorders. Later the sufferers' plight would be classified as PTSD— post-traumatic stress disorder. Many others, however, were unscathed and even strengthened by what they had been through. At a family gathering held by our grandparents, the changes in my mother amazed a sister-in-law. Lorna was warmer, more outgoing and vibrant than the coolly shy woman she remembered. Anne Balfour, too, thought that my mother "blossomed" in the camp and became more independent.[15]

Many carried from the camp a variety of complexes and quirks. My occasional tantrums continued for nearly a year after liberation; we don't know what mixture of insecurity and frustration produced them. During our American summer, Mary June dreamed more than once that Japanese soldiers were coming in revenge for her escaping them. And for several years Angus Lorenzen, liberated at age nine, wanted to dive underground when low-flying planes appeared — the result of a near escape from the camp's shelling. Remembering the fate of the camp's first escapers also gave him "a sense of foreboding" when he broke even a minor traffic law.[16] Some ex-internees thought the camp's forced lack of privacy made them more introverted, even emotionally cut off from others. Peter Wygle, a young teenager at liberation, later said he found it hard to make close friends. He attributed this to the mayhem of the shelling, which calloused him against grievous loss; the shelling severed the arm of a beloved aunt figure and killed her husband. Wygle also hated locked doors and, like others, he detested throwing away food; in hotels his wife Nancy had to restrain him from raiding the trays left outside the doors of other guests. And my mother never kicked the occasional habit of drinking hot water instead of tea or coffee, as we had done in the camp. Many internees thought that the camp made them appreciate the simplest pleasures and what really mattered in life.

What did matter? The camp's effects on attitudes are hard to disentangle from predispositions. Without internment, would a person have valued this or that anyway? Liz Lautzenhiser Irvine felt that internment and liberation made her and her friends "more patriotic" and "pro-military." Edward McCreary, another camp teenager, believed that gratitude to his liberators led him to sign up for the army in Korea, though later he resisted a corporate career: being his own person was important. Several ex-internees said that the camp made them value freedom more, a treasure to be defended but not blindly or uncritically. Sylvia Williams (aged 7–10 in camp) believed that the suffering wrought by war, especially the stress visited on her father, helped her become a Quaker and psychotherapist, working for peace and the bereaved.[17]

My own liberalism was reinforced by moving from what had seemed a classless camp society to the sharp class distinctions and inequalities of England: "rough" neighborhood boys who spoke differently to me; the small dwellings of my grandparents' gardeners compared to the great house where I lived. I felt I did not deserve it. In fact, I was more used than I realized to class differences in the Philippines, but they were most obviously racial. When our ship docked at San Pedro, I was surprised to see that the dockworkers were white. (For more on race, see the next chapter.)

As they looked back on camp life, some former internees actually thought the experience worth it. The extent of this is hard to judge. Those I asked were not a scientific sample and they were mostly teenagers or children in camp, suffering less, on the whole, than adults. It is also difficult to allow for bias. People often don't like believing that "investments" of time or money — even forced ones — have been wasted.

Some ex-internees, my sister included, did *not* think it was worth it; they could have done so much more if free. Others had a mixed view. Cecily Mattocks Marshall, whose childhood odyssey took her from late internment on Mindanao island to Santo Tomás, "wouldn't want to relive it" but thought the war gave her a baseline of strength. When life got tough later, it was "not as tough as in the camp." Edward McCreary went further: the camp was a lot more "educational" than going to an American high school.

I myself valued my camp past less as an education than as an exotic, quasi-heroic experience to be proud of. But my mother told a niece it was the "best thing" that happened to her — for two reasons: she "had to manage" and she met people more varied and different from her than she otherwise would have done. Geege Wootten, interned in her early twenties, called it a "good experience" and an "education" in spite of the boredom and hunger. Like other women, she noted, she came from a "very protected circle" before the war.[18] In a way, the camp expanded the lives of women while diminishing those of men (not counting the overworked internee officials). For the first time, women had to cope without servants, sometimes on their own, while men lost prewar careers as well as their traditional role of family provider.

Memories of the camp have been nurtured by a vigorous association, BACEPOW — Bay Area Civilian Ex-Prisoners of War. Its founding officers largely came from the San Francisco area but its signed-up membership is far wider. It focuses mainly on the Philippine camps. Santo Tomás, the biggest camp, is its centerpiece.

BACEPOW reunions, including group visits to Santo Tomás itself, have perpetuated the bonds between ex-internees that Curtis Brooks and others missed right after the war. Aging army liberators of the camp have also joined in, continuing their strong emotional ties with the liberated. BACEPOW officers adopted the military titles of veterans' organizations: commander, vice-commander, even adjutant.

A founding purpose of BACEPOW, like other internee associations, was to get compensation for its members, including medical support. It was an uphill struggle. In the Cold War, the United States of America and Britain saw Japan as an ally against Russia and China, so they did not want to weaken it with big reparations. The small sums eventually paid came from Japanese overseas assets frozen in the war and from Western governments.[19]

A wider aim of BACEPOW was to document the camp's history and make sure it was not forgotten; it signed up internees' children and grandchildren, who helped perpetuate interest. Several BACEPOW members made camp history an avocation (to the benefit of this book). They wrote, collected, and sifted accounts of camp life, adding to books and articles produced by others. Many of the shorter accounts appeared in BACEPOW's four-monthly newsletter, *Beyond the Wire* (henceforth *Wire*).

Like BACEPOW reunions, *Wire*'s narratives featured the positive and funny in camp life as well as the somber. *Wire*'s editorials, on the other hand, were more apt to stress the bad side. They made *Wire* a bristling watchdog against anything that seemed to excuse Japan's inflictions on internees or slight their suffering. And they took the camp association into political positions that went beyond seeking reparations.

In the May 2011 issue, for example, an editorial attacked the federal government for funding a University of Hawaii conference on the Pacific war. It objected to a pro–Japan view presented at the conference and later picked up by Fox News. It implied wrongly that the conference (which included U.S. war veterans' relatives) largely took Japan's side against alleged Western imperialism and American militarism.[20]

In an editorial a year later, BACEPOW's commander, Angus Lorenzen, complained that far more of his lecture audiences knew of the controversial wartime internment of West Coast Japanese Americans than of Japan's camps for civilians. An earlier editorial had already called the Pacific camp civilians "the 'Forgotten POWs.'" But instead of concentrating his wrath on American ignorance — a failure of education on the Pacific war — he took it out on the experience of the Japanese Americans. He briefly recognized the "difficulty [of being] forcibly relocated" and "losing free will," but then stressed how much better off they had been than Far Eastern internees. In two subsequent issues, he ran articles by Lee Allen, ex–Santo Tomás internee, arguing that signs of espionage by some Japanese Americans meant they had to be interned, and they were better cared for than is usually claimed. Actually, many lost homes and businesses — by act of their own government — and were inadequately and tardily compensated, whereas most Americans prospered in a war boom.

Whatever the facts of their treatment, the whole focus on Japanese Americans — spanning a year of newsletters — amounted to one war-afflicted group (BACEPOW) seeking historical recognition at the expense of another. Lorenzen even put Japanese American "internees" into quotation marks and used the original government euphemism, "relocation," instead of "internment," to distance them from his constitutents.[21]

In his own boyhood memoir, published four years earlier, Lorenzen had taken a different line. An Americanized Briton, he wrote of bonding with Japanese American students at his American high school after the war. Like him, they had been imprisoned and were outsiders to mainstream America. Autobiographer and group advocate were not the same.[22]

The subject of Filipinos was a different matter again. BACEPOW continued the gratitude felt by internees for the support and affection they got from the Philippine population. *Wire* articles recognized Filipino suffering in the war and recorded their heroic assistance to internees. At a big reunion in San Diego in 1999, BACEPOW honored the local Filipino American community. Later, under Lorenzen, it gave prizes for Filipino student essays on a war subject.

All in all, BACEPOW was an important part of the Santo Tomás aftermath. If its political statements sometimes veered into self-pity ("the forgotten POWs"), it nevertheless provided community and historical memory. Inevitably, though, it has meant more to some than to others. Not everyone is a "joiner," and even in early postwar Manila, many ex-internees did not talk much about the camp. Life moved on.

13

Significance

There was no one World War II. Different people experienced it very differently. This was true even at a single prison camp such as Santo Tomás. I want in this final chapter to recognize the variety but also ask general questions. In what ways were our Japanese overlords particularly cruel, and why? Who was responsible for how they behaved: the Japanese people as a whole or their militarist elites? Ex-internees have divided on this. But what was our own responsibility? As prisoners given some scope to run our own affairs, how successfully did we cope with oppression? And beyond this, how did the Santo Tomás experience fit into the sequence of events that led American power back to the Philippines and on to Japan?

Right up to the end, internees differed in the assets they had from the years when they could bring in private food and money. They differed, too, in how they conserved, or did not conserve, the big Red Cross food kits that went equally to everyone fourteen months before liberation. But differences in genetic makeup were also important. The extra food bought by ex-banker Fay Bailey, and the diverse vegetables grown by his young daughter, Caroline, did not stop him getting beriberi. Malnutrition generally hit men worse than women (for physiological reasons explained in Chapter 9), but beriberi did not afflict some other men in their late forties (Bailey's age).

Whatever their biological stars, internees found different ways to survive, mentally as well as physically. Few would have seen them as conscious strategies, but they included the following:

- *Acquiring support groups.* Many came in with a coterie of friends to begin with, but support groups were made, not just inherited. Personality as well as luck helped the pregnant "sinner," Margaret Sherk, acquire friends who stood by her when she needed them.
- *Cautious, practical acceptance.* My mother, Lorna Wilkinson, epitomized this. Though she lost her house and was separated from her husband, she never once showed self-pity or rancor at what the Japanese had inflicted on her. She disliked them for what they had done, but she treated invasion and internment almost as a natural cataclysm. Not assuming that rescue would come soon, she planned for the long term, making our Red Cross kit food last all the way. She was not unique.
- "*The activity cure.*" This approach recommended by a camp poster was apt. Internee historian A.V.H. claimed that the busiest people were generally the happiest. Some

internees, such as mothers with young children, had no choice about being busy, but others threw themselves into work to feel they were doing something constructive. Active curiosity helped too, from the voracious reading of Fay Bailey and Paul Esmérian to teenagers who seemed to be on hand whenever something interesting happened.
- *Ingenuity and making do.* Necessity was indeed the mother of invention, from using Red-Cross kit face cream for frying food to boiling weeds as vegetables, or even Robin Prising making shoelaces as a gift to his father by blacking lengths of twine. Lack of Filipino servants and services encouraged internees to do things for themselves, from mending leaks in shanty roofs to making clothes out of bits and pieces of fabric.
- *Business enterprise.* The camp's mix of cash economy and barter rewarded old skills and developed new ones. Sophie Gibb brought in her hair-cutting skill. Geege Wootten sketched internee children in return for cash or a cake when she found she could draw. People who missed their servants and had the money created jobs for teenagers and others who cut grass around shanties, cleaned dorm spaces, and did other handyman jobs.
- *Finding beauty in small things.* Piped music in the Fathers' Garden or on the plaza, moonlight on the shanties, early morning sunshine after rain—all gave solace to those open to it.
- *Irreverent mischief.* Subversive jokes on the loudspeakers ("better leyte than never") made many feel good, but some daring people went further: Peter Wygle and friends sabotaging Japanese truck tires; Jerry Sams mis-repairing Japanese radios so he could get them back.
- *Loan sharking, profiteering, and stealing.* It would be nice to report that those who lent money at exorbitant rates, bought Red Cross kit food cheap to sell dear later, or stole from dorms and shanties came to no good, but life is not like that. We don't know how many knaves prospered and survived, as they were the least likely of internees to leave a record.

Privation — Real and Relative

Between a quarter and a third of Allied troops taken prisoner by the Japanese died in captivity, mostly from physical abuse, executions, forced labor, malnutrition, and disease with little or no treatment. Civilian internees under the Japanese fared better: 11 percent died, yet this was nearly three times the 4 percent death rate of British and American soldiers captured by the Germans and Italians.

"Only" 8 percent of civilian internees died in the Philippines. In Santo Tomás, 10–12 percent died, more than at other Philippine civilian camps generally because all but three of them closed earlier (by January 1944).[1] Most of their inmates were transferred to Santo Tomás for the last months, which was when near-starvation made deaths accelerate.

Japan's bad treatment of prisoners reflected brutal policies toward its own soldiers—except that "brutal" in the Japanese military lexicon meant instilling "spirit" versus Western decadence. Knowing that Japan could never match the American armaments industry, the country's military leaders sought a counterbalance in their human material. The soldier was to be hardened to endure all in the service of his emperor; he must be determined to prevail; if he couldn't, he must fight "to the death" rather than surrender. Right to the end, some generals and admirals did not accept the possibility of defeat; for others, there was still an invincible Plan B: "glorious" death for the emperor.

Contempt for surrender extended to the enemy, encouraging atrocious treatment of military POWs and sidelining planning for *any* kind of prisoners. Japan's wartime economics played into this. Unable to send food to its troops overseas, it made them buy or loot from the countries they occupied. Even when the Japanese belatedly took on the task of feeding interned "enemy aliens," their own soldiers came first. As food ran short in the occupied countries, whose agriculture they had helped to wreck, they cut internee rations.

Compared with other civilian camps, Santo Tomás was by no means the worst. Internees transferring from Bacolod in March 1943 and Davao in January 1944 thought it almost a "country club" compared to what they had come from. The camp's position in Manila gave it unusual access to hospitals and to aid from non-interned business people and internees' servants, before it was sealed off in early 1944 and the whole city moved toward mass starvation. Isolated rural camps gave more scope to individual commandants to decide conditions — for the worse at Los Baños under its cruel, de facto commandant, Lieut. Konishi, but for the better at Baguio, whose commandants were mostly humane. Elsewhere, the Indonesian camps were particularly bad, for reasons not yet well explained. Sex-segregated, they often forced children as well as women to work far more than the 2–3-hour daily norm for adults and older teenagers at Santo Tomás. But none of the southeast Asian camps suffered from the cold like Shanghai's Lunghua, made famous by J. G. Ballard, where temperatures fell to freezing in January and the buildings were unheated.

What did affect Santo Tomás internees as much as anyone was *relative* deprivation: hardship relative to what they were used to and expected. This happened in two stages. First, racial top dogs accustomed to luxurious living before the war suddenly became a subject people, herded into prison by alien usurpers. Then, after two years of relative prosperity in a "porous prison,"[2] where goods could be brought in and some people could even live at home "on pass," the screws were turned. As outside contacts were severed and feeding reduced, the regime grew more threatening and food became everyone's obsession.

Inequality

There was another kind of relative deprivation too. The "have nots" envied the "haves," those who could afford shanties and get private food and other goodies through the gate until the last year. The camp's large and spread-out population discouraged a total pooling of resources. When people faced each other in a much smaller community, it was harder *not* to share equally. While internee Grace Nash was expecting a baby, she shared a maternity ward out of camp with three other internees. A group of friends, living out of camp because they had babies, offered to send her a hot meal a day. Nash appreciated the offer but demurred: "I couldn't possibly eat when the others are just as hungry as I am." So the friends sent in meals for all four of them once a week.[3]

Among the Philippine camps, pooling for equality was strongest when leaders sought it from the start and the camp was small enough to reach a clear consensus. Bacolod, numbering under 150, met a delay in Japanese feeding by pooling the different amounts of food internees brought in. Harvey Pope, a Scots lumber-company manager, proposed this with Japanese support and was elected camp "director." It helped that he had brought in more food than anyone else, though other business executives bought food for the camp on their firms' credit. Over time, though, the sharing weakened. Internees coming in later often left food at home, arranging with Filipinos and friends to bring it in gradually as private gifts.

Other, smaller camps made various collective arrangements to feed themselves, from equal taxation to contributions according to means.[4] Much depended, again, on the initial setup and leadership. Embedded in a commercial city with lots of private assets, the new prisoners of Santo Tomás were immediately allowed to bring in food and other items from friends and servants for their own use. This served the Japanese camp administrators. They soon had over 3,000 internees on their hands, and maximizing private sources got them off the hook for the first six months before the army started giving money for food and other camp expenses. Once established, a private economy of buying and selling was well entrenched, lasting alongside the free-food "chow-lines" until the Japanese banned private importing in early 1944.

The camp's shanty system, too, morphing from rudimentary shacks to organized townships, involved inequality. A good third of internees could not afford shanties, but they reduced overcrowding in the dormitories, especially after internees were allowed to move into them overnight. Their effect on inequality was two-sided. Like economic segregation in modern housing, they made differences in wealth less visible, as better-off people could eat privately and keep possessions in their shanties. That meant, though, that inequality was not confronted.

The Japanese themselves were uneasy about internee inequality. Some did not like the way their prisoners separated themselves into disparate groups centered on private homesteads. They believed a more uniform and public way of life would make for better order and control. Like other brands of fascism, Japanese nationalism harbored a paradox. Though its militarist organization was harshly hierarchical, its stress on social unity valued collectivism over economic class differences. (The Nazis were not simply lying when they called themselves National Socialists, and Mussolini tripled welfare spending in ten years as a percentage of the Italian budget.) In this spirit, a camp commandant had proposed that the internee government take over camp stores rather than simply taxing their profits as a contribution to the camp.

Internee "campitalism" took a different route. Like a modern liberal state, it encouraged private enterprise, relying on the camp budget and voluntary contributions to aid some of the poorest. Until the front-gate "package line" closed in early 1944, private imports by internees maximized the camp's total assets: outside friends would probably have sent in less food and other goodies if they knew it would be pooled. And food coming in through the gate made camp chow-line food go further. Some of the camp's better-off internees did not use the line every day until well into 1943.

On two occasions, though, a more socialist policy might have paid off. When the big Red Cross food kits arrived in December 1943, the internee government might have pooled them and fed them gradually into the camp chow-line. A small women's camp, Kuching, in Borneo did exactly that. It would have prevented the big disparities — unfair for the children, if not the adults — that occurred when some families ate up their kits too fast. Three months later, when the army closed the package line but allowed Japanese buyers to bring in food for sale, the internee government might have bought and sold the food, controlling its prices by rationing, as it did for some basics. Camp treasurer Fay Bailey belatedly regretted the camp had not done this (see Chapter 9). It would have gone, though, against the grain of the camp's culture. Even the "have nots," who got nothing through the package line, did not propose widespread sharing. The internees were inventive and adaptive; along with that, they valued private enterprise. Rebuild a society they did, but they could not remake their values, and did not want to.

Government by Businessmen

Inequality aside, the record of the business executives who ran the camp is largely a success story and, indeed, a lesson for modern corporate managers. It shows what business leaders can do when short-term profit is off the map.

The challenges facing internee management were formidable. Internee leaders were responsible for governing and preserving a newly created society of over 3,000 people, standing between them and their Japanese overlords. The job included meticulous budgeting and food administration; financial arrangements with outside creditors and benefactors; rigorous public health measures; and planning for a future that might bring anything from starvation to an attack by the Japanese army.

The leaders even operated a "foreign aid" policy, sending help to the non-interned Filipino families of internees and secretly aiding Cabanatuan POWs, some of whom had families in the camp. It was the Cabanatuan aid, involving contact with guerrillas, that probably got the internee leaders Carroll Grinnell and Alfred Duggleby, along with others, tortured and killed by the Kempeitai.

The camp's governing structure — an array of committees and sub-committees — showed that management by committee did not have to mean stultifying groupthink. Committees widened the leaders' support and reduced the workload of individuals, an important factor when malnutrition became widespread. It is easy to forget that the camp, especially in its last year, was run by hungry men working far longer than the 3-hour daily norm for males.

Among the top leaders, Earl Carroll was particularly successful in using diplomacy to head off conflict; it was he who persuaded the Santa Catalina convent nuns to give over most of their building as a hospital. Some other internee leaders were not so good at communicating, in spite of the public notices and information broadcasts. When the Executive Committee suddenly fenced off the main gate so that internees could no longer see visitors bringing in gifts to the "package line," the committee offended internees running the package line. The committee did not tell them in advance what they were doing and that it was being done to protect the whole arrangement after the commandant discovered smuggled messages.

Carroll Grinnell, committee chairman at the time, and some other colleagues were not natural democrats: they valued managerial efficiency over widespread debate and had to be pressured to hold more elections. They did meet calls for more open government, but as the town-meeting row showed, they feared that vociferous argument might upset their Japanese masters and give away too much information. Always they felt they had to make difficult choices, opposing some Japanese demands and acquiescing in others. It was a camp version of the "collaboration" issue — how much was prudent, how much disloyal? — played out in the Philippines as in other occupied countries. At Santo Tomás, cooperation between internee leaders and commandants deterred interference by the army outside and the dreaded Kempeitai: commandants could show they were running an orderly camp, though that did not allay all army fears of internee subversion and revolt.

Race and Blame

At the start of internment, a white man objected to being in the same dorm as a black internee. Another man, the banker Alexander Calhoun (soon to be camp finance chief), would have none of it. "We are all Americans here," he said, "and we have only one enemy."[5] His opinion prevailed in this situation — and in the camp generally. Later in the year, when a black internee and a white one, both merchant seamen, came to blows in an ugly fight, camp leaders asked the fifty or so black Americans if they wanted a committee to represent them. The internees' Executive Committee was worried that the Japanese might score propaganda points by charging internees with racism; a visiting official had already denounced Japanese American internment in the United States of America. The black Americans declined the offer in the same language as Calhoun's: "We are all Americans here." They did not want different treatment.

The camp's general lack of white-black racism was not true everywhere. In the last few months, internee interpreter Frank Cary said that some black and mestizo Americans hung around the commandant's office complaining about "prejudice." But nothing came of it; Commandant Hayashi did not seem to take it seriously. Privately, some internees talked of "niggers" and even "coons." But they kept it quiet, especially as the black Americans included formidable people, such as Dr. Barker Brown, who lectured on Oriental philosophy, and the outspoken military widow, Millie Sanders.[6]

The big divide in racial feeling was between grateful affection for Filipinos and hate of the Japanese invaders. Even those who had condescended to Filipinos before the war appreciated the loving help given them by Filipino servants and friends through the gate. They were appreciated all the more when internees learned of the horrors befalling the city outside. When Tressa Roka first discovered that servants had sold some of her belongings to keep alive, she resented it, but she forgave them at the end when the servants disappeared, possibly killed.

Internees' general dislike of the Japanese was to be expected. It was not always deeply racist, in the sense of believing Japanese people to be innately inferior or despicable. Derogatory labels for the enemy — "Japs" or "Nips," like "Krauts" for the Germans — are common among people at war; what else should one call the foe? And the way some Japanese and Taiwanese strutted around, sloppily dressed with uncovered bellies, invited disrespect, whatever one's racial beliefs. Guarding a prison camp was a low-status job in the Japanese army, often filled by low-standard recruits.

Experiencing their enemies close-up made Santo Tomás internees less lavishly racist than the American media back home. The internees found there were "good" as well as "bad" Japanese, whereas the U.S. media often lumped all Japanese together as fiendish monkey-like animals, an image that continued in comic books after the war. Occasionally, internees even recognized that hate itself could imprison. When eight-year-old Margaret Olsen died of meningitis in the camp, her mother Florence confided to her diary, "Thank God I can't blame the Japanese for the death of my little daughter."[7]

Still, the internees inherited a language of prewar racism, not just derogatory terms for blacks but also phrases such as "yellow peril," an American term first applied to Chinese immigration and then to Japanese militarism. Camp diaries contrasted Japanese short stature ("little runts") with their bullying power, while a camp drawing by James McCall portrayed the Japanese aggressor as a monstrous quasi-gorilla. Just after the war McCall published a camp poem by another internee calling the Japanese "ape-men" and "filthy vermin." (McCall, who also made digs at the British, showed that racism was not all of a piece: he had a Filipino wife, not interned, and after the war he ran UNICEF aid for Asian children.) At liberation, some internees extended their loathing of the Japanese to the U.S. Army's Japanese American interpreters — to the disgust of Emily Van Sickle.[8]

After liberation, Tressa Roka found it took time "to stop hating" — to discover that "hate, greed, and prejudice were not confined to the enemy alone" and that "yesterday's enemy could be today's ally."[9] Some ex-internees never reached that point, goaded by Japan's resistance to acknowledging war crimes, unlike Germany. Again people varied. Some former internees did not consciously blame contemporary Japanese for what their country had done in the war, but emotionally they preferred to stay away from them. Others, like Nick Balfour, who worked in Japan after the war, had no problem.

In looking back at Japan's responsibility for what they and others had suffered, former internees divided into two groups. One group blamed the Japanese generally for a warlike spirit that they all willingly shared. The other group stressed the ability of "gangsters" at the top to indoctrinate the people and propel them into aggression. They blamed powerful, militarist leaders rather than the people as a whole.

The first group stressed the enormous commitment of Japanese soldiers to fight "to the death" and their shame when, rarely, they did surrender. The home front supported this. The Japan that produced *kamikaze* pilots and suicide attacks by infantry also produced mothers who told their military sons to die rather than give up: surrender would bring ostracism on their families. Long before Pearl Harbor, too, the Japanese people generally supported the invasion of China: after all, why should only westerners be allowed to have empires?

"A people gets the government it deserves," an ex-internee told me. This view was not necessarily racist in a biological sense: blaming a whole culture did not invariably mean blaming a Japanese DNA. In wartime America, though, blaming the Japanese as a whole produced genocidal hate in the press — "the only good Japanese is a dead one" — whereas media hatred of Germans was more focused on the real Nazis. And long after the war, Robin Prising's Santo Tomás memoir was still unusual among camp narratives in recognizing that oppressors could be victims too, including rank-and-file Japanese soldiers.[10] More than half a million Japanese died in the Philippines, many from hunger; some resorted to cannibalism.

The second group of ex-internees, which includes me, has stressed totalitarian power:

the ability of Japan's military leaders to indoctrinate and intimidate the people. No ex-internees have elaborated the full argument, but it runs like this: From long before the war, Japan's rulers tried to isolate the people from knowledge of other countries. Through "voluntary" local associations, they regulated behavior and linked veneration of the emperor to a warlike spirit. When war came, the Kempeitai secret police punished suspected dissenters. Government propaganda persuaded many Japanese that Western soldiers were depraved monsters who would do things worse than death to the people if they were allowed to invade. When U.S. troops took the island of Saipan in the Marianas, many of the Japanese families living there killed themselves, hurling first their babies and then themselves off cliffs to avoid falling into American hands. Within the military, no-surrender indoctrination was still fiercer. As the war came to wreak havoc on Japanese soldiers and civilians, they sometimes complained bitterly about their leaders' privileges and mistakes, but they did so privately. They saw no real alternative to fighting the war.

Admittedly, Japanese military fascism gained traction in a culture of obedience and conformity. But the Japanese were not uniquely susceptible to being bullied and brainwashed. As we saw in Chapter 1, Americans in the prewar Philippines made no fuss about State Department efforts to stop them from leaving, even impounding passports. After the war, Communist witch-hunts frightened many Americans into a terror of being associated with any left-wing activity. More recently, the Milgram experiments, starting with Yale students and replicated around the world, have shown that people are often prepared to inflict intense pain on others if commanded to do so by respected authority.[11] So it is not surprising that in the closed society of Japan, the government's combination of threats, propaganda, and instilled emperor worship could wield immense psychological power over the Japanese people. Both government and people came, in the long run, out of the same culture, but the individual soldier or civilian did not invent Japanese militarism.

In the Philippines, abusive Japanese treatment of Filipinos — much of it racist — did not just spring from the mental knapsack of ordinary soldiers; it came from higher up. At Santo Tomás, even the most humane commandants — humane at least to their charges — let their soldiers at the gate abuse Filipinos much more than internees. Internees "on pass" out of camp also noticed the harsher treatment of Filipinos. Some of this was the bad behavior of occupying troops in general, far from home and ignorant of local customs. But their rulers had made it worse. Japan's leadership had landed them in a hastily occupied country, without education about anything outside Japan, while telling them they came from a superior "Yamato" race. Racism may explain why the camp's commandants permitted more abuse of Filipinos and why Commandant Hayashi ignored complaints about "prejudice" by black and mestizo internees.

Ordinary soldiers, who did not get to know Westerners, were more likely than the camp commandants to swallow the official line that Westerners were arrogant and decadent. This made them all the angrier when their Filipino "inferiors" showed affection for Americans rather than gratitude at being "liberated" from them. As I explained in Chapter 3, it all became a vicious circle. Face-slapping, the standard discipline meted out to the soldiers themselves, alienated Filipinos still further, leading to more abuse.

When some of the soldiers got to know Filipinos and became friendly with them, visiting brass from Tokyo worried that the local troops were getting too soft, just as officials had worried that the Santo Tomás garrison was getting too "lax" (see Chapter 10). In Manila, the Japanese Propaganda Corps encouraged good relations with the locals, but the Kempeiai and other, fascistic officers wanted a hard line against any sign of disrespect — which, again, was self-defeating. Fascists make bad imperialists.[12]

Stressing the political and social conditioning of the Japanese may seem to excuse too many Japanese for what their country did. The problem is not confined to the Pacific war. What we are faced with is the dilemma of blame and individual responsibility in an age of social and scientific explanation. To be culpable of doing wrong, a person must have free will to choose what he or she does. Our legal and moral codes are mainly based on this concept. Since the 1920s, however, the rise of the behavioral sciences — followed more recently by studies of the brain — have reduced the play of free will by showing how social and neurological forces shape behavior. Did the sinner really choose to sin, or was he or she conditioned to do it? In which case was it blameworthy sin?[13]

The dilemma is not wholly modern. In the sixteenth century John Calvin argued anxiously, tortuously, and (I think) unsuccessfully that divine "predestination"—God's advance selection of sinners and saved—was compatible with the sinner's "free will" in choosing to sin. Calvin's anxiety flourishes in our own time, except that social and scientific "determinism" has replaced religious predestination as a threat to free will and moral responsibility. In the 1960s, President Lyndon Johnson used the inner-city black riots, and the deprivation they reflected, to promote his "war on poverty." In doing so he was at pains to say that *understanding* the riots' causes was not to *excuse* them. But the problem of understanding without excusing did not go away. We see it today when trying to understand the background of a criminal offender is often suspected of excusing criminal behavior — and slighting its victims.

In 2005, James Nelson published a study of the infamous Bataan Death March, in which up to 20,000 Filipino and American POWs died — many from torture, executions, starvation, and thirst along the way — as they were marched from their Bataan surrender to the atrocious Camp O'Donnell. Nelson, whose POW father survived transport on a "hellship" to Japan, vividly described the atrocities. They appalled him as much as anyone but he went beyond blaming individual soldiers. He stressed the military training that brutalized death march guards as well as a massive logistical failure to anticipate the needs of the prisoners, many of whom were already wounded and/or weakened by malaria. Nelson's article angered one of my correspondents, Frederico Baldassarre, the son of a death march survivor. Dismissing the article as "just one more apology" (i.e., excuse) for Japanese behavior, he argued that officers in charge of the march could have resisted brutality. The same applied, he said, to the Japanese people. Whether or not he was right about that, he implicitly feared the same elision of *understanding* and *excuse* that Lyndon Johnson had tried to head off.[14]

Baldassarre recognized the problem. To the extent that brutal policies from above conditioned the death march abusers, the abusers were not culpable. Many people will find this hard to take. They might point to the fact that some of the death march guards and officers did show kindness rather than cruelty to the POWs — just as some guards at Santo Tomás and other camps tried to mitigate the suffering of internees, especially little children. Did this not mean that many others also had the free will to choose, and so were culpable when they *were* abusive? Or did it take special circumstances, perhaps going back to childhood, to mold the kind ones so that they resisted the army's general brutality? Nobody knows. We really don't, but that uncertainty is hard to accept.

Atrocities

Most Santo Tomás internees did not see or experience "atrocities" in the usual sense of that term. There is no record of rape by Japanese in the camp. The closest thing to atrocity suffered by most internees was the slow-motion assault of increasing starvation. Atrocities, nevertheless, were on their minds. Images of the 1937 Nanjing massacres frightened many on the eve of internment. During internment, reports of Japanese cruelties affected people differently, from the stories of torture methods told with gusto in the Boys' Club to adult fears of massacre. Fear became reality when the first three escapers were horrifically executed, and the Kempeitai seized other internees suspected of subversion. At the end, the brutalization of war reached into the camp when internees themselves mutilated and kicked the guard commander, Lieut. Nanakazu Abiko, as he lay dying in agony.

Outside the camp, on a more horrific scale, news of the Palawan massacre, burning POWs alive at the Puerto Princesa camp, may have speeded the camp's rescue. Liberation prefaced the even more horrendous "rape" of Manila when the city's Japanese defenders ran the gamut of atrocity from burning people alive to using their bayonets to pierce infants and "open up" women. For ex-internees and many others, this confirmed the exceptional cruelty of the Japanese. They were right, too, in that Japanese soldiers were generally readier than Allied ones to inflict pain on victims right in front of them. Judged on effects, though, American bombing and shelling killed and maimed more civilians than the Japanese did.

In March 1945, as the Battle for Manila was ending, the U.S. air force general, Curtis LeMay, intensified the firebombing of Japanese cities. It incinerated over 180,000 Japanese men, women, and children, not counting Hiroshima and Nagasaki. The Japanese media denounced LeMay's use of incendiary bombs as "fiendish" and uncivilized in much the same language that Americans used against the Japanese, but American opinion generally did not see the raids as atrocities — not after the much-publicized Bataan Death March, followed by Manila. Douglas MacArthur himself detested bombing cities; he banned it in the Battle for Manila, and a close aide denounced LeMay's raids as "barbaric." But other top commanders did not share MacArthur's view.[15]

What distinguished the Japanese atrocities that surrounded and threatened Santo Tomás from Allied cruelties? Dictionaries define atrocities as one of two things: they are very cruel acts or appallingly wicked ones. Common usage requires both elements for an act to qualify as an atrocity. The second element is more subjective: it allows people to excuse or partly excuse an action (i.e., reduce its wickedness) for extenuating reasons. When Filipino guerrillas caught Japanese soldiers, they often cut them up before killing them; the Philippines has a strong knife culture. After liberation, Santo Tomás internee Alice Bryant told a Filipino acquaintance that she opposed all American torture of Japanese. But she became more understanding of *Filipino* torturing when he reminded her of the many Japanese abuses of Filipinos in addition to wrecking their country. Even Bryant, who later became a peace activist, recognized revenge for past ill treatment as a mitigating factor.[16]

Many people also exempt cruel attacks from being atrocities if they seemed at the time to be ultimately life-saving or otherwise served humane purposes. This "ends justify the means" argument, which underlies most defensive wars ("good wars"), has been applied to Allied bombing of cities, most obviously Hiroshima and Nagasaki, but not just to them. Bloodthirsty as he seemed, Curtis LeMay claimed sincerely, and plausibly at the time, that his firebombing would shorten the war and save lives by weakening Japanese morale and war production. Quite recently, one of my ex–Santo Tomás correspondents (a kindly man) argued that total war made the whole Japanese population fair game for air raids. The Japanese equivalent of "Rosie the Riveter" was as much part of the war machine as a soldier. (Rosie's children he did not mention.)

Western opinion in World War II and since has also tended to associate atrocities with *personal behavior*: individuals, whether en masse or not, torturing, raping, murdering other individuals, in contrast with the pilot and bombardier thousands of feet up who never see the agony they inflict. As the Pacific war mounted in ferocity, both sides killed and sometimes tortured captives in the stress of battle; American and Australian soldiers were especially goaded by the suicidal "treachery" of Japanese, who would play dead or wounded, doing more killing before getting killed themselves. But the Japanese also used massacre and torture as part of military and police procedure. In that sense, they produced far more atrocities. In the long run, technological killing at a distance, insulating killers from the horror of what they do, may be as much a threat to humanity, but abusing individuals when you can actually see them and hear their cries often seems worse.[17]

At the border between technological and personal killing was strafing survivors of sunken Japanese troopships. One proponent of this practice was Air Force Major Paul ("Pappy") Gunn, whose family was in Santo Tomás. On the basis of the 1929 Geneva Convention, which banned injury to "fallen" and "unarmed" enemies, Gunn and others who did or authorized it were war criminals — all the more as it was deliberate policy. It was an assault on the pilots, too, because they could see the frightened faces of their victims and often felt distressed and guilty about it. Gunn's motives included revenge for what the Japanese had done in the Philippines, but he had a rationale. "Better we kill them in the water than let them kill our boys on the land," he told his pilots.[18] This, too, was an "ends justify the means" argument: winning and ending the war by killing enemy troops.

Military training on both sides whipped up aggressive hatred. But the anguish of Gunn's pilots — which he respected but overrode — was far from the personal sadism deliberately enlisted by the Japanese against civilians. In the Nanjing atrocities, raping, massacring, and pillaging by Japanese soldiers gathered its own momentum, but government propaganda had encouraged them with images of the Chinese as dangerously treacherous. The army also instigated the atrocities to terrorize and control the population.

In Manila, as elsewhere, systematic torturing by Kempeitai interrogators employed sadists who enjoyed the work. The Manila atrocities of 1945 looked at first more spontaneous. Often drunk, the Japanese soldiers came to realize they would die, so why not enjoy themselves first against a distrusted and disliked population? Their cruelty to babies is the hardest to understand, in view of the traditional Japanese love of children, demonstrated in Santo Tomás. One explanation is that you attack in your enemy what you prize most if you want to give your enemy maximum hurt.

Whatever hellish psychology operated, we now know that the Manila atrocities did not arise *only* from personal rage, fear, and lust. Military orders *utilized* these feelings by commanding the massacres: they declared that "even women and children [had] become guerrillas"; all non–Japanese should be killed. The orders reflected the bewilderment of urban warfare in which anyone might be the enemy, but they also drew on extreme violence in Japanese military traditions, even against their own soldiers. The orders specified "suicide attacks" and commanded "friends of the wounded [to] make them commit suicide" so they would not be taken prisoner.[19]

Compared with these enormities, the abuse of a dying guard commander, Lieut. Abiko, by Santo Tomás internees may seem trivial. But it wasn't. It showed how irrational cruelty gets justified. The attack on Abiko was mainly one of revenge — a powerful human motive. As internee Tressa Roka said at the time, he was attacked as a scapegoat for all Japanese actions against the internees, but he was also attacked for his own bullying and humiliating behavior.

Reporters covering the camp's liberation did not mention his abuse. It would not do for the folks back home to think of the internees as anything other than innocent victims. To this day, however, some ex-internees have said he deserved all he got. "He was such a bastard ... such a monster," one of them told me, as if he were a Himmler or a Kempeitai torturer, which he was not.

Other internees were appalled at the time, or disapproved in retrospect. In his recollections published half a century later, camp teenager Peter Wygle said he was not at all proud to have been one of a mob kicking Abiko on the ground. He even allowed himself some respect for the fighting spirit showed by Abiko at the end, "doing what he felt a soldier was supposed to do."[20]

Whatever their views later, Abiko's attackers demonstrated a universal truth about human cruelty: people find added license to attack others when they see their victims not as the vulnerable underdogs they are (in this case, a man dying on the ground) but as oppressive overdogs (a powerful guard commander). Self-deception is a robust human tendency. In China's "cultural revolution" of the 1960s, the Red Guards showed this in spades when they persecuted and humiliated their own parents and teachers as supposed agents of an old, oppressive order.

Against this proposition, a defender of Abiko's abuse told me that one could not expect his attackers to adjust so fast from oppressor image to victim image after all the suffering they had been through. Yet internee opponents of the abuse, and the "gloating" over his body afterward, made this adjustment: they did not lose their moral compass. To avoid a double standard, we should ask the same "free will" question posed about humane Japanese on the Bataan Death March, even though we don't know the answer. Did those who opposed Abiko's abuse show that the abusers could have chosen otherwise? Or were abusers and their opponents conditioned differently? Or could it just be that the objectors to his abuse had fewer bad experiences of Abiko?

There was also the secondary motive of trophy-seeking: the attempt to cut off Abiko's ear as well as buttons and insignia. Taking enemy body parts, especially ears, as well as gold teeth, was a particular American practice; other Allied troops seldom went in for it. Did it come from a folk memory of frontier scalping? Or was it just a macabre form of souvenir collecting, a degraded consumerism? Again, there is no sure answer.[21]

Lieutenant Abiko himself could be cruel. When internees, caught watching American air raids, were made to stand all day looking toward the sun, Abiko as guard commander was responsible for the harsh way the punishment was enforced, making the victim stand without moving. But that was not why internees attacked him at the end. Few of them had seen or undergone the abuses that many Filipinos had received from other Japanese. Internees attacked Abiko because of the lengthy bowing practices he put them through, his bullying of labor gangs, and his intimidating manner. The abuse of Abiko was akin to killing between rival youth-gang members for not showing "respect." He was attacked for assaulting the ego, not the physical person. It was a deeper version of the Japanese concern with "face" that internees had sometimes scoffed at.

A Bloody Sequence

The liberation of Santo Tomás heralded the only U.S. Army ground attack on a big defended city in the Pacific war. And that was bound to be a formidable and bloody enterprise. "Never do it if you can avoid it" was the advice of the ancient Chinese military sage, Sun Tzu, on attacking "fortified cities."[22]

Although the camp's rescue *led to* the tragedy that befell Manila, it did not *cause* that tragedy. The Santo Tomás liberation differed here from the liberation of the camp's offshoot, Los Baños. The 11th Airborne Division, which whisked away the Los Baños internees in amtracs across the nearby lake, Laguna de Bay, could not stay to hold the area; Japanese forces there were too strong. This enabled the Japanese to massacre in reprisal the Filipinos of a nearby barrio, though guerrillas had warned the locals to leave.[23]

In Manila's case, the U.S. attack on the city and the subsequent slaughter would have probably happened anyway, Santo Tomás or no Santo Tomás, due to the military importance of the Manila harbor and the symbolic significance of taking the capital. MacArthur's subordinate general, Walter Krueger, a less political animal, wanted to postpone attacking Manila while he went after the main Japanese forces in the hills. But even if his choice had prevailed, it would have just prolonged the agony of a starving city held by vengeful soldiers, since it would have meant isolating and blockading Manila. We now know what happened when American and Australian forces bypassed and bottled up Japanese garrisons, leaving them to "wither on the vine," in the comfortable euphemism of war planners. On Pacific islands not invaded but instead blockaded by the Allies, Japanese and islanders alike starved to death. Elsewhere, when starving Japanese resorted to cannibalism, they sometimes killed prisoners and local people for food. Given the state of mind of Manila's defenders, this might well have happened there too, on top of the atrocities that did happen.[24]

Though MacArthur's eagerness to liberate Santo Tomás was not responsible for Manila's suffering, the camp had a place in the events that led to the Battle for Manila. In late July 1944, America's top Pacific commanders met with President Franklin Roosevelt in Honolulu to discuss future strategy. The commanders divided over whether to bypass the Philippines, or most of it, and attack Formosa (Taiwan) as a stepping-stone to Japan or to take Luzon first as the springboard for an advance. MacArthur passionately advocated "Luzon first." Behind his detailed military case lay personal reasons — a wish to vindicate himself triumphantly in the Philippines after his humiliation there two years before, plus a genuine love of the country. In a private moment with the president, he made it political. Bypassing the Philippines in favor of Formosa would, he said, mean abandoning "millions of [Filipino] wards of the United States and thousands of internees and prisoners of war." This would damage American prestige throughout the Far East and bring punishment in the U.S. elections that fall.[25]

13. Significance

Memorare — Manila 1945 monument. Unveiled in February 1995. This sculpture, near Manila Cathedral, commemorates victims of the horrendous Battle for Manila, February–March 1945. Created by Peter de Guzman, its weeping mother represents the Philippines and motherhood. She is surrounded by dead children, a rape victim (right), a distraught young man (left) and a dead elderly man (bottom). The inscription is by the author Nick Joaquin. A nearby plaque says that the civilian dead were "victims of heinous acts perpetrated by the Japanese imperial forces and the casualties of the heavy artillery barrage of the American forces" *(courtesy of Memorare — Manila 1945 Foundation, Inc.)*.

No decision was made then; Washington did not give "Luzon first" the green light until early October. It did so on the basis of new, logistical calculations and military events, including the Japanese capture of Chinese airfields near Taiwan. It is hard to imagine, though, that FDR would have countenanced a total bypassing of Luzon as his fears grew about the fate of the prison camps with their substantial American populations.

Long after MacArthur invaded the Philippines, he continued to think he could liberate *both* Manila's internees and its general population without great loss of life. Unlike General Krueger, he did not believe he would meet much resistance in the city. His intelligence advisers, plus his own wishful thinking, completely missed the resolve of Manila's Japanese commander, Admiral Sanji Iwabuchi, to defend the city. As late as 4 February 1945, the day after MacArthur's tanks broke into Santo Tomás, he was planning an early victory parade in Manila.

It was not to be. The inmates of Santo Tomás, and the smaller Bilibid prison close by, were saved, but not the city. Santo Tomás indeed became one of the safest places to be in the city — after its brief shelling. That, in fact, was not new. By 1944, Santo Tomás offered more security from starvation and abusive soldiers than many could count on outside. Pleas to let in the Filipino families of internees, usually women and children, came from more than a wish to be reunited with interned husbands and fathers.

For all their losses and tribulations, the internees of Santo Tomás were a protected people.

Appendix I: Chronology

Events outside the camp are in italics.

1941

8 December	*News of Pearl Harbor attack reaches Manila, followed by Japanese bombing.*
22 December	*Japanese forces land at Lingayen Gulf, 115 miles up the Luzon coast from Manila.*
24 December	*US/Philippine commander, Gen. Douglas MacArthur, and staff leave Manila for Corregidor island fortress, as army evacuates to the Bataan peninsula and Corregidor.*

1942

2 January	Japanese troops enter Manila.
4 January	Allied nationals ("enemy aliens") start arriving at Santo Tomás.
6 January	"Package line" begins: private food, other supplies, and money are allowed through the main gate, but only minimal messages. "Pass" system also starts, allowing some internees to leave camp on a temporary "pass," to visit or stay in hospitals or live at home on grounds of illness or having small infants.
January	Whirlwind of clearing, building, repairs, plumbing latrines and establishing cooking facilities.
February	First "shanties" are built, initially used just during the day. First planting in camp vegetable garden also takes place.
15 February	First atrocity against internees: flogging and execution of three escapers.
20 February	Internees enter the camp from Sulphur Springs, a hotel outside Manila, used as a holding center for transients from China.
6 May	Corregidor falls to the Japanese, completing their occupation of the Philippines. Corregidor nurses mostly go to Santo Tomás. Last GIs surrender on 12 May on Mindanao, though some join guerrillas.
2 July	Japanese army starts cash payments to the camp for food and other supplies. Camp buyers are allowed outside the camp. Before this, the Red Cross was the main provider for the whole camp.
27 July	Internee-run jail is permitted, in place of sending miscreants outside to military police.
28 July	Elections for new internee Executive Committee, approved by the commandant on 6 July. Later the Committee becomes increasingly unelected as members leave and are replaced by the commandant's appointees.
Late August	Main camp hospital is transferred to Santa Catalina convent-dormitory for nuns and women students, across the street along the camp's east wall, after initial resistance by the Japanese. Nuns retain a wing of the building.
November–December	Internee anger erupts when Executive Committee cancels "town meetings" for fear of inflaming dissension and revealing too much to the Japanese.

1943

5 January	Following jail sentences for persistent drunkenness offenders, a camp vote supports continued naming-and-shaming of all punished internees by broadcasting their names and sentences, whatever the offence. A quarter of the vote opposes it and the camp announcer resigns.
11 January	Comments by a discontented troublemaker lead the commandant to require all internees with military records to identify themselves to him. Thirty are taken out. Most end up in military camps. Some die en route to Japan when the U.S. Navy attacks their unmarked ships.
20–21 January	Four "pregnant papas" are jailed when new internee pregnancies are revealed. In a row about illegal sex in shanties, the commandant temporarily suspends shanty use for most occupants, and "indefinitely" cancels elections to the Executive Committee.
	Late January Commandant shuts down the *STIC Gazette*, the internee newspaper that succeeded *Internews* (started January 1942). *Internitis* (stories and humor) was closed in November 1942 for using scarce paper to "frivolous purpose."
	February Men get permission to sleep in shanties.
8–10	March Japanese authorities outside the camp, concerned about contacts with Filipinos, suddenly arrest over 100 internees out on "on pass" (see 6 January 1942). About 60 are held for two days in bad conditions at Fort Santiago police prison/HQ and interrogated before release.
10 March	After closure of Bacolod Camp on Negros, its 119 internees arrive in Santo Tomás. The internees of other civilian camps in the Philippines are moved to Santo Tomás by early January 1944, leaving only Baguio (Camp Holmes), Santo Tomás, and Los Baños (see 13 May below). Baguio internees go to Bilibid Prison near Santo Tomás on 29–30 December 1944.
May	General recall of internees with passes to live at home due to illness or infants, except for some seriously ill or disabled. Space problems prompt commandant to allow children to sleep with fathers in shanties. Shanty regulations of August 1943 restrict girls to eight years old or younger.
13 May	786 men and 12 women nurses move to new, rural camp at Los Baños. 207 (mostly wives and "sweethearts") follow in December, and 511 men, women, and children in early April 1944, but not "able-bodied" men. 150 more go in early December 1944.
26 September	127 internees are repatriated as part of a prisoner exchange. Confusion and suspicion abound about how they were selected, but two days before they go, camp impresario Dave Harvey and others give a farewell show, revealing "The Lost Tribes of the Philippines," a.k.a. STIC internees, to a bewildered anthropologist. Earlier evacuations in 1942, mainly diplomatic or transfers of Shanghai people back there, were less controversial.
September–December	Disquiet at unelected status of most Executive Committee members pressures the committee to hold an election (4 October) for a place vacated by repatriation of its vice-chairman. Don Holter, leading critic of the committee (and future Methodist bishop), wins the place by a landslide. Some non-elected members are replaced at intervals by elections — permitted by the commandant but ended by army takeover (6 January below).
14 October	*Japanese Military Administration of the Philippines establishes a puppet republic under President José Laurel, officially replacing the Philippine Executive Commission and Japanese Military Administration. The republic's constitution was promulgated on 4 September.*
14–17 November	Big typhoon floods out shanties, causing massive overcrowding in the Main Building.
16–19 December	Last delivery of Red Cross "comfort kits" — boxes of food for each internee (including children), plus medicines, vitamins and other supplies for the whole camp. But distribution is delayed when guards find U.S. patriotic labels on cigarette packs in the boxes.

1944

6 January	Santo Tomás is transferred to direct army control under the army's War-Prisoner Headquarters, from a quasi-civilian authority, where it has been since transfer from the military police in February 1942.
15 January	Camp population is recorded as reaching 3,945 (from 3,359 at the end of January 1942 and 3,700 in late May 1943). This excludes 614 still with passes to be outside, mainly in hospitals; most are recalled later but 360 internees go to Los Baños in April. At liberation (3 February 1945), the camp numbers about 3,900.
1 February	Women are allowed to sleep in shanties along with men of the same family. Reveille on camp loudspeakers plays "Here Comes the Bride." Special permission was given on 10 January to a woman, newly re-interned, to join her husband in his shanty overnight. By late March 1944, over 1,000 internees are sleeping in shanties.
February	Japanese army takes over direct food supply to the internee administration, under protest by latter. The army stops private food imports through the main gate (the "package line"), though sending private laundry out of the camp is allowed until 10 July! Internee committee can provide "supplementary" food and other items from food reserves or cash reserves (bought via Japanese agents), and outlets selling some items for cash remain open, but serious food cuts follow later.
	Shanties near walls are ordered to be taken down or moved. More shanty removal, from within 20 meters of the walls, follows in late April.
	Various other measures to seal off, control, and inspect internees are taken this month, including a second, 8 A.M. roll call, started 28 February, in addition to the evening roll call.
	Inmates at four outside hospitals and the Holy Ghost College children's home are returned to Santo Tomás. Other hospitals are mostly closed to internees by October 1944. Internee leaders protest the internment of seriously ill people.
18 February	Commandant replaces the internee Executive Committee with a smaller, appointed Internee Administration Committee of just three members (one British).
23 February	A new commandant, S. Onozoki, permits the election of three "Agents" as internee representatives (one British), in the absence of elections for the Internee Committee.
23, 28 February	Military police brutally interrogate, take out, and jail four internees suspected of bringing in news from outside. They are joined in April by a fifth, initially in the camp hospital due to abuse by the interrogators. One dies in prison. The other four return to camp after liberation, having escaped a mass execution at Muntinlupa Prison, 3–4 February 1945, which was interrupted by approaching U.S. forces and a guerrilla rescue. The internee Agents had repeatedly inquired and protested about the arrests.
3 March	Many internees are thrilled to get mail and food parcels from American relatives and friends, including toiletries and children's clothes.
20 March	Commandant closes off the Fathers' Garden beside the seminary, used for concerts and church services.
April	Scheme for smuggling in extra money for the camp is started via university administrator Luis de Alcuaz, following some money and medicine smuggling by two American seminary fathers and others. Food smuggling for the camp starts in September.
April–May	Internees resist a Japanese loyalty oath, but sign a weakened version.
28 May	A Sunday remembered as "Roll Call Day." Two snap roll calls are held, lining up internees for over two hours from noon and an hour before supper. At other times Lieut. Abiko and others rehearse internees in "proper" bowing. They slap objectors and an old man found sitting in a chair.
Mid-June	The last issue of *Manila Tribune* (Japanese-controlled) is allowed into camp, having been temporarily banned from 22 February to 1 May. Some copies still come in unofficially.
1 July	Commandant ends theatrical performances after a big variety show makes fun of internee conditions and hints that Paris will soon fall to the Allies.

8 July	407 clergy and their families, out "on pass," are brought into camp, kept apart from other internees, and trucked to Los Baños the next day.
27 July	*Honolulu meeting between President Roosevelt and his top Pacific war commanders focuses on the strategy and logistics of "Formosa first" versus "Luzon first"—attacking Japan via Formosa (Taiwan) or first taking Luzon. Gen. MacArthur makes a political and moral as well as military argument for liberating the Philippines and its internees, but the issue is not finally decided until October (see 3 October below).*
Early August	Under Japanese army orders, the commandant requires internees to turn in cash above 50 pesos per person for deposit in their own accounts at Manila's Bank of Taiwan. The Internee Committee and Agents protest; most people comply, but some hide cash. Some give from their surplus money to camp funds. Individuals can draw 50 pesos a month from their accounts via the internee administration but the money is rapidly depreciating and items to buy are dwindling. The commandant also sets up closer oversight of money taken out of the camp's own bank account.
9–10 August	Japanese guards start building air-raid shelters for their own use. Later in the month they start training for "enemy" invasion and other "emergencies," including floods.
August	The camp gambles on meat reserves. Based on a divided vote by camp doctors, the Internee Committee decides to use up the reserves by the end of October. Extra weekly provision of 6 ounces of corned beef per internee, or other meat, starts on 6 September, running out in late October.
Mid-September	Typhoid outbreak among Japanese guards is followed by new Japanese hygiene requirements governing the garrison. Internees are not affected due to their own public health measures.
21 September	*Big U.S. air raid on Manila docks takes place*, the first one visible to internees, and a great spectacle. Intermittent air raids and air-raid warnings occur from then on. Internees caught watching are made to stand all day in the sun looking upward.
3 October	*"Luzon first" finally beats "Formosa first." A directive by the U.S. Joint Chiefs of Staff authorizes a move on Japan via Luzon, Iwo Jima, and Okinawa rather than invading Formosa (Taiwan).*
6 October	Commandant orders a stop to commercial selling in the camp. Prices are by now astronomical, but private smuggling and profiteering continue, much of it by bribing guards.
10 October	*Gen. Tomoyuki Yamashita ("the Tiger of Malaya") assumes command of the Japanese army defending the Philippines.*
14 October	Clyde DeWitt, lawyer among the Agents and a thorn of complaint to the Japanese, is made to join a transfer of internees to Los Baños, under protest by the Agents and others.
20 October	*U.S. forces land in the Philippines at Leyte island.* Informed by secret radio, the camp's morning broadcaster says, "Better leyte than never."
October–November	Over 50 "civilian employees" and "civilian *military* employees," many of them Taiwanese, replace Japanese guards, who leave for active service elsewhere. Commandant urges weakened internees to grow more vegetables.
22 November	Camp milk ended for children over 3.
30 November	Japanese guard logbook reports vitamin B injections for 23 guards with beriberi symptoms.
5 December	Reg Spear (OSS special forces) gets into Santo Tomás for a few hours to discuss rescue scenarios and Japanese intentions with camp leaders.
14 December	*Approximately 140 U.S. POWS are massacred at a camp on Palawan island when the local Japanese commander believes a U.S. landing is imminent. A few escape.*
15 December	*U.S. forces land on Mindoro island, just south of Luzon. By the end of the month, Americans and Australians build two airbases for land-based aircraft to cover an assault on Luzon.*
23 December	Two camp leaders and two others are suddenly jailed on suspicion of contact with guerrillas and U.S. forces, and then taken out by the Kempeitai. Their bodies, beheaded, are found after the camp is liberated.
25 December	*U.S. planes drop leaflets on Manila*, including the camp, from the "Commander in

Chief" and "the American Forces of Liberation," wishing "their gallant allies, the People of the Philippines, all the blessings of Christmas, and the realization of their fervent hopes for the New Year."

December–January 1945
Gen. Yamashita (Philippine army commander) pulls troops out of Manila, preferring to fight in the hills, but leaves some units behind when two admirals (Okochi and Iwabuchi) commit naval soldiers to Manila's defense.

1945

6–8 January	Some of the Japanese garrison leave the camp, having burned documents and trucked out supplies. On 7 January Commandant Hayashi holds a long secret meeting with top internees, saying his staff and soldiers will leave the camp to fight in the hills, but the decision is reversed that afternoon.
9 January	*U.S. 6th Army lands at Lingayen Gulf, Luzon, where the Japanese landed three years before. At the end of January, U.S. 8th Army units land on Luzon west coast, north and south of Manila.*
16 January	Internee Joseph Eisenberg escapes from the gym male dormitory near the wall and gets to U.S. army lines. Commandant Hayashi transfers men under 50 from the gym and gives a suspended prison sentence to the dorm monitors, with dire warnings against it happening again.
30 January	*U.S. special forces and Filipino guerrillas rescue 489 military POWs and 33 civilian prisoners from their camp at Cabanatuan, behind Japanese lines 75 miles north of Manila.*
31 January	Ted Stevenson, a camp doctor, is jailed for refusing to take "malnutrition" off death certificates. Deaths more than double from 15 in December to 32 in January. Camp "chow-line" in January provides under 1,000 calories a day per internee: under 800 from the army, plus some from camp and private stocks.
31 January–2 February	Japanese garrison again shows signs of leaving: burning documents, trucking out supplies, killing their livestock, and stealing from the camp gardens. Some soldiers depart.
3 February (Saturday)	U.S. flier, an internee's brother, drops goggles with a note: "Roll out the barrel. Santa Claus is coming Sunday or Monday." (Other wordings reported.)
3 February (evening)	*A "flying column" of the 1st Cavalry Division enters Santo Tomás,* joyously liberating most internees, but faces a siege in one building where the Japanese garrison holds some internees hostage (including young boys). Some internees savage the hated guard commander, Lieut. Abiko, after he is mortally wounded.
4 February	*A few blocks from the camp, the 37th Infantry Division liberates military POWs and civilian internees at Bilibid Prison just after the division closes in on Santo Tomás. The prison's guards left earlier the same day.*
5 February	The siege in Santo Tomás ends with "safe conduct" for the Japanese garrison out of the camp. Many are believed to have died soon after in the fighting. A few return to the camp as captured prisoners.
7–11 February	Japanese shelling kills over 20, mostly internees but also Filipino workers and one GI.
23 February	*Over two thousand internees at Los Baños, the spin-off from Santo Tomás, are rescued in a combined operation behind Japanese lines by local guerrillas, paratroops, and amphibious forces who whisk the captives away in amphibious "amtracs" across a nearby lake, Laguna de Bay. In reprisal, Japanese later massacre some 1,500 Filipinos in the local barrio.*
Early March	*The Battle for Manila ends, leaving much of the city destroyed and over 100,000 Filipinos killed by massacres and shelling.*
9 April	Main exodus of internees for ships to the United States of America begins. Some leave earlier (including to Australia), some later, and some stay in the Philippines.
14 July	The camp is officially closed, having been under U.S. Army administration since liberation.

Appendix II: The Camp's "Ten Commandments"

    I. Thou shalt have no other interest greater than the welfare of the Camp.
    II. Thou shalt not adopt for thyself, or condone in others, any merely selfish rule of conduct, or indulge in any practice that injures the morale of the Camp. Thou shalt not violate the procedures agreed upon by the authorities or by the majority, for punishment can surely be visited upon all — innocent and guilty alike — because of the misdeeds of a few.
    III. Thou shalt not betray the ideals and principles which thou was taught, so that in the future thou wilt not be condemned for neglecting the heritage.
    IV. Remember the work of the Camp, to do thy share. Six days shalt thou labor and do all thy work assignment, and also on thy rest day, refresh thy mind and heart with worship. For thy work will be satisfying and effective only when it is done in the right spirit.
    V. Honor thy forefathers by recalling vividly their struggle for better things, that though mayest contribute now and in the days to come to the realization of their ideals.
    VI. Thou shalt not hinder the best development of youth in the Camp.
    VII. Thou shall not break down family relationships.
    VIII. Thou shalt not steal.
    IX. Thou shalt not injure thy neighbor's reputation by malicious gossip.
    X. Thou shalt not covet thy neighbor's shanty or his room space. Thou shalt not covet thy neighbor's wife, nor his fiancée, nor his influential position, nor anything that is thy neighbor's.

Though "the welfare of the Camp" replaced God in the first commandment above, "The Ten Commandments for Santo Tomás" were issued by the internee administration's Department of Religion under its first chairman, the Rev. Walter Foley, who had been minister of Manila's interdenominational Union Church. The public-address "radio station," KGST, broadcast them in the camp's first year. Foley was no simple believer in obedience — hence his vehement opposition to the canceling of camp "town meetings." (Foley was killed in the post-liberation shelling, and his wife lost an arm.)

If you have read this book, the motives and worries behind the camp commandments will be obvious. But in case you are interested in comparing the camp version with the Old Testament's original Ten Commandments, I print them below, abridged down to their basic injunctions.

    I. Thou shalt have none other gods before me.
    II. Thou shalt not make any graven image, or any likeness of any thing that is in heaven above or that is in the earth beneath.... Thou shalt not bow down thyself unto them, nor serve them....
    III. Thou shalt not take the name of the Lord thy God in vain....
    IV. Keep the Sabbath day to sanctify it.... Six days thou shalt labour and do all thy work: but the seventh day is the Sabbath of the Lord thy God: in it thou shalt not do any work....
    V. Honour thy father and thy mother....

VI. Thou shalt not kill.
VII. Neither shalt thou commit adultery.
VIII. Neither shalt thou steal.
IX. Neither shalt thou bear false witness against thy neighbour.
X. Neither shalt thou desire thy neighbor's wife, neither shalt thou covet thy neighbor's house, his field, or his manservant, or his maidservant, his ox, or his ass, or any thing that is thy neighbor's.[1]

Appendix III: The Literature of Santo Tomás

Full titles and publishing details are in the bibliography. Camp names of women are given before their married names if they differ.

The size and variety of Santo Tomás literature — especially the memoirs — merits this commentary. It is not a detailed review, and I don't analyze the writers by their age at internment or by the period in which they wrote, as a fuller review should. I focus on books but this is not to disregard articles, unpublished narratives, or even emails among the gems I have found. For example, no one seriously interested in the camp's governance and politics should ignore the prodigiously researched and thoughtful article "Legitimate Collaboration" (2008), by James Mace Ward. A student of European "collaboration" in World War II, Ward understated internee committee resistance to Japanese demands, but cogently argued that committee-commandant cooperation benefited internees and the Japanese army alike. At the other end of the spectrum, one of the best camp diaries, unpublished, is by Lydia Macleod, interned at thirteen, written with all the vim and vigor of a teenager who can tell bad things, as well as good ones, about herself and others. Six decades later, another camp teenager now in his eighties, Curtis Brooks, wrote me emails of such eloquence that I sent one of them — on postwar entry into mainstream America — around to my family.

The number of published camp diaries and memoirs — over twenty-five books — far exceeds civilian memoirs of wartime Manila, where a much larger population suffered more than the camp. No camp diary or memoir is better than Marcial Lichauco's brilliant Manila diary, *Dear Mother Putnam* (1949), or Fernando Mañalac's *Manila* (1995), but they are rare items. (Both include observations of Santo Tomás.)

The large number of camp memoirs reflects the talent pool of the country's largest civilian camp and the wealth of many ex-internees. Most of the memoirs were privately published, often before low-cost self-publishing took off, and their photographs were not all cheap. However, a large minority of the authors — more than their proportion of internees — were not from the "Manila elite," but either lived in the provinces or were transients from China, caught in Manila by the war. Did the outlook of the migrant sharpen their eyes and pens, or were they less inhibited about exposing their thoughts and feelings to fellow expats from the same city?[1]

Women wrote most of the memoirs, though men outnumbered them in the camp. Camp life was largely a domestic story — making do in dorm and shanty — and women probably felt they had more time and space at home afterward to write it all up. In postwar America and Britain, the men were more apt to have busy professional careers.

The richness of camp culture and history made good grist for memoirs, even though internment life often felt boring at the time. Book blurbs and marketing tend to exaggerate the horrors.

Tressa Roka Cates' *Drainpipe Diary* (1957) was even reissued as *Infamous Santo Tomas* (1981), as if the camp were an Auschwitz or a Tdijeng.

Several memoirs give more than one perspective. *Surviving a Japanese P.O.W. Camp* by Peter Wygle (1991) reproduces the memoir by his father Robert—some of it in diary form with drawings—but he includes his own commentary as a camp teenager, and the two don't always agree. Peter Wygle's writing is among the best on the camp. A natural at comic writing, he shows that a spontaneous, knock-about style does not have to be lightweight. His profile of his talented, eccentric, racist father is a masterpiece of critical love. Another rich mixture is *Surviving the Rising Sun* by Liz Lautzenhiser Irvine (2010), which moves between the diary entries of three people—the author herself as a camp teenager, her father, and her grandmother—plus historical infilling and a variety of camp documents, from ration cards to notices.

It is easy to assume that retrospective memoirs are less reliable than day-by-day diaries—more vulnerable to flawed memory and back projection of feelings not felt so much at the time. Camp diaries, though, like other memoirs, are sometimes inaccurate on what the writer did not actually see. This is especially true of the jumbled events of the camp's liberation. Paul Esmérian's diary (published in 1980) keeps clear of this by mentioning almost nothing he did not witness, except for reports and rumors about the war affecting his native France. The very different diary kept by Fay Bailey, camp treasurer and Red Cross official (published by his daughter, Caroline Bailey Pratt, in 2001), is equally reliable because of his meticulous mind and his dual standpoints—private internee and camp officer. His diary is too laconic to be a great read, but he gave important facts and figures, and was not averse to criticizing high-placed colleagues. Pratt's edition of his diary includes documents and a roster of internees with their prior occupations.

Other diaries were not always immune to later tinkering by their authors. This led Tressa Roka Cates (now deceased) into an outright error. Her diary entry for 2 February 1944 reports the arrival of a "new, pint-sized Commandant, an ardent baseball fan, and something of an eccentric." This could only be Commandant Yoshie, and it was an accurate description, but he did not arrive until late April. Maybe her papers got mixed up and she stuck it in the wrong place, but it suggests that her diary was adjusted later. (I did not fire her on that account from the book's A-team of author witnesses, described in the introduction; her observations about camp life and her own survival are too telling.)

Only two authors before me have written book-length histories mainly focused on Santo Tomás, though there is also a DVD narrative by Lou Gopal and Michelle Bunn (2006). Internee A.V.H.'s three volumes, published in the 1960s and already mentioned in the introduction, are a goldmine of detail and commentary. His month-by-month narrative is useful for chronology but not very readable. And like many writers, he exaggerates the power of camp commandants and their officers as against the army's power outside the camp. He also makes little mention of the fact that most camp guards were Taiwanese, not Japanese, by the end. Only Frank Cary, internee interpreter, writes about the nature of the Taiwanese in his diary (written as letters to relatives).

The other camp history book is Bruce Johansen's *So Far from Home* (1996), based partly on the experience of his in-laws in the camp; he himself was not interned. He, too, writes month-by-month. He does so lucidly and vividly but says little about the politics of the camp and does not add much to the work of Hartendorp. Two "potpourri" books by internees, published soon after internment, are better supplements to Hartendorp's history. Frederic Stevens' book (*Santo Tomas Internment Camp*, 1946) is a collection of fact-packed essays on camp life and governance, mostly by himself, with a roster of internees and a chronology mainly based on committee minutes. J.E. McCall's book, with the same main title (1945), is a splendid medley of documents, statistics, cartoons, and poetry by the camp's best artist and versifier. Another internee artist, Donald Dang, produced a book of drawings titled *Survival in Santo Tomas* (1991); he was not as good an artist as McCall, but his long, pithy captions give nuggets of camp life seen with a fresh eye.

Among histories that *include* Santo Tomás, the most informative on the camp is Frances

Cogan's *Captured* (2000), on civilian internment throughout the Philippines. By restricting herself to American internees, she misses some important non-American stories, not to mention American-British tensions, but her "Notes on Sources" contain a superb essay on the pitfalls of diaries and memoirs, which she nonetheless uses. Two other books on Japan's civilian internees, Theresa Kaminski's *Prisoners in Paradise* (2000) and Bernice Archer's *Internment of Western Civilians under the Japanese* (2004), say a lot about male-female differences and (in Archer's case) children. Santo Tomás features still more in Elizabeth Norman's *We Band of Angels* (1999), following army nurses from Bataan and Corregidor to internment in Santo Tomás and Los Baños. Norman skillfully blends personal stories into the flow of history, the wider context of what was happening.

There is no really good military history of Santo Tomás' liberation. Robert Holland, in *The Rescue of Santo Tomas* (2003), tells much of it very readably but is too confined to the perspective of one participant: Holland was a Marine aircraft coordinator riding in the flying columns. The same is true for two journalists embedded with the columns, Carl Mydans and William Dunn. (Dunn's book actually starts the columns off in the wrong place, thirty miles south of where they formed up.) Rose Contey-Aiello's fiftieth anniversary "album" includes unique narratives by troopers and tank crews, but they are no substitute for an overall history. At the other end of the scale, Robert Ross Smith's more formal military history, *Triumph in the Philippines* (1963), is good on strategy and tactics but loses the reader in a procession of unclearly located Luzon towns, ill served by confusing maps. The clearest flying-column narrative is B.C. Wright's account in *The 1st Cavalry Division in World War II* (1947), but it lacks strategic context (what were the generals thinking?). Shorter summaries, as in D. Clayton James' biography of MacArthur, tend to exaggerate the speed and ease with which the columns got by the Japanese. No account, indeed, gives a real sense of how it all felt, be it fatigue, excitement, fear, horror at comrades wounded or killed, or the shock and pain at getting wounded oneself. Nothing gets anywhere near E.B. Sledge's classic Marine memoir of Peleliu and Okinawa: *With the Old Breed* (1981).

I end with a self-indulgence, not strictly on the camp's literature but on how the camp affected one writer. In 1984 I published a book, *American Tough* (illustrated paperback, 1986), on tough-guy and pseudo-tough-guy styles in American history and culture, as well as their sources. Like subsequent books by me on American social character, the idea for it started among the American tough guys of the Boys' Club, Education Building, Santo Tomás Internment Camp.

Chapter Notes

The bibliography gives fuller details of publications cited below. The authors' names for some women's memoirs differ from their internee names because of marriages after the war.

The bibliography takes care of this with cross-references. In the notes here, family surnames in parentheses follow authors' and other informants' names where they are different. "Santo Tomás" is spelled without an accent where the author omits it. "RW" indicates the present author, Rupert Wilkinson.

Introduction

1. The one exception is an unpublished memoir of Lt. Chiyomi Toyota, which is almost entirely about service elsewhere, referring very briefly and vaguely to good relations with Santo Tomás internees.

Chapter 1

1. Williams, *To the Angels* (1985), 19–20. "Auto-calesas" are from Connaughton et al., *The Battle for Manila* (1995, 2002), 21.
2. Karnow, *In Our Image* (1989), 9, 209, 223–24; José and Yu-José, *The Japanese Occupation of the Philippines* (1997), ch. 4; Setsuho and José, eds., *The Philippines under Japan* (1999), ch. 6. by Ricardo José.
3. Cates (Roka), *The Drainpipe Diary* (1957), 17, diary 7 January 1942.
4. Our relationship with Evie was not a happy one for reasons by no means all her fault. I will say little about her, as it does not bear much on our camp experience. Soon after internment, our mother was in the camp hospital with bronchitis, so Evie must have been in charge of us, but neither Mary June nor I remember this. Also, Mary June's and my memories of our servants regarding who did what and lived where is not perfectly reliable, but the picture given is not unusual.
5. On causes of "Nanking," see Chapter 13, section on atrocities.
6. Stevens, *Santo Tomas Internment Camp* (1946), 5; U.S. Court of Federal Claims and U.S. Court of Appeals: *Achenbach v. United States* (2004). For other views, see Buss, "Claude Buss in, 1941–1942" (1990), 240–41; U.S. State Department papers, letter by Sayre to Secretary of State Cordell Hull, 14 August 1941.
7. Curtis, "Extra-Curricular Activities, 1940–1945" (unpublished diary), 16. "Never volunteer" was standard, jocular usage in American and British armies in the war and after; but in this situation and to a volunteering civilian?

8. Nash, *That We Might Live* (1984), 14–16; Stafford, *Roosevelt and Churchill* (1999), 174, quoting from Gerald Wilkinson's war diary.
9. Lichauco, *Dear Mother Putnam* (1949, 1997, 2005), 2–3.
10. Vorster, *Me* (2005), 58.
11. Esmérian, "War Years in the Philippines 1941–1945" (1980), 11, diary 2 January 1942.
12. Buss, "Claude Buss in Manila, 1941–1942" (1990), appendix report (1943), 274.
13. This account mainly draws on Alcuaz's papers, especially his "Memorandum to Brig. Gen. Courtney Whitney" (19 March 1945). I could find no testimony by Frs. Tascon and Jordan; the University of Santo Tomás archives apparently have nothing on the controversy. The Spanish historian Florentino Rodao gave me information on the government-university conflict over fascism. Frederic Stevens, chairman of the American Emergency Committee (then a part of the American Philippine Red Cross), claimed briefly that the university "readily agreed" to an internment-camp proposal from him and the U.S. Army's property chief, Christian Rosenstock. Stevens, *Santo Tomas Internment Camp* (1946), 6. Before that, however, as documented by Alcuaz, the university leaders turned down a similar request from Claude Buss and the Red Cross, having consulted the Spanish consul general; they then disbanded the Emergency Committee after "disagreements" with it. See also Buss, "Claude Buss in Manila, 1941–1942" (1990), appendix report (1943), 273–74, 280–81; Connaughton et al., *The Battle for Manila* (1995, 2002), 31.

Chapter 2

1. Mañalac, *Manila* (1995), 15; Vorster, *Me* (2005), 60–61. The reference to armored cars is from Lichauco, *Dear Mother Putnam* (1949, 1997, 2005), 12, diary 3 January 1942.
2. Cates (Roka), *The Drainpipe Diary* (1957), 33–34, diary 4 January 1942. She calls the officer an NCO but the sword indicates that he was probably an officer.

3. Mary June Pettyfer (Wilkinson) to RW, email 5 May 2010. Unlike Mary June but more vaguely, I remember staying with the Rev. Harold Spackman, not the Shannons. Like other clergy, Spackman, a British Anglican, was not initially interned, but he and his wife chose to be so by early July 1942.

4. Poston (Wootten), *My Upside-Down World* (2002), 110, diary 7 January 1942.

5. Cates (Roka), *The Drainpipe Diary* (1957), 14, diary 6 January 1942, quotes both the small boy and the old lady. Cates reported three washbowls, one shower, and three toilets for 500 women in her part of the Main Building (which she renamed "the Big House"). The bathroom numbers in the text are from Wetmore (Mathews), *Beyond Pearl Harbor* (2001). I have not established what happened if you had "the trots" and faced a big toilet line, but Bobbie Olsen (interned at 9) believed you could go to the head of the line. Olsen, interview transcript (2002), 23. Earl Carroll, the initial internee leader, said that on the first night, all Japanese left the camp, holding him responsible for any escapes (none happened), but subsequently internees reported guards coming into rooms at night. Jesus and Quirino, *Earl Carroll* (1980), 74–75.

6. Santo Tomás Internment Camp, Executive and Internee Committee Minutes and Proceedings, 16, 21 January 1942; Santo Tomás Internment Camp, *Internews* (4 February 1942) and *STIC Gazette* (4 February 1943), chronology 1; Stevens, *Santo Tomas Internment Camp* (1946), 78; Jesus and Quirino, *Earl Carroll* (1980), 75, 82; Whitesides, "The Economics of Internment" (1988), 16; Sams (Sherk), *Forbidden Family* (1989), 62–63, 70n.–71n; Cogan, *Captured* (2000), 61–62; Wetmore (Mathews), *Beyond Pearl Harbor* (2001), 25; Bailey, *Only a Matter of Days* (2001, 2008), 29, 30, diary 8, 18–19 January 1942; Irvine (Lautzenhiser), *Surviving the Rising Sun* (2010), 39.

7. Various committee minutes in January and February 1942 record impatience with allegedly slow Red Cross (Philippine) progress in feeding the camp, plus requests for an appeal to the Red Cross outside the Philippines (endorsed by the commandant) and contributions from internees themselves (May 1942). Santo Tomás Internment Camp, Executive and Internee Committee Minutes and Proceedings.

8. Hartendorp, *The Santo Tomas Story* (1964), 8.

9. Hartendorp, *The Santo Tomas Story* (1964), 11.

10. Esmérian, "War Years in the Philippines 1941–1945" (1980), 17, diary 14 January 1942; Hartendorp, *The Santo Tomas Story* (1964), 32; Irvine (Lautzenhiser), *Surviving the Rising Sun* (2010), 125: "Dyeing Doesn't Pay," English class theme, 11 March 1943. Still out of camp due to his French nationality, Esmérian had visited the camp to help his friend, Anne Balfour, obtain leave to live out (explained in Chapter 3).

11. Hartendorp, *The Santo Tomas Story* (1964), 24; Stevens, *Santo Tomas Internment Camp* (1946), 16–17, 20.

12. My numbers for previous occupations are rough estimates based on an "occupations census" published by J.E. McCall for 6,874 people who were in Santo Tomás at some time, including those transferred in and out. This was roughly double the camp's population in its early months, so I approximately halved his numbers, assuming the proportions from different occupations would be about the same. Curiously, McCall reported only four men who called themselves "plumbers," although there must have been more who did plumbing. McCall, *Santo Tomás Internment Camp* (1945), 65–66.

13. My abridgment, with some change in verse order, of "The American Way" (15 October 1942) in McCall, *Santo Tomás Internment Camp* (1945), 6–7.

14. Doolan, "My Life in a Japanese Prison Camp during World War II" (2004), 15–17. Doolan agrees with me about our age and the early date of this event. Roy Doolan Jr. to RW, email 3 June 2010.

15. Accounts differ as to what school books came in, from whom, and when. Hartendorp, *The Santo Tomas Story* (1964), 26; Irvine (Lautzenhiser), *Surviving the Rising Sun* (2010), 9, diary 7 October 1942.

16. Different accounts locate teen social centers, square dances, and so on in different places, including the Main Building. At various times, teenagers used the Main Building's mezzanine floor for sitting out and socializing.

17. Mary June Pettyfer (Wilkinson), taped interview by RW, 1 September 2009, Victoria, BC, Canada.

Chapter 3

1. Waterford, *Prisoners of the Japanese in World War II* (1994), 48n6 and appendix A. The 1929 Geneva Convention, which covered military POWs in World War II, forbade punishment for escape attempts and required a three-month gap between sentencing and execution for a capital offence, with notification of the prisoner's national government as soon as possible in that period.

2. This history of the event draws on briefings given by Earl Carroll to A.V.H. and other interned journalists and editors the evening following the execution; Carroll's biography, including interviews with an anonymous Hearst Syndicate reporter in 1945; and testimony of the Rev. Owen Griffiths reported to the British Foreign Office on 30 August 1942 by Stanley Wyatt-Smith, British consul general, Manila, who somehow obtained and transmitted Griffiths' account while he was under house arrest before diplomatic repatriation. Together these accounts give more detail than mine does while differing from each other in some particulars. According to Wyatt-Smith, the coercion of unwilling Filipino gravediggers was "confirmed by a Spaniard named Gascunana" who was at the (Chinese) cemetery for a relative's burial. I have been cautious in using Carroll's Hearst interviewer, as he was clearly given to racist melodrama. Wyatt-Smith, "Execution by Japanese Military Authorities in the Philippines of three British subjects ..." (1942); Hartendorp, *The Santo Tomas Story* (1964), 39–44; Hartendorp, *The Japanese Occupation of the Philippines*, Vol. I (1967), 88–94; Jesus and Quirino, *Earl Carroll* (1980), 16–19, 79–80. See also Ward, "Legitimate Collaboration" (2008), 165–66, citing testimony by Ernest Stanley and others. Stanley said he told the three their fate.

3. Krass, "Will the Morning Ever Come?" (1942) in Krass papers (my abridgment). The poem, in the papers of Iris Krass, a camp teenager, was by her mother.

4. Executive Committee minutes, 12 February 1945, excerpted by Stevens, *Santo Tomas Interment Camp* (1946), 386–87. Several internee memoirs repeat the "dug own grave" myth, as does Connaughton et al., *The Battle for Manila* (1995, 2002), 42. After the war, a Japanese Filipino liaison official quoted the colonel handling the case: "according to Japanese army law we must show the example because others might do the same." Lt. Col. Naki, quoted by Enrique Umamuka: War Crimes Interrogations, Report 91, 132ff.

5. Paul Esmérian, peddling in Manila markets, claimed that local produce was still widely affordable through 1942. Esmérian, "War Years in the Philippines 1941–1945" (1980), 29, diary 25 December 1942. Steinberg, in *Philippine Collaboration in World War II* (1967), 86–91, gives a brilliant, encompassing account of what happened, and why, to the

Philippine economy under the Japanese. See also Parsons, "Report of Mr C. Parsons to the U.S. Department of State" (1942), 32ff, which, despite its early writing, is penetrating on the way Japanese policy disrupted business, stripped factories, and so forth. According to Fay Bailey, internee treasurer at the time and traveling into the city on camp business in August 1943, many Filipinos were moving to Manila, as prices there at that time were lower, especially for rationed food such as meat. He presciently feared, though, what would happen when Manila was "cut off" by war. Bailey, *Only a Matter of Days* (2001, 2008), 166, 168, diary 23 August, 1 September 1943.

6. Hartendorp, *The Japanese Occupation of the Philippines*, Vol. II (1967), 18–19. The Bessmer donations totaled P975,000, which I have expressed in dollars at three pesos to the dollar, not two, due to Philippine inflation, and then multiplied by 15 to reach today's U.S. dollar values. Bessmer had a lot of trouble getting repaid after the war; there were questions about which Red Cross organization should pay. Cay Pratt (Bailey) to RW, email 16 December 2011.

7. The watermark story comes from Edgar Kneedler, a Manila hotelier before internment in Santo Tomás. Kneedler, "The Internees' Own Story" (2003), 81. John Dos Passos reported hearing the story on reaching the camp just after its liberation. Dos Passos, *Tour of Duty* (1946), 153. The "Mickey Mouse" pesos fell from initial par with the old "Commonwealth" peso (officially banned but used in black markets) to 1.44 to the old peso in June 1943, 20 in July 1944, and 120 in January 1945 — reflecting the hyper-inflation of 1944. On Manila inflation above increases in Japanese money allowances to the camp, see Stevens, *Santo Tomas Internment Camp* (1946), 136. See also Pratt (Bailey), "The Internees' Own Story" (2003), 104.

8. Cates (Roka), *The Drainpipe Diary* (1957), 44, diary 12 January 1942. I have found no camp account or informant clarifying when imports of money were restricted or stopped. Internees had so much money it seems unlikely it was all brought in initially or smuggled. In April 1942, internees were told they could withdraw 50 pesos a month, or 100 pesos per family, from bank accounts via the commandant, and 50 pesos a month from firms, though that was later discontinued or suspended. Santo Tomás Internment Camp, Executive and Internal Committee Minutes and Proceedings, 14, 23 April 1942. Fay Bailey, camp "disbursing officer," describes bringing money for the camp from IOUs as illegal, but not inspected, between July 1942 and November 1943. Bailey, *Only a Matter of Days* (2001, 2008), 22–23 (written 1946). According to camp internee/historian A.V.H., Commandant Kuroda told camp leaders in early October 1943 that he was turning a blind eye to major imports of money, having satisfied himself it was not for guerrillas. Luis de Alcuaz reported "a rigid inspection of packages entering the camp to stop the entrance of money (Mickey Mouse)." He dates this as late October but the year is not clear. Hartendorp, *The Santo Tomas Story* (1964), 186–87; Alcuaz papers: "Memorandum to Brig. Gen. Courtney Whitney" (19 March 1945), 6. In August 1944, well after the package line ended and internees had to bank money above 50 pesos a month (see Chapter 8), a bank branch was set up in the gym for drawing out funds. Bailey, *Only a Matter of Days* (2001, 2008), 273, diary 5, 6 October 1944.

9. Van Sickle, *The Iron Gates of Santo Tomás* (1992), 45.

10. Poston (Wootten), *My Upside-Down World* (2002), 190–91, diary 30 September 1942; Esmérian, "War Years in the Philippines 1941–1945" (1980), 48, diary 31 July 1943. As early as May 1942, an internee's mother, herself not interned due to age (see note 15 below), was happily surprised that internee officials at the gate were able to "let [her daughter] come and talk with me ... across the line." And spoken messages via internee officials continued after the crackdown. Irvine (Lautzenhiser), *Surviving the Rising Sun* (2010), 64–65, 100, diary of Belle Norton, 10 May, 1 November 1942. As mentioned elsewhere, Akida Kodaki was in fact a kind of super-commandant, based outside the camp and working with S. Kuroda inside.

11. Esmérian, "War Years in the Philippines 1941–1945" (1980), 54, diary 11 September 1943.

12. Bryant, *The Sun Was Darkened* (1947), 146–47, 148; Van Sickle, *The Iron Gates of Santo Tomás* (1992), 44–45, 307, 312; Cates (Roka), *The Drainpipe Diary* (1957), 160–61, 201, 232, diary 21 April 1943, 7 February, 6 December 1944.

13. Sams (Sherk), *Forbidden Family* (1989), 72–73. In November 1943, the Relief and Welfare Council raised cash relief, because of inflation, to 30 pesos per month per needy adult (about $140 today), P25 per teenager, and P20 per younger child. In early October 1944, it was cut to P25 a month for adults (only about $3.75 today due to the peso's hyper-inflation) and P15 for children, on the grounds of fewer spending opportunities in the camp. Aid to internees' non-interned families was doubled against inflation, pending commandant's approval. Santo Tomás Internment Camp, Internee and Executive Committee Minutes and Proceedings, 27 November 1943; Stevens, *Santo Tomas Internment Camp* (1946), 456, minutes 3 October 1944. See also Vaughan, *The Ordeal of Elizabeth Vaughan* (1985), 277–78. The Executive Committee minutes "held over for further study" a proposal to borrow from individuals to aid needy mothers without husbands for three months. Stevens, *Santo Tomas Internment Camp* (1946), 416, entry 9 July 1944. No outcome was given. Just before liberation, the internee interpreter, Frank Cary, on leaving the camp hospital where he met Philippine-American War veterans, said "camp funds" paid them $60 (not 60 pesos?) against future arrears of pension. Cary, *Letters from Internment Camp* (1993), 117, letter 29 January 1945. I have seen no other report of this.

14. Curtis, "Extracurricular Activities, 1940–1945," installment 23 June 1943. This and most of Curtis' account was written as a letter to his wife but he also called it a "diary" and a "journal" (25). He wrote it only after transfer from Santo Tomás to Los Baños in May 1943, hiding it under the floorboards of his barrack room.

15. Cates (Roka), *The Drainpipe Diary* (1957), 86, diary 19 April 1942. Sometimes looking old without illness enabled a person to stay out without being initially interned. So it was for Belle Norton, who was 69 in early January 1942. Irvine (Lautzenhiser), *Surviving the Rising Sun* (2010), 8.

16. Sams (Sherk), *Forbidden Family* (1989), 71n. See also Lewis (Kerns), chapter in *Interrupted Lives* (1995), 86–88, on unhappiness at the Holy Ghost school.

17. Stevens, *Santo Tomas Internment Camp* (1946), 379; Vaughan, *The Ordeal of Elizabeth Vaughan* (1985), 207, 215–16, diary 19 April, 1 May 1943. Later in 1943, Elizabeth Vaughan went into a hospital outside the camp and her children stayed with a kind Swiss couple, until all three were reunited in the Holy Ghost Convent, where Elizabeth, still weak from fever, did kitchen work. The three later returned to Santo Tomás.

18. "Producer gas" buses, replacing gasoline or diesel oil with gas from another burned fuel, were actually in use in Europe by 1938. The contraption I noticed had two chambers. The bottom one burned charcoal or alcohol. This heated the chamber above it, which probably contained

charcoal, though it could be coal, coke, and so forth. As the charcoal in the top chamber got hot, it produced gas piped through to the motor in front, where it was ignited by the spark plugs as in a gasoline engine.

19. It is not certain if this took place at the Franciscos' own home or that of a friend. Pancho described it as "the Wing's house" [*sic*], but his grandchildren remember accounts of Japanese visits to their own home. L.J. Francisco (Pancho) to "Hank," letter, 3 April 1945, in Francisco papers; Anthony de Alcuaz, Marie Kish, and Jeanne Siegel, interview with RW and Mary Wilkinson, 12 September 2009, Belmont, California.

20. Dower, *War without Mercy* (1986), 200 and ch. 8. Japanese control of Manila culture was never complete and took time to develop. Even the Japanese-controlled *Manila Tribune* was criticized in November 1942 by the authorities for reporting 40 Japanese aircraft lost in the Solomons campaign. Bailey, *Only a Matter of Days* (2001, 2008), 94, diary 19 November 1942. Fay Cook Bailey, internee food supply chief, had contact with Manila when he went out to get supplies, do Red Cross business, and pay hospitals from camp funds.

21. Prising, *Manila, Goodbye* (1976), 93–96.

22. Hartendorp, *The Santo Tomas Story* (1964), 135–38; Wilkins, "Close-up Report on the Japanese" (1945). Over a hundred people were initially taken to Fort Santiago, where they had to stand for several hours before some were released. Presumably, any living at home on a pass were allowed to return there, as no fuss on that score was reported. Fay Cook Bailey, part of the camp administration, reported 57 coming into camp from Fort Santiago. Bailey, *Only a Matter of Days* (2001, 2008), 129, diary 10 March 1942.

Chapter 4

1. Van Sickle, *The Iron Gates of Santo Tomás* (1992), 109.

2. Bryant, *The Sun Was Darkened* (1947), 145–46; Vaughan, *The Ordeal of Elizabeth Vaughan* (1985), 201–2, diary 19 April 1943. See also Esmérian, "War Years in the Philippines 1941–1945" (1980), 31, diary 14 February 1943, on a camp scene looking like a "Sunday outing in the woods!" Bryant, in *The Sun Was Darkened*, 141, says the boat's very public toilets were three "terrifyingly large holes" in a platform off the stern. Japanese on the boat were demanding but quite kind. The eight days aboard were mainly in port.

3. Cates (Roka), *The Drainpipe Diary* (1957), 59, diary 10 February 1942; Hartendorp, *The Santo Tomas Story* (1964), 399. Abram Hartendorp, camp historian, did not give their names, and Tressa Cates' diary gave them a pseudonym ("Greenshoes"). I have not identified exactly who they were, nor how they got away with their resistance. Did the wife's Buddhism play a part? The Japanese handled religion quite carefully (see Chapter 7). By today's standards, the husband at least was not very old. Hartendorp says that he died at 68, though Cates says she was "many years older." It seems they were moved into the university museum on the Main Building's second floor, where, according to Cates, he slaved for her while she read, talked Buddhism, and wrote remarkably sensitive poetry. Cates (Roka), *The Drainpipe Diary* (1957), 176, diary 20 July 1943.

4. Lucy Evans (Evie) may have joined us in Room 33 but Mary June, aged not quite ten on re-internment, has no memory of it.

5. Curtis Brooks to RW, email 13 June 2010. According to May Berenbaum, entomologist and bedbug expert, the bugs were reported in 1948 to have developed resistance to DDT, which was widely used against them during World War II. "Maybe Curtis Brooks actually discovered the first pesticide-resistant bed bug!" Berenbaum to RW, email 23 August 2010; Berenbaum, "This Bedbug's Life" (2010).

6. Esmérian, "War Years in the Philippines 1941–1945" (1980), 42, diary 7 July 1943. Early on, a "congenial crowd" of 32 in a men's dorm room managed to fit in a table for playing poker until 10 P.M. Bailey, *Only a Matter of Days* (2001, 2008), 34, diary 17 February 1942.

7. Poston (Wootten), *My Upside-Down World* (2002), 188–90, diary 28 September 1942; Wetmore (Mathews), *Beyond Pearl Harbor* (2001), 21–22; Shiels (Tonkin), *Bends in the Road* (1999), 42. Almost all descriptions of dorm room relations are by women internees.

8. Vaughan, *The Ordeal of Elizabeth Vaughan* (1985), 281–82, diary 15 July 1944. Lehman's comments are in the words of my father, Gerald Wilkinson, reporting a phone call from her on getting back to the United States earlier than our family. Wilkinson, "War diary," 25 April 1945.

9. Sams (Sherk), *Forbidden Family* (1989), 91–92; Cates (Roka), *The Drainpipe Diary* (1957), 109, diary 26 July 1942.

10. Sascha Jean Jansen (Weinzheimer) to RW, email 13 May 2010.

11. Bailey, *Only a Matter of Days* (2001, 2008), 123, 133, diary 11, 12 February, 12 March 1943; Hartendorp, *The Santo Tomas Story* (1964), 154. A.V.H. said the permission included "older children." But shanty regulations of 16 August 1943 said that girls up to age eight could sleep in shanties if accompanied by an adult; boys up to that age and older could too. McCall, *Santo Tomás Internment Camp* (1945), 80, General Code of Regulations, Article 31.

12. Hartendorp, *The Santo Tomas Story* (1964), 54; Bailey, *Only a Matter of Days* (2001, 2008), 135, diary 7 April 1943; Templer, "Internment Diary," 14, entry for May 1943; Poston (Wootten), *My Upside-Down World* (2002), 254, diary 25 August 1943.

13. Vaughan, *The Ordeal of Elizabeth Vaughan* (1985), 205–6, diary 19 April 1943.

14. Hall, "Roderick Hall's Narrative" (2008), 62–63. Hartendorp, in *The Santo Tomas Story* (1964), 35, refers to "democratic" abstentions from "shanty aristocracy." The inferences about adults without families in the camp and some families out of camp are mine.

15. Hartendorp, *The Santo Tomas Story* (1964), 35; McCall, *Santo Tomás Internment Camp* (1945), 72, 78–80: "Shanty Area Regulations," 16 August 1943. There were fewer rules at first.

16. Templer, "Internment Diary," 13–14, entries for May and June 1943; Esmérian, "War Years in the Philippines 1941–1945" (1980), 40–41, diary 20 June, 14 October 1943; Prising, *Manila, Goodbye* (1976), 125.

17. Jesus and Quirino, *Earl Carroll* (1980), 28; Hartendorp, *The Santo Tomas Story* (1964), 119–21.. Like others, I refer to Kuroda as commandant, but he worked so closely with Akida Kodaki, chief of external affairs in the Japanese Military Administration, that Kodaki was a super-commandant, so to speak (described further in Chapter 7). Some writing refers to Kodaki as commandant.

18. Hartendorp, *The Santo Tomas Story* (1964), 119–21, 125–27; Van Sickle, *The Iron Gates of Santo Tomás* (1992), 102; Cates (Roka), *The Drainpipe Diary* (1957), 150, diary 20 January 1943; Nash, *That We Might Live* (1984), 85–89.

19. Cates (Roka), *The Drainpipe Diary* (1957), diary 21

January 1943; Poston (Wootten), *My Upside-Down World* (2002), 216-17, 219, diary 7, 11, 14 January 1943. See also Bailey, *Only a Matter of Days* (2001, 2008), 118, diary 23 January 1942, again on the innocent suffering with the guilty.

20. Stevens, *Santo Tomas Internment Camp* (1946), 408, Executive Committee minutes 22 January 1943; Irvine (Lautzenhiser), *Surviving the Rising Sun* (2010), 123, giving a shanty regulation for late January 1943, rephrased in shanty regulations of 16 August 1943, in McCall, *Santo Tomás Internment Camp* (1945), 79.

21. The 137 pregnancies are reported by Stevens in *Santo Tomas Internment Camp* (1946), 228, but his own list of new babies and birth dates for Santo Tomás internees (485) gives only 75 births and, I estimate, 32 conceptions, including six during the period of maximum shanty restrictions. The list, however, does not include births after 15 February 1945 (two weeks after liberation), nor, it seems, those who subsequently moved to the Los Baños camp. Some pregnancies, of course, began before internment, and we don't know how many started outside camp on pass.

22. Hartendorp, *The Santo Tomas Story* (1964), 74; Kaminski, *Prisoners in Paradise* (2000), 143; Poston (Wootten), *My Upside-Down World* (2002), 184, diary 1 September 1942; Sams (Sherk), *Forbidden Family* (1989), 97; Wetmore (Mathews), *Beyond Pearl Harbor* (2001), 31; Van Sickle, *The Iron Gates of Santo Tomás* (1992), 65; Johansen, *So Far From Home* (1996), 129; Nash, *That We Might Live* (1984), 121; Sascha Jean Jansen (Weinzheimer) to RW, email 30 December 2010. Geege Poston (Wootten) suggested that food shortage at the very beginning, as well as stress for the more "nervous," may have stopped menstruation. Phone conversation with RW, 29 March 2011. But more research is needed on Santo Tomás birth rates, allowing for the camp's age distribution, proportion married, and so forth (see note 21 above).

23. Cates (Roka), *The Drainpipe Diary* (1957), 37, 42, 55, diary 8, 11 January, 1 February 1942; Ward, "Legitimate Collaboration" (2008), 164-65.

24. Curtis Brooks to RW, email 24 January 2012; Hartendorp, *The Santo Tomas Story* (1964), 126; Ward, "Legitimate Collaboration" (2008), 164-65; Prising, *Manila, Goodbye* (1976), 74; Santo Tomás Internment Camp, Executive and Internee Committee Minutes and Proceedings, 24 January 1942; Stevens, *Santo Tomas Internment Camp* (1946), 399, Executive Committee minutes, 4 August 1942.

25. Parsons, "Report of Mr C. Parsons to the U.S. Department of State" (1942), 33; Parfet, "Dancing in the Dark" (1999); Curtis Brooks to RW, email 29 March 2011; Irvine (Lautzenhiser), *Surviving the Rising Sun* (2010), 158; Shiels, *Bends in the Road* (1999), 37, 33-34. Parsons was released from camp in June 1942 for special diplomatic reasons (see Chapter 10) — hence the early date of his report. Margo Tonkin and Roger Schade were reunited in April 1944 when her family moved to Los Baños. But another wrench came six months later when he had to leave his Los Baños friends to rejoin his family in Santo Tomás; they did not meet again for fifty years but remained good friends. Shiels, *Bends in the Road* (1999), 45, 47, 50, 62; Roger Schade to RW, email 5 April 2011.

26. Van Sickle, *The Iron Gates of Santo Tomás* (1992), 152; Poston (Wootten), *My Upside-Down World* (2002), 202, 217, diary 11 November 1942, 11 January 1943; Bailey, *Only a Matter of Days* (2001, 2008), 115, diary 12 January 1943.

27. Esmérian, "War Years in the Philippines 1941-1945" (1980), 48-49, diary 2 August 1943; Dang, *Survival in Santo Tomas* (1991), 20, "The Busybodies."

28. According to Margaret Sams (now deceased) and their daughter, Gerry Schwede, he also went over the wall to help guerrillas set up a radio station eleven miles east of Manila, but she says he was away 8 days and one wonders how this would get by roll calls without putting a room monitor at risk, even though his bed on the museum landing had a staircase separate from dorm rooms. Sams (Sherk), *Forbidden Family* (1989), 112-13, including footnote additions in 1987 to her original memoir completed in the 1950s; Schwede to RW, email May 2011. Most of the iguana jape got into the camp newspaper. Santo Tomás Internment Camp, *Internews* (28 April 1942), 2. The only other account I know of having a baby during Santo Tomás internment is by Grace Nash, wife of one of the "pregnant papas," who says nothing about how and where she got pregnant. Nash, *That We Might Live* (1984), especially chs. 6-8.

29. Sams (Sherk), *Forbidden Family* (1989), especially 12 (introduction by Lynn Z. Bloom), 103, 110-11, 119-22, 178.

30. Sams (Sherk), *Forbidden Family* (1989), 133, 154, 286-87.

31. Sams (Sherk), *Forbidden Family* (1989), especially 158-78. See also Kaminski, *Prisoners in Paradise* (2000), 142-43, on the Los Baños period. Grace Nash, another pregnant internee at Hospicio, said it was normal procedure to go to another hospital for delivery, but described a hostile nurse anxious that no baby would be born at Hospicio. Nash, *That We Might Live* (1984), ch. 7.

32. Jesus and Quirino, *Earl Carroll* (1980), 103; Poston (Geege Wooten), *My Upside-Down World* (2002), especially 106, 118, 127-28, 194-95, including diary 11, 14 October 1942; phone conversations with Geege Poston, 31 December 2010, 18 July 2011.

Chapter 5

1. Sams (Sherk), *Forbidden Family* (1989), 109-10; Cates (Roka), *The Drainpipe Diary* (1957), 56, diary 4 February 1942; Montefiori, "A Bit of Camp 1942-1945" (no date), 38-39 in Hearnden papers; Poston, *My Upside-Down World* (2002), 133, diary 25 April 1942. Cates, given to pseudonyms, refers to Dave Harvey as Harvey Jones.

2. The USS *Hornet* was sunk in the Battle of the Santa Cruz Islands, in the Solomons, on 27 October 1942, after fighting in the Battle of Midway. Before that, in April 1942, it launched the first U.S. air raid on Japan — the famous Tokyo raid by Lt. Col. Jimmy Doolittle (U.S. Army Air Force), using medium bombers, never carrier-launched before. In the Santa Cruz battle, a Japanese task force beat a smaller American one, but at costs the Japanese could ill afford. A new Hornet carrier went into operation in 1944.

3. Stevens, *Santo Tomas Internment Camp* (1946), 196-99; Enriquez, "Coping with War" (2010), 13-14. In November 1942, the diary of Fay Cook Bailey, who preferred more silence, reported nightly recorded music from 7:15 to 8:45 P.M., sometimes interspersed with fifteen-minute "'news' broadcasts" (presumably camp news). A keen reader, he also reported a "radio" play version of Joseph Kesseling's *Arsenic and Old Lace* (1939, later made into the Frank Capra movie), well acted by internees over the broadcast system. Bailey, *Only a Matter of Days* (2001, 2008), 94, 122, diary 19 November 1942, 9 February 1943.

4. Hartendorp, *The Santo Tomas Story* (1964), 270; Templer, "Internment Diary," 15, entry for February 1944; Vaughan, *The Ordeal of Elizabeth Vaughan* (1985), 279, diary 14 July 1944; Esmérian, "War Years in the Philippines

1941–1945" (1980), 50, 62, 63, diary 8 August, 5 September, 22 December 1943.

5. Editorial in late September 1942, quoted by Hartendorp in *The Japanese Occupation of the Philippines*, Vol. I (1967), 372, with reference to *Time* by Hartendorp. The full text of Dave Harvey's "Cheer Up!" is printed in various places, including Jesus and Quirino, *Earl Carroll* (1980), 93–95; Center for Internee Rights, *Civilian Prisoners of the Japanese in the Philippine Islands* (2002), 43–44; and Enriquez, "Coping with War" (2010), 19–20. Enriquez and Jesus/Quirino say that Dave Harvey wrote it, but others have said it is not known.

6. Irvine (Lautzenhiser), *Surviving the Rising Sun* (2010), 147–54, gives the text and cartoons, which were printed as a program. Paul Esmérian said it was followed by "funny tableaux" sung or played by internees on the theme of repatriation via Goa ("I want to Go-a"), with a chorus by the audience. Esmérian, "War Years in the Philippines 1941–1945" (1980), 55, diary 27 September 1943.

7. Hartendorp, *The Santo Tomas Story* (1964), 280–81; Bryant, *The Sun Was Darkened* (1947), 161–62.

8. Prising, *Manila, Goodbye* (1976), 126, 146; Stevens, *Santo Tomas Internment Camp* (1946), 200, 452–53; Van Sickle, *The Iron Gates of Santo Tomás* (1992), 268, 287; Hartendorp, *The Japanese Occupation of the Philippines*, Vol. II (1967), 158; Irvine (Lautzenhiser), *Surviving the Rising Sun* (2010), 185; Enriquez, "Coping with War" (2010), 12–28. Van Sickle says that regular evening music broadcasts had been banned by late 1944, but Liz Lautzenhiser's diary reports "sitting out in front" to recorded music in early January 1945. Irvine (Lautzenhiser), *Surviving the Rising Sun* (2010), 205, diary 4 January 1945. On Christmas Day 1944, Anne Balfour said she heard "two airs of Messiaen [on] the radio ... it was good to hear music after all this time." Balfour, "Diary of Anne Balfour, Manila," 47, entry 15 December 1944. Perhaps air raids had just suspended it.

9. Lorenzen, *A Lovely Little War* (2008), 128; Stevens, *Santo Tomas Internment Camp* (1946), 177.

10. Stevens, *Santo Tomas Internment Camp* (1946), 254–60; Parsons, "Report of Mr C. Parsons to the U.S. Department of State" (1942), 32; Doolan, "My Life in a Japanese Prison Camp during World War II" (2004), 12, 32; Prising, *Manila, Goodbye* (1976), 144; Sams (Sherk), *Forbidden Family* (1989), 87; Poston (Wootten), *My Upside-Down World* (2002), 134; Curtis Brooks to RW, email 28 May 2010.

11. Stevens, *Santo Tomas Internment Camp* (1946), 259–60, quoting from a show, 9 May 1942. Irvine (Lautzenhiser), *Surviving the Rising Sun* (2010), 63–64, gives the full words. The quoted lines of "We'll Be Out Tomorrow" are my abridgment from Lucas, *Prisoners of Santo Tomas* (1975, 1988), 37–38, based on the diary of Isla Corfield, who also noted (and maybe coined) the term "rumortism" (author is unknown).

12. Curtis Brooks to RW, email 28 May 2010; Cates (Roka), *The Drainpipe Diary* (1957), 185, diary 2 October 1943.

13. Sams (Sherk), *Forbidden Family* (1989), 87–88, 92–96. It sounds extraordinary that people would pay for bookmending in a prison camp, but her customers may have included quasi-private subscription libraries. At the general camp library three months into internment, rapid turnover of books left 125 of about 900 volumes at the menders. The books mainly came from Manila's YMCA, Union Church, and American School. Santo Tomás Internment Camp, *Internews* (28 April 1942), 1.

14. Irvine (Lautzenhiser), *Surviving the Rising Sun* (2010), 151; Vaughan, *The Ordeal of Elizabeth Vaughan* (1985), 212, diary 1 May 1943; Cates (Roka), *The Drainpipe Diary* (1957), 162, diary 26 April 1943.

15. Vaughan, *The Ordeal of Elizabeth Vaughan* (1985), 263, diary 1 March 1944; Cates (Roka), *The Drainpipe Diary* (1957), 162, diary 26 April 1943.

16. Hartendorp, *The Santo Tomas Story* (1964), 53–54, 208–9, commenting on the camp in early 1942 and early 1944; Van Sickle, *The Iron Gates of Santo Tomás* (1992), 223–24. See also James Halsema, former Baguio mayor and Baguio camp internee, on "dog eat dog," thefts, and so on in Santo Tomás after liberation: reported in Crouter, *Forbidden Diary* (1980), 482–83, diary 12 February 1945; Halsema, "The Internment Camp at Baguio" (1987), 11–12.

17. Wygle, *Surviving a Japanese P.O.W. Camp* (1991), 81; Vaughan, *The Ordeal of Elizabeth Vaughan* (1985), 205–6, diary 19 April 1943; Cates (Roka), *The Drainpipe Diary* (1957), 138, diary 14 December 1942. Poston (Wootten), *My Upside-Down World* (2002), 171, 179, diary 8, 14 August 1942. See also in this book J.E. McCall's cartoon, "The Haves and the Have Nots," and Commandment X in "The Camp's Ten Commandments," Appendix II.

18. Vaughan, *The Ordeal of Elizabeth Vaughan* (1985), 278–79, diary 14 July 1944, and 233–36, diary 10 July 1943; Poston (Wootten), *My Upside-Down World* (2002), 192–93, 243, 273, including diary 7 October 1942, 30 May 1943.

19. I have not established when camp work became effectively required. A survey of males working as of 1 August 1942 found 1,542 men working, 325 men between 18 and 60 "unassigned," and 23 "refusing assignment." The following month, the camp's Education Committee reported the two-hour norm as a Work Assignment Committee "aim." Camp historian A.V.H. implied that work was not required of all fit adults until May 1944, but in November 1942, an internee was given 30 days extra labor for "refusing work detail." In August 1943 the Education Committee reported new "Work Assignment Regulations," declaring all men over 17 and all women over 16 "subject to assignment of camp duties" that they must "accept" unless declared unfit by the Department of Hygiene. I do not know why the age was lower for women, but their work was often lighter physically. The Education Committee wanted the age raised to 18, but did not apparently succeed. Hartendorp, *The Japanese Occupation of the Philippines*, Vol. II (1967), 306–7; Santo Tomás Internment Camp, *Internews* (15 August 1942), 1; Santo Tomás Internment Camp, Education Department Committee Minutes, 4 September 1942, 6 August 1943; Stevens, *Santo Tomas Internment Camp* (1946), 404, Executive Committee minutes, 16 November 1942. McCall, in *Santo Tomás Internment Camp* (1945), 88–90, prints the September 1944 labor rules.

20. Cates (Roka), *The Drainpipe Diary* (1957), 96, diary 1 June 1942.

21. Poston (Wootten), *My Upside-Down World* (2002), 118, 244–46, 263, including diary 3 June 1943.

22. Vaughan, *The Ordeal of Elizabeth Vaughan* (1985), 202, diary 19 April 1943; Bryant, *The Sun Was Darkened* (1947), 155; Poston, *My Upside-Down World* (2002), 167, diary 2 August 1942.

23. Wygle, *Surviving a Japanese P.O.W. Camp* (1991), 5–6, 83–90; Santo Tomás Internment Camp, *STIC Gazette* (8 November 1942), 2. Wygle's book is by Peter Wygle, his son (interned at age eleven); it includes Robert Wygle's memoir and observations by Peter, who spent time with his father at work. The Community Service Award was dated 16 October 1942. Several ex-internees have mentioned using twine or string to knit clothes. After the war a relative of Robert Wygle, not interned, criticized him for wanting

to "look noble" in not taking money that could have bought more food and extras for his wife and two children in the camp, as they had no shanty other than his workshop.

24. Sams (Sherk), *Forbidden Family* (1989), 97. The reference to a "society lady" is from Stevens, *Santo Tomas Internment Camp* (1946), 25.

25. "The Padre" (12 November 1944) in McCall, *Santo Tomás Internment Camp* (1945), 23, abridged by me.

Chapter 6

1. Irvine (Lautzenhiser), *Surviving the Rising Sun* (2010), 205, diary 4 January 1945. With permission from the writer, I have slightly abridged and reworded the diary entry to clarify what happened where. Other children kept diaries, but I have found no other published one except for entries in the Mindanao and Manila memoir of Cecily Marshall (Mattocks), who reached 11 in June 1942. See Marshall, *Happy Life Blues* (2007).

2. The revised "Labor Codes" of September 1944 said that boys "in good physical condition" should work "as assigned" and that "exemption or modification" could be applied to work by "persons under 16 year of age ... due to conflict with school-work." McCall, *Santo Tomás Internment Camp* (1945), 88–90. Hartendorp, in *The Santo Tomas Story* (1964), 66, describes "children" doing camp jobs twice a week in the early months. Nine months after the camp started, the Work Assignment Department reported that no one under 18 had "regular camp duties" but thirty-five had "regular jobs." Santo Tomás Internment Camp, *STIC Gazette* (25 October 1942), 2. The number of eight- to seventeen-year-olds approached 300.

3. Wygle, *Surviving a Japanese P.O.W. Camp* (1991), 70.

4. Nicholas Balfour to RW, email attachment 7 July 2008; Irvine (Lautzenhiser), *Surviving the Rising Sun* (2010), 217, 17 January 1945. For a boy's impressions of latter-day hostility, see Prising, *Manila, Goodbye* (1976), 144. Angus Lorenzen's boyhood account of the camp says that friendliness between guards and children ceased after the traumatic execution of escapers in February 1942 — chiefly, he implies, on the part of children — but other memories indicate that this was not so sudden or total. Lorenzen, *A Lovely Little War* (2008), 86.

5. Irvine (Lautzenhiser), *Surviving the Rising Sun* (2010), 113; Cates (Roka), *The Drainpipe Diary* (1957), 217–18, diary 20 September 1944. Poston, in *My Upside-Down World* (2002), 128–29, dates the squad bowing trick to mid-1942. The anonymous Hearst interviewer of Earl Carroll has him dating a similar episode, or maybe the same one, in 1944. Jesus and Quirino, *Earl Carroll* (1980), 8. Doolan's "My Life in a Japanese Prison Camp during World War II" (2004), 19–20, tells of the trick on a single guard. Doolan says the commandant thereupon forbade bowing by children, but I remember having to bow in 1944–1945. By late 1944, though, guards often gave up bowing back, especially (perhaps) to children. Hartendorp, *The Santo Tomas Story* (1964), 247; Nicholas Balfour, conversation with RW, 1 July 2011.

6. Prising, *Manila, Goodbye* (1976), 153–54; Morse (Brooks), "The Internees' Own Story" (2003), 129. Charles Land-Reeves, about the same age as Robin Prising, recounts the same kind of encounter as Prising's, though not with Abiko. Land-Reeves, "...*Boy!*" (1996), 123–24. And Jannis Robb Gared tells of getting an egg from a guard when she was about ten; he showed her a worn photo of his own little girl. Gared, "In Loving Memory" (1999). See also Lewis (Kerns), chapter in *Interrupted Lives* (1995), 87–88.

7. Tyrer, *Stolen Childhoods* (2011), especially 56, 175ff, 334ff; Krass, BBC interview (2011); Krass, phone conversations with RW, 6 July, 5 August 2011. The more positive aspects came out in my conversations with Krass. Her younger brother, Peter, who came in with her, was a loner and more unhappy but not enough is known to elaborate. The missionary Frank Cary spent a month taking care of a mentally disabled thirteen-year-old boy without parents in the camp, after they came in together from the Davao prison camp, and the boy had distressed everyone in a "boys' dormitory" by wetting and soiling his bed. Cary does not say what became of him, but he does note the concern of internee leaders. Cary, *Letters from Internment Camp* (1993), 48, letter 8 January 1944.

8. Prising, *Manila, Goodbye* (1976), 73–74, 99, 125–33, 134, 145–46, and picture of Sanders following page 80; Margaret Ball to RW, email 8 January 2011, on Elsie Harrington, her grandmother, and Robin Prising. Kneedler, in "The Internees' Own Story" (2003), 83, gives some background on Millie Sanders, though he misspells her name as "Saunders" as well as being inaccurate on dates of air raids. Edgar Kneedler was a Manila hotel manager before the war. Sanders' husband apparently served with the 9th Cavalry Regiment, one of four black regiments sent to the Philippines in the Philippine-American War in the belief that they were especially suited to the tropics. Prising said that in the hospital a nurse told him she had said she was moving to Los Baños, but internee lists indicate she did not go, while confirming that her occupation had been "Boarding House." Bailey, *Only a Matter of Days* (2001, 2008), 454.

9. Santo Tomás Internment Camp, Education Department Committee Minutes, 27 November 1942, with circular ("memorandum") from Executive Committee, 1 December 1942; Cates (Roka), *The Drainpipe Diary* (1957), 73, diary 16 March 1942; Santo Tomás Internment Camp, *The Internitis* (September 1942), 11.

10. Printed "Boxing Program" for 26 February 1943 (including stick-figure cartoon of a vanquished boxer escaping into a tree) in Bailey, *Only a Matter of Days* (2001, 2008), 343–46; Len Baker, phone conversation with RW, 27 July 2011.

11. This description is mainly taken from a long Education Committee memo in March 1943, seeking a new education shed. The commandant turned this down, though a new "study hall" (located in the Main Building's grade-school rooms after school finished there) was obtained by the end of the year after much casting about for a place to do homework other than in crowded, noisy corridors. Santo Tomás Internment Camp, Education Department Committee Minutes, memorandum attached, 19 March 1943. See also Alice Bryant's account of teaching in the school in Bryant, *The Sun Was Darkened* (1947), 153. On library access, Len Baker, phone conversation with RW, 27 June 2011. Liz Irvine (Lautzenhiser), in *Surviving the Rising Sun* (2010), 137–38, prints a vivid first aid final test and a congratulatory letter, 12 June 1943. The Education Committee minutes make frequent mention of first aid. The long memo referenced above says that grade-school classes through sixth grade (presumably age eleven) were taught on the Main Building ground floor, but Robin Prising, my sister Mary June, and my friend Nick Balfour recalled classes on the top floor before the age of 12 in 1944.

12. Lewis (Kerns), chapter in *Interrupted Lives* (1995), 84; Len Baker, phone conversation with RW, 27 June 2011; Baker, "A Teenager at Santo Tomas, 1942–1945" (1974), 5–7.

13. Bryant, *The Sun Was Darkened* (1947), 152–54; Cur-

tis Brooks and Dorothy Brooks (Mullaney in camp), phone conversation with RW, 1 August 2011; Wygle, *Surviving a P.O.W. Camp* (1991), 67–69; Prising, *Manila, Goodbye* (1976), 127, 147, 159. Santo Tomás Internment Camp, Education Department Committee Minutes, 27 August 1943, gives more mixed views, and Liz Irvine, daughter of school administrator Roscoe Lautzenhiser, reprints several good English "themes" that she wrote (see Irvine [Lautzenhiser], *Surviving the Rising Sun* [2010]).

14. The Education Department developed three libraries of its own, including a "Children's Library," in addition to a general library, several privately run rental libraries, and "limited access" for teachers to the university's library. Santo Tomás Internment Camp, Education Department Chairman, "To Any Education Official Concerned" (1945). On reading, Nicholas Balfour to RW, email 2 June 2009. The Annex had story-tellers too.

15. Nicholas Balfour to RW, email 4 February 2010. My mother thought my attacks on Mary June were getting my own back for being bossed before the war, but my tantrums recurred until well after liberation, as Chapter 12 notes.

16. Lorenzen recorded the extra hit of being wrongly accused of having a pro-Nazi father (in fact, a World War I veteran) mainly because he had previously lived in Shanghai's German quarter. Lorenzen, *A Lovely Little War* (2008), 82–85. My Boys' Club memories were amplified by Nicholas Balfour, nine months older than me, in very full emails and conversations, with some information from older Boys' Club members such as Mike Browning, Jay Crawford, Tom Crosby, and Bill Tonkin. The "club" started in one room — Leake's. Charles Land-Reeves (then just Reeves) gives a very different account of entering the Boys' Club in 1943, aged nine or ten, as apparently the only English boy in his room, rejected by the Americans, and getting no support from Brother Abrams. Land-Reeeves, "...*Boy!*" (1996), 112–14.

17. I have met no one else who remembers this, but an ex-Filipino informant has told me quite recently that what I remembered vaguely as large, brown, molassassy cookies were indeed a Filipino favorite: *panucha* or *pinocha* cakes made of "thick unprocessed sugar-cane juice that is normally dried into brown sugar." Yolanda Cruz to RW, email 3 August 2011.

Chapter 7

1. My account of Tjideng Camp is based on Clara Olink Kelly's camp memoir, *The Flamboya Tree* (2003), especially 156–64. She was interned at only four, but see also van der Kuil, "Tjideng Camp" website (bibliography, last section on DVDs, etc.). On maneuvering for survival and the play of different interest groups even in horrifically oppressive camp regimes, see especially the classic, first-hand study by Eugene Kogan, *The Theory and Practice of Hell* (2006), based mainly on Buchenwald.

2. Japanese chains of command are confusing, in part because so many documents have been destroyed, but also because the military had its own competing structures while infiltrating civil government all the way to the top. Though the camp's first commandant, Hitoshi Tomayasu, was a military police lieutenant, the camp was soon put under a General Affairs Office, headed by a military officer, which had a foreign affairs team or section in charge of civilian camps. The office was located in the Japanese Military Administration of the Philippines until that was replaced by the puppet Republic of the Philippines in November 1943. The General Affairs Office then continued as the State Affairs Office, in charge of civilian camps until the army took over in January 1944, putting civilian camps, along with military POW camps, under an army War-Prisoner Headquarters (not the "military police," as some have claimed). The War-Prisoner Headquarters reported directly to the commanding general in the Philippines until June 1944, when it reported to him via a newly created supply corps, though the camps were still subject to separate army inspections and Kempeitai raids. Officially, too, the War-Prisoner Headquarters was part of the War-Prisoner Department in Tokyo commanded by a general who also ran a Bureau of POW Intelligence, both of which sent recommendations to the Philippines.

3. Nagai, "The Internment of Western Civilians under the Japanese" (2006), focusing on Santo Tomás from a partly Japanese perspective, stresses the two motives of prisoner protection and Japanese security and the tension between them. The same two motives even appear in a Taiwan camp guideline giving the circumstances for killing POWs in the event of an Allied invasion. Taihoku POW Camp, Taiwan, entry from journal (1944). See also Hartendorp, *The Santo Tomas Story* (1964), 41, on a Tokyo critic encouraging the army to take responsibility for feeding the camp. Jesus and Qurino, in *Earl Carroll* (1980), 94–98, discuss the Santo Tomás broadcast.

4. The secrecy of the activities and lack of Japanese documents mean we will perhaps never know the full story. I have pieced together my brief account from War Crimes Information Series, Monthly Report [by Japanese Army] for Military Internment Camp, no. 1 (December 1944); Hartendorp, *The Santo Tomas Story* (1964), 369–70, 378, 395, 424–25; Hartendorp, *The Japanese Occupation of the Philippines*, Vol. II (1967), 351–52, 511, 539, 589–90; Jesus and Quirino, *Earl Carroll* (1980), 40, 42–45; Ward, "Legitimate Collaboration" (2008), 179, 187–88; Chris Larsen Jr., blog 14 June 2006, at Gopal and Bunn, "Victims of Circumstance: Santo Tomás Internment Camp." On the basis of war trial affidavits, James Ward gives some credence to suggestions by Earl Carroll and others that a camp informer helped expose Grinnell and the others. But a key event was the arrest and torture (and subsequent execution) of the Mencarinis, a Manila couple active in the underground and aid to military POWs. Less certain is the suspicion that Grinnell and Duggleby were blamed for a well-informed San Francisco broadcast on Santo Tomás conditions. Johnson is reported to have operated a radio (not apparently found) and to have been in contact with guerrillas when he was in an outside hospital. Hartendorp says he was "frank and somewhat careless of speech" (*The Santo Tomas Story*, 370). The Kempeitai took him out of camp immediately whereas they left the other three in the internee-run camp jail for twelve days, enabling Earl Carroll to speak with them before they were taken out.

5. Hartendorp, *The Japanese Occupation of the Philippines*, Vol. I (1967), 226–67; Setsuho and José, eds., *The Philippines under Japan* (1999), ch. 7 by Terada Takefumi; Lichauco, *Dear Mother Putnam* (1949, 1997, 2005), 173, diary 10 July 1944; Cogan, *Captured* (2000), 223–24; Butcher, "Wartime Memoirs" (2002), 63–65. To some extent, the Japanese favoring of Catholics may have been due to a link between Philippine Catholic leaders and Franco Spain, neutral but pro-Axis, as seen in a banquet and political speech given by the country's top Dominican, Fr. Thomas Tascon, to a visiting Japanese Catholic bishop. Hartendorp, *The Japanese Occupation of the Philippines* (1967). The Protestant clergy leader, Bishop Norman Binsted, was away from the bullying sessions but got his own pledge accepted, tactfully drawing a line much as Arch-

bishop O'Doherty had. Binsted later went into the camp and then to Los Baños. However, not all missionaries were unpopular. Tressa Roka noted the impact of some young Irish and French Canadian missionaries, on and off the softball field. Cates (Roka), *The Drainpipe Diary* (1957), 203, diary 2 March 1944.

6. Hartendorp, *The Japanese Occupation of the Philippines*, Vol. I (1967), 57–60, quoting from *Internews*. On armbands and colors, see also Hartendorp, *The Santo Tomas Story* (1964), 23. Dan Raleigh, first chief of internee police, may have initiated the issuing of armbands but it conformed to Japanese bureaucratic customs of the times. With regard to the dual commandants, Kodaki and Kuroda, the latter continued as deputy to Kodaki's successor, Kitaro Kato, who held both of Kodaki's jobs at least temporarily. Later, in 1944, Commandant Onozoki stayed on as aide to his successor, Lt. Col. Yoshie, and then acting commandant in June–August between Yoshie's departure and the arrival of the last commandant, Lt. Col. Hayashi.

7. Wyatt-Smith, "Internment of Consuls" (1942); Mydans, *More than Meets the Eye* (1959, 1974), 111–12.

8. Vaughan, *The Ordeal of Elizabeth Vaughan* (1985), 268, diary 30 April 1944; Hartendorp, *The Santo Tomas Story* (1964), 259–60; Bailey, *Only a Matter of Days* (2001, 2008), 232, diary 2 May 1944. However, Bailey also reports Yoshie giving him special permission to cook in the shanty—generally forbidden then—due to his wife Althea's ailing condition. Bailey, *Only a Matter of Days* (2001, 2008), 288, diary 25 May 1944. He also proposed, unsuccessfully, bringing in pigs and carabaos to feed the camp, as well as internee efforts to make and sell things outside. Santo Tomás Internment Camp, Executive and Internee Committee Minutes and Proceedings, 29 May, 6 June 1944.

9. Paul Esmérian's description is in Esmérian, "War Years in the Philippines 1941–1945" (1980), 58, 8 November 1943. On the package line's final day, a sergeant or officer of the guard suddenly let in the outside throng but I assume this had Kato's approval. Kato's thank-you letter is quoted from Hartendorp, *The Santo Tomas Story* (1964), 301–2. He unfairly calls it "fawning."

10. On Japanese officials and internee inequality, see Lucas, *Prisoners of Santo Tomas* (1975, 1988), 123. See also Vaughan, *The Ordeal of Elizabeth Vaughan* (1985), 206, diary 19 April 1943; Sams (Sherk), *Forbidden Family* (1989), 149, 151; Van Sickle, *The Iron Gates of Santo Tomás* (1992), 201.

11. Hartendorp, *The Santo Tomas Story* (1964), 188–89, 389–90; Hartendorp, *The Japanese Occupation of the Philippines*, Vol. I (1967), 544; Stevens, *Santo Tomas Internment Camp* (1946), 479, digest of Executive Committee minutes, 17–19 January 1945; Bailey, *Only a Matter of Days* (2001, 2008), 180, diary 16 October 1943; Poston (Wootten), *My Upside-Down World* (2002), 244, including diary 31 May, 2 June 1943. There is some confusion about names and dates for several escapes. Ruan may have escaped the harshest punishment by acting or being crazy. Eisenberg's case is a mystery: at the start of the war he was involved with the military, having been a radio engineer, and was suspected in some quarters of being a double agent. James Zobel (MacArthur Memorial library) to RW, email 2, 9 December 2009.

12. Cates (Roka), *The Drainpipe Diary* (1957), 53, diary 29 January 1942; U.S. Court of Federal Claims (2004), 36: claim by Georgia Barnes' brother, Thomas (not interned), with some corroboration by Hartendorp, *The Japanese Occupation of the Philippines*, Vol. II (1967), 186. See also Santo Tomás Internment Camp guard, *Diary*, 18 August, 8 September 1944.

13. Lucas, *Prisoners of Santo Tomas* (1975, 1988); Arthur, *Deliverance at Los Baños* (1985), 30–31; Bailey, *Only a Matter of Days* (2001, 2008), 222, diary 18 March 1944. Arthur dates Konishi at Santo Tomás from 1942 but other accounts indicate early 1944 (or at least not of importance until then).

Hartendorp, *The Santo Tomas Story* (1964), 224; War Crimes Interrogations, testimony of Gerald Rimmer. My account of Konishi versus Kato is based on observations by internee interpreter Frank Cary in the commandant's office. See Cary, *Letters from Internment Camp* (1993), 133, letter 28 June 1945.

14. Santo Tomás Internment Camp guard, *Diary*, 30 November 1944. Accounts differ as to whether Abiko started at the camp in 1943 or 1944. Arthur, in *Deliverance at Los Baños* (1985), 30, said he was a 1936 Olympic swimmer, but the International Olympic Studies Center's list of Japanese swimmers from that year does not include him.

15. Prising, *Manila, Goodbye* (1976), 152–53.

16. Prising, *Manila, Goodbye* (1976), 153; Edward McCreary, phone conversation with RW, 31 July 2012. The Weinzheimer stories are from my phone conversation with Sascha Jean Jansen (Jean Weinzheimer), 22 September 2011. There are other, mostly vaguer accounts of Abiko, not equally unfavorable. Hartendorp, *The Santo Tomas Story* (1964), 240, 309 and elsewhere; Cogan, *Captured* (2000), 274; Glass, "Lieutenant Abiko" (1999). See also Hartendorp, *The Japanese Occupation of the Philippines*, Vol. II (1967), 311–12, transcript of Abiko and others in a committee meeting. The Guadalcanal reference was made by William Grimm (see War Crimes testimony).

17. War Crimes Interrogations, testimony of Gerald Rimmer, Frank Foley, and Shizua Ohashi; Hartendorp, *The Santo Tomas Story* (1964), 266–67.

18. Prising, *Manila, Goodbye* (1976), 134–43.

Chapter 8

1. Hartendorp, *The Santo Tomas Story* (1964), 60.

2. The Agents came out of elected representatives of room and floor monitors. When new monitors were elected in October 1943, shanty "district supervisors" and "assistant supervisors" remained appointed by the internee Shanty Department, as laid down by "Shanty Area Regulations" of 16 August 1943. A shift from the initial election of shanty area monitors or mayors does not seem to have caused much protest, perhaps because the appointees were popular. McCall, *Santo Tomás Internment Camp* (1945), 72, 78–80; Bailey, *Only a Matter of Days* (2001, 2008), 182, diary 25 October 1943.

3. Nash, *That We Might Live* (1984), 38. J. E. McCall, internee chronicler, sketcher, and poet, expressed a continuing dislike of alleged British advantages and superciliousness. McCall, *Santo Tomás Internment Camp* (1945), 18, 28, and Plate LXIV following page 96.

4. The drunken soldiers episode was experienced by Dorothy Main, interned daughter of Thomas Harrington, internee agent and former British consul. Main also told of a long walk and talk by Stanley and Harrington near the end, about which Harrington kept silent; it probably concerned future scenarios. Margaret Ball (Main's daughter) to RW, email c. 20 March 2010. See also Holland, *The Rescue of Santo Tomas* (2003), 167, using research on Stanley by Maurice Francis. British intelligence never divulges the identities of its agents, living or deceased. The claim, repeated by Connaughton et al. in *The Battle for Manila* (1995, 2002), 94–95, that the front liberators of Santo

Tomás called for Stanley and gave him a rifle, is denied by Lt. Col. Walter Landry (captain in 1945), who was right there.

5. Cogan, *Captured* (2000), 162. As Frances Cogan and others reported, 18% of camp children scored positive on a TB skin test in March 1942, reinforcing moves to send children away to the Holy Ghost College school. The test, though, showed exposure to TB with some build-up of immunity in response, not TB itself.

6. Who paid what for outside hospital service is far from clear. The hospitals' allocation of Japanese payments to the camp per internee, from July 1942 to February 1944, probably covered only accommodations, feeding, and basic nursing. It seems that operations were sometimes done for free and sometimes charged for on the basis of ability to pay, accepting IOUs as well as partial down payments and help from benefactors. Stevens, *Santo Tomas Internment Camp* (1946), 114–15; Nash, *That We Might Live* (1984), 62, 114–15; Wygle, *Surviving a Japanese P.O.W. Camp* (1991), 62–63.

7. Stevens, *Santo Tomas Internment Camp* (1946), 414, quoting committee minutes.

8. McCall, *Santo Tomás Internment Camp* (1945), 72–85, gives most of the articles.

9. Irvine (Lautzenhiser), *Surviving the Rising Sun* (2010), 94; Wygle, *Surviving a Japanese P.O.W. Camp* (1991), 204; Santo Tomás Internment Camp, *STIC Gazette* (4 October, 8 November 1942). The October editorial followed the temporary closure of the front-gate "package line" following illegal messages in laundry going out (referenced in Chapter 3). See Appendix II for the camp's Ten Commandments as well as the original, biblical ones.

10. Stevens, *Santo Tomas Internment Camp* (1946), 106; Enriquez, "Coping with War" (2010), 7; Prising, *Manila, Goodbye* (1976), 126, 146.

11. Santo Tomás Internment Camp, Executive and Internee Committee Minutes and Proceedings, 31 January, 2 February 1942.

12. We know little about the jails; another one at the back of the Main Building may have been used when space was needed for solitary confinement. Dr. Ted Stevenson, jailed near the end, gave a smaller dimension for the front jail. Stevenson, *Recollections* (1997); Karen Lewis (Kerns), phone conversation with RW, 31 October 2011; Sonia Francisco, phone conversations with RW, June 2009. On a previous cage-like jail near the gym, see Hartendorp, *The Santo Tomas Story* (1964), 118.

13. Hartendorp, in *The Santo Tomas Story* (1964), 73, says the Committee on Order was set up at the same time that the jail was authorized, late July 1942, but committee minutes show it was operating by 9 July. Stevens, *Santo Tomas Internment Camp* (1946), 379. As reported by Earl Carroll's anonymous Hearst interviewer, Carroll implied—unlike Hartendorp—that the pressure against due process came from the Japanese, not the Executive Committee. It may have come from both. Jesus and Quirino, *Earl Carroll* (1980), 27; Hartendorp, *The Santo Tomas Story* (1964), 84–85. James Ward's detailed political history of the camp says that the Committee on Order's "charter" limited jail sentences to 90 days but longer, "'indeterminate'" sentences were sometimes given. Earl Carroll reportedly claimed that the camp reduced sentences to 30 days after a smuggled-in copy of the Geneva Convention gave that number as the maximum for POWs, but he does not give a date for this event. Ward also says that the vote on broadcasting sentences occurred in the "fall" of 1942, but minutes indicate January 1943. Ward, "Legitimate Collaboration" (2008), 169, 169n; Jesus and Quirino, *Earl Carroll* (1980), 28; Stevens, *Santo Tomas Internment Camp* (1946), 407, entry for 7 January 1943.

14. Hartendorp, *The Santo Tomas Story* (1964), 93–95; Foley, "Department of Religion" (1946), 171; Ward, "Legitimate Collaboration" (2008), 170. Foley's strictures against malicious rumors are also in the camp's "Ten Commandments," located in Appendix II of this book.

15. "Important people" is quoted from Hartendorp, *The Japanese Occupation of the Philippines*, Vol. II (1967), 141, on early 1944. See also Lucas, *Prisoners of Santo Tomas* (1975, 1988), 41, citing Isla Corfield, who served as woman member of the court. There were also charges that internee Wally King, appointed sole shanty materials importer to control quality and prices, favored some contractors over others for extra payments. Van Sickle, *The Iron Gates of Santo Tomás* (1992), 201–2. Favoritism in negotiating outside passes and giving other help is sometimes hard to distinguish from care for individual cases, especially when the administrator knew the internee. Getting medical passes out was also complicated by the inconsistent and arbitrary action of a Japanese doctor. Hartendorp, *The Santo Tomas Story* (1964), 95–96.

16. Sams (Sherk), *Forbidden Family* (1989), 149–51; Van Sickle, *The Iron Gates of Santo Tomás* (1992), 201, 203. By late October 1944, Carroll Grinnell said he had personally obtained a million pesos for camp, though by then hyperinflation was minimizing the peso's value. Some of the million may have been his loans to individuals, usually to be repaid at an increasingly lucrative one dollar for two pesos (the prewar rate), but, unlike some big camp creditors, he did not hope his payments to the camp budget would be underwritten by the American Red Cross. Bailey, *Only a Matter of Days* (2001, 2008), 279, diary 26 October 1944; Cay Pratt (Caroline Bailey) to RW, email 23 November 2011.

17. Hartendorp, *The Santo Tomas Story* (1964), 289–92, 330; Hartendorp, *The Japanese Occupation of the Philippines*, Vol. II (1967), 310–12; Bailey, *Only a Matter of Days* (2001, 2008), 256–57, 260, 287, 383–84, diary August (various dates), 23 November 1944; Agents to Commandant, 14 August 1944; phone conversation with Cay Pratt (Bailey) 4 October 2011. The initial amount given the camp was about 245,000 pesos but the proportion of the total handed in—my calculation—varies, as Hartendorp and Bailey seem to differ on that total. By July 1944, the value of the Japanese Philippine peso had fallen to a fifth of the prewar peso, which was fifty U.S. cents.

18. On nurses' arrangements and group behavior, see Hartendorp, *The Santo Tomas Story* (1964), 60, 82, 123. See also Norman, *We Band of Angels* (1999), 151, 155–57, 306n12; Kaminski, *Prisoners in Paradise* (2000), 96–98; Poston (Wootten), *My Upside-Down World* (2002), 263–64; Bailey, *Only a Matter of Days* (2001, 2008), 116, diary 13, 14 January 1943; Sperry (Lee), *Running with the Tiger* (2009), 243, diary 14 January 1943. The army nurse, Denny Williams, said the nurses had to move to a noisy room near the kitchen but that did not cause the strike. Williams, *To the Angels* (1985), 137. On nurses' personal styles, see Prising, *Manila, Goodbye* (1976), 134. See also Esmérian, "War Years in the Philippines 1941–1945" (1980), 75, diary 25 November 1944; Nash, *That We Might Live* (1984), 110; Sams (Sherk), *Forbidden Family* (1989), 159, 67; Susan Trout, phone conversation with RW, 11 July 2011, on her mother, army nurse Frankie Lewey, said by a Philippine Scout soldier to be the only U.S. Army nurse he ever saw smile. Van Sickle, in *The Iron Gates of Santo Tomás* (1992), reported a more favorable experience by herself and many others but not all. She also observed disdain by ex–China

Rockefeller foundation doctors for local interned ones (57–58 and elsewhere).

19. Manila expats often did such embroidery as a gift for departing friends at their *espedidas* (farewell parties), and the practice continued into the camp — for example, on a handkerchief or blouse. Bill Davidson, grandson of Elizabeth Cunningham, believes she embroidered the signatures in the camp. Davidson to RW, email 1 December 2010. There was also a Taiwanese signature and one in Japanese as well as in English by Ernest Stanley, the interpreter.

20. Kneedler, "The Internees' Own Story" (2003), 82–83. Edgar Kneedler told this as a firsthand story; he was eating at a bench outside the kitchen. See chapter 6, note 8, for more on Sanders and Kneedler.

21. Rutter, *The Long March into Oblivion* (2006), 16–26; Stevens, *Santo Tomas Internment Camp* (1946), 43–44; Hartendorp, *The Santo Tomas Story* (1964), 121–22; Hartendorp, *The Japanese Occupation of the Philippines*, Vol. I (1967), 361–62; Cates (Roka), *The Drainpipe Diary* (1957), 149, diary 12 January 1943; Bailey, *Only a Matter of Days* (2001, 2008), 115–16, 132, diary 11–14 January, 22, 24 March 1943; Poston (Wootten), *My Upside-Down World* (2002), 217–18, diary 11–14 January 1943; Irvine (Lautzenhiser), *Surviving the Rising Sun* (2010), 120. It is unclear how many military internees returned to camp at different times. Bailey says they had to pay varying fines or stay longer at Fort Santiago. I do not know how many survived. Hartendorp, in *Japanese Occupation of the Philippines*, records a calm but incisive interrogation of Owens by Carroll Grinnell, apparently establishing he had not named names. Later, civilians who had worked at some point for the military had also to report to the commandant. Some 250 did so but nothing happened to them.

22. Stevens, *Santo Tomas Internment Camp* (1946), 52–53; Hartendorp, *The Santo Tomas Story* (1964), 178–84; Van Sickle, *The Iron Gates of Santo Tomás* (1992), 173–75; Ward, "Legitimate Collaboration" (2008), 173. Stevens summarizes earlier evacuations in 1942 (less fraught, as camp conditions were better then, with more optimism about early rescue). Mydans, *More than Meets the Eye* (1959, 1974), 82. Jesus and Quirino, in *Earl Carroll* (1980), 25–26, report Earl Carroll's concern in 1942 about keeping Filipinos on their side by staying.

23. Stevens, *Santo Tomas Internment Camp* (1946), 63–65, 278–80, 461–62; Hartendorp, *The Santo Tomas Story* (1964), 254–56; Hartendorp, *The Japanese Occupation of the Philippines*, Vol. II (1967), 218–21; Ward, "Legitimate Collaboration" (2008), 178; Santo Tomás Internment Camp, Executive and Internee Committee Minutes and Proceedings, 27, 28 April 1944. Geege Poston (Wootten) told me about patching up Lee's clothes: phone conversation with RW, 31 December 2011. Stevens notes that demands for an oath started in December 1943 for internees working at the main gate. Unlike Hartendorp, Stevens says that internees were ordered to sign an oath in February, but copies were returned when some signers wrote "under duress" beneath their signatures. The Internee Committee minutes give the original "letter of reservations"; the minutes also reported that the previous commandant, lawyer Gonshichi Onozoki, who had stayed on to advise his successor, assured the committee that "conspiracy" would be narrowly construed.

Chapter 9

1. Cates (Roka), *The Drainpipe Diary* (1957), 235, diary 17 December 1944.

2. Stevens, *Santo Tomas Internment Camp* (1946), 155–56: chow-line menus to mid-January 1945. Memoirs and memories differ on whether they included lunch; mine accords with Stevens in that they did. But a meal ticket for April 1943, reissued (it seems) for April 1944, shows only two servings, AM and PM. The original two meals a day were initially expanded to lunch servings for children and men doing heavy work, with scraps for others.

3. Stevenson, "Statement before U.S. Congress" (1947). The initial letter by Commandant Kato to the internee finance and supplies chairman on 24 January 1944, announcing direct supply by the "Japanese Military Authorities," did not mention calories but grams, totaling 766 grams (1.68 pounds) per adult per day, broken down by food categories, including 200 grams of vegetables, "if and when available," 400 grams of cereals (progressively reduced to 187), and various amounts of fish, sugar, and cooking oil or fats, all later eliminated. Irvine (Lautzenhiser), *Surviving the Rising Sun* (2010), 172. Frederic Stevens' big chapter on "food" at Santo Tomás said the Japanese "ration" fell from 400 to 300 calories per adult internee in September 1944, but he apparently confused calories with grams. Stevens, *Santo Tomas Internment Camp* (1946), 157, 433 (15 September 1944 entry). Calories are only one factor in preventing malnutrition. In addition to *composition* (e.g., enough protein and key vitamins), food *bulk* is important.

4. The quotations are from Internee Committee minutes, paraphrasing Commandant Onozoki. Stevens, *Santo Tomas Internment Camp* (1946), 448, excerpting minutes of 16 August 1944. Onozoki was filling in as "acting" commandant, June–September 1944, between the tenures of Lt. Cols. Yoshie and Hayashi, having been commandant before Yoshie. A tally of food purchases shows that small amounts of fruit and vegetables were again bought in November 1944. Stevens, *Santo Tomas Internment Camp* (1946), 149.

5. Hattie Brantley quoted by Norman, *We Band of Angels* (1999), 186; Santo Tomás Internment Camp guard, Diary, 30 November 1944 and other entries in September–November 1994; Cogan, *Captured* (2000), 189; Collingham, *The Taste of War* (2011), 189. Nagai, in "The Internment of Western Civilians under the Japanese" (2006), 167, says that some Santo Tomás Japanese actually died of malnutrition, presumably due to reduced immunity to disease. The guards suffered a typhoid outbreak in September 1944, leading to new hygiene rules. As early as June 1944, the Japanese "war camps" administration in the Philippines admitted a failure to meet food allocation targets and a need to bring in some food "from distant points." War Crimes Information Series, Monthly Report (30 June 1944). Long before that, though, Japanese guards stole food from the camp's central kitchen. Santo Tomás Internment Camp, Executive and Internee Committee Minutes and Proceedings, 11 April 1942.

6. Cates (Roka), *The Drainpipe Diary* (1957), 209, diary 12 July 1944. The ban was lifted or bypassed for Christmas 1944 (see later in this chapter).

7. Lorenzen, "A Desperate Drug Smuggler" (2012); Wanda Damberg (Werff), phone conversations with RW, 19 January, 10 February 2012. When Ahern went to Los Baños, a Spanish father, Pedro Mateos, succeeded him in the operation. Werff later went to Los Baños too.

8. Hartendorp, *The Santo Tomas Story* (1964), 272–73; Jesus and Quirino, *Earl Carroll* (1980), 30–31, 34–36; Van Sickle, *The Iron Gates of Santo Tomás* (1992), 212; Bailey, *Only a Matter of Days* (2001, 2008), 388–98: camp documents (some secret) and post-liberation memo to American National Red Cross. Fay Bailey succeeded Alex Calhoun

as camp treasurer and was an officer of the American Red Cross, Philippine subsidiary. I have not pursued the obscure paper trail on what Red Cross branch, if any, repaid the loans and at what rate of exchange.

9. Hartendorp, *The Santo Tomas Story* (1964), 292–93, 404; Hartendorp, *The Japanese Occupation of the Philippines*, Vol. II (1967), 318, 539; Dos Passos, *Tour of Duty* (1946), 203–6; Jesus and Quirino, *Earl Carroll* (1980), 34–41; Alcuaz papers: "Memorandum to Brig. Gen. Courtney Whitney" (19 March 1945), 8–14, and several press and interview reports; Jeanne Siegel, Anthony de Alcuaz, and Marie Kish (adult children of Luis de Alcuaz), taped interview by RW and Mary Wilkinson, Belmont, California, 12 September 2009. Most accounts say Alcuaz went into hiding around 23 December, when Carroll Grinnell and his companions (as well as their secret Manila contacts) were arrested, but his family suggested it was later. It is also unclear whether the encounter with Abiko happened before or later, or even on 3 February, half a day before the camp's liberation, when he went back to his office. Brave Filipino helpers of Alcuaz, including his cousin, Manuel Mañosa, assistant director of Manila's water board, may have continued some smuggling after Alcuaz left.

10. Hartendorp, *The Santo Tomas Story* (1964), 373.

11. Hartendorp, *The Santo Tomas Story* (1964), 201.

12. Private selling and buying of ice was stopped in early 1944, but the corned beef and pork were "cured," so they could keep for a while after opening. In mid-December 1944, Fay Bailey's family of three, down to their last three corned beef cans, made one 8-ounce can last for two lunches. Bailey, *Only a Matter of Days* (2001, 2008), 291, diary 10, 11 December 1944. Each internee's kit included 32 cans of meat or fish. Hartendorp's *Santo Tomas Story* (1964), 202, lists the kit contents per internee but does not give can sizes.

13. Nash, *That We Might Live* (1984), 123–24, 138–40; Crabb, "Santo Tomas Diet Slow Starvation" (1945); Van Sickle, *The Iron Gates of Santo Tomás* (1992), 303. The adage that beer specifically helps breastfeeding (e.g., by "relaxing" the milk supply) has been disproven, but beer does contain nutrients. "Liberation" for the Nashes did not come until 23 February 1945, as they moved to Los Baños in April 1943.

14. Cary, *Letters from Internment Camp* (1993), 81, letter of 21 September 1944. On calories versus results, camp treasurer Fay Bailey, Caroline's father, made this point against Japanese "pressure" to grow more quick-harvest talinum. Bailey, *Only a Matter of Days* (2001, 2008), 287, diary 15 November 1944. Liz Irvine, the Lautzenhisers' daughter, suggested lack of know-how and experience of hard physical labor in breaking new ground. Phone conversation with RW, 20 September 2011; also airmailed answer to questions sent 7 June 2011. Mary June and I do not recall planting at our shanty in addition to our mother's work in the camp vegetable garden, though at least one shanty (we moved) had banana trees.

15. Bailey, *Only a Matter of Days* (2001, 2008), 283, 291–92, diary 7 November, 12 December 1944; Van Sickle, *The Iron Gates of Santo Tomás* (1992), 298–99; Hartendorp, *The Santo Tomas Story* (1964), 391; McCall, *Santo Tomás Internment Camp* (1945), 134. Bailey's records are particularly valuable on prices, as he often gives them in U.S. dollars or "good" pesos — illegal, prewar "Commonwealth pesos," which circulated secretly. Internee memoirs usually give prices in deflated, Japanese "Mickey Mouse" pesos, making it hard to allow for general depreciation of the currency against the dollar. Bailey's spending given here exceeds the 125 pesos a month officially allowed his family of three (including his wife and child) but some of it was by IOU checks, and some may have been extra hidden money. Van Sickle says the smugglers took a third of the food obtained; Hartendorp claims that customers took the risk and implies internee smugglers sometimes did not deliver.

16. Mary June Pettyfer (Wilkinson), taped interview with RW, 1 September 2009, Victoria, BC, Canada; Sebastian Balfour, conversation with RW, 3 January 2011; Nicholas Balfour to RW, email 2 June 2009; Anne Balfour, "Diary of Anne Balfour, Manila," entries 21 December 1944, 11 January 1945; Esmérian, "War Years in the Philippines 1941–1945" (1980), diary 18 December 1944.

17. Landry, taped interview by Lou and Michelle Gopal (2005); Wygle, *Surviving a Japanese P.O.W. Camp* (1991), 133; Cary, *Letters from Internment Camp* (1993), 111, letter 27 January 1945. Contey-Aiello, in *The 50th Anniversary Commemorative Album of the Flying Column* (1994), gives GI comments on internee appearances by sex and age (see, for example, 88–89, 96, 98).

18. Adams, letter and report to U.S. Army Judge Advocate General (1945); Stevens, *Santo Tomas Internment Camp* (1946), 125–26, including statistics on weight losses. Percentage losses are my calculation. Internee Marie Adams, an American Red Cross social worker, was responsible for records of deaths. On hormones, gender, age, and weight loss, I am indebted to biologist Yolanda Cruz, an expert on proteins. Cruz to RW, email 3, 4 February 2012. Santo Tomás women over 60 actually lost more weight proportionally than men: 36% versus 33%. They had bulked up so much fat before the war that they could lose more weight, largely in fat (though fat is lighter per volume than muscle). The value of fat remained important, being a more "compact source of energy" than carbohydrates and transformable into glucose for energy. Cruz to RW, email 6 February 2012. Other aspects of female versus male longevity — much discussed by scientists — may well be relevant.

19. Cates (Roka), *The Drainpipe Diary* (1957), 234, diary 15 December 1944.

20. "Wet" beriberi is distinguished from "dry" beriberi (impaired nerve endings). Expanded and "saggy" blood vessels also demanded more blood flow, straining the heart. Impaired heart muscle can, in turn, promote beriberi by failure to circulate blood, not supplying enough blood protein and leaving fluid to collect at extremities. Beriberi and myocarditis could each be a cause of death without the other. Of the fifteen deaths in the last four months attributed at least in part to beriberi, nine were attributed to myocarditis too. Numbers and percentages are my calculation from Adams, letter and report to U.S. Army Judge Advocate General (1945). I am grateful to emails from Yolanda Cruz (see note 18 above) on 12 February 2012 and phone conversations with ex-internee Iris Krass, a physician, on 5 August 2011 and 15 February 2012. Krass noted out that some older people would be dying anyway of heart failure.

21. Lichauco, *Dear Mother Putnam* (1949, 1997, 2005), 195, diary 10 December 1944. The Lichaucos made their home a makeshift hospital in the ensuing Battle for Manila.

22. Cates (Roka), *The Drainpipe Diary* (1957), 242, diary 26 January 1945. The "Santo Tomás stare" was more widely known in the Pacific as "the stare," induced by stress.

23. Mary June Pettyfer (Wilkinson), taped interview by RW, 1 September 2009, Victoria, BC, Canada; Montefiori (Hearnden), "A Bit of Camp 1942–1945" (no date), 30–31, in Hearnden papers.

24. Tika Balfour, conversation with RW, 1 September 2010, and email to RW, 24 February 2012. Morse (Brooks),

"The Internees' Story" (2003), 129, also tells of a quarrel involving theft and double-crossing.

25. Jansen (Weinzheimer), chapter in *Interrupted Lives* (1995), 42; Elizabeth Norman to RW, email 25 July 2009, on her interviews with interned army nurses for her book, *We Band of Angels* (1999). See also Poston (Wootten), *My Upside-Down World* (2002), 269.

26. Prising, *Manila, Goodbye* (1976), 62–64.

27. Balfour, "Diary of Anne Balfour, Manila," 46, 47, entries 19 December 1944, 4 January 1945; Tika Balfour to RW, email 5 March 2012.

28. Bailey, *Only a Matter of Days* (2001, 2008).

Chapter 10

1. War Crimes Information Series, Monthly Reports (June 1944). The report also attributed laxity to a "civilian ... majority of the personnel"—civilian army workers recruited as guards—but the big influx of such workers, mostly Taiwanese, at Santo Tomás seems to have been later. The other two camps were probably Baguio (Camp Holmes) and Los Baños.

2. War Crimes Information Series, Monthly Reports (December 1944); Cary, *Letters from Internment Camp* (1993), 117, letter 29 January 1945.

3. Taihoku POW Camp, Taiwan, entry from journal (August 1944); Utsumi, "'Annihilation Plan' [for] the Allied POWs" (2005). Wilkinson, in "Was There a Massacre Plan?" (2013), says more about the Japanese Army Ministry's guidelines ("notification") of September 1944, *Radio Riku AMitsu, No. 1633*, in relation to Santo Tomás. They were first reported to me by Professor Aiko Utsumi in correspondence between her, Yukako Ibuki and myself. The Army Ministry was often called the Ministry of War, but there was also a Navy Ministry.

4. The quotation is a paraphrase in Frederic Stevens' "chronology," largely drawn from committee minutes. Stevens, *Santo Tomas Internment Camp* (1946), 475, entry 1 January 1945, 151–52.

5. Hartendorp, *The Santo Tomas Story* (1964), 237–41, 250, 275–79, 295; Hartendorp, *The Japanese Occupation of the Philippines*, Vol. II (1967), 210–14; Ward, "Legitimate Collaboration" (2008), 176–77; International Committee of the Red Cross, Convention Relative to the Treatment of Prisoners of War (1927); Utsumi, "Japan's World War II POW Policy" (2005). Article 31, the convention's article on military labor, was not a watertight defense against the use of internees for this task. POW work, it said, should have "no *direct* connection with the operations of war. *In particular*, it is forbidden to employ prisoners in the manufacture or transport of munitions" (my emphasis). Committee protests also claimed or implied wrongly that the Geneva Convention forbade any compelling of POWs to work. From August 1944, if not earlier, Japanese guards themselves spent a lot of time working on patrol walkways, perhaps to keep them flood-free for fast action and maybe to keep the garrison busy. Santo Tomás Internment Camp guard, *Diary* (1944). In January 1944 internees agreed to build a guards' shack in a new garden area, presumably to keep out thieves (the committee minutes don't give the reason). Santo Tomás Internment Camp, Executive and Internee Committee Minutes and Proceedings, 21 January 1944.

6. Vaughan, *The Ordeal of Elizabeth Vaughan* (1985), 295, diary 21 September 1944; Hartendorp, *The Santo Tomas Story* (1964), 321.

7. Nicholas Balfour to RW, email 7 July 2008; Balfour, phone conversation with RW, 12 February 2009; Curtis Brooks to RW, email 21, 22 February 2011. The dip in the wing of the Vought Corsair (called a "broken wing" more gloomily by an internee) sat over the undercarriage, raising the wing so that the outsized propeller, needed by the powerful engine, did not scrape the deck. Without the dip, the landing gear's legs would have been too long, and too bulky when folded.

8. Wygle, *Surviving a Japanese P.O.W. Camp* (1991), 114. Internees debated before and after liberation what the heavy bombers were; several accounts even claim they were the new Boeing B29 Superfortress, much talked about in February 1945, though they did not generally operate over the Philippines. Nick Balfour is sure he saw Boeing B17 Flying Fortresses, which he distinguished by their high single tailfin versus the B24's small twin rudders, but B24s with a bigger range were the main ones. Only Donald Dang, camp artist, claimed there were serious injuries from the antiaircraft shell fragments. Dang, *Survival in Santo Tomas* (1991), 102.

9. Hartendorp, *The Santo Tomas Story* (1964), 372.

10. "Regulations Governing Internees (revised Sept. 27, 1944)," in McCall, *Santo Tomás Internment Camp* (1945), 86–87; Stevens, *Santo Tomas Internment Camp* (1946), 565, report from minutes of 15 November 1944. I have not read of any book getting banned.

11. Bailey, *Only a Matter of Days* (2001, 2008), 274–76, 386–87, diary 9–14 October 1944; letter from Internee Committee to Commandant, 12 October 1944; meeting between the same, 12 October 1944, including commandant's response to be posted immediately on bulletin boards; Stevens, *Santo Tomas Internment Camp* (1946), 459–60, report from Internee Committee minutes, 19 October, 3 November 1944; Hartendorp, *The Santo Tomas Story* (1964), 331–32, 347–48, 380; Wygle, *Surviving a Japanese P.O.W Camp* (1991), artendor 110–11; Cary, *Letters from Internment Camp* (1993), 96, letter 23 November 1944.

12. Hartendorp, *The Santo Tomas Story* (1964), 134–35; Santo Tomás Internment Camp, Executive and Internee Committee Minutes and Proceedings, 9 February 1944. Hartendorp, describing the situation in March 1943, reported plans already in place for defending the camp when Manila was being retaken. The Internee Committee minutes mentioned above, reporting a later reorganizing of special forces, referred to the "possibility of civil disorder and mass hysteria," not overtly to defense against the Japanese, which, of course, it could not say.

13. Chambers, *OSS Training in the National Parks and Service Abroad in World War II* (2008, e-book), ch. 9; Spear, letter to RW, 8 June 1994; Spear, transcripts of interviews by Peter Parsons and Morgan Cavett (1998) and James Zobel (2010); address to Manila (Santo Tomás) Liberation Reunion, San Diego, 5 February 1999; meeting with RW and others, San Diego, 6 February 1999; phone conversations with RW, 19, 26 April 2010; earlier conversations with Mary June and Stephen Pettyfer; Peter Parsons to RW, email 14, 15 December 2011, including a summary from videotape of Spear's San Diego address; Edward McCreary, phone conversation with RW, 31 July 2012. Chambers' book is the only publication to date Spear's mission: it gives good background on Spear but is inaccurate on some details of his mission. Spear, who died in October 2011, and his widow, Robin, are the only sources of information on his mission, except that teenager Edward McCreary saw a person who was presumably Reg Spear come in and leave (McCreary differed in some details from Spear's account of how he entered the Main Building). OSS secrecy can explain

the lack of sources but several ex-internees of Santo Tomás, well informed on the camp, disbelieve his story. However, their claim that Spear made it up is less plausible than the case for its truth, to say the least. In reply to their question of why he waited for nearly fifty years to tell his story, he said that FDR and others had sworn him to secrecy: he only went public when "Bill Colby" (William Colby, then executive director of the CIA) told him that other OSS people had done it. James Zobel, MacArthur Memorial Library, has confirmed that Spear worked for OSS in World War II. Robin Spear told me she was present at a lunch a few years ago with RS, Bartolomeo Cabangbang, the guerrilla radio operator at Victory Hill and an associate of Chick Parsons, and several confederates, authenticating much of the story. She also said she had copies of letters from "POTUS" (codename for the president of the United States) and from William Donovan, OSS director, saying the president wanted him for "the job" (unspecified). Robin Spear to RW via email from Reg's assistant, Rachel Wagoner, 29 March 2012; Robin Spear, phone conversation, 5 July 2012. Peter Parsons, Chick's son, who interviewed Spear for a TV documentary on his father (interview cited above), believes the story and says Spear revealed a family detail that he could only have heard from Chick. Edward McCreary also says he saw the same man he originally spotted talking with Carroll Grinnell and other internee officials outside the Main Building before he left toward the main gate. Spear's story did change on some details in his various accounts, but no more than aged memory could account for a long time after a fast-paced event. The account of his Executive Committee conversation is true both to his character and to that of Earl Carroll. My own account infers that plans discovered for moving or killing internees (told to me and others by Spear) were the Tokyo guidelines. Disbelievers ask (as I have) why Washington could not have gotten the camp information it needed from local covert sources, but that assumes much trust of local guerrillas or a readiness to involve a potential informant such as university official Luis de Alcuaz (a prewar acquaintance of my father) in dangerous contact with U.S. intelligence. Disbelievers also underestimate the active imaginations of spymasters in hatching schemes, as OSS and CIA history shows. On Spear's alleged seeing of my mother, he initially said he also saw my sister, Mary June, but she denied this and he later mentioned only my mother. Mother never mentioned it to us before she died in 1992, but she did not volunteer much about the camp until asked. The secret war diary of our father, revealed after he died in 1965, deliberately did not describe covert operations, though it mentions Konrad Hsu, a Chinese American businessman/scientist, who also features in Spear's account of a later mission into China (see Chambers, *OSS Training*). My father quixotically and unsuccessfully badgered MacArthur to let him do army guerrilla training to return to the Philippines.

14. Santo Tomás Internment Camp, Executive and Internee Committee Minutes and Proceedings, 7 January 1945; Cary, *Letters from Internment Camp* (1993), addendum 135–36, letter 28 June 1945; McCall, *Santo Tomás Internment Camp* (1945), 131; Hartendorp, *The Santo Tomas Story* (1964), 379–82, 385–86. My summary of the 7 January meetings is taken from slightly differing accounts in the committee minutes, interpreter Frank Cary's letter, and Earl Carroll's report to internee journalists, 12 January, as given by Hartendorp. The commandant's 9 January broadcast is quoted by Hartendorp, *The Santo Tomas Story*, 382, and McCall, *Santo Tomás Internment Camp*. Stevens' *Santo Tomas Internment Camp* (1946), chronology 476–77, gives a different sequence of announcements after 7 January from that provided by Hartendorp and McCall. Van Sickle's *The Iron Gates of Santo Tomás* (1992), 304–5, which also quotes the 9 January announcement, says that Carroll vigorously and controversially wanted the whole garrison to stay in order to protect the camp. A shanty neighbor of the Van Sickles knew one of the civilian officials, Mr. Hirose, who visited him at the time.

15. Smith, *Triumph in the Philippines* (1963), 240–42. Smith quotes Yamashita's tactical and humane reasons for wishing to leave Manila, but these are taken from possibly biased war crimes trial testimony.

16. Hartendorp, *The Santo Tomas Story* (1964), 383–84; Van Sickle, *The Iron Gates of Santo Tomás* (1992), 305.

17. Mary June Pettyfer (Wilkinson), taped interview by RW, 1 September 2009, Victoria, BC, Canada, and an earlier comment on the phone; Poston (Wootten), *My Upside-Down World* (2002), 271. Poston's account seems to be from October 1944 (not a diary entry) but the same attitude carried on.

18. My account of livestock slaughtering comes from four slightly differing sources: Santo Tomás Internment Camp, Executive and Internee Committee Minutes and Proceedings, 2 February 1945; Stevens, *Santo Tomas Internment Camp* (1946), 482, chronology 1, 2 February 1945; Cates (Roka), *The Drainpipe Diary* (1957), 244–45, diary 1, 2 February 1945; Hartendorp, *The Santo Tomas Story* (1964), 400–404. The garrison had expanded in late 1944 and/or early 1945.

19. Holland, *The Rescue of Santo Tomas* (2003), 51, 166n53; Cecily Marshall (Mattocks) to RW, email 15 February 2012; phone conversation with RW, 21 March 2012. The message's wording differs a bit in some accounts.

Chapter 11

1. Mary June Pettyfer (Wilkinson), taped interview by RW, 1 September 2009, Victoria, BC, Canada; conversations with RW, London, October 2012. Other accounts describe colored flares, even before the tanks came in. Accounts differ, too, on whether the first tanks came down the right or left side of the camp.

2. Drea, in *MacArthur's ULTRA* (1992), 186–97, discusses differences between MacArthur's and Krueger's intelligence estimates as well as contradictory signals from decoded intercepts concerning Yamashita's intentions. Drea's estimate of total Japanese troops in Manila is higher than that of other accounts and is more authoritative.

3. James, *The Years of MacArthur*, Vol. II (1975), 632–33; Walter Landry (1st Cavalry), taped interviews by Richard Seron, 1 March 2010, 29 August 2012. See also Irvine (Lautzenhiser), *Surviving the Rising Sun* (2010), 227, quoting Brig. Gen. William Chase on Santo Tomás as the priority; U.S. Army, "Japanese Defense of Cities as Exemplified by the Battle for Manila" (1945), 19. On Palawan and massacre fears, see James Zobel (MacArthur Memorial Library) to RW, email 26 October 2010, 19 March 2012. See also MacArthur, *Reminiscences* (1964), 246; Mydans, *More than Meets the Eye* (1959, 1974), 183: reported comment by MacArthur to photographer Carl Mydans. Landry's interviews reported briefing by Brig. Gen. Chase on guerrilla warnings, but guerrillas may have had an incentive to promote an early attack on Manila.

4. Reported flying-column numbers vary. My count is mainly based on a detailed breakdown by unit made by Walter Landry (flying-column captain), 14 November 2012, and sent me via Richard Seron. Officially the 5th and 8th Cavalry columns were called the first and second "serials";

the reconnaissance column was the third, but Landry says the soldiers did not use this term.

5. I totaled 26 deaths from U.S. Army "After Action" Operations Reports, but I may have undercounted a few from attached units. Wright, *The 1st Cavalry Division in World War II* (1947), 134, reported 36 killed and 141 wounded, but that included post-liberation fighting through 7 February. It is not clear if it included 44th Tank Battalion losses.

6. On "P.K." origins, see Richard Seron (flying-column researcher) to RW, phone conversation, 18 July 2010. On "front line general," see Chase, *Front Line General* (1975). Brig. Gen. Hugh Hoffman retained nominal oversight of the 8th Cavalry column, and some contact with it as it came from his brigade, but its real commander was Lt. Col. Hackett Conner. Gen. Mudge stayed involved too.

7. George Fisher, phone conversations with RW, 16, 25 November 2009. On sleep and driving through, see also Walter Landry, taped interview by Lou and Michelle Gopal, DVD (2005).

8. U.S. Army, "After Action" Operation Reports, 8th Cavalry Regiment (1945), makes no reference to Far Eastern University; it refers briefly to "meeting sniper and machine gun fire," in contrast to its fuller description of the successful Malacañan capture, an official objective. A brigade headquarters report says more but minimally about the Far Eastern battle and seems inaccurate on which unit brought rescue. U.S. Army, "S-3 Periodic Report, Headquarters 1st Cavalry Brigade" (1945). No published account mentions the Far Eastern episode as a wrong route taken and ambushed. My figure of ten troopers killed is from Walter Landry, commander of the troop, who identified the dead later but was not at the Far Eastern battle. Landry, taped interview by Richard Seron, 14 November 2012. The 8th Cavalry report says 15 of the regiment's troopers were killed that day. My account, especially of the rescue, draws on Wright, *The 1st Cavalry Division in World War II* (1947), 130, but he wrongly says it was part of a sally to take the Legislative Building. My other sources are Landry's interview with Richard Seron, plus a handwritten account by Landry, and many phone conversations with Susan Trout (daughter of Lt. Jerrett) and Richard Seron (flying-column researcher in association with Trout and Landry). I have singled out Lt. Jerrett for the experience of being badly wounded, but there were heroic actions by others too, including Sgt. John Gallagher. Wright, *The 1st Cavalry Division in World War II* (1947), 130.

9. Between differing witnesses, it is almost impossible to verify the sequence of movements inside and outside the Main Building. Macleod, "Camp diary," 3 February 1945; Mydans, *More than Meets the Eye* (1959, 1974), 188–89.; Walter Landry (1st Cavalry), taped interview by Seron, 1 March 2010. Rescue times have been disputed. Several accounts say the tanks entered at 8:50 P.M. but that was by the Main Building clock, which was on Tokyo time, an hour later than Western-based time for Manila.

10. England, "My Story of Santo Tomas" (1950, January 2010); Hartendorp, *The Santo Tomas Story* (1964), 407; Prising, *Manila, Goodbye* (1976), 184–85; Williams, *To the Angels* (1985), 208–10; Wygle, *Surviving a Japanese P.O.W. Camp* (1991), 132; Van Sickle, *The Iron Gates of Santo Tomás* (1992), 315; Cary, *Letters from Internment Camp* (1993), 125, postscript 23 March 1945 to letter of 11 February 1945; Stevenson, *Recollections* (1997); Poston (Wootten), *My Upside-World* (2002), 274; Cates (Roka), *The Drainpipe Diary* (1957), 315; Richard Seron, phone conversation with RW, 13 May 2010; Walter Landry (1st Cavalry), taped interviews by Richard Seron, 13 October 2010, 23 March 2011; Geege Poston (Wootten), phone conversation with RW, 21 February 2012; Edward McCreary, phone conversation with RW, 31 July 2012. Accounts differ on timing and some other aspects. Decades later, internee Robert Smiley, who had helped in the aid station, claimed "in his cups" that he had cut Abiko's throat there. Sascha Jansen (Jean Weinzheimer), phone conversation with RW, 19 September 2011. This does not easily fit other accounts. Regarding the second grenade, the Japanese model required a wire to be pulled out before hitting it sharply on a hard surface.

11. Santo Tomás Internment Camp, Executive and Internee Committee Minutes and Proceedings, 3 February 1945; Cary, *Letters from Internment Camp* (1993), 121–25, 137–43, letters 11 February, postscript 23 March, and 28 June 1945; Hartendorp, *The Santo Tomas Story* (1964), 405–10; Chase, *Front Line General* (1975), 89; Wygle, *Surviving a Japanese P.O.W. Camp* (1991), 131–32; Cogan, *Captured* (2000), 272, quoting internee hostage Robert Robb. My only source for Joan Meredith's appeal is my mother. Memories differ on the order of events and I do not detail all movements. Regarding tipping off the Japanese outside, Chase and others never mentioned a fear of this being done by radio or phone. Japanese army radios worked badly and were not widely distributed, and there were breakdowns in battery supply. There is no report of the camp having a two-way version. Phone lines may have been cut or blocked by a power failure.

12. Stevens, *Santo Tomas Internment Camp* (1946), 363–66, including a two-page quotation from William Weidmann, an Education Building internee; Hartendorp, *The Santo Tomas Story* (1964), 408–11. See also Crosby, "Remembrance and Thanks" (2002); Brooks, diary fragment (in DVD section of bibliography); Wrinch, "Peter and Tom's Story" (c. 2007), 12–13. Much of the personal experience is from Nicholas Balfour (emails and phone conversations, especially a long email from 7 July 2008), as well as emails and phone comments from Curtis Brooks, Mike Browning, Tom Crosby, and Peter Wrinch. I am not sure of the sequence of movements and orders, and my informants do not agree on whether the Boys' Club included a room across the corridor. Others moved into the center section's big storeroom when told to move to the back. Charles Land-Reeves, also in the Boys' Club, gives an account of the siege that differs sharply and more scarily from my memory and Nick Balfour's. Land-Reeves, *"...Boy!"* (1996), 134–40.

13. On the final negotiations and walkout, see Hartendorp, *The Santo Tomas Story* (1964), 412–13; Mydans, *More than Meets the Eye* (1959, 1974), 193–97; Hencke, interview transcript (2002), 10. The report that Sgt. Uyesugi accompanied Brady into the Education Building comes only from Uyesugi, in Contey-Aiello, ed., *The 50th Anniversary Commemorative Album of the Flying Column* (1994), 76. Connaughton et al., in *The Battle for Manila* (1995, 2002), 95, claim that Hayashi and others were killed by soldiers from Malacañan but give no source. Internee administrator Gerald Rimmer said he "read in the newspapers" of Hayashi's body being found in northern Luzon mountains (War Crimes Interrogations). According to Uyesugi, General Chase said the same. Another report says Commandant Hayashi's uniform was found some distance from Manila. Susan Trout, phone conversation with RW, 22 January 2013. It is possible, as some have speculated, that guerrillas got wind of the "safe-conduct" agreement, but I do not believe that General Chase engineered this. His autobiography is defensive about "turning [them] loose." He later boasted of being a "Jap" killer but he had a sense of honor toward the Japanese. At Cabanatuan, en route to

Manila, he found boxes of Japanese soldiers' ashes and wanted to get them back to Tokyo. Chase, *Front Line General* (1975), 83, 89, 108.

Chapter 12

1. Mary June Pettyfer, taped interview with RW, 1 July 2009, Victoria, BC, Canada.
2. Patrick DiMatteo, phone conversation with RW, 20 December 2012; Walter Landry, interview by Lou and Michelle Gopal, DVD (2005); Geege Poston (Wootten), phone conversation with RW, 10 August 2012. See also Jansen (Weinzheimer), "Freedom" (2011), which vividly describes GI-internee relations.
3. Montefiori (Hearnden), "A Bit of Camp 1942–1945" (no date), 67–68; Cates (Roka), *The Drainpipe Diary* (1957), 248–49; Sascha Jansen (Jean Weinzheimer), phone conversation with RW, 30 January 2012. On trooper attitudes, see written answers by then-Capt. Walter Landry (1st Cavalry) to RW's questions, December 2012.
4. Hartendorp, *The Japanese Occupation of the Philippines*, Vol. II (1967), 529–30; Lorenzen, *A Lovely Little War* (2008), 149–50; Curtis Brooks to RW, email 11 January, 13 June 2010.
5. U.S. Army, "After Action" Operation Reports, 61st Field Artillery (5 February 1945); Stevens, *Santo Tomas Internment Camp* (1946), 453, Internee Committee minutes, 18 September 1945; Hartendorp, *The Santo Tomas Story* (1964), 317–18, 419; Wygle, *Surviving a Japanese P.O.W. Camp* (1991), 137; Walter Olson (37th Infantry Division "fire direction" and "survey"), phone conversation with RW, 28 March 2011; Curtis Brooks to RW, email 16 February 2012. In the incipient battle for Manila, the Japanese shelled other clearly non-military institutions too, including the Quezon Institute Hospital.
6. Esmérian, "War Years in the Philippines 1941–1945" (1980), 85, diary 11 February 1945. Abridged by me sometimes without ellipses (...).
7. Earlier that day the garrison started loading trucks outside the Education Building, evidently aiming to leave when U.S. forces appeared. Curtis Brooks to RW, email 3 March 2013.
8. MacArthur, *Reminiscences* (1964), 26. The most detailed later claims are by Strong, *A Ringside Seat to War* (1965), 89, and Lorenzen, *A Lovely Little War* (2008), 135–36, 151–52. Herman Strong, an internee who is now deceased, said that he, interpreter Ernest Stanley, and "the American commander" (unnamed) saw a 4 February massacre plan in the commandant's office on the evening of 3 February, but that office had been in the Education Building, not yet liberated, from October 1944. He also dubiously attributes to the commander a midnight (3 February) deadline for reaching the camp. Angus Lorenzen quotes alleged messages from Tokyo and from a "secret transmitter" in the camp, printed in a history textbook, c. 1949–1951, whose author(s) and title he could not remember. Lorenzen to RW, email 13, 18 February 2010. On moving shanty people to the Main Building, see Cary, *Letters from Internment Camp* (1993), 122, 138, letters 11 February, 28 June 1945. I explore massacre-plan claims and counter-claims in Wilkinson, "Was There a Massacre Plan?" (2013), an unpublished "memo to self" but available on request.
9. Sascha Jansen (Jean Weinzheimer), phone conversation with RW, 1 September 2012. Other accounts stress more the initial succor of many refugees—for example, Balfour, "Diary of Anne Balfour, Manila," entry 19 February 2012.

10. Hartendorp, *The Santo Tomas Story* (1964), 423; Sascha Jansen (Jean Weinzheimer), phone conversation with RW, 30 January 2012.
11. Mary June Pettyfer (Wilkinson), taped interview by RW, 1 September 2009, Victoria, BC, Canada; Mydans, *More than Meets the Eye* (1959, 1974), 198.
12. Vaughan, *The Ordeal of Elizabeth Vaughan* (1985), 302–4, diary 9–12 March 1945, including having to sign IOUs for the passage home. Only some ended up paying. I have not followed the murky paper trail on who paid what, the disputes involved, and transactions between the United States and other governments. Montgomery, "Capital Circus" (1950).
13. Bryant, *The Sun Was Darkened* (1947), 261–62.
14. Curtis Brooks and Dorothy Brooks (Mullaney), phone conversations with RW, 27 May 2009, 3 August 2009, 1 August 2011; Curtis Brooks to RW, email 28 June 2012, 5 September 2012; Dorothy Brooks (Mullaney) to RW, email 6 September 2012. Barney Brooks had died before I contacted them. Dorothy Mullaney, interned at age nine, married Curtis in 2000 and reported somewhat the same feelings.
15. Cogan, *Captured* (2000), 311–18; Mary Guillemard, conversations with RW, early 2000s. Quotation from Tika Balfour, conversation with RW, 1 September 2010.
16. Lorenzen, *A Lovely Little War* (2008), 86, 172–73.
17. Liz Irvine (Lautzenhiser), phone conversation with RW, 29 September 2011; Edward McCreary to RW, email 23, 27 September 2012; Cates (Roka), *The Drainpipe Diary* (1957), 270; Wygle, *Surviving a Japanese P.O.W. Camp* (1991), 192; Van Sickle, *The Iron Gates of Santo Tomás* (1992), 340–41; Tyrer, *Stolen Childhoods* (2011), 338–39.
18. Phone conversations with RW: Jay Crawford, 22 February 2012; Cecily Marshall (Mattocks), 21 March 2012; Edward McCreary, 31 July 2012; Susan Douglas, citing Lorna Wilkinson, 7 August 2010; Geege Poston (Wootten), 31 December 2011.
19. Archer, *The Internment of Western Civilians under the Japanese* (2004), 239–45; Felton, *Children of the Camps* (2011), ch. 13.
20. Lorenzen, "From the Commander" (May 2011). www.pacifichistoricparks.org/teacher_workshop/2010/NEHcontroversy.html. If the editorial did not mean a pro-Japanese predominance at the conference, then it meant that including any pro-Japan view was heinous. *Wire* did not accept reader responses. *Wire*'s political assertiveness reached into the camp's governance too. "A Demonic Commandant" by Lorenzen in the *Wire*, January 2013, was one-sided regarding the last commandant, Lt. Col. Hayashi, omitting his bids to pull the garrison out, distorting his role in the final siege, and attributing to him actions that came from the army and Kempeitai outside.
21. Lorenzen, "From the Commander" (May 2010, May 2012); Allen, "The Other 'Internees'" (September 2012, January 2013). No Japanese Americans were caught for espionage (unlike some Caucasians, mainly of German origin). Japan's Los Angeles consulate had called Japanese Americans unreliable "cultural traitors" to Japan. Roger Daniels, historian and critic of the internment, to RW, email 24 November 2012; Dower, *War without Mercy* (1986), 79. Daniels also detailed the second article's exaggeration of living conditions and reparations. Daniels to RW, 29 January 2013.
22. Lorenzen, *A Lovely Little War* (2008), 211.

Chapter 13

1. Cogan, *Captured* (2000), 151, 334n2. Santo Tomás estimates vary due to changing camp totals as internees

came in from other camps and left for Los Baños. The Nazi civilian killer camps, of course, dwarfed these proportions, and up to two-thirds of Russian POWs died in German camps, largely due to anti-Slavic racism.

2. "Porous prison," the title of Chapter 3, was coined for Santo Tomás by Norman, *We Band of Angels* (1999).

3. Nash, *That We Might Live* (1984), 96–97, 183–84, 197, on small-group sharing later in Los Baños.

4. Vaughan, *Community under Stress* (1949), 37–38, 43–44; Stevens, *Santo Tomas Internment Camp* (1946), 295–323 (including essay on Iloilo camp by Fr. Koelman).

5. Approximate quotation by Geege (Wootten) Poston, who knew Calhoun. Phone conversation with RW, 18 July 2011.

6. Hartendorp, *The Santo Tomas Story* (1964), 92–93; Poston (Wootten), *My Upside-Down World* (2002), 202, diary 11 November 1942; Cary, *Letters from Internment Camp* (1993), 79, letter 21 September 1944; Bryant, *The Sun Was Darkened* (1947), 198–99; Prising, *Manila, Goodbye* (1976), 134; Bailey, *Only a Matter of Days* (2001, 2008), 85, diary 16 October 1942; Lorenzen, *A Lovely Little War* (2008), 99–100 (on the unconscious racial bias of a teacher).

7. Olsen, transcript of interview by Goldhagen (2002).

8. McCall, *Santo Tomás Internment Camp* (1945), 48–49, including verse by "L.A.C." dated 22 October 1944. See also Stevens, *Santo Tomas Internment Camp* (1946), 69; Van Sickle, *The Iron Gates of Santo Tomás* (1992), 338.

9. Cates (Roka), *The Drainpipe Diary* (1957), 260–61, 270, diary 10, 14 March 1945.

10. Prising, *Manila, Goodbye* (1976), 207.

11. Schreker, *No Ivory Tower* (1986); Milgram, *Obedience to Authority* (1974); Wikipedia, "Milgram Experiment." See also Derren Brown's TV experiments with crowd conformity: Brown, " Gameshow" (2011, in Bibliography, section on DVDs, etc.).

12. I am grateful to Philippine historian Ricardo José for an encompassing account of changing and differing Japanese policies toward Filipinos. José to RW, email 24 September 2012.

13. Eagleman, *Incognito* (2011), ch. 6, on brain studies and "blameworthiness." Debates about a space for free will go back through the atom theories of the early Greek philosopher Epicurus versus the total determinist Democritus.

14. Nelson, "The Causes of the Bataan Death March Revisited" (2005); Frederico Baldassarre to RW, email 8 February 2011. The two writers differed at length on the roles of the Japanese commander, Gen. Masaharu Homma, and his staff, but both criticized Homma.

15. Dower, *War without Mercy* (1986), ch. 3, especially 72; Hastings, *Nemesis* (2007), 341, quoting Brig. Gen. William Fellers.

16. Bryant, *The Sun Was Darkened* (1947), 235–36.

17. American troops did massacre and bomb civilian villages suspected of pro-Japanese collaboration but Japanese reprisals were more common. On American atrocities, including rape on Okinawa, see Schrijvers, *Bloody Pacific* (2010), 210–12, and on Japanese trickery, 189.

18. Gunn, *Pappy Gunn* (2004), 236–38. Dower, in *War without Mercy* (1986), 66–67, reported the same practices by others — no secret in the United States — as well as the distress of pilots.

19. José, "'Death for Honor,' Part 2" (February 2011), 22–23, 33, especially quoting orders of 13 and 15 February 1945. It is not clear if the total-kill order came from Manila defense chief, Adm. Sanji Iwabuchi, or only a local army commander, or both. Psychotherapist Susan Douglas suggested the explanation of Japanese violence against children.

20. Wygle, *Surviving a Japanese P.O.W. Camp* (1991), 132.

21. Dower, *War without Mercy* (1986), 64–66; Sledge, *With the Old Breed on Peleliu and Okinawa* (1981, 2010), 118, 131, 151; Wilkinson, *American Tough* (1984, 1986), 101, on the American frontier and hunter-hunted relations; Michael Snape, phone conversation with RW, 14 November 2012. Dr. Snape, widely informed on the war for his research on U.S. military chaplains, found no widespread examples of human trophy-seeking in other Allied armies.

22. Sun Tzu, *Art of War* (trans. 1994), 17: "attacking fortified cities [should be] adopted only when unavoidable." He did not directly say why.

23. Cogan, in *Captured* (2000), 263, 286–91, explores the uncertain question as to whether impending massacre prompted the rescue. The internees in Los Baños were closer to total starvation than those in Santo Tomás.

24. Collingham, *The Taste of War* (2011), ch. 13. Homicidal cannibalism was the only kind of Japanese atrocity not cited at the Tokyo war crimes trials, for fear of upsetting POW relatives and others. One idea attributed to Gen. Krueger was to take just Manila's port area but that sounds unrealistic.

25. Larrabee, *Commander in Chief* (1987), 346–47, quoting Gen. Courtney Whitney, and also a cable from MacArthur to U.S. Army Chief of Staff, Gen. George Marshall.

Appendix II

1. Foley, "Department of Religion" (1946), 168–70, prints the commandments and gives their camp religious background. I have abridged the original Ten Commandments from Deuteronomy 5:6–21 in the King James version of the Bible.

Appendix III

1. Margaret Ball, knowledgeable about postwar expat Manila, noted to me the high non-Manila proportion of writers and suggested inhibition by Manila expats.

Bibliography

Cross-references usually direct the reader to women authors' names where these differ from wartime names due to postwar marriage. The occasional book-format memoir without any publisher or printer information, and not designed for sale, is listed below under "Unpublished Memoirs and Papers." "Santo Tomás" is spelled without an accent where the author omits it.

Publications

Allen, Lee. "The Other 'Internees.'" *Beyond the Wire* (Bay Area Civilian Ex-Prisoners of War, September 2012, January 2013). Title and introduction by Angus Lorenzen.

Annasenz, Henry J. [8th Cavalry Regt.]. Letter. *Los Angeles Times* (2 February 1985), Part II, p. 2.

Archer, Bernice. *The Internment of Western Civilians under the Japanese 1941–1945: A Patchwork of Internment.* London: RoutledgeCurzon, 2004.

Arthur, Anthony. *Deliverance at Los Baños.* New York: St. Martin's, 1985.

Bailey, Caroline. See Pratt, Caroline Bailey.

Bailey, Fay Cook. *Only a Matter of Days: The World War II Prison Camp Diary of Fay Cook Bailey.* Edited by Caroline Bailey Pratt. Bennington, VT: Merriam, 2001, 2008.

Ballard, J. G. *Miracles of Life: Shanghai to Shepperton: An Autobiography.* London: HarperCollins, 2008.

Beevor, Antony. *The Second World War.* London: Weidenfeld and Nicholson, 2012.

Bennett, Joan. "Children of Japs' Santo Tomas Camp Learn How to Shout and Laugh Again." Associated Press (11 February 1945).

Berenbaum, May. "This Bedbug's Life." *International Herald Tribune* (21–22 August 2010): 7.

Bloom, Lynn Z. "Till Death Do Us Part: Men's and Women's Interpretations of Wartime Internment." *Women's Studies International Forum* 10, no. 1 (1987): 75–83.

Breuer, William B. *Retaking the Philippines: America's Return to Corregidor and Bataan: October 1944–March 1945.* New York: St. Martin's Press, 1986.

Brooks, Curtis. Civilian Committee column [on *Achenbach et al. v. United States*]. *EX-POW Bulletin* (American Ex-Prisoners of War, 25 April 2005).

Brooks, Curtis, Karen Kerns Lewis, and Ted Cadwallader. "Going Home." *Beyond the Wire* (Bay Area Civilian Ex-Prisoners of War, January 2011).

Brooks, Mary Jane. See Morse, Mary Jane.

Bryant, Alice Franklin. *The Sun Was Darkened.* Boston: Chapman and Grimes, 1947.

Buss, Claude. "Claude Buss in Manila, 1941–1942" and appendix report, 1943. In *Forgotten Heroes: Japan's Imprisonment of American Civilians in the Philippines, 1942–1945*, edited by Michael P. Onorato. Westport, CT: Meckler, 1990.

Butcher, Henry Hale. "Wartime Memoirs (1941–1945)." In *Civilian Prisoners of the Japanese in the Philippine Islands: Years of Hardship, Hunger, and Hope, January 1942–February 1945*, edited by the Center for Internee Rights. Paducah, KY: Turner, 2002.

Cary, Frank. *Letters from Internment Camp: Davao and Manila.* Ashland, OR: Independent Publishing, 1993.

Cates, Tressa R. *The Drainpipe Diary.* New York: Vantage, 1957.

Center for Internee Rights, ed. *Civilian Prisoners of the Japanese in the Philippine Islands: Years of Hardship, Hunger, and Hope, January 1942–February 1945.* Paducah, KY: Turner, 2002.

Chambers, John Whiteclay, II. *OSS Training in the National Parks and Service Abroad in World War II.* Washington, DC: U.S. National Park Service, 2008. E-book edition.

Chase, William C. *Front Line General: The Commands of William C. Chase.* Houston: Gulf Publishing, 1975.

Clausen, Henry C., and Bruce Lee. *Pearl Harbor: Final Judgment.* New York: Crown, 1992.

Clear, Barbara. "Women and Children." In *Santo Tomas Internment Camp*, main author Frederick H. Stevens. "Printed in the U.S.A." by Stratford House, "limited private edition," 1946.

Cogan, Frances B. *Captured: The Japanese Internment of American Civilians in the Philippines, 1941–1945.* Athens: University of Georgia, 2000.

Cohen, Stan. *Wings to the Orient: Pan American Clipper Planes 1935 to 1945.* Missoula, MT: Pictorial Histories, 1985.

Collingham, Lizzie. *The Taste of War: World War Two and the Battle for Food*. London: Penguin, 2011.

Connaughton, Richard. *MacArthur and Defeat in the Philippines*. Woodstock, NY: Overlook, 2001.

Connaughton, Richard, John Pimlott, and Duncan Anderson. *The Battle for Manila*. Novato, CA: Presidio, 1995, 2002.

Contey-Aiello, Rose, ed. *The 50th Anniversary Commemorative Album of the Flying Column 1945–1995*. Tarpon Spring, FL: Marrakech Express, 1994.

Corfield, Isla. See Lucas, Celia.

Cowie, Teedie. See Woodcock, Teedie Cowie.

Crabb, Robert. "Santo Tomas Diet Slow Starvation." *New York Times* (6 February 1945).

Crosby, Frank Thomas Speir. "Remembrance and Thanks: Santo Tomas Internment Camp, Manila, PI 1942–45." In *Civilian Prisoners of the Japanese in the Philippine Islands: Years of Hardship, Hunger, and Hope, January 1942–February 1945*, edited by the Center for Internee Rights, 37–38. Paducah, KY: Turner, 2002.

Crouter, Natalie. *Forbidden Diary: A Record of Wartime Internment, 1941–1945*. Edited by Lynn Z. Bloom. New York: Burt Franklin, 1980.

Dang, Donald M. *Survival in Santo Tomas: A Portfolio of Sketches and Commentaries*. Kailua, HI: "Limited Private First Edition," 1991.

Doolan, Roy [Sr]. Four articles on internment in Santo Tomás. *Healdsburg Tribune* (23 July, 6 August, 13 August, 27 August 1953).

Dos Passos, John. *Tour of Duty*. Boston: Houghton Mifflin, 1946.

Dower, John W. *War without Mercy: Race and Power in the Pacific War*. New York: Pantheon, 1986.

Drea, Edward J. *MacArthur's ULTRA: Codebreaking and the War against Japan, 1942–1945*. Lawrence: University Press of Kansas, 1992.

Dunn, William J. *Pacific Microphone*. College Station: Texas A & M University Press, 1988.

Eagleman, David. *Incognito: The Secret Lives of the Brain*. New York: Vintage, 2011.

Elphick, Peter. *Far Eastern File: The Intelligence War in the Far East, 1930–1945*. London: Hodder and Stoughton, 1997.

Emerson, Geoffrey Charles. *Hong Kong Internment, 1942–1945: Life in the Japanese Internment Camp at Stanley*. Hong Kong: Hong Kong University Press, 2008.

England, Sarah. "My Story of Santo Tomas." *Beyond the Wire* 3, no. 1 (Bay Area Civilian Ex-Prisoners of War, January 2010, written 1950): 4, 8.

———. "My Story of Santo Tomas." *Beyond the Wire* 3, no. 2 (Bay Area Civilian Ex-Prisoners of War, May 2010, written 1950): 1, 3.

Enriquez, Elizabeth L. "Coping with War: KGST 'Radio' and Other Media Strategies of Civilian Internees in the Philippines in World War II." *Social Science Diliman* 6, no. 2 (Quezon City, Philippines, December 2010): 1–28.

Esmérian, Paul. "War Years in the Philippines 1941–1945." From Esmérian, *Journal D'Extreme-Orient 1940–1945*. Paris: Editions Entente, 1980. Translated from the French by Nicholas Balfour, Sebastian Balfour, Tika Balfour, Hazel Cripps, Jenny Kyle, and Nellita Geoffroy-Dechaume. Copy held by Rupert Wilkinson, courtesy of Balfour family.

Ewing, Alice Damberg. *Courage & Deliverance: Our Mother's Story*. Coralville, IA: F.E.P. International, 2006.

Felton, Mark. *Children of the Camps: Japan's Last Forgotten Victims*. Barnsley, UK: Pen & Sword, 2011.

First Cavalry Division Association. *1st Cavalry Division: A Spur Ride through the 20th Century: "From Horses to the Digital Battlefield."* Paducah, KY: Turner, 2002.

Flanagan, Edward M. *Angels at Dawn*. New York: Berkley, 2002. Previously published as *The Los Baños Raid: The 11th Airborne Jumps at Dawn*. Novato, CA: Presidio, 1986.

Foley, Walter Brooks. "Department of Religion." In *Santo Tomas Internment Camp*, main author Frederic H. Stevens. "Printed in the U.S.A." by Stratford House, "limited private edition," 1946.

Fung, Cornelia Lichauco. *Beneath the Banyan Tree: My Family Chronicles*. Hong Kong: CBL Fung, 2009.

Garcia, Mauro, ed. *Documents on the Japanese Occupation of the Philippines*. Manila: Philippine Historical Association, 1965.

Gared, Jannis Robb. "In Loving Memory." In *Eye Witness: The Memories of Ex-POWs in the Philippines*, edited by Virginia Glass and Herbert Riley. N.p.: Bay Area Civilian Ex-Prisoners of War, 1999.

Gawne, Jonathan. *Finding Your Father's War: A Practical Guide to Researching and Understanding Service in the World War II US Army*. Drexel, PA: Casemate, 2006.

Glass, Virginia McKinney. "Lieutenant Abiko." In *Eye Witness: The Memories of Ex-POWs in the Philippines*, edited by Virginia Glass and Herbert Riley, 30. N.p.: Bay Area Civilian Ex-Prisoners of War, 1999.

Glass, Virginia McKinney, and Herbert Riley, eds. *Eye Witness: The Memories of Ex-POWs in the Philippines*. N.p.: Bay Area Civilian Ex-Prisoners of War, 1999.

Goldhagen, Juergen R., ed. *Manila Memories: Four Boys Remember Their Lives Before, During and After the Japanese Occupation*. Exeter, UK: Old Guard Press, 2008.

Greene, Dennis. "The Liberation of Santo Tomas Prison Camp in WWII." In *Civilian Prisoners of the Japanese in the Philippine Islands: Years of Hardship, Hunger, and Hope, January 1942–February 1945*, edited by the Center for Internee Rights, 11–15. Paducah, KY: Turner, 2002.

Gunn, Nathaniel. *Pappy Gunn*. Bloomington, IN: AuthorHouse, 2004.

Hall, Roderick. "Roderick Hall's Narrative." In *Manila Memories: Four Boys Remember Their Lives Before, During and After the Japanese Occupation*, edited by Juergen R. Goldhagen. Exeter, UK: Old Guard Press, 2008.

Halsema, James R. "The Internment Camp at Baguio." Interview by Michael P. Onorato. Fullerton: California State University Oral History Program, 1987.

Harries, Meirion, and Susie Harries. *Soldiers of the Sun: The Rise and Fall of the Imperial Japanese Army 1868–1945*. London: Heinemann, 1991.

Hartendorp, A.V.H. *The Japanese Occupation of the Philippines*. 2 vols. Manila: Bookmark, 1967.

———. *The Santo Tomas Story*. Abridged from a larger manuscript by Frank H. Golay. New York: McGraw-Hill, 1964.

Hastings, Max. *Inferno: The World at War, 1939–1945*. New York: Knopf, 2012.

———. *Nemesis: The Battle for Japan, 1944–45*. New York: Harper, 2007.

Helphand, Kenneth I. *Defiant Gardens: Making Gardens in Wartime*. San Antonio: Trinity University Press, 2006.

Hewlett, Frank. "66 Japanese Freed to Save Hostages." *New York Times* (6 February 1945).

Heyashi, Sabiro, with Alvin D. Coox. *Kogun: The Japanese Army in the Pacific War*. Quantico, VA: Marine Corps Association, 1959.

Hoeflein, Hans. "Hans Hoeflein's Narrative." In *Manila Memories: Four Boys Remember Their Lives Before, During and After the Japanese Occupation*, edited by Juergen R. Goldhagen. Exeter, UK: Old Guard Press, 2008.

Holland, Robert B. *The Rescue of Santo Tomas, Manila, WWII: The Flying Column: 100 Miles to Freedom*. Paducah, KY: Turner, 2003.

Hoyt, Edwin P. *Davies: The Inside Story of a British American Family in the Pacific and Its Business Enterprise*. Honolulu: Topgallant, 1983.

Hoyt, Eve Foss. "Three Years in Santo Tomas." *The Ave Maria: Catholic Home Weekly* 80, no. 6 (7 August 1954): 8–12.

Huber, Thomas M. "The Battle of Manila." In *Block by Block: The Challenges of Urban Operations*, edited by William G. Robertson. Leavenworth, KS: U.S. Army Command and General Staff College Press, 2003.

Ienaga, Saburo. *The Pacific War, 1931–1945: A Critical Perspective on Japan's Role in World War II*. New York: Pantheon, 1978.

Irvine, Liz Lautzenhiser, with Debbie Irvine Hammock. *Surviving the Rising Sun: My Family's Years in a Japanese POW Camp*. San Antonio: PILiz, 2010.

James, D. Clayton. *The Years of MacArthur*. Vol. II, *1941–1945*. Boston: Houghton Mifflin, 1975.

Jansen, Sascha Jean. Chapter in *Interrupted Lives: Four Women's Stories of Internment during World War II in the Philippines*, edited by Lily Nova and Iven Lourie. Nevada City, CA: Artemis, 1995.

———. "Freedom." *Beyond the Wire* (Bay Area Civilian Ex-Prisoners of War, September 2011).

———. "Going Home" [quoting a serviceman's poem on children in the ship back]. *Beyond the Wire* (Bay Area Civilian Ex-Prisoners of War, January 2011).

———. "Heroes." In *Eye-Witness: The Memories of Ex-POWs in the Philippines*, edited by Virginia M. Glass and Herbert Riley. N.p.: Bay Area Civilian Ex-Prisoners of War, 1999.

———. "Heroes Unseen." *Beyond the Wire* (Bay Area Civilian Ex-Prisoners of War, May 2012).

———. "The Internees' Own Story." In *The Rescue of Santo Tomas, Manila, WWII*, main author Robert B. Holland. Paducah, KY: Turner, 2003.

Jesus, Ed. C. de, and Carlos Quirino. *Earl Carroll: Colossus of Philippine Insurance*. Manila: Underwriters Publications, 1980.

Johansen, Bruce E. *So Far From Home: Manila's Santo Tomás Internment Camp, 1942–1945*. Omaha: PBI Press, 1996.

Johnstone, William. *The Modern Epidemic: A History of Tuberculosis in Japan*. Cambridge, MA: Harvard University Press, 1995.

José, Ricardo Trota. "'Death for Honor,' Part 1." *Philippines Free Press* (19 February 2011): 20–33 passim.

———. "'Death for Honor,' Part 2." *Philippines Free Press* (26 February 2011): 18ff.

José, Ricardo Trota, and Lydia Yu-José. *The Japanese Occupation of the Philippines: A Pictorial History*. Manila: Ayala Foundation, 1997.

Jurika, Louis. "A Philippine Odyssey." *Beyond the Wire* 4, no. 1 (Bay Area Civilian Ex-Prisoners of War, January 2011).

Kaminski, Theresa. *Prisoners in Paradise: American Women in the Wartime South Pacific*. Lawrence: University of Kansas Press, 2000.

Karnow, Stanley. *In Our Image: America's Empire in the Philippines*. New York: Random House, 1989.

Kelly, Clara Olink. *The Flamboya Tree: A Family's War-Time Courage*. London: Arrow, 2003.

Kerns, Karen. See Lewis, Karen Kerns.

Klaäs, M. D. *The Last of the Flying Clippers: The Boeing B-314 Story*. Atglen, PA: Schiffer, 1997.

Kneedler, Edgar Mason. "The Internees' Own Story." In *The Rescue of Santo Tomas, Manila, WWII*, main author Robert B. Holland. Paducah, KY: Turner, 2003.

Kogan, Eugene. *The Theory and Practice of Hell: The German Concentration Camps and the System Behind Them*. 1st rev. ed. New York: Farrar, Straus, and Giroux, 2006.

Land-Reeves, Charles E. "…Boy!" *A Passage to Manhood*. Worthing, UK: Guildings, 1996.

Larrabee, Eric. *Commander in Chief: Franklin Delano Roosevelt, His Lieutenants, and Their War*. New York: Harper and Row, 1987.

Lautzenhiser, Liz. See Irvine, Liz Lautzenhiser.

Leary, William M., ed. *We Shall Return! MacArthur's Commanders and the Defeat of Japan*. Lexington: University of Kentucky Press, 1988.

Lee, Ansie. See Sperry, Ansie Lee.

Legarda, Benito J., Jr. *Occupation: The Later Years*. Manila: Vibal, 2007.

———. *Occupation '42*. Manila: De La Salle University Press, 2003.

———. "Yamashita's First Interview: Manila Was Not an Open City, Part 1." *Philippines Free Press* (5 February 2011): 21–33 passim.

———. "Yamashita's First Interview: Manila Was Not an Open City, Part 2." *Philippines Free Press* (12 February 2011): 26–32 passim.

Lewis, Karen Kerns. Chapter in *Interrupted Lives: Four Women's Stories of Internment during World War II in the Philippines*, edited by Lily Nova and Iven Lourie. Nevada City, CA: Artemis, 1995.

Lichauco, Marcial P. *Dear Mother Putnam: A Diary of the Second World War in the Philippines*. Hong Kong: CBL Fung, 1997; Manila: Green Pagoda Press, 2005. "First published privately by the author in 1949."

Lorenzen, Angus M. "A Desperate Drug Smuggler." *Be-

yond the Wire (Bay Area Civilian Ex-Prisoners of War, January 2012): 2.
_____. *A Lovely Little War: Life in a Japanese Prison Camp through the Eyes of a Child*. Palisades, NY: History Publishing, 2008.
_____. "From the Commander." *Beyond the Wire* (Bay Area Civilian Ex-Prisoners of War). Editorials: January 2010, May 2010, September 2010, May 2011, May 2012.
Lucas, Celia. *Prisoners of Santo Tomas*. Based on the diary of Isla Corfield. London: Leo Cooper, 1975; Exeter, UK: David and Charles, 1988.
MacArthur, Douglas. *Reminiscences*. New York: McGraw-Hill, 1964.
Magnuson, Frieda. *Out in '45, If We're Still Alive*. Sisters, OR: One-Book Company, 1984.
Mañalac, Fernando J. *Manila: Memories of World War II*. Quezon City, Philippines: Giraffe Books, 1995.
Manila Tribune [*The Tribune*]. 7 January, 3 February, 4 February 1945. Copies held by Rupert Wilkinson, courtesy of Curtis Brooks.
Marshall, Cecily Mattocks. *Happy Life Blues: A Memoir of Survival*. Clinton, MA: Angus MacGregor, 2007.
Marshall, H.E. *Our Island Story: A History of Britain for Boys and Girls from the Romans to Queen Victoria*. Tenterden, UK: Galore Park with Civitas, 2005. First published in 1905.
Marx, Trish. *Echoes of World War II*. Hemel Hemstead, UK: MacDonald Children's Books, 1989; Minneapolis: Lerner, 1994.
Mathews, Clio. See Wetmore, Clio Mathews.
Mattocks, Cecily. See Marshall, Cecily Mattocks.
McCall, J.E. *Santo Tomás Internment Camp: STIC in Verse and Reverse; STIC-toons and STIC-tistics*. Lincoln, NE: Woodruff, 1945.
McKinney, Virginia. See Glass, Virginia McKinney.
Milgram, Stanley. *Obedience to Authority: An Experimental View*. New York: Harper, 1974.
Montgomery, Ruth. "Capital Circus" (1950). In *Civilian Prisoners of the Japanese in the Philippine Islands: Years of Hardship, Hunger, and Hope, January 1942–February 1945*, edited by the Center for Internee Rights, 39. Paducah, KY: Turner, 2002.
Morse, Mary Jane. "The Internees' Own Story." In *The Rescue of Santo Tomas: Manila, WWII*, main author Robert B. Holland. Paducah, KY: Turner, 2003.
Mydans, Carl. *More than Meets the Eye*. New York: Harper, 1959; Westport, CT: Greenwood, 1974.
_____. "My God! It's Carl Mydans." *Life* 18, no. 8 (19 February 1945): 20–100 *passim*.
Nagai, Hitoshi. "The Internment of Western Civilians under the Japanese: A Case Study of the Japanese Occupation of the Philippines." *Iwanami Koza: Asia-Pacific War* 4 (Tokyo, February 2006): 145–76. Summarized and partially translated from the Japanese by Ralph Turner for Rupert Wilkinson.
Nash, Grace C. *That We Might Live: A Story of Human Triumph during World War II*. Scottsdale, AZ: Shano, 1984.
Nelson, James. "The Causes of the Bataan Death March Revisited." *Bulletin of the American Historical Collection* (Manila) 39, no. 1 (2005): 9–35.
Norman, Elizabeth M. *We Band of Angels: The Untold Story of American Nurses Trapped on Bataan by the Japanese*. New York: Random House, 1999.
Olink, Clara. See Kelly, Clara Olink.
Owens, William A. *Eye-Deep in Hell: A Memoir of the Liberation of the Philippines, 1944–45*. Dallas: Southern Methodist Press, 1989.
Parfet, Buck. "Dancing in the Dark." In *Eye Witness: The Memories of Ex-POWs in the Philippines*, edited by Virginia M. Glass and Herbert Riley, 27. N.p.: Bay Area Civilian Ex-Prisoners of War, 1999.
Paust, Gilbert, and Milton Lancelot. *Fighting Wings: A Pictorial History of Aerial Combat*. New York: Essential Books, 1944.
Petillo, Carol Morris. *Douglas MacArthur: The Philippine Years*. Bloomington: Indiana University Press, 1981.
Poston, Madeleine. *My Upside-Down World*. Gladstone, OR: Benneta, 2002.
Pratt, Caroline Bailey. "The Internees' Own Story." In *The Rescue of Santo Tomas, Manila, WWII*, main author Robert B. Holland. Paducah, KY: Turner, 2003.
Prising, Robin. *Manila, Goodbye*. London: Heinemann, 1976.
Reeves, Charles. See Land-Reeves, Charles E.
Reischauer, Edwin O. *The Japanese*. Cambridge, MA: Harvard University Press, 1977.
Reyes, Pedrito, Mercedes Grau-Santamaria, et al. *Pictorial History of the Philippines*. Manila: Capitol, 1953.
Richards, Peter C., ed. *The Liberation Bulletin of Philippine Internment Camp No. 1 at Santo Tomas University, Manila, Philippines*. Manila: No. 6 ULI-ULI, 1945.
Robb, Jannis. See Garred, Jannis Robb.
Roka, Tressa. See Cates, Tressa R.
Sams, Margaret. *Forbidden Family: A Wartime Memoir of the Philippines, 1941–1945*. Edited by Lynn Z. Bloom. Madison: University of Wisconsin Press, 1989. Written in the late 1940s, but page footnotes are from interviews with Bloom in the 1980s.
Sayre, Francis Bowes. *Glad Adventure*. New York: Macmillan, 1957.
_____. Statement before U.S. Congress, House of Representatives, Interstate and Foreign Commerce Committee, Hearings (22 March 1947).
Schreker, Ellen. *No Ivory Tower: McCarthyism and the Universities*. New York: Oxford University Press, 1986.
Schrijvers, Peter. *Bloody Pacific: American Soldiers at War with Japan*. New York and Basingstoke, UK: Palgrave Macmillan, 2010. First published as *The GI War against Japan* in 2002.
Setsuho, Ikehata, and Ricardo Trota José, eds. *The Philippines under Japan*. Manila: Ateneo de Manila University Press, 1999.
Sherk, Margaret. See Sams, Margaret.
Shiels, Margo. *Bends in the Road*. Bowen, Queensland, Australia: Margo Shiels, 1999.
Silen, Bert. "Silen Denies Americans Told to Leave Islands." *American Internees Bulletin* (November 1946).
Sledge, E.B. *With the Old Breed at Peleliu and Okinawa*. Introduction by Victor Davis Hanson. Novato, CA: Presidio, 1981; London: Ebury, 2010.

Smith, Robert Ross. *Triumph in the Philippines: The War in the Pacific.* Honolulu: University Press of the Pacific, 1963.

Spector, Ronald H. *Eagle against the Sun: The American War with Japan.* New York: Random House, 1985.

Speir, Frank Thomas. See Crosby, Frank Thomas Speir.

Sperry, Ansie Lee. *Running with the Tiger: A Memoir of an Extraordinary Young Woman's Life in Hong Kong, China, the South Pacific and POW Camp.* N.p.: Sperry Family Trust, 2009.

Stafford, David. *Roosevelt and Churchill: Men of Secrets.* London: Little, Brown, 1999.

Steinberg, David Joel. *Philippine Collaboration in World War II.* Ann Arbor: University of Michigan Press, 1967.

Steinberg, Rafael, and the editors of Time-Life Books. *Return to the Philippines.* New York: Time-Life Books, 1979.

Stevens, Frederic H. *Santo Tomas Internment Camp.* "Printed in the U.S.A." by Stratford House, "limited private edition," 1946.

Stevenson, Theodore D., MD. Statement before U.S. Congress, House of Representatives, Committee on Interstate and Foreign Commerce, Hearings on HR 873, 1823 and 1000, and 2823 (20–21 March and 21 April 1947).

Strong, Herman E. *A Ringside Seat to War.* New York: Vantage, 1965.

Sun Tzu. *The Art of War* [c. 450–223 B.C.]. Translated by Ralph Sawyer. Boulder, CO: Westview, 1994; Philadelphia: Running Press, 2003.

Syjuco, Ma. Felisa A. *The Kempei Tai in the Philippines: 1941–1945.* Quezon City, Philippines: New Day, 1988.

Tachikawa, Kyoichi. "The Treatment of Prisoners of War by the Imperial Japanese Army and Navy: Focusing on the Pacific War." *NIDS Security Reports*, no. 9 (December 2008). Tokyo: National Institute for Defense Studies. Japanese original published in *Boueikenkyuosho Kiyo* [*NIDS Security Studies*] 10, no. 1 (September 2007).

Tonkin, Margo. See Shiels, Margo.

Trumbull, Robert. "Manila Internees Ate Grass, Leaves." *New York Times* (8 November 1945).

Tutt, Bob. "MacArthur Returns to Manila: Highlands Veteran Was Part of Mighty Force in Philippines." *Houston Chronicle* (15 July 1995): 26a.

Tyrer, Nicola. *Stolen Childhoods: The Untold Story of the Children Interned by the Japanese in the Second World War.* London: Weidenfeld and Nicolson, 2011.

Ugaki, Matome. *Fading Victory: The Diary of Admiral Matome Ugaki, 1941–1945.* Translated by Masataka Chiyaha. Edited by Donald M. Goldstein and Katherine V. Dillon. Pittsburgh: University of Pittsburgh Press, 1991.

Ullom, Madeline."The Internees' Own Story." In *The Rescue of Santo Tomas, Manila, WWII*, main author Robert B. Holland. Paducah, KY: Turner, 2003.

U.S. Court of Federal Claims and U.S. Court of Appeals for the Federal Circuit. *Marcia Fee Achenbach et al., Plaintiffs, v. United States* (2004). Complaint by Anthony D'Amato, David G. Duggan, and Susan M. Keegan. Appeal by Anthony D'Amato.

U.S. War Department, Ordnance Office. *Medium Tank M4A4: Technical Manual No. 9–754.* Washington, DC, 29 August 1942.

Utsumi, Aiko. "'Annihilation Plan' [for] the Allied POWs." Excerpt from Utsumi, *Nihon.gun no Horyo Seisaku* [POW Policy of the Japanese Army], translated by Yukako Ibuki, edited by Ricardo José, 317–26. Tokyo: Aoki Bookstore, 2005. Excerpt held by Rupert Wilkinson, courtesy of Yukako Ibuki.

_____. "Japanese Army Internment Policies for Enemy Civilians during the Asia-Pacific War." In *Multicultural Japan: Paleolithic to Postmodern*, edited by Donald Denoon, Mark Hudson, and Tessa Morris-Suzuki. Cambridge: Cambridge University Press, 1996.

_____. "Japan's World War II POW Policy: Indifference and Irresponsibility." *Asia-Pacific Journal: Japan Focus* (May 2005), e-journal.

van der Post, Laurens. *The Night of the New Moon.* London: Hogarth, 1970; London: Vintage, 2002.

Van Sickle, Emily. *The Iron Gates of Santo Tomás: The Firsthand Account of an American Couple Interned by the Japanese in Manila, 1942–1945.* Chicago: Academy Chicago, 1992.

Vaughan, Elizabeth Head. *Community under Stress: An Internment Camp Culture.* Princeton, NJ: Princeton University Press, 1949.

_____. *The Ordeal of Elizabeth Vaughan: A Wartime Diary of the Philippines.* Edited by Carol M. Petillo. Athens: University of Georgia Press, 1985.

Ward, James Mace. "Legitimate Collaboration: The Administration of Santo Tomás Internment Camp and Its Histories, 1942–2003." *Pacific Historical Review* 77, no. 2 (May 2008): 159–201.

Waterford, Van [Walter F. Wanrooy]. *Prisoners of the Japanese in World War II: Statistical History, Personal Narratives, and Memorials Concerning POWs in Camps and on Hellships, Civilian Internees, Asian Slave Laborers and Others Captured in the Pacific Theater.* Jefferson, NC: McFarland, 1994.

Weinzheimer, Jean. See Jansen, Sascha Jean.

Werff, Wanda. See Ewing, Alice Damberg.

Wetmore, Clio Mathews. *Beyond Pearl Harbor: Civilians Imprisoned at Santa Tomas, Manila 1942–1945.* Haverford, PA: Infinity Publishing, 2001.

Whitesides, John G. "The Economics of Internment: Life in a Japanese Internment Camp in the Philippines during the Second World War: An American View." *Papers in Southeast Asia Business History*, no. 1 (Ann Arbor: University of Michigan Center for Southeast Asian Studies, September 1988).

Wilkins, Ford. "Close-Up Report on the Japanese." *New York Times* (4 March 1945): 18, 42–43.

_____. "Santo Tomas Hit by Foe's Artillery." *New York Times* (25 February 1945).

Wilkinson, Rupert. *American Tough: The Tough-Guy Tradition and American Character.* Westport, CT: Greenwood, 1984; New York: Harper and Row, 1986.

Williams, Denny. *To the Angels.* San Francisco: Denson, 1985.

Woodcock, Teedie Cowie. *Behind the Sawali: Santo Tomás in Cartoons, 1942–1945.* Greensboro, NC: Cenografix, 2000.

Wootten, Geege. See Poston, Madeleine.
Wright, B.C. *The 1st Cavalry Division in World War II*. Tokyo: Toppan, 1947.
Wygle, Peter R. *Surviving a Japanese P.O.W. Camp: Father and Son Endure Internment in Manila during World War II*. Ventura, CA: Pathfinder, 1991.
Wygle, Peter R., and Robert Howard Wygle. "The Internees' Own Story." In *The Rescue of Santo Tomas, Manila, WWII*, main author Robert B. Holland. Paducah, KY: Turner, 2003.

Unpublished Memoirs and Papers

Adams, Marie. Letter and report to U.S. Army Judge Advocate General on deaths in Santo Tomás Internment Camp, 20 July 1945. College Park, MD: National Archives.
Alcuaz, Luis de. Papers. Selected copies held by Rupert Wilkinson, courtesy of de Alcuaz family.
Baker, Len. "A Teenager at Santo Tomas, 1942–1945" (1974). Copy held by Rupert Wilkinson, courtesy of Len Baker.
Balfour, Anne. "Diary of Anne Balfour, Manila" [19 June 1943–27 April 1945]. Translated from French original by Sheila Whitfeld. Copy held by Rupert Wilkinson, courtesy of Balfour family and Hazel Cripps.
Campbell, Lydia. See Macleod, Lydia.
Curtis, John. "Extra-Curricular Activities, 1940–1945." In papers of John Curtis and others, selected copies held by Rupert Wilkinson, courtesy of Penny Mellor.
Curtis, Penny. See Mellor, Penny.
Doolan, Roy F. [Jr]. "My Life in a Japanese Prison Camp during World War II: Santo Tomas University Internment Camp, Manila, Philippines, January 6, 1942 to February 3, 1945" (2004). Copy held by Rupert Wilkinson, courtesy of Roy Doolan.
Fisher, George. *Military Memoir*. Quincy, MA: Flying Column Writing Project, n.d.
Francisco, Louis J. Papers. Selected copies held by Rupert Wilkinson, courtesy of de Alcuaz and Francisco families.
Gibb, Sophie. See Jensen, Addie Gibb.
Guytingco, Diasdado. "Liberation of STIC." Long email to Carl Potts (1 April 2005). Copy held by Rupert Wilkinson, courtesy of Sue Trout.
Hall, Roderick. Bibliography of the "Roderick Hall Collection of Books on Manila and the Philippines during World War II in Memory of Angelina Rico de McMicking, Conseulo McMicking Hall, Lt. Alfred L. McMicking, and Helen McMicking, Executed in Manila, January 1945." Manila: Filipinas Heritage Library, Ayala Foundation. Copy held by Rupert Wilkinson.
Hearnden, Phyllis. See Montefiori, Phyllis.
Hencke, John [44th Tank Battn.]. Transcript of interview by Eddie Graham. Fredericksburg, TX: National Museum of the Pacific War [formerly Admiral Nimitz Museum], 31 January 2002.
Holland, Robert [U.S. Marine Corps]. Transcript of interview by James Zobel. Norfolk, VA: MacArthur Memorial Foundation Oral History Project, 23 April 2005.
Hodsoll, Frank. "Britain in the Philippines." Address to the American Association of the Philippines. Manila: U.S. Embassy, 1 December 1954. Copy held by Rupert Wilkinson, courtesy of John Hawkins.
Horner, Layton. "Japanese Military Administration in Malaya and the Philippines." University of Arizona, History Department, doctoral dissertation, 1973.
Izod, Sally. Papers. London: Imperial War Museum.
Japanese Imperial Army. See Santo Tomás Internment Camp; Taihoku POW Camp; War Crimes Information Series; War Crimes Interrogations Series.
Jensen, Addie Gibb. *A Child Called Allie: Memories of My Life as Allie* (2009). Copy held by Rupert Wilkinson.
José, Ricardo T. "Civilians in Bataan and the Death March." Address at commemoration of the Battle of Bataan, Capas, Tarlac, Philippines, June 2009. Copy held by Rupert Wilkinson, courtesy of James Litton and J. Michael Houlahan.
Krass, Iris. Papers. London: Imperial War Museum.
Kyde, George Douglas. Report of G.D. Kyde on Internment in Japan until 31st July 1942, to Chartered Bank, London, 1943. Copy held by Rupert Wilkinson, courtesy of Sally Hirst.
Landry, Walter J. [8th Cavalry Regt.]. See Seron, Richard, and Susan Jerrett Trout.
Macleod, Lydia. "Camp diary" [21 September 1944 to 15 March 1945]. Copy held by Rupert Wilkinson, courtesy of Danielle Bruce and Margaret Ball.
Mellor, Penny. "A Family History" (1998). Copy held by Rupert Wilkinson, courtesy of Penny Mellor.
Mendez, Frank [8th Cavalry Regt.]. Transcript of interview by Tim Darley. Norfolk, VA: MacArthur Memorial Foundation Oral History Project, 23 April 2005.
Montefiori, Phyllis. "A Bit of Camp 1942–1945" (no date). Based on her diaries written as Phyllis Hearnden. Hearnden/Montefiori papers. London: Imperial War Museum.
Ohdaira, Shinichiro [civilian official, Los Baños]. "The Ohdaira Story," edited by James J. Halsema, n.d. Copy held by Rupert Wilkinson, courtesy of Liz Irvine.
Olsen, Roberta (Bobbie). Transcript of interview by Juergen R. Goldhagen, 14 February 2002. Copy held by Rupert Wilkinson, courtesy of Juergen R. Goldhagen.
Olson, Walter [37th Infantry Division]. "My Time in World War II" (no date). Copy held by Rupert Wilkinson, courtesy of Walter Olson.
Parsons, Charles (Chick). "Report of Mr C. Parsons to the U.S. Department of State" (12 August 1942). Copy held by Rupert Wilkinson, courtesy of Frederico Baldassarre.
Philippine Red Cross [American National Red Cross subsidiary]. Reports and letters regarding Santo Tomás Internment Camp. Box 1170. College Park, MD: National Archives.
Prismall, Mrs. J. "Internment of Civilians." Account by Secretary, British Consulate General, Manila, 1942. In papers of John Curtis and others, selected copies

held by Rupert Wilkinson, courtesy of Penny Mellor.
Relief for Americans in the Philippines (New York). Newsletters, April and June 1944. Copies held by Rupert Wilkinson, courtesy of Liz Irvine.
Santo Tomás Internment Camp. Education Department Chairman, Don W. Holter, "To Any Education Official Concerned" [report on the camp school for student credentials], 17 January 1945. Copy held by Rupert Wilkinson, courtesy of Liz Irvine.
_____. Education Department Committee Minutes, 20 August 1942–21 November 1943. Copies held by Rupert Wilkinson, courtesy of Liz Irvine.
_____. Executive and Internee Committee Minutes and Proceedings, January 1942–September 1945. Record Group 331. College Park, MD: National Archives.
_____. Food and Supplies Department. Memo [long report] by G. M. Bridgeford for Mr. Earl Carroll, Vice-Chairman, Internee Committee, 29 May 1944. Copy held by Rupert Wilkinson, courtesy of Cay Pratt.
_____. *Internews*, *STIC Gazette*, and *The Internitis*, selected issues. Copies held by Rupert Wilkinson, courtesy of Michael Browning and Liz Irvine.
_____. List of Internees. Manila: Ateneo de Manila University, Rizal Library, American Historical Collection.
Santo Tomás Internment Camp guard. *Diary [logbook] of the Internment Camp in the Philippines, Branch No. 1, 6 July–31 December 1944.* Translated by Yukako Ibuki. Edited by Rupert Wilkinson. Japanese title: *Yokuruyo Sho Daiichi Bunsho Jinchu Nish.* Copies held by Rupert Wilkinson and Yukako Ibuki, with summary/commentary by Rupert Wilkinson. Courtesy of National Institute of Defense Studies Library, Tokyo.
Seron, Richard, and Susan Jerrett Trout. "Career Summary: Lt. Col. Walter J. Landry." Quincy, MA: Flying Column Writer's Project, n.d.
Spear, Reginald. Transcript of interview by Peter Parsons and Morgan Cavett, 13 October 1998, with "footnote" information added by Mark Lewis to Parsons, email, 14 November 2006. Copy held by Rupert Wilkinson, courtesy of Maurice Francis.
_____. Transcript of interview by James Zobel. Norfolk, VA: MacArthur Memorial Foundation, Oral History Project, 17 June 2010.
Stevenson, Theodore D. *Recollections: A Life of Medical Service Overseas* (1997). Selected chapters held by Rupert Wilkinson, courtesy of Donald Stevenson.
Taihoku POW Camp, Taiwan. Entry from journal of the camp on "extreme measures for POWs" (August 1944). London: Imperial War Museum. New translation from the Japanese by Ralph Thompson with translator's notes, held by Rupert Wilkinson.
Templer, Angela M. "Internment Diary, 1940–1945." Reconstructed by author from her diary left behind in Los Baños during its hasty liberation. Copy held by Rupert Wilkinson, courtesy of Jenny Kyle.
U.S. Army. "After Action" Operations Reports for 5th Cavalry Regiment, 8th Cavalry Regiment, 44th Tank Battalion, 61st Field Artillery Battalion, and 8th Engineer Battalion, January 1944–February 1945. College Park, MD: National Archives.
_____. "After Action Report" of XIV Corps, 6th Army, 29 July 1945. College Park, MD: National Archives.
_____. "Japanese Defense of Cities as Exemplified by the Battle for Manila." Report by XIVth Corps, 6th Army, 1 July 1945. College Park, MD: National Archives.
_____. "S-3 Periodic Report, Headquarters 1st Cavalry Brigade," 2–3 February 1945. College Park, MD: National Archives.
U.S. State Department. Papers. Francis Sayre to Secretary of State, 7 January, 27 June, 14 August, 9 October 1941. Special Division Memorandum, "Evacuation of Americans from Philippines in Emergency," 17 March 1941. Copies held by Rupert Wilkinson, courtesy of Liz Irvine and Frederico Baldassarre.
Vorster, Erwin. *Me: The Memoir of Erwin Vorster.* Vorster family, 2005.
War Crimes Information Series. Monthly Reports on [three] Military Internment and Prisoner of War Camps in the Philippines, by the Japanese Army War-Prisoner Headquarters, April to December, 1944. College Park, MD: National Archives.
War Crimes Interrogations (various). College Park, MD: National Archives.
Wilkinson, Gerald. "War diary, 1941–1945." Copies held by Rupert Wilkinson and Mary June Pettyfer. Original in Churchill College Archives, Cambridge University (subject to partial closure by British Government Cabinet Office).
Wilkinson, Rupert. "Was There a Massacre Plan? Santo Tomás Internment Camp, Manila, 1944–45" (2013). Copy held by Rupert Wilkinson.
Wrinch, Peter. "Peter and Tom's Story: STIC 1941 to 1945" (c. 2007). Copy held by Rupert Wilkinson, courtesy of Peter Wrinch and Margaret Ball.
Wyatt-Smith, Stanley. "Execution by Japanese Military Authorities in the Philippines of three British subjects for escaping from civilian internment camp." Report to British Ambassador and Australian Charge d'Affaires, [formerly at] Tokyo, 20 August 1942. In papers of John Curtis and others, selected copies held by Rupert Wilkinson, courtesy of Penny Mellor.
_____. "Internment of Consuls by the Japanese." Report to British Foreign Office. Probably 1942. In papers of John Curtis and others, copy held by Rupert Wilkinson, courtesy of Penny Mellor.
YMCA. Memorandum by H. A. Janson concerning the activities of the Neutral Warfare Committee of the International YMCA, 15 April 1945. Copy held by Rupert Wilkinson, courtesy of Frederico Baldassarre.

DVDs, Tapes, Websites, and Broadcasts

Batty, Daniel. *Japan's War in Colour.* DVD, 2005. Based on book and author of same name: London: Carlton Books, 2004.
Bay Area Civilian Ex-Prisoners of War (BACEPOW). Camp Profiles on Santo Tomás, Los Baños, and Baguio/Bilibid. www.bacepow.net.
Brooks, Curtis. Diary fragment, 4 February 2012. In Gopal and Bunn, "Victims of Circumstance: Santo Tomas Internment Camp." www.cnac.org/emilscott/santotomas01.htm.

Brown, Derren. "Gameshow." Channel Four Television, London, 28 October 2011.
Buensuceso-Oebanda, Maita. "Keep the Flame Burning — Faith and Fortitude: Santo Tomas Internment Camp." Website for blogs, from 2006. http://stic.wordpress.com/2006/01/05/hello-world/.
Burns, Ken, and Lynn Novak. *The War*. PBS Home Video. DVD, 2008 (movie, 2007).
Cassera, Tony. Blog no. 23 (9 January 2008). See Buensuceso-Oebanda, Maita.
Gopal, Lou, and Michelle Bunn. *Victims of Circumstance: Santo Tomas Internment Camp*. DVD, 2006. www.lougopal.com.
_____. "Victims of Circumstance: Santo Tomas Internment Camp." www.cnac.org/emilscott/santotomas01.htm.
International Committee of the Red Cross. Convention Relative to the Treatment of Prisoners of War. Geneva: 27 July 1929. ICRC Web page.
Krass, Iris. Interview by Libby Purves. "Midweek," BBC Radio 4, London, 15 June 2011.
Landry, Walter. Interview by Lou and Michelle Gopal. Norfolk, VA: MacArthur Memorial Foundation, 2005. DVD.
_____. Taped interviews by Richard J. Seron. Quincy, MA: Flying Column Writers' Project, 1 March, 13 October 2010; 23 March 2011. Including questions by Rupert Wilkinson.
Lewis, Jonathan. *Hell in the Pacific*. Carlton for Channel 4, TV (UK). DVD, 2001.
Rutter, Donald. "The Long March into Oblivion" (2006). Long blog at *Victims of Circumstance: Santo Tomas Internment Camp* (website), edited by Lou Gopal and Michelle Bunn. www.cnac.org/emilscott/rutter01.htm.
van der Kuil, Peter. "Tjideng Camp: A Women and Children's Internment Camp." http://members.innet.au/-vanderkp/tjideng.html.
Wikipedia. "Milgram Experiment." http://enwikipedia.org/wiki/Milgram_experiment.

Index

Numbers in ***bold italics*** indicate pages with illustrations.

Abiko, Nanakazu 5, 85, 100–3, 120, 133, 135, 139, 157, 169; death of 3, 151–52, 160–61, 187, 189–90
Abrams, John 90–91
Achenbach v. United States 16–17
Agents 104–5, 111, 112, 115, 134
Aguinaldo, Emilio 11
Aguinaldo's department store 42
Ahern, Hilary 37, 119
air raids: American, near the camp 116, 134–36; American, on Japan 187–88; Japanese 19
Alamo Scouts 144
Alcuaz, Luis de 39, 119–20, 157, ***171***; helping select camp site 21–23, 25–26; resignation 5, 170–71
Allen, Lee 177
amahs (nannies) 14, 18, 85
American Coordinating Committee 16, 95
American Emergency Committee 16, 21, 28–29, 30
American School 18, 21, 85
American Tough (Rupert Wilkinson) 202
Amorsolo, Fernando 46
Andrews Sisters 71
Angat River 146, ***147***
anti-Communism 185
Anti-Imperialist League 11
Archer, Bernice 202
Atabrine 46, 155
athletics 33, 82, 87, 98
atrocities 3, 15, 20, 35–37, 95, 100, 101, 167, 187, 189–90; defined 7, 187–88
Australia 4, 28, 116, 140, 169
Axe, Delvin 72

Bacolod 17, 57; camp 6, 49, 57, 180, 181, 194
Baguio 13, 137; camps 194
Bailey, Althea 96
Bailey, Caroline 41, 123, 131, 178, 201
Bailey, Fay 74, 96, 123, 128, 131, 178, 179, 182; writing by 181, 201
Baker, Leonard (Len) 87, 88
Baldassarre, Frederico 186

Balfour, Anne 63, ***64***, 69, 103, 124, 131, 140, 154; after liberation 157, 175; food ingenuity 122, 128, 131; outside camp 45, 103
Balfour, Nicholas (Nick) 4, ***64***, 71, 85, 89, 124, 128; after liberation 160, 163, 184; in Boys' Club 90–92; in Education Building siege 154–56; on U.S. air raids 135
Balfour, Sebastian ***64***
Balfour, Stephen 63
Balfour, Tika ***64***, 124, 130, 131
Ballard, J.G. 180
Barnes, Georgia 100
Barrow, Tom ***156***
Bataan 18, 113; "Death March" 65, 186, 187, 189
"Battlin' Basic" tank 1, ***147***, 150, 151
Bay Area Civilian Ex-Prisoners of War (BACEPOW) 175–77
bedbugs 51–52, 87, 206n5
Bell, Don 72
Benguet gold mines 137
beriberi 2, 82, 123, 124, 126, 127, 178, 214n20; among guards 118
Bessmer, J.O. 38–39
Beyond the Wire 176–77, 218n20
Bilibid prison 71, 134, 155, 192, 197
Binsted, Norman 36, 210–11n5
births and pregnancies 61, 130; and Margaret Sherk 5, 63, 65–66; "pregnant papas" issue 60–61
black Americans 86–87, 113–14, 183, 185, 186
blame *see* culpability
Boeing 314 Clippers ***10***, 10–11
Bordner High School 89
Borneo 181
Bowen, Deede 50
bowing 37–38, 101–2
Brady, Todd 155
Brantley, Hattie 118
Brent School 13
Bridgeford, George 40
Brines, Russell 106
British Columbia 137
British in Santo Tomás 1–2, 4, 15, 26, 27, 35–37, 88, 90–92, 106; in internee government 30, 104–5, 106

Brooks, Bernard, Jr. (Barney) 52, 166, 169, 172–73
Brooks, Bernard, Sr. 166
Brooks, Curtis 52, 62, 63, 89, 121, 126, 166; on U.S. air raids 135; after internment 169, 172–73, 200
Brooks, Emilie 166
Brooks, Mary Jane 85
Brown, Barker 183
Browning, Mary ***58***, 128
Browning, Michael (Mike), Jr. ***58***, 128
Browning, Michael (Mike), Sr. ***58***
Bryant, Alice 42, 49, 80, 89, 122, 128, 172, 187
Bryant, William (Bill) 6, 122, 128
B17 Flying Fortresses, Boeing 17
B24 Liberators, Consolidated 135
Bunn, Michelle 201
Bushido 102
businessmen as camp leaders 2, 28–29, 30, 104, 106, 182–83
Buss, Claude 16, 20–21
Butenko, Helen 43
"By Babylon's Wave" (Charles Gounod) 70

Cabanatuan 146; POWs 3, 38, 40, 44, 56, ***58***, 63, 65–66, 78, 108, 144, 182, 197
Calhoun, Alexander (Cal) 77, 105, 183
Calvin, John 186
Camp O'Donnell 186
"campitalism" 42, 99
cannibalism 184, 190
Captured (Frances Cogan) 201
carabaos (water buffaloes) 9, 11, 141–42
Carroll, Earl 5, 28–30, ***29***, 39–40, 60, 95, 104, 105, 107, 182; and execution of escapers 35–37; on Internee Committee 120, 138, 139, 152
Cary, Frank 201, 123, 133, 139, 169, 183; affected by malnutrition 124, 128; in Education Building siege and negotiations 106, 152–54, 155

229

Cassera, Francis 96
Castleton, Iris 131
Cates, Lowell 24
Cates, Tressa *see* Roka, Tressa
Catholicism 11, 22–23, 90–91, 97; *see also* religion
Cavite naval base 18
Central Committee 30
Chase, William 146, 149–50, 154, 155
"Cheer Up! Everything's Going to Be — Lousy" (Dave Harvey) 68
children and teenagers 5, 28, 33–34, 82–93; boarded out 44, 44, 60–61, 85, 86, 92; in Boys' Club 6, 85, 90–92, 131, 187; feeding 38, 121, 124–26; games 5–6, 82–83, 91; and guards 83–85; jobs by 82–83, 86, 88, 209n2; and relationships 85, 87, 92; and sex/romance 52, 62–63; *see also* athletics; education; reading
China, Chinese 15–16, 47, 184
cigarettes 121–22, 128, 138, 157
Civilian Emergency Administration 19
Clark Field airbase 144
Clemson, Lynwood **160**
Cochran, Melmuth (Mel) 130
Cogan, Frances 201–2
Colayco, Manuel 1, 150
"collaboration" 92, 183, 200
community 70, 75, 78, 80–81, 173, 198–99
Conner, Hackett (Hack) 1, 146, **158**
Contey-Aiello, Rose 202
Coote, Betty **160**
Corfield, Gill 57
Corfield, Isla 57
Corregidor 4, 18, 19, 113, 193
Corsairs, Vaught 135, 215n7
culpability 7, 184–86
Cunningham, Elizabeth 113
Curtis, John 17, 19, 43

Daly, David 120, 130
Dang, Donald 201
Davao 95, 180
Davies, Clive 15
Davies, Theophilus (Theo) 15
Davison, Maude 113
Dear Mother Putnam (Marcial Lichauco) 200
deaths, internee 127; compared with other camps 179; gender and age differences 124; after liberation 2, 131, 162, 167
deaths, non-internee: Filipino 2, 11, 16; Japanese 145; U.S. "flying column" 145, 148, **159**
del Mundo, Fe 44
deprivation, relative 74, 170, 180
DeWitt, Clyde 31, 109, 134
diaries as history 7, 200–1
DiMatteo, Patrick (Pat) 159
dive-bombers 134, 135, 145; dropping goggles 142
doctors 12, 28, 32, 35; during the camp's liberation 152–53; Filipino 12, 97; meat decision 121; reports and protests by 105–6, 120–21
Dominicans 1, 9, 22–23, 107
Donovan, Willliam ("Wild Bill") 137
Doolan, Roy ("TNT") 33, 83, 87, 128
dormitories 4, 26, 27, 29, 49–55, 85–8; pictures of **50**, **52**, **53**, **54**; *see also* gym dormitory
The Drain Pipe Diary (Tressa Cates) 5, 201
drunkenness 30, 109–110
Duggleby, Alfred (Dug) 66, 105, 108, 137–38; arrest and killing of 97, 105, 182
Dunn, William 202
Dyer, Phyllis 68
dysentery 77, 107, 114, 127

USS *Eberle* 172
education 33–34, 82, 85, 87–91
Education Building siege and hostages 1, 2, 150, 152–55
8th Army 197
8th Cavalry Regiment 145–50; route map **141**
Eisenberg, Joseph 100
elections 30, 104, 105, 106, 111
11th Airborne Division 100, 190
Elks Club 13, 16
entertainment 32, 68–71, 75
escapes 35–37, 99–100
Esmérian, Paul 5, 19, 31, 41, 44–45, 52–53, 59, 63, **64**, 74, 90, 98, 103, 140; and jobs in camp 78, 124; on liberated camp 166; on malnutrition 124; outside camp 24, 44–45
Evans, Lucy (Evie) 14, 25, 51, 85, 203n4
Executive Committee 30, 35–37, 77, 105, 108; issues for 60, 110–11, 114–15, 182, 183; organization 30, 104

face-slapping (*binto*) 47, 185
"family aid" (to Filipino relatives) 38, **79**
Far Eastern University, battle at 148–50, 155
fascism 3, 5, 15, 23, 181, 185, 186
Fathers' Garden 34, 69, 96, 119, 179
5th Cavalry Regiment 145–48; route map **141**
fights 54, 60, 130
Filipinos: prewar 9, 11–12; and Santo Tomás 27, 40, 47, 116, 122, 128, 183, 192; under the Japanese 2, 46–47, 185–86
1st Cavalry Division 144, 152–56; "flying columns" 144–50; route map **141**; after liberation 157–59, 166
The 1st Cavalry Division in World War II (B.C. Wright) 202
Fisher, George 146–47
Fletcher, Lindsay 60, 152–53
Fletcher, Tom 35–37
Foley, Walter 110–11, 198
food and feeding 2, 123, **167**, **168**; and "chow-line" meals 28, 30, 68, 75, 82, 116, 126, 213n2; at Christmas 1944 121, 122, 131; and the Japanese army 27, 116–19; in prewar Philippines 12; *see also* children and teenagers; malnutrition; Red Cross; smuggling
Ford, Joyce 86
Formosa *see* Taiwan
Fort McKinley 142
Fort Santiago 3, 47, 95, 96
44th Tank Battalion 144
Francisco, Louis, Sr. (Pancho) 22, 46
Francisco, Marie 46
Francisco, Pomponette 22, 39; marriage to Luis de Alcuaz **171**, 172
Francisco, Sonia 126
Franco, Francisco 3, 9, 23
free will *see* culpability

Gallagher, John 217n8
gardens and growing 6, 30, 59, 76, 82, 123, 178; commandants on 98, 117, 122, 139; ingenuity 122–123
Gearhart, James 151, 152–53
gender differences 4, 14, 32, 33, 77, 107, 170, 176, 200, 206n11; and camp administration 104, 111; and camp work 78, 117; in malnutrition 124, 214n18
General Electric 40, 105
General Motors 56, 119
Geneva Convention 36, 134
Germany 17
Gibb, Allie 17
Gibb, Sophie 17, 57, 179
Gibb, William (Bill) 17, 57
giving 6, 28, 43, 67, 86, 105, 112, 128, 130–31; from outside camp 28, 38–39, 40, 43, 98, 118, 12; shanties and shanty space 55, **58**, 67
Goa 114–15
"God Bless America" (Irving Berlin) 70, 72, 143, **164**
Godolphin, Francis ("Frisco") 145
Goldsborough, Edwin 37
Goodyear Tire 30
Gopal, Lou 201
Gounod, Charles 70
Greater East Asia Co-Prosperity Sphere 46, 97
Griffiths, Owen 36–37
Grimm, Peter 170
Grinnell, Carroll 66, 99, 104, 105, 108, 113, 134, 135, 182–83; arrest and killing of 3, 96, 105, 133, 182; criticized 105, 110–12

Index

Guam 10
guerrillas 3, 37, 133, 134, 182, 187; helping liberate Los Baños camp 101, 190, 197; Japanese fear of 45, 47, 105, 132–33; and Manila economy 118, 127; and Reg Spear 137–38; in the Santo Tomás liberation 1, 144, 150, 160
Guimba 144, 146
Gunn, Paul ("Pappy") 188
Guytingco, Diosdado 150
gym dormitory 26, *50*, 59, 128, 130; and food smuggling 120

Hall, Alaistair ("Shorty") 58, 119
Harrington, Elsie 86
Harrington, Thomas 104–5
Harris, Everett 134
Hartendorp, Abraham (A.V.H.) 30, 31, 61, 69, 75, 142, 178; as camp historian 4, 201; on liberated camp 169
Harvard University 11
Harvey (MacTurk), Dave 5, 68–71, 74, 78, 87, 111
Hawaii 15, 17, 28–29
Hayashi, Juichiro 100, 112, 136–37, 185; departure moves (Jan. 1945) 139–42; in final siege and negotiations 152–55; leading garrison out of camp *156*
health care 12, 31, *79*, 88, 107–8, 109
Hearnden, James (Jag), and Phyllis 27
heart-muscle inflammation (myocarditis) 119, 127; and beriberi 214*n*20
"hellships" 65–66, 114, 137, 186
Hencke, John 150
Hewlett, Frank 150–51
Hewlett, Virginia 150–51
Hirose, Toshio 123, 151
Hiroshima 187
Hoeflein, Hans 18
Holland, Albert (Bert) 43–44, 48
Holland, Robert (Bob) 145, *147*, 202
Holter, Don 97, 104
Holy Ghost College school 44, 85
Hong Kong 14, 16, 45, 63; internees from 27, 34, 57
Honolulu 10, 28–29; July 1944 meetings 190
USS *Hornet* 69
Hospicio de San José 58, 66, 119
hospitals 12, 38, 43–44; at Santo Tomás 47, 60, 87, 103, 107, 113, 128, 130
humor 2, 32, 53, 55, 58, 60, 68, 70–72, 109; against the Japanese 2, 70–72, 179
hunger *see* malnutrition

Indochina 17
Indonesia 17; camps 4, 94, 180, 181
inequality 6, 42–43, 44, 70, 75–77, *76*, 78, 111–12, 113, 180–82;
and camp aid 6, 42–43, *79*, 205*n*13; Japanese attitudes to 76, 99, 181; and shanties 56, 57–58, 61, 76, 181; *see also* community; "family aid"
International Harvester 41, 112, 131
Internee (Administration) Committee 104, 115, 137–38; and commandant's departure move (Jan. 1945) 139; food policies 119, 121; protests to Japanese 94, 117, 132, 134, 137
Internews 194
Internitis 70, 87, 194
Internment of Western Civilians under the Japanese (Bernice Archer) 202
Ipekdjian, Adolphe, and Alice 44
Irvine, Liz *see* Lautzenhiser, Liz.
isolation hospital *21*, 107
Iwabuchi, Sanji 139, 191
Iwanaha, Maj. 101
Iwo Jima 116

jails 30, 60–61, 108, 110; Japanese outside the camp 95, 96
James, D. Clayton 202
Japan, Japanese: attitudes to Filipinos 40, 46–47; civilian-camp policies 95–96, 180; internee and ex-internee views of 37–38, 184–85; invasion of the Philippines 18–20; prewar 15–16, 17, 102; *see also* Japanese army; Japanese in Santo Tomás; Japanese navy
Japanese Americans 1, 155, *163*, 177, 183, 184
Japanese army 15–16, 17–24, 27, 133–34, 166; brutalizing of 47, 102, 136, 179–80, 186, 188–89; and Santo Tomás administration 94–97, 132, 210*n*2; treatment of Filipinos 2, 46–47, 100, 185–86, 189
Japanese in Santo Tomás 3, 5, 29, 94–103, 108, *153*; civilian officers 103, 105, 112, 115, 123; commandants 5, 29, 71, 97–100, 201; guards 3, 29, 38, 83–85, 112, 121–22, 132, 140–42; lieutenants 35, 36, 98; *see also* Abiko, Nanakazu (Lieut.); Hayashi, Juichiro; Kato, Kitaro; Kodaki, Akida; Kuroda, S.; Onozoki, Gonshichi; Yoshie, Yasunska
Japanese navy 139
Jerrett, Francis 149–50
Johansen, Bruce 201
Johnson, Ernest 96
Johnson, Lyndon 186
Jordan, Eugenio 23, 25–26

kamikaze suicide attacks 145, 184
Kaminski, Theresa 202
Kato, Kitaro 98–99, 100–1, 122
Keiffer, Anne 61
Keiffer, Patricia 61
Kempeitai police 3, 46, 47, 94, 95, 105, 120, 166, 185, 187, 188; efforts to keep out 99, 108, 115
Kerns, Bryan 110
Kerns, Karen 83, 110
KGST 69, 198
Kodaki, Akida 41, 97, 106, 114–15
Komatsu, Lieut. 98, 135
Konishi, Sadaaki 100–1, 102
Korea 15, 137
Krass, Ethel 3
Krass, Iris 85–86
Krass, Patricia 86
Krueger, Walter 143–44, 190, 191
Kuching camp 181
Kuroda, S. 60–61, 97, 104

Laguna de Bay 169, 190
Landry, Walter 124, 146, 149, 159
latrines and shower rooms 2, 4, 26, 27, 53, 55, 75, 78; in the Education Building siege 154; after liberation 166
Laurel, José 46
Laurent, Gustav 41
Lautzenhiser, Liz 31, 82, 84, 101, 109, 123
Lautzenhiser, Mamie 109, 123, 131
Lautzenhiser, Roscoe 87, 123, 131, 175
law and order 29–30, 106, 108; court controversy 110
Laycock, Blakey 35
Leake, Bertram 90, 131
Lee, Tun Yem 5, 115
Legislative Building 144
Lehman, Christopher (Chris) 55
Lehman, Elizabeth (Betty) 54–55
LeMay, Curtis 187–88
Leney, Harold *125*
Leyte 72, 116, 143, 144, 169
Lichauco, Marcial 11, 18, 127, 200
Linder, Cortland (Cort) 69
lines *see* queuing
Lingayen Gulf 116, 140, 143, 144, 145, 193, 197
Lloyd, Samuel (Sam) 106, 135, 139; in siege and hostage negotiations 152
Lodovica, Anastasia 14
Lodovica, Angel 14, 41
Lodovica, Estolita 14
Loft, Tom *125*
Lorenzen, Angus 11, 59, 71–72, 83, 91; after internment 175, 177, 218*n*8, 218*n*20
Los Angeles 77, 172
Los Baños camp 43, 59, 63, 65, 66, 67, 81, 101, 104, 130, 134, 180, 195; clergy sent to 97; as proposed new site for Santo Tomás 105–6; rescue 101, 169, 190, 197; started 194
loyalty oaths 5, 115; clergy 97
Lunghua camp 180
Luzon 82, 116, 136, 138, 140, 143–44; "Luzon first" 190–91
Luzon Stevedoring 138, 170

MacArthur, Douglas 72, 116, 136, 138, 140, 143, 145, 187; and Battle for Manila 190–92; postwar 169, 172; prewar 3–4, 12, 17, 18, 19, 46; and Santo Tomás 2, 144, 161, 169
Macleod, Lydia 126, 157, 200
Malacañan Palace 144, 148, 155
malaria 18
malnutrition 2, 3, 4, 126–27; after-effects of 173; and behavior 61, 63, 127–31; gender and age differences in 92, 124–26, *125*, 178, 214n18
Mañalac, Fernando 24, 200
Manchuria 15
Manila: Battle for 2, 167, 169, 187, 188–89, 190–92, *191*; entered by 1st Cavalry 148–50; and the Japanese invasion 3–4, 18–23, 24; prewar 9–11, 13–14, 17–18; under the Japanese 38, 47, 127
Manila (Fernando Manalac) 200
Manila, Goodbye (Robin Prising) 5
Manila Tribune 53, 72, 195
Mariana Islands 116, 185
Marine Corps, U.S. 145, *147*
Marshall, Cecily *see* Mattocks, Cecily
massacre plans 133, 137; alleged 6–7, 97, 168–69, 218n8; fears of 2, 133, 140, 150
Mathews, Clio 27
Mattocks, Cecily 142, 176
McCall, James 32, 80, 184
McCreary, Edward 138, 175, 176
McKinley, William 11
McSorley, Frank 142
Meadows, Martin 99
memoirs as history 7, 200–1
Memorare-Manila 1945 monument *191*
Meredith, Joan 152
Merriam, Robert 65
mestizos 9, 22, 183, 185
Milgram experiments 185
Military Administration of the Philippines (Japan) 46, 210n2
military background issue 114
Milne, George 42
Mindanao 176
Mindoro 196
money and prices 38, 12, 205n8; and banking controversy 112, 196; and escapes 35–37, 100; in IOUs outside camp 39–40, 119–20; "Mickey Mouse" *39*, 39–40, 118; monitors (dormitory and floor) 27, 29, 43; shanty 57
Morotai 116
Morrison, Geoffrey 62
mosquitoes, mosquito nets 27, *50*, 51, 154
"Mousey" 91–92, 128, 135
Mudge, Verne 144, 146
Muntinlupa prison 134
music 69–70, 71, 74, 77, 179
Mussolini, Benito 181

Mydans, Carl 98, 150, 202
Myers, Terry 84

Nagasaki 187
Nanjing atrocities 15, 20, 187, 188
Nash, Gale 130
Nash, Grace 18, 61, 102, 122, 122–23, 128, 180
Nash, Ralph 18
Nash, Stanley (Stan) 130
National City Bank 77, 105
National Socialism 181
Nazis, Naziism 17, 181, 184
Nazurawa, T. 97
Negros 49
Nelson, James 186
New Guinea 116
Newman, George 72
newspapers: internee 70, 87, 109, 194; Japanese-sponsored 53, 72, 195
Nimitz, Chester 116
nipa huts 11, 55
Nixon, Eva 27
Nogi, Dr 127
Norvell, David *125*
Novaliches 147
nuns 34, 120, 182
nurses 5, 12, 107–8; army 9, 62, 66, 112–13; Filipino 97; treating wounded GIs 152

O'Doherty, Michael 97
O'Donnell camp 95
Office of Strategic Services (OSS) 137
Ohashi, Shizua 103, 105, 112, 115, 139, 151
Ohta, Siechi 25
Okinawa 116
Okinawa 116, 202
Okochi, Denshichi 139
Olsen, Florence 184
Olsen, Margaret 184
Onozoki, Gonshichi 98, 99, 101, 118
"Orange" plans 15
Oroso, Maria 120
Owens, Richard James (Jack) 63, 114

"package line" 27, 40–42, 43; ended 77, 96, 99, 181; suspended 41, 182
Palawan massacre 133, 144, 187
Pampanga River 146
Pan American Airways 10–11, 37, 77, 91
Parsons, Charles ("Chick") 62, 72, 138
Pasig River 9, 20–21, 144; oil tanks burning 19–20
"passes" out of camp 42–46, 47–48, 105
Pearl Harbor 3, 17, 18, 193
Pedder, Gerald 36
Peleliu 202
Philippine-American War and veterans 11, 28, 58, 150

Philippine General Hospital 107
Philippine Republic (under Japanese power) 46, 210n2
Philippines: geography and population of 11; under American control 11–19; under Japanese occupation 38, 127, 117–18, 127
Polo Club 13, 21
Pontejo, Eustaquio 14, 19, 46
Pope, Harvey 181
Poston, Mac 67
POWs, military 4, 5, 42, 55, 95; Japanese and Taiwanese 155, 161, *162*, *163*; *see also* Bataan; Cabanatuan; "hellships"
Pratt, Caroline *see* Bailey, Caroline
Princeton University 145
Prising, Frederick 26, 86–87, 136
Prising, Marie 26, 47, 86–87, 102–3, 136
Prising, Robin 5, 26, 44, 47, 85, 89, 109, 130, 136, 179; in and out of camp 86–87, 103; and Lieut. Abiko 85, 101, 151; on war victims 184
Prisoners in Paradise (Theresa Kaminski) 202
profiteering 122, 123, 128, 179
P38 Lightnings, Lockeed 135, 136
public address and broadcast system 62, 69–72, 109, 110
Puerto Princesa massacre 133, 187
Punahou Academy 17

queuing 4, 27, 74–75
Quezon, Manuel 12, 13, 16, 19
Quezon City 169

racism: American and Western 13–14, 15, 16, 26, 46, 62, 105, 183–84; Japanese 46–47, 185
radios 72, 108, 132, 140; military 138, 145, *147*, 149
Raleigh, Daniel (Dan) 30
Ralston, Marion 52, 92
reading 74, 89–90, 91, 179
recipe-mania 128
Red Cross 5, 30, 172; aid to Santo Tomás (1942–43) 3, 26, 107, 38–39, 42, 43, 38–39, 95; "comfort kits" 6, 73, 115, 121–22, 126, 157, 178, 181–82; other aid in 1944 107, 111, 118, 119; pre-invasion 3, 14, 16
Red Guards 189
religion 34, 70, 80–81, 140, 198; Japanese treatment of 37, 97, 210–11n5
Remedios hospital 103
repatriation 43, 138, 150–51; after liberation 169, 172; 1943 controversy 114–15, 194; prewar policies toward 16–17
The Rescue of Santo Tomas (Robert Holland) 202
Richards, Harriett 88
Rimmer, Gerald 103

Roka, Tressa 5, 24, 40, 41, 50, 55, 68, 201, 75, 100, 117, 127; and fiancé "Catesy" 26, 62, 76, 122; as a nurse 5, 14, 19, 31, 78, 125–26; social views of 42, 183, 184, 189
roll calls 29, 35, 38, 71, 74, 96–97, 101–2, 142; on "Roll Call Day" 101, 195
Roosevelt, Franklin 17, 137, 190, 191
Rosenbaum, Rose (Rosie) 89
Rosenstock, Christian 21
Ross, Tom 144
Rotary Club 13
rumors 36, 72–74, *73*, 140, 161; causes of 74
Russo-Japanese War 15
Rutter, Don 114

Saipan 185
Sams, Jerry *52*, 65–66, 71, 111–12, 179
San Francisco 10, 42, 77, 172
San Miguel 146
San Pedro 172
Sanders, Millie 86–87, 113–14, 183
Santa Catalina hospital 107, 113, 120, 130, 137, 152, 182
Santo Tomas Internment Camp (Frederic Stevens) 201
Santo Tomas Internment Camp (J. E. McCall) 201
Santo Tomás Internment Camp: after-effects on ex-internees 173, 175; after liberation 157–72; compared with other camps 1, 6, 4, 49, 94, 177, 179–81; demographics 1–2, 31–32, 195; financing of 38–40, *79*, 112, 181, 196; location and layout of 9, *20–22*, 26; liberation of 1, 6, 143–56; major changes at 2, 3, 45, 55, 61, 94–95, 96–97, 104, 116; organization of 29–30, 49, 94, 106, 108, 182; reflections on experience at 175–76, 177; selected as a camp 21–23, 25–26
Sayre, Francis 16, 19
Schade, Roger 63, 143
Schafer, Gladys *58*
Schafer, Paul *58*
Schoendube, Charles 150
Secret Intelligence Service, British 3, 15
Seewald, Hughes 146
self-pity 4, 70, 177, 178
servants 6, 13, 14, 25, 27, 40, 41, 128, 183; loss of 126, 179; Wilkinson family's 14, 41, 170
sex and romance 45, 48, 55, 60–67, 113; and malnutrition 61, 127–28; restrictions on 26, 29, 49, 60–62, 67; with army liberators 157, 159
Shanghai 14, 63, 77, 150, 180; internees from 27, 43, 114
Shannon, Eileen 41

Shannon family 19, 25
shanties 49, 55–61, 181; pictures of *56*, *57*, *58*, *64*
Shaw, John 86
shelling of Santo Tomás 2, 198, 162–63, 166
Sherk, David 5, 43, 44, 55, 63, 65, 66, 74
Sherk, Gerry Ann 5, 63, 65–66
Sherk, Margaret 5, 44, 55, 68, 73, 74, 77, 80; on inequality 43, 111–12; pregnancy of 5, 63, 65–66, 178
Sherk, Mildred (Mickie) 66
Sherk, Robert (Bob) 65–66
Sherman tanks 1, 143, 144–48, 150, 152; photographed *147*, *149*, *161*
6th Army 143–44, 145, 197
Sledge, E.B. 202
Smith, Mary Ellen 137
Smith, Robert 88
Smith, Robert Ross 202
smuggling 119, 123, 128, *129*, 133; to Cabanatuan POWs 38, 40, 96; by Luis de Alcuaz 5, 39, 119–20, 157; messages 41
So Far from Home (Bruce Johansen) 201
Sousa, John Philip 71
Spain, Spanish 3, 5, 9, 23
Spanish-American War 11
Spear, Reginald (Reg) 137–38, 215–216n13
Sperry, Christine 66–67
Sperry, Hank 61, 66–67
Spratley Islands 16
Staight, Lettye *174*
Stanley, Ernest 36, *52*, 106, 139; in Education Building siege and negotiations 106, 152, 153, 155, *156*
"Star Spangled Banner" (Francis Scott Key) 70
"Stars and Stripes Forever" (John Philip Sousa) 71
State Department, U.S. 16–17, 114–15, 185
stealing 128, 130, 179; by Filipinos from outside 100, 116; by Japanese/Taiwanese 2, 117, 139, 141–42
Stevens, Frederic 16, 95, 201
Stevenson, Theodore (Ted) 151, 152; *173*; and death certificates 3, 127
Stevenson, Walter 131
STIC Gazette 70, 109, 194
Stolen Childhoods (Nicola Tyrer) 92
stuttering 91–92
sugar industry 3, 12, 15
Sulphur Springs 193
Sun Tzu 190
support groups 66, 77–78, 173, 178
Survival in Santo Tomas (Donald Dang) 201
Surviving a Japanese P.O.W. Camp (Peter Wygle) 201

Surviving the Rising Sun (Liz Irvine) 201
Sutton, James 147

Taft, William Howard 11–12
Tagalog 9, 72, 75, 88
Tait, Stewart Edward (Eddie) 32
Taiwan (Formosa), Taiwanese 133, 190–91; guards 6, 83, 118, 201, 123, 133, 154, *162*, 183
Takahashi, Lieut. 35–36
Tarlac 138
Tascon, Thomas 23, 25–26, 170
Templer, Angela 34, 45, 59, 69; outside camp 45
Templer, Hazel 59
Templer, James 45, 59
Templer, Jenny 34, 59
Templer family 45
Ten Commandments 109, 198–99
Theo H. Davies & Co. 15, 41
37th Infantry Division 144, 155; after liberation 159, 166
Thompson, Pendleton ("Bumblebee") 70
Thorson, Roy 107, 120
Time-Life 10, 70, 150
Tjideng camp 94
Tocqueville, Alexis de 140
Tokyo 102; government directives 119; war-crimes trials 4, 169
Tomayasu, Hitoshi 5, 29, 35–37, 40, 60, 98, 100
Tonkin, Marguerite (Margo) 63, 82
Tonkin, William (Bill) 82
"town meeting" issue 110–11, 182–83
Triumph in the Philippines (Robert Ross Smith) 202
trophy-seeking 189
Tsurumi, Ryozo 98, 104
tuberculosis (TB) 131; Japanese fear of 45
Tuliahan River 147
Tulloch, James (Jim) 74
typhoon flood (Nov. 1943) 59–60, 107–8
Tyrer, Nicola 92

United States: and the Philippines prewar 9–14, 15–17; war policies 15–19, 116, 187, 190–91
United States Armed Forces in the Far East (USAFFE) 17, 23
United States Navy 137, 147, 169
University of Hawaii 177
University of Santo Tomás 1, 2, 5, 9, 25–26, 119–20
Uyesugi, Ken 155

Valdefuente Bridge 146
Van Sickle, Charles 5, 41, 112, 131
Van Sickle, Emily 5, 49, 63, 140; social views of 5, 42, 105, 112, 131, 151, 184
Van Vorhees, Edwin 56, 119, 163
Vaughan, Beth 44, 77, 135

Vaughan, Clay 44, 75, 135
Vaughan, Elizabeth 5, 44, 49, 55, 57–58, 75, 76, 78, 98, 133; and death of husband Jim 77
Vorster, Erwin 24

Wake 10
War-Prisoners Headquarters, Japanese 71, 96, 132–33, 210*n*2
Ward, James 200
Warner, Barnes & Co. 40, 43
"We'll Be Out Tomorrow" (anon.) 73
Weeks, Henry 35–37
Weinzheimer, Jean 46, 83, 110, 130
Weinzheimer, Roy 123
Weinzheimer, Sascha 102, 123, 124
Weinzheimer, Walter 130
Weinzheimer family 55, 78, 169
Werff, Wanda 119
Whitesides, John 17–18
Wilkins, Ford 47
Wilkinson, Gerald 3–4, 18, 19, 138–37, 172
Wilkinson, Lorna 4, 24–25, 54, 89–90, 122, 124, 138, 139, 178; after internment 156, 157, 175, *174*, 176; before internment 3, *12*, 14–15, 18, 19–20; outside camp 45–46, 89
Wilkinson, Mary June 4, 24–25, 55, 85, 89, 131, 136, 143; after internment 157, 163, 170, 172, 175, 176; before internment *13*, 14, 18, 20; and hunger 124, 128, 130, 170; outside camp 45–46; spiritual faith of 34, 140
Wilkinson, Rupert 4, 19–20, 25, 33, 46, 83, 89, 107, 130, 131, 134, 136; after internment 157, 159–60, 162–63, 166, 170, 172, 175, 176, 202; before internment *13*, 18, 19–20; in the Boys' Club 90–92; in the Education Building siege 2, 143, 154–56; outside camp 45–46
Willard, Douglas (Doug) 91
Williams, Denny 9, 151
Williams, Sylvia 175
Williamson, Arthur *125*
Winkler, Hugo *125*
With the Old Breed (E.B.Sledge) 202
Wolff, Thomas (Tommy) 28
Wootten, Madeleine (Geege) 5, 26, 42, 50, 54, 76, 77–78, 108, 135, 140; on the camp experience 176; and Hank Sperry 66–67, 78; jobs and trading by 78, 80, 179; and liberation 151, 159
work and jobs 31, 74, 78–81, 178; for the Japanese garrison 94, 133–34; for money or bartering 5, 57, 74, 78, 82; requirements 31, 78, 82, 117
Wright, B.C. 202
Wrinch, Peter 163
Wyatt-Smith, Stanley 98
Wygle, Peter 50, 82, 83, 89, 113, 124, 135, 179; after internment 175, 189, 201
Wygle, Robert (Bob) 50, *51*, 75, 80, 109, 201

Yamashita, Tomoyuki 139, 143–44
"Yankee Doodle" 70
YMCA 28, 118, 118, 121
Yoshie, Yasunska 5, 98, 115, 134, 201
Yule, Sheila 35
Yule, Susan (Susie) 45
Yule, Tom 45